MW01641354

Conflict and Peace in Eurasia

Focusing on a range of Eurasian conflicts, including Nagorno-Karabakh, South Ossetia and Abkhazia, this book offers contemporary perspectives on the ongoing conflicts in Eurasia, with an emphasis on the attempts towards peace.

The book brings into focus how various factors such as ethnicity, religion, border disputes, resources and animosities inherited from the past play crucial roles in these conflicts. It questions whether developments in Eurasia affect other conflicts across the globe, and if differences between parties can be resolved without pulling the relations beyond adjustable limits. The book goes on to look at how tricky the path to peace could be, and furthers the development of a framework of study of Eurasian conflicts in the post-Soviet world, while taking into account both internal and external variables in analysing these conflicts. It is a useful contribution to Central Asian Politics and Security Studies.

Debidatta Aurobinda Mahapatra is Assistant Professor of South and Central Asian Studies at the Central University of Punjab, India. His areas of expertise are conflict, peace and development and strategic aspects of Eurasian politics.

Central Asia research forum
Series Editor: Shirin Akiner
School of Oriental and African Studies, University of London

Other titles in the series:

Sustainable Development in Central Asia
Edited by Shirin Akiner, Sander Tideman and John Hay

Qaidu and the Rise of the Independent Mongol State in Central Asia
Michal Biran

Tajikistan
Edited by Mohammad-Reza Djalili, Frederic Gare and Shirin Akiner

Uzbekistan on the Threshold of the Twenty-first Century
Tradition and survival
Islam Karimov

Tradition and Society in Turkmenistan
Gender, oral culture and song
Carole Blackwell

Life of Alimqul
A native chronicle of nineteenth century Central Asia
Edited and translated by Timur Beisembiev

Central Asia
Aspects of transition
Edited by Tom Everrett-Heath

The Heart of Asia
A history of Russian Turkestan and the Central Asian Khanates from the earliest times
Frances Henry Skrine and Edward Denison Ross

The Caspian
Politics, energy and security
Edited by Shirin Akiner and Anne Aldis

Islam and Colonialism
Western perspectives on Soviet Asia
Will Myer

Azeri Women in Transition
Women in Soviet and post-Soviet Azerbaijan
Farideh Heyat

The Post-Soviet Decline of Central Asia
Sustainable development and comprehensive capital
Eric Sievers

Prospects for Pastoralism in Kazakhstan and Turkmenistan
From state farms to private flocks
Edited by Carol Kerven

Muslim Reformist Political Thought
Revivalists, modernists and free will
Sarfraz Khan

Economic Development in Kazakhstan
The role of large enterprises and foreign investment
Anne E. Peck

Energy, Wealth and Governance in the Caucasus and Central Asia
Lessons not learned
Edited by Richard Auty and Indra de Soysa

The Politics of Knowledge in Central Asia
Science between Marx and the market
Sarah Amsler

The Economics and Politics of Oil in the Caspian Basin
The redistribution of oil revenues in Azerbaijan and Central Asia
Edited by Boris Najman, Richard Pomfret and Gaël Raballand

The Political Economy of Reform in Central Asia
Uzbekistan under authoritarianism
Martin C. Spechler

Religion and Security in South and Central Asia
Edited by K. Warikoo

Conflict and Peace in Eurasia
Edited by Debidatta Aurobinda Mahapatra

Conflict and Peace in Eurasia

Edited by
Debidatta Aurobinda Mahapatra

LONDON AND NEW YORK

First published 2013
by Routledge
2 Park Square, Milton Park, Abingdon, Oxon OX14 4RN

Simultaneously published in the USA and Canada
by Routledge
711 Third Avenue, New York, NY 10017

Routledge is an imprint of the Taylor & Francis Group, an informa business

British Library Cataloguing in Publication Data
A catalogue record for this book is available from the British Library

Library of Congress Cataloging in Publication Data
A catalog record has been requested for this book

ISBN: 978-0-415-63278-2 (hbk)
ISBN: 978-0-203-08103-7 (ebk)

Typeset in Times New Roman
by Wearset Ltd, Boldon, Tyne and Wear

Printed and bound in the United States of America by Publishers Graphics, LLC on sustainably sourced paper.

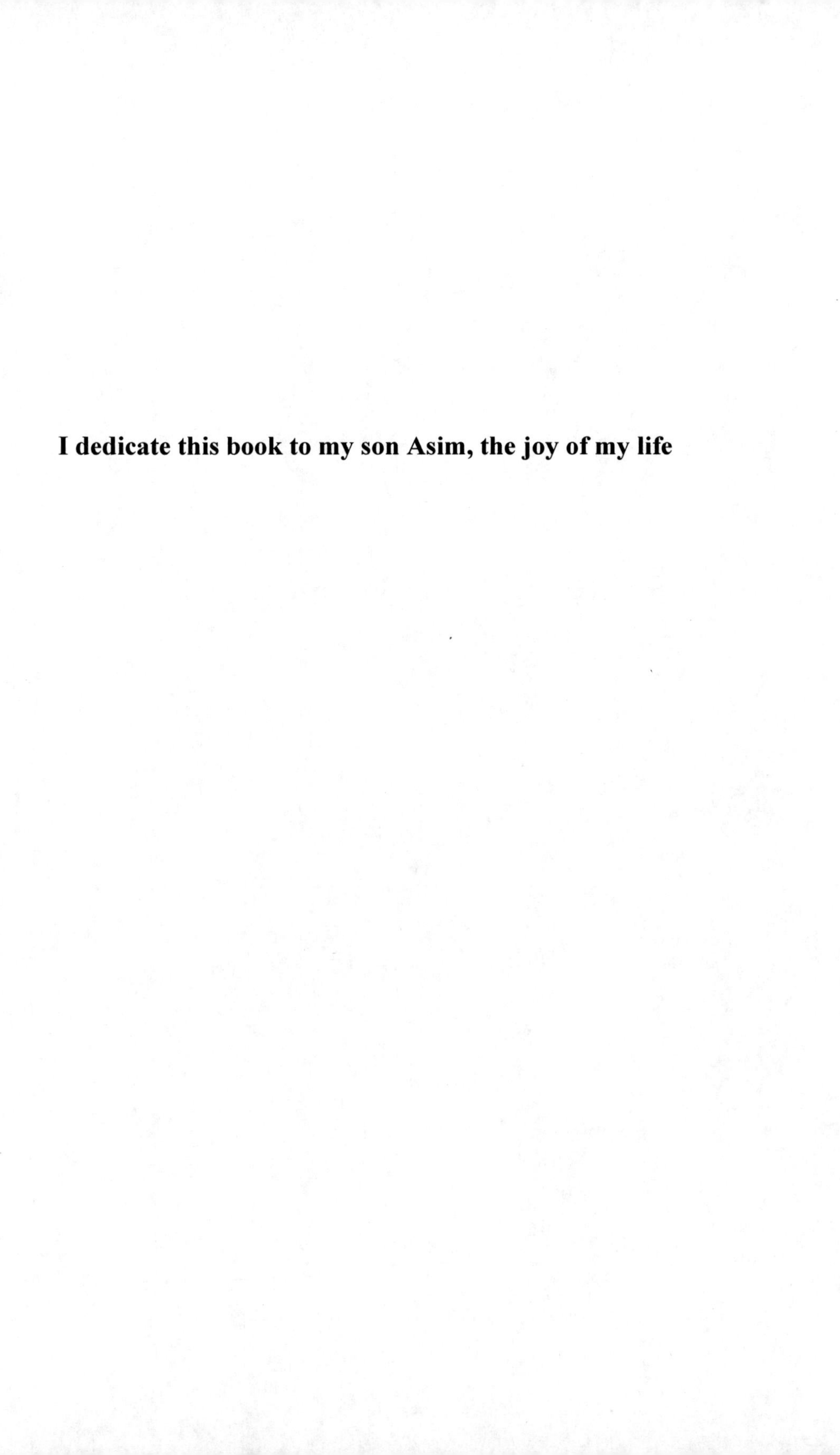

I dedicate this book to my son Asim, the joy of my life

Contents

List of illustrations xi
Notes on contributors xii
Acknowledgements xv

Introduction: contextualising Eurasian conflicts and prospects of peace 1
DEBIDATTA AUROBINDA MAHAPATRA

1 **A perspective on conflict and peace** 23
JOHAN GALTUNG

2 **From the Balkans to the Caucasus: paradoxes of the precedents in a post-Balkan perspective** 36
EMANUELA C. DEL RE

3 **Mapping ethnic relations: cartography and conflict management in the North Caucasus, Russia** 54
ANDREW FOXALL

4 **Complexities of the peace process in Nagorno-Karabakh** 73
FRANÇOISE COMPANJEN

5 **Subtle line between self-defence and war: South Ossetia 2008** 88
FRANÇOISE COMPANJEN AND ABEL POLESE

6 **Chechen conflict viewed through the prism of National Bolshevism: parallels and incongruities** 103
DMITRY SHLAPENTOKH

7 **Kyrgyzstan: conflict and prospects of peace** 119
SÉBASTIEN PEYROUSE AND MARLÉNE LARUELLE

8 **Southern Kurdistan: from conflict zone to subregional integration in Greater Eurasia** 134
JASON E. STRAKES

9 **Prospects of inclusive peace, perception of players and stakes involved in the post-9/11 Afghanistan** 159
DEBIDATTA AUROBINDA MAHAPATRA

10 **Resolving Uyghur conflict through a participatory rights-based approach to development** 176
HENRYK SZADZIEWSKI

11 **Linking peace and development: an imperative for conflict transformation in Kashmir** 194
SEEMA SHEKHAWAT

Index 210

Illustrations

Figure

8.1 Model of conflict and cooperation in Iraqi Kurdistan, 2003–present 138

Map

3.1 Stavropol' krai and the North Caucasus 60

Tables

1.1 Probable inter-regional relations 26
1.2 Regional relations profiles 26
3.1 Ethnic Russian population in the subjects of the North Caucasus Federal District, 2010 Russian Census 58
3.2 Ethnic composition of Stavropol' krai population, 2010 Russian Census 61
8.1 Level of subregional integration in Erbil province 150
8.2 Level of subregional integration in Dohuk province 151
8.3 Level of subregional integration in Sulaymaniyah province 152

Contributors

Françoise Companjen is affiliated to the Vrije Universiteit Amsterdam, Faculty of Social Sciences as a lecturer. She specialises in civil society and democracy building in the South Caucasus. As the managing director of Caucasus Interconnect, she organises debates on the South Caucasus, Georgia in particular, connecting academics, civil servants and consultants.

Emanuela C. Del Re is a professor at the University Niccolò Cusano of Rome (Italy), teaching political sociology. She has expertise in the areas of geopolitics, conflict studies and security issues, with a focus on the Balkans, Caucasus and North Africa. She has become a consultant for many international institutions and a member of prominent networks and think-tanks. She has worked as an international electoral observer for the UN, EU and OSCE on many missions. She is a contributing editor to the leading Italian geopolitical review *Limes* and the *Italian Review on Intelligence Gnosis*. She is the founding chairperson of EPOS International Mediating and Negotiating Operational Agency.

Andrew Foxall is a lecturer in Human Geography at Queen's University Belfast. He holds a BSc (Hons) from the University of Plymouth, an MSc from the University of Birmingham, and completed his DPhil at the University of Oxford in 2011. His research focuses primarily on the post-Soviet North Caucasus, although he has also published on Russian politics, energy and the environment in post-Soviet Eurasia and geopolitics in the Russian Arctic.

Johan Galtung was born in 1930 in Oslo, Norway and is widely known as the 'father of peace research', having about 150 books published on peace and social science in general, and mediating the same number of conflicts around the world. He is holder of the Right Livelihood Award (aka the alternative Nobel peace prize), the Korean peace prize, the Abdul Ghaffar Khan peace prize from the American Muslim Association and 14 honorary professorships and doctorates. Galtung and his Japanese wife, Fumiko Nishimura, live in France, Spain, the United States and Japan.

Marléne Laruelle is director of the Central Asia Program, and a research professor of International Affairs at the Institute for European, Russian and Eurasian Studies (IERES), the Elliott School of International Affairs, George

Washington University. On Russia, her main areas of expertise are political and social evolution, identity issues, nationalism, citizenship and migration. Previous works include *Russian Eurasianism: An Ideology of Empire* (2008) and *In the Name of the Nation: Nationalism and Politics in Contemporary Russia* (2009). On Central Asia, her main areas of expertise are political and social evolution, identity issues and geopolitics.

Debidatta Aurobinda Mahapatra works at the Centre for South and Central Asian Studies, Central University of Punjab, India. Previously, he worked at the University of Mumbai and University of Jammu. He was a visiting fellow at Queen's University Belfast and Institute of Oriental Studies Moscow in 2010. He has received awards such as the Scholar of Peace (WISCOMP, New Delhi, 2007) and Kodikara (RCSS, Colombo, 2010). His publications include *Central Eurasia: Geopolitics, Compulsions and Connections* (2008) and *World Order, Multipolarism and Terrorism* (2011). His areas of expertise are conflict, peace and strategic aspects of Eurasian politics.

Sébastien Peyrouse is a senior research fellow with the Central Asia-Caucasus Institute and Silk Road Studies Program, a centre affiliated with Johns Hopkins University, Washington, DC, and the ISDP, Stockholm. He is an associate scholar with the Institute for International and Strategic Relations, Paris, and with the Fundación para las Relaciones Internacionales y el Diálogo Exterior, Madrid and a member of the Brussels-based Europe-Central Asia Monitoring. He has authored or co-authored *Turkmenistan: Strategies of Power, Dilemmas of Development* (2011) and *The 'Chinese Question' in Central Asia* (2012). He has also co-edited *China and India in Central Asia* (2010) and *Mapping Central Asia: Indian Perceptions and Strategies* (2011).

Abel Polese is a Marie Curie research fellow at the Institute of Political Science and Governance of Tallinn University. Prior to this endorsement he has been a research fellow at the University of Edinburgh and at Dresden Technical University. His most recent publications include *The Colour Revolutions in the Former Soviet Union: Successes and Failures* (2010) (co-editor) and 'Surviving Post-socialism', a special issue of the *International Journal of Sociology and Social Policy* (2011) (co-editor). He is currently working on informal economic practices in post-socialist spaces.

Seema Shekhawat is a post-doctoral fellow at the Centre for African Studies, University of Mumbai, India. She was recipient of the Scholar of Peace award from WISCOMP in 2007. She has been a consultant to various international organisations, including the Internal Displacement Monitoring Centre, Geneva. Her areas of research are conflict, peace and gender. Her publications include *Conflict and Displacement in Jammu and Kashmir* (2006) and *Contested Borders and Division of Families in Kashmir* (2009) (co-author).

Dmitry Shlapentokh is associate professor of History at Indiana University, United States. He is the author of several books and approximately 100 articles and chapters.

Jason E. Strakes is a researcher and visiting lecturer at the International School for Caucasus Studies (ISCS), Ilia State University, Tbilisi, Georgia. Earlier he served as a Greater Middle East analyst and consultant to the US Army and government personnel, focusing on Kurdish affairs. He completed an MA and PhD in international studies and political science at the School of Politics and Economics, Claremont Graduate University, United States. He also serves as the Eurasia/Developing North representative on the Executive Council of the International Studies Association on Global South Caucus. His research interests include foreign policy, defence and security policy, Central Eurasia and the international relations of former Soviet states.

Henryk Szadziewski is the manager of the Uyghur Human Rights Project, a non-governmental research entity. Mr Szadziewski has a BA (Hons) in Modern Chinese and Mongolian Studies from the University of Leeds and an MSc (Econ) in Development Management from the University of Wales, where he was awarded a distinction for his work on Uyghur economic, social and cultural rights. He has authored numerous research and opinion articles on Uyghurs, Central Asia and development economics. He lived in China for five years, three of those in Kashgar, and has travelled widely across Central Asia. He is proficient in Mandarin, and has also studied the Uyghur language.

Acknowledgements

The volume is a compendium of chapters contributed by well-known scholars on conflicts in Eurasia – all of whom either lived or worked in the field for extended periods, and remain committed through their work to a dispassionate analysis of a particular conflict and its peace prospects. The work is a collective endeavour of all of the contributors, to whom I remain indebted for their patience and trust reposed in me. I express deep appreciation and gratitude to Johan Galtung for contributing a chapter. I am very grateful to Neil Jarman, Florian Farkas, Ned Bertz, Janette Davies, Elizabeth Hanson and Otto F. von Feigenblatt for their invaluable help during preparation of this manuscript.

I thank Dorothea Schaefter and her team members, particularly Jillian Morrison, at Routledge for their unfailing support towards the publication of this volume. I am indebted to Professor Shirin Akiner, series editor, Central Asia, for her valuable cooperation.

Finally, I thank my wife Seema for providing much needed support and love that allowed me to work on the book with peace of mind. She read and reread the manuscript and made valuable suggestions, without which this book would have taken longer to produce. To my parents and parents-in-law, I remain indebted for constant encouragement and support.

Introduction

Contextualising Eurasian conflicts and prospects of peace

Debidatta Aurobinda Mahapatra

Eurasia emerged as a crucial theatre in international politics after the collapse of the Soviet Union. The uncertainty that ensued in Europe's east and Asia's west following the end of bipolar politics at the termination of the Cold War led emerging countries of the region to search for ways to address their concerns and meet challenges and opportunities posed by internal and external factors. Two trends emerging in the post-Soviet space altered the balance of power in the Eurasian region: first, the emergence of new nation-states with diverse potentials and an array of developments marked by instability, violence and competing spheres of influence. Second, new vistas opened up for nation-states outside the Eurasian landmass to interact and shape relations in the region. The region's growing openness to the outside world in terms of new relations, transportation links and cultural and linguistic transformations has led to clashes between old and new approaches in the region. The old relations erected by imperial domination were challenged by internal and external forces. In order to cope with the emerging scenario, with few exceptions, the countries of Eastern Europe looked west, while countries in Central Asia and the Caucasus found themselves in a dilemma of whether to maintain old relations with Russia – without a formal command system in place – or look westwards to realise their potentials. These changes have impacted politics of the emerging nation-states in various ways in terms of revival of irredentist claims over territory, clashes of identities and conflicts over resources, with spill-over effects in the surrounding regions and beyond.

This volume brings together some carefully selected conflicts in the Eurasian region, both from post-Soviet space and its extended neighbourhood. The focus is on the underlying factors, both kinetic and potential, that fuel and sustain conflicts. The book constitutes a tentative step in furthering the development of a framework of study of Eurasian conflicts in the post-Soviet space and its extended neighbourhood, while taking into account both internal and external variables in analysing these conflicts. It offers a number of perspectives on Eurasian conflicts, while unravelling some of the intriguing aspects of Eurasia in a broader framework of conflict and peace. Eurasia is a debated and contested term. It is important to admit its complicated nature while analysing developments in the region. There are diverse perspectives as to what exactly constitute the contours of Eurasia, and these add to the ambiguity in defining the geographical, political, social and economic patterns characterising the region. A lack of a universally accepted definition makes the concept amenable to differing, and at times contradictory, interpretations. The purpose of this volume is not to discuss these interpretations of the concept and its dynamics; rather, it charts a safe course by accepting a less contested interpretation of the term as the post-Soviet space and its peripheries. The book aims to remove the strait-jacket of geopolitical considerations and rivalries of the region and in turn focus on conflicts and prospects for peace, thus bringing into focus some of the neglected aspects of the region overshadowed by traditional realistic discourse. The view that conflicts in the Eurasian space could be considered 'frozen' as they did not witness intense violence, except during the initial years of the Soviet collapse, has been challenged by recent developments. The Russia–Georgia war in 2008 brought into focus the dynamic nature of the hitherto frozen conflicts in the region.

Early research on Eurasian studies focused on grand themes involving the region, but conflict itself was rarely a primary variable of analysis. Hence, area scholars' reticence to problematise conflicts as another subject for study plays a part in a lack of in-depth study of Eurasian conflicts. Studies of Eurasian conflicts (Brook 1992; Fowkes 1998; Goldenberg 1994; Seely 2001; Waal 2003; Heathershaw 2009) are isolated as they do not account for broad parameters which shape conflicts and their peace prospects in the region. Besides the issue of a lack of commonly agreed definitions of Eurasia, there appears a couple of other factors responsible for the neglect of conflict studies in the region: (1) looking at the developments from a post-Cold War prism, without according due importance to the unique characteristics of the conflicts; (2) ascribing all problems to the evils of transition from socialist to capitalist societies; (3) a somewhat recent development, which is focusing on the region in a wider framework of the 'global war against terrorism;' and (4) focusing on aspects such as energy resources, power rivalries and other components of international politics, while neglecting conflicts as core element of focus. The more scholars of Eurasia objectify conflicts in the region as mere offshoots of the post-Soviet transformation, the less able they will be to trace underlying factors and interactions within them in shaping conflicts. There is also a misconception about what might be theorised, particularly in the context of conflicts in the region which are diverse and heterogeneous. The theoretical importance of Eurasian conflicts lies primarily in what it might reveal about various factors shaping the differences and discontents by situating them in the past, present and future of Eurasian nations. As such, a theory on Eurasian conflicts sits squarely within the broader framework of Eurasian studies.

This edited volume will significantly contribute to the literature on Eurasian studies, as there is no single volume that provides a contemporary perspective on the ongoing conflicts and the peace prospects in the region. The chapters in the book bring into focus how various factors such as ethnicity, religion, boundary disputes and animosities inherited from the past play crucial roles in the conflicts. They provide a prism to look at instability and volatility in the region from close quarters. The chapters explore a range of Eurasian conflicts to address some relevant questions. Will developments in Eurasia affect other conflicts across the globe? What will be the future international order as other discontented regions in different parts of the world aspire to independent status in the aftermath of Kosovo's independence in February 2008 and the subsequent crisis in the Caucasus? Does every distinct unit in a federation possess the right to self-determination? This is a matter of common concern for all pluralistic and multi-ethnic states. How can differences between different parties be resolved amicably without pulling the relations in the opposite direction beyond adjustable limits? In the context of ethnic conflicts, whether it is Nagorno-Karabakh, South Ossetia or Abkhazia, ethnic identities have resurfaced in the post-Cold War period. The discussion then revolves around the possibility of harmonious coexistence of diverse identities within a broader framework of national ideal, or the inevitability of fragmentation of existing state structures along divisive lines. For instance, South Ossetia and Abkhazia, with their distinct identities, posed a dilemma as to whether these regions could be reconciled within the broader framework of Georgia (which Georgia argues for), or whether, as Russia has argued, the Kosovo precedent should guide their aspirations. Another major question the volume seeks to address is whether piecemeal approaches to peace undertaken by local, regional and international players for conflict resolution can yield positive results in managing conflicts, if not resolving them.

While analysing the hows and whys of conflict and peace in Eurasia, the aim was neither to be geographically rigid in the sense of only covering the former Soviet Union, nor was it to provide a compendium of randomly selected Eurasian conflicts. I chose to work closely with select scholars with long and close experiences of studying conflicts in the broader Eurasian space. I have chosen to include conflicts from both within and beyond post-Soviet space, principally sparked by one or more of the following causes: ethnic factors, disputed borders, religious or ideological factors, underdevelopment, past legacies and interests of international and regional powers. While admitting the lacuna in the book in terms of not covering each and every conflict in the region, which may not be possible in a single volume, it needs to be stressed that this sacrifice in breadth of coverage is significantly remunerated by the depth and intimacy of the case studies that have been included. The volume has not encouraged a particular research methodology on the premise that the diverse conflicts in the region may be treated in divergent manners. Contributors have been given liberty to innovate their own analytical strategies to explore such a variety of case studies, which has helped bring out the crucial aspects of conflict and peace in the region. From a broader perspective, the case studies in the book respond to the call: if there is conflict, what are its dynamics and how tricky is the path to peace?

What is Eurasia?

Eurasia is a porous region, in part an imagined territory and in part a contested political space. It is a 'subjective vision', to use Black's phrase, and remains ensnared in a 'geographist ideology' (Black 1997). The landscape is vast, encompassing several time zones, making it difficult to discern attributes of the region in a simplistic fashion. The complexity of the nature of description of the Eurasian landscape emerged clearly after the collapse of the Soviet Union as scholars and policy-makers focused attention on this hitherto neglected space. The collapse not only marked the end of an epoch, but also marked the emerging confusion in crafting a new discipline in the debris of the Soviet Union. The dominant discourse revolving around the Soviet Union under the broad rubric of Sovietology (Cohen 1985) found itself decaying in the last years of the Soviet Union, and it remained a puzzling task for the experts of Soviet studies to define the newly emerging post-Soviet space. Cohen pointed out how, during the decaying years of the Soviet Union, it was not intellectual discourses but rapid political changes that led to development of new approaches in the study of the region (ibid.: 7). Scholars struggled to choose between the labels of Europe or Asia to characterise the emerging states in the post-Soviet space, but gradually settled on Eurasia with the appearance of the journal *Kritika*, which was one of the first to appear with 'Russian and Eurasian' in its subtitle, followed by *The Slavic Review* and *The Russian Review* (Hagen 2004: 445–468).

There were attempts to define Eurasia, as a result of which one can come across a large and growing literature on the subject. One of the notable attempts to define and focus evolving contours of Eurasia is the ten-volume series produced by the Russian Littoral Project in the 1990s, sponsored by the University of Maryland at College Park and Paul H. Nitze School of Advanced International Studies of the Johns Hopkins University and directed by Karen Dawisha and Bruce Parrott. The project included studies by Starr (1994), Dawisha and Dawisha (1995), Parrott (1995) and Tismaneanu (1995). Another comparatively recent attempt to explore various dimensions of the region is the initiative under the rubric 'Eager Eyes Fixed on Eurasia' by the Slavic Research Centre, at Hokkaido University, Japan. Other initiatives, like the Central Eurasian Studies Society based at Indiana University, Bloomington, have spearheaded the movement to transcend a state-centric focus on the region by analysing microelements within the region. The popular usage of the term Eurasia, Hagen (2004: 445) argues, leads to a kind of 'decentering of historical narratives from the powerful perspectives of the former capitals, whether imperial St. Petersburg or tsarist-Soviet Moscow'. This decentring of narratives allows the aspirations of emerging states in post-Soviet space to escape the isolation of decades of domestically and internationally reinforced division and containment.

The schools of classical Eurasianism and neo-Eurasianism as developed by émigré Russian scholars led by Nikolai Trubetskoi (Trubetskoi 1952; Shlapentokh 2007) during the inter-war years and later by Aleksandr Dugin (Dugin 1997; Shenfield 2001) envisaged a Eurasian identity as distinct from Europe and Asia, with characteristics not identifiable with either of the two. The Eurasian doctrine as developed by these scholars, despite crucial differences, mainly argues that Eurasia comprises the territory of the former Soviet Union and Russian empire. It has evolved as a civilisation over the past 700 years since the Mongol conquest of Russia in the thirteenth century, and its most significant cultural constituents are Orthodox Christianity, Buddhism and Islam, all combined in the 'symphonic personality of Eurasia' (Palat 1993: 2799). Both schools insist upon the significance of multiple layers of identity within the broader Eurasian concept. In addition to the single 'Eurasian' identity of Eurasia's consolidated totality – what Nikolai Trubetskoi called Russia-Eurasia's 'upper level' – there is also an elaborate mosaic of more localised identities at the lower levels (Bassin 2008: 287). Aleksandr Dugin further extended the concept and provided it with a geopolitical spin by positing a primordial, dualistic conflict between 'Atlanticism' (led by the United States and the United Kingdom) and 'Eurasianism' (led by Russia) (Dunlop 2004: 13). Neo-Eurasianism gained increasing currency in the post-Soviet period in the late 1990s and afterwards as its advocates, particularly Dugin, enjoyed proximity to policy circles in the Kremlin.

Defining Eurasia is a complex task not only in terms of geography, but also in terms of socio-cultural aspects. Its diversities preclude the possibilities of a rigorous generalisation. The concept can be seen as more interactive than integrative (Weisbrode 2001: 11). Analysts who emphasise the interactive aspect argue that the region witnessed the dawn of civilisation and its gradual proliferation to other parts of the globe (Diamond 1997: 176–192). According to one argument, ancestors of the Turkic tribes inhabited parts of Eurasia some 10,000 years ago, later migrating in all directions (Khidribekughli 2004: 4–5). The historical chronology of the region shows that diverse empires and cultures traversed the region, making it a zone of hybrid identity and culture. These migratory people impacted the cultures of Europe as well as the cultures of Asia. They also conditioned the history of the region. Some of the distinct characteristics of the Eurasian region include: the historic confrontation between nomadic horsemen and settled agriculturalists; the lands where Turkic, Iranian, Caucasian, Mongolian, Tungusic and Tibetan people proliferated; the Inner Asian religions of Islam, Buddhism and Shamanism; and the emergence of newly independent states from the disintegration of the Soviet Union (Schoeberlein 2002: 4–5). The region as a whole is not homogenous in terms of ethnicity, religion, culture or language. The vision of Eurasia as a theatre of interaction between diverse cultures, religions, languages and empires has given rise to the prospects of coexistence of diverse identities but without imposed assimilation. Varied approaches to account for the developments in the aftermath of the Soviet collapse notwithstanding, there has not been a particular theory developed so far that can account for the myriad diversities of the region and the consequent identity clashes. There is uncertainty about current politics and the future possibilities for the region. This propels the countries of the region to search for ways to address their security needs and meet new challenges in the post-Soviet era (Kupchan 1994).

The constructivist approach to the study of Eurasia analyses the fluidity and multiplicity of identities as they function in nation formation and the practice of domestic and foreign policy. Rather than conceiving of nations and states as possessing single identities from which their interests and behaviour follow, the approach evaluates political actors as capable of employing various identities, constituted both historically and by elites, who shape their attitudes and actions in domestic and international arenas (Suny 1999–2000: 139). This approach does not rely solely on grand narratives or dogmas, but is guided by factors already existent, such as insecurity and danger and fear of an uncertain future. It assumes there is a lack of any 'guiding visions' or conception of a 'national idea' towards defining the region as it hosts diverse ethnic communities and clashing interests, and suffered 'most economically, politically, and in terms of ethnic and civil conflict after the breakup of the Soviet Union'. For instance, the Caucasian region – highly ethnically diverse, with about 130 ethnic groups living together under the Soviet command system (Souders and Kanet 1994: 134) – found itself in the vortex of instability and violence as the system of forced peace was ruptured after the collapse of the Soviet edifice in 1991, thus allowing old conflicting identities to resurface. As a result, one can witness conflicts in the wider Eurasian landscape as in Kosovo, South Ossetia and Abkhazia, Chechnya and many others that transcend the borders of the emerging nation-states.

Another enduring change shaping Eurasia is its growing openness to the outside world after the collapse of the Soviet Union (Hunter 1996: 313). Often associated with the terms 'heartland', 'great game', 'new great game' and 'grand chess board', Eurasia was a factor in the imperial rivalry in the nineteenth and early twentieth centuries between the British and Russian empires. The British colonialists were apprehensive of a possible Russian advance towards the important Indian colony, and so stepped up geopolitical manoeuvres to control the geopolitically important region of Central Asia through Afghanistan. The Russians perceived the whole area as their natural sphere of influence. The Eurasian heartland had enticed outside powers to influence the politics of the vast geopolitical landmass. In his ground-breaking research *The Geographical Pivot of History*, Halford J. Mackinder emphasised the crucial significance of the region as it can emerge as a strategic springboard. For the enhancement of European power, he argued: 'Europe is but a small corner of the great island which also contains Asia and Africa … only to the south-east [present day Central Asia] were there practicable oasis-routes leading to the outer world' (Mackinder 1919: 70; Kearns 2009).

The post-Cold War world was not free from the calculations of geopolitics; rather, new dimensions were added to the calculations. Post-Soviet Eurasia witnessed multiple players, both global and regional, with divergent geo-strategic and economic objectives getting involved in the region, as earlier the Soviet domination kept it almost closed to international scrutiny. It was only after the collapse of the Soviet Union, with the 'parade of sovereignty' in 1991–1992, that Eurasia was opened to scrutiny from a de-ideological, post-Cold War perspective whereby the region's importance as an energy source, a ground for religious extremism and an experiment in liberalisation, democratic and market reforms and nation-building became prominent. This complex scenario provides the occasion to study the region in an interdisciplinary framework. It also necessitates an approach which transcends mono-causal explanations and analyses 'the relation between political power and geographical space in terms that take into account disparate processes shaping contemporary Eurasian space' (Labban 2009: 3).

Contextualising Eurasian conflicts

The term 'conflict', owing to its fluid nature, is applied generically to various kinds of situations. From a broader perspective the term implies the pursuit of incompatible goals by different people or groups. These goals can range from contradictory needs within a family to competition over scarce resources between members of a community or between neighbouring countries, or to opposing factions seeking political or economic control (Coser 1956; Dessler 1980; Horowitz 1985; Moore 1986; Pruitt and Rubin 1986). When conflict becomes violent and includes weapons of destruction, the term used is 'armed conflict'. The Uppsala Conflict Data Project defines a major armed conflict as a

> contested incompatibility that concerns government and/or territory over which the use of armed force between the military forces of two parties, of which at least one is the government of a state, has resulted in at least 1000 battle-related deaths in any single year.
>
> (*SIPRI Year Book 2002* [2003]: 77)

Though the end of the Cold War led to the decline of interstate warfare, it inversely led to the rise of conflicts confined within nation-states, or on the boundaries of neighbouring states. Modern conflicts are complex in nature, as most of them are intrastate with, at times significant amount of, aid and fuel coming from across the formal boundaries of the state. According to Skelsbaek and Smith, from the beginning of 1990 until the end of 1999, the world witnessed 118 armed conflicts, most of which were civil wars, often confined to one region of a country but internationalised through the involvement of outside powers (Skelsbaek and Smith 2001: 3).

In the post-Cold War era one of the locales of inter- and intrastate conflicts has been the Eurasia region, in which the diversities and volatilities have challenged the existing structures and patterns of state formation, governance, security and peace prospects with global implications. A study by the Interdisciplinary Research Project on the Root Causes of Gross Human Rights Violations (PIOOM), based in Leiden, covering the year from summer 2000 to summer 2001, found that a total of 59 violent political conflicts were located in the Asian region, out of which 38 were in Central Asia and South Asia (Jongman 2003: 19). Many of the conflicts in Eurasian space are deeply embedded in the debris of the Soviet Union, but in many cases the parties are without clear identities (Suny 1999–2000: 140). The issue of ethnic diversity and conflicting interests along ethnic lines is quite crucial. In an age of increased global awareness with advanced means of communication beyond state control, ethnicity cutting across borders has become a major issue for multiethnic states to confront.

The countries of Central Asia and the Caucasus are rich in ethnic heterogeneity, a characteristic common to neighbouring states including Turkey, Iran, Afghanistan and Pakistan. All Central Asian states are to varying degrees multiethnic and have ethnic linkages with each other: Kazakhstan, Kyrgyzstan, Uzbekistan and Turkmenistan are, to varying degrees, Turkic-speaking nations; only Tajikistan differs by its Persian ethnic and cultural roots. As Sébastien Peyrouse and Marlène Laruelle, in their study of Kyrgyzstan conflict, argue, the deteriorating socio-economic conditions and unstable political life coupled with unemployment, recession and migration flows have intensified interethnic conflicts in the region (Chapter 7). The political borders between these states correspond poorly to ethnic settlement patterns. Afghanistan's role as a bridge between Central and South Asia is illustrated most clearly in its ethnic divisions. Afghanistan shares borders with three countries of Central Asia – Tajikistan, Uzbekistan and Turkmenistan – and with Pakistan and Iran. The convergence of Afghan Taliban and Pakistani Taliban could become possible partly due to their predominantly ethnic Pashtun origin. Roughly half of the Afghan population is Pashtun; nevertheless, more Pashtuns live in Pakistan than in Afghanistan. On the other hand, over one-quarter of Afghanistan's population comprise Tajiks, Uzbeks and Turkmens, inhabiting the northern parts of the country on the border with Central Asia. Hence, developments in Afghanistan impact these countries. This same pattern can be observed in other parts of Eurasia. The ethnic Kurds are spread over the territories of Iraq, Iran and Turkey. Their demand for autonomy has wide-ranging implications for the policies of these countries. The 2008 violence between ethnic Tibetans – spread across Tibet, Sichuan and Gansu – and the Chinese forces brought into the open the clashes among the diverse ethnic communities in China. China's trouble does not end with Tibet. Its northwestern Xinjiang province is the home of the Uyghurs, close to ten million Turkic people speaking a language almost identical to Uzbek. Interestingly, Kazakh, Kyrgyz and Uzbek communities also exist in Xinjiang. As Henryk Szadziewski argues, Han Chinese migration to the region, political and economic marginalisation of the Uyghur people, as well as curbs on Uyghur cultural rights, such as religious and linguistic freedoms, are all issues of contention between Uyghur civil society and the Chinese government (Chapter 10).

The Caucasus region is also prone to ethnic conflicts. The whole Caucasus region is confined not only to the post-Soviet trans-Caucasus states of Armenia, Azerbaijan and Georgia, but also includes parts of southern Russia. The three trans-Caucasus countries remained under Czarist rule for about two centuries before coming under the control of the Soviet socialist regime in the early twentieth century. These countries had experienced imperial rule under Persian, Roman and Ottoman empires. After the collapse of the Soviet Union these countries emerged independent, but found themselves in disarray. The peace imposed from Moscow ended with the collapse of the Soviet Union. Thomas de Waal, analysing the Nagorno-Karabakh conflict, raised the question of why and how the mass peaceful coexistence of decades turned so suddenly into conflict, and argued that despite coexistence, trade and intermarriage between Armenians and

Azerbaijanis, there was astonishingly little dialogue between them, so 'both held on to two sharply contradictory narratives on the question of conflict' (Waal 2003: 125). Hence, it was no surprise that the issue of boundary disputes, ethnic turbulence and the lack of stable and vibrant political systems confronted all these countries. This whole region from the Black Sea in the east to the Caspian Sea in the west and from southern Russia in the north to Turkey and Iran in the south is inhabited by numerous ethnic communities but with little reconciliation and dialogue. Whether it is Nagorno-Karabakh (Chapter 4), South Ossetia (Chapter 5) or Chechnya (Chapter 6), the region is known as a zone of instability. The politics of assimilation and expulsion of ethnic communities from each others' territories is one of the fundamental issues that the states in the region face. It not only changes demographic structures, but also fuels violent clashes and leads to parallelisms between various conflicts (Chapter 2). The conflicts in the region are embedded in structural factors as well as impacted by agency, with perceptions of space and power being conflictual. As Françoise Companjen and Abel Polese argue, such an approach moves away from the neo-realist state-centred approach to provide a more socio-cultural and economically embedded vision of the conflict (Chapter 5).

The identity search by emerging countries of Eurasia has been further complicated by developments that took place in the post-Soviet era. One such development is religious fundamentalism and extremism and the realisation that countering extremism through force has not been successful, as the case of Afghanistan reveals (Chapter 9); instead, the phenomenon has spill-over effects in parts of the Eurasia region. The Taliban in Afghanistan, and its spread to Central Asian states, particularly Tajikistan and Uzbekistan (which also have ethnic links with Afghanistan), has created a dangerous platform for terrorism and Islamic extremism in Central Asia. While under Soviet control religion was subdued by communist ideology; the post-Soviet phase generated a great interest in Islam in former Soviet republics (Rakhimov 2010: 36). The emerging trend in post-Soviet space is oriented more towards changing society through religious proselytising than through political mobilisation as shown by the Hizb ut-Tahrir movement (Roy 2003: 97–108). A revival of Islamic traditions unique to these societies could not be considered harmful, but its transformation to extremism and intolerance can challenge multiethnic structures of these societies. Whether it is the Afghan Taliban, Tehrik-e-Taliban Pakistan, the Islamic Movement in Uzbekistan, Hizb ut-Tahrir in Kyrgyzstan or the idea of establishing a Caucasian Caliphate mooted by Chechen radical leader Doku Umarov, all these forces have not only challenged prospects for democracy and stability in the region, but also ignited the desire for a religion-based resolution of conflicts (Chapter 6). Operation Enduring Freedom in 2001 might have stalled Taliban activities, but their recent resurgence in Afghanistan and Pakistan has generated fear of Taliban-like activities engulfing the whole region. A study by the PIOOM predicted that the war against terrorism might result in escalation of conflict in Chechnya, the Middle East, Pakistan, Kashmir and other parts of Asia (Jongman 2003: 19). A careful reading of the statement by former Kyrgyz President Kurmanbek Bakiyev at the Collective Security Treaty Organization (comprising former Soviet republics of Armenia, Belarus, Kazakhstan, Kyrgyzstan, Russia, Tajikistan and Uzbekistan) summit on 14 June 2009 reveals how concerned the regional leaders are about the Taliban surge in Pakistan and Afghanistan. Bakiyev observed:

> The situation in Pakistan is very grave; the situation in Afghanistan is serious.... If the conflict against the Taliban deepens further in Afghanistan, which direction will people head in? God help us, they will move toward Tajikistan, Kyrgyzstan, Uzbekistan, and beyond.
>
> (Radio Free Europe/Radio Liberty 2009)

The resilience and strength of institutions in a state also determine the nature and scope of conflict. In a democracy where the institutions are strong to counter anti-social and anti-state activities, the potential for violent conflict is minimal because grievances are channelled through well-functioning civil society groups, media, political parties and other democratic mechanisms, thus reducing the scope for expressing dissatisfaction and disagreement in non-democratic ways. But democratic political institutions or ethnic and religious homogeneity and high military spending alone are insufficient to defend the state against large-scale violence in the absence of economic development (World Bank 2003). The mere establishment of democratic mechanisms without addressing the concerns of the people may not transform the conflict (Chapter 7). The Kashmir situation brings into focus the linkage between economic development and peace, which cannot be substituted by mere establishment of formal democratic structures (Chapter 11). Political factors related to leadership and governance have their own share in fuelling conflicts. Lack of state legitimacy, greed of rulers and armed groups and militias with vested interests all contribute to violent conflicts (Berdal and Malone 2000). John Schoeberlein (2003: 66–69) has emphasised the following factors that enhance conflict potentials in the Central Asia region: failure of leadership in areas of governance and economy; a confrontational stance and aggressive policies by leaders; conflict over resources; decline of education; weak civil society; and lack of strong linkage between populations and their governments. The signs were quite apparent even before the collapse of the Soviet Union, the most prominent being the 1989 pogrom carried out against Meskhetian Turks in Uzbekistan, resulting in hundreds of deaths and the exodus of 100,000 Meskhetians from the region. In summer 1990, even more severe violence broke out in southern Kyrgyzstan in clashes between the Uzbek and Kyrgyz communities, which resulted in perhaps 1,000 deaths (ibid.: 67). The 1998 incident at the Tajikistan–Uzbekistan border, in which insurgents led by Mahmud Khudayberdiev entered Tajikistan from Uzbekistan, and the 1999 and later campaigns by the Islamic Movement of Uzbekistan from the territory of Tajikistan, or the 2010 violence at Osh in Kyrgyzstan are some of the other striking developments in this context.

The interplay between the countries of the region and their asymmetrical relations with the external powers have impacted the politics of the region. Unlike in the past, many countries in the region have asymmetric relationships with Russia. The relations between Russia and former Soviet republics in the continental sphere of Europe and Asia became subject to diverse factors, among which two are prominent. First, Russia no longer enjoyed imperial status nor the ideological weapon and control of the Soviet Union; its geography squeezed, the new Russian foreign policy (Mandelbaum 1998) searched for alternatives. Second, the collapse provided the emerging nations with the freedom to seek partners to suit their national interests. The play of conflicting currents of politics, culture and economics between Russia and the West make Eurasia a contested space. The emerging countries, without any overarching socialist control, preferred the course which their leaders considered appropriate for their national interests. While countries like Georgia and Azerbaijan expressed an interest in joining the North Atlantic Treaty Organization (NATO) to counter Russian influence, countries like Kazakhstan attempted to maintain relations with Russia in a collaborative framework, while simultaneously trying to develop relations with the West. To a significant extent, the 11 September 2001 terrorist attack, which shattered a number of myths related to security and order, led the West to evince a major interest in the region (Lederach 2003: 9–13). The post-Soviet space emerged to occupy a 'front-stage geopolitical location hardly imaginable before the event' (Allison 2004: 277). The United States established military bases in Central Asian countries after 9/11, thereby making it possible for Washington to shape regional affairs effectively. Broadly, the projected US interest in the region is three-fold: to promote democracy and human rights; to have another source of energy for it and its allies; and to enhance its influence and relations in the region. Through various mechanisms such as the partnership for peace (PfP) programme of NATO, it aims to expand cooperation with the countries of the region. The interests of the European Union (EU) in the region are similar to those of the United States, though the geographic proximity makes it more vulnerable to the volatility in the region. The member countries of the EU individually have also attempted to develop relationships in the region. While the West has enhanced its activities in the Eurasian region, Russia perceives it as encroachment into its sphere of influence. This Russian perception has been strengthened by the viewpoint that the United States has used the massive military build-up in Central Asia to seal the 'Cold War victory against Russia, to contain Chinese influence and to tighten the noose around Iran' (Kleveman 2003). Russia considers the region its backyard, to be watched and nursed carefully and sometimes to be tackled with force, while the West aims to 'consolidate and perpetuate the prevailing geopolitical pluralism on the map of Eurasia' (Brzezinski 1997: 51). The 'constrained' Russia perceives the West, especially NATO, 'as an intruder and competitor in its western borderlands', while the West perceives itself as a 'partner and also a revolutionary', aiming to bring political stability and economic prosperity to the region (Garnett 1998: 91).

During the Cold War and initial post-Cold War years, the energy potential of the region was not adequately highlighted. Developments like the Arab–Israeli conflict, the Iranian issue, terrorism and volatile regimes in the Gulf have raised concerns about the strategic consequences of losing control over the oil supplies from the region. These developments, coupled with geo-strategic imperatives and the importance of Eurasia, have evinced the attention of players in this post-Soviet space. The nascent focus on Eurasia as a hub of energy is reflected in the statement:

> it is ironic that the Western community of nations, while not hesitating to wage a costly war in order to keep the Kuwaiti oil fields from changing hands, virtually ignores the possibility of what may happen in the event of the rich oil and gas fields of Western Siberia (Russia), Kazakhstan, Turkmenistan and Azerbaijan falling into unfriendly, anti-Western hands.
>
> (George 1992: 25)

According to estimates, the Caspian Sea basin alone contains the second largest source of oil and the largest source of natural gas in the world. Rising oil prices and energy consumption make certain that the conflicts in the Eurasian region will not be untouched by energy politics, as the pipelines (such as Baku–Tbilisi–Ceyhan, South Stream and Nabucco) and politics involving them spark rivalries and shape regional and international relations. Some of the pipelines pass through or border conflict-prone areas such as Nagorno-Karabakh, Abkhazia, South Ossetia, Chechnya, Dagestan and Afghanistan (Bahgat 2002: 323). The conflict in Nagorno-Karabakh or the 2008 war in Caucasus cannot be viewed in total isolation from the pipeline politics of the region. Companjen rightly argues that, among various factors, 'energy politics is also chipped in the negotiations around Nagorno-Karabakh' (Chapter 4).

Besides reviving traditional linkages with the region, China has attempted to further its geo-strategic objectives and cultivate economic relations with the energy-rich region. It has clinched major deals with countries in the region to import oil and gas. Through the Shanghai Cooperation Organization (SCO), military pacts and joint exercises, China is ready to play a decisive role. In comparison, India appears to have adopted a less competitive approach despite its traditional linkages with this region, though there is an increasing realisation in Indian policy circles that it cannot remain aloof from the developments in the region. The Indian subcontinent has geographic proximity with the region. Past linkages, including the silk route, not only carried trade but also religion, culture and migration. The silk route passed through an undivided Kashmir towards Central Asia and China (Mahapatra 2008). The Kashmir conflict, primarily with an unsettled border dimension, continues to witness intermittent violence (Chapter 11), thereby minimising the chances of a revival of the silk route trade that can help India to reach out to other parts of Eurasia. The resolution of this conflict could be crucial for energy-hungry India in terms of reviving ties and thereby raising the stakes in this energy-rich region.

Two other major influences from the immediate periphery include Turkey and Iran. While Russia significantly bases its influence on its long control over the major part of the region, Iranian and Turkic influences stem from their geographical contiguity and historical and cultural ties. Eurasian languages have either Turkic or Persian roots, with later Russian influence. Most of the people living in the region – such as Tatars, Bashkorts, Azeris, Turkmens, Kyrgyz, Kazakhs, Uyghurs and Uzbeks – share a common Turkic language heritage. Tajiks and Afghans derive their language from Persian roots. The influence of Arabic is also considerable. It was only in the twentieth century that the Arabic writing system and calendar were replaced with Russian-derived ones for the Turkic and Iranian languages of Central Asia (Lehrman 2004: 5–6). Turkey's membership of NATO and its cultural and linguistic affinity with the countries of the region has put it in a special position in Eurasian politics. In the aftermath of independence in the region, Turkey, through its trade relations, energy projects, education relations and people-to-people contacts, has attempted to drive these countries westward. Iran has three major objectives in the region: to expand its infrastructure; to gain political and economic influence through organisations like the Economic Cooperation Organization (ECO); and to acquire shares in a number of Caspian oil and gas developments and export ventures. While the Iranian influence is more distinct in Central Asian countries, the influence of Turkey is more prominent in Caucasian states such as Azerbaijan. But this impact has also led to sullen memories of rivalries, conquest and empire-building. Unlike Turkey, Iran's close relations with Russia put it in a different orbit. Turkey–West relations and Iran–Russia relations have been perceived as antagonistic to each other. Maintaining and consolidating stability in the region thus remains a formidable task, involving both domestic developments in the new states and their external interactions. As Jason Strakes has emphasised in his study on Kurdistan (Chapter 8), the relations between powers like Turkey, Iran and Iraq have shaped regional developments. The complex developments have led to cycles of reciprocal misunderstanding, explained by perceptions that what one is doing is legitimate, defensive and benign, but what the other is doing is improper, aggressive and dangerous (Mandelbaum 1998: 6).

Exploring peace

The sharp rise in the number of conflicts in various regions in the post-Cold War period enhanced the significance of peace studies as a discipline to impact on actions of parties in a conflict towards its transformation. While one can trace the origin of the discipline of conflict resolution to the 1950s and 1960s, the study gained increasing currency in the 1980s (Miall *et al.* 2003: 29). The 1990s witnessed the emergence of a robust discipline of conflict resolution and peace studies (Barash 1991; Smoker *et al.* 1990; Rapoport 1992; Sandole and Merwe 1993; Galtung 1996). The emerging field of peace studies attempted to locate conflict beyond a state-centric realist paradigm. Conflict, the new field argues, does not emerge solely from political crisis as the traditional view holds, but from other deep-seated factors – economic, political or social, or a varied combination of them all. Studies indicate that conflict, among other things, is linked to economic retardation (Collier and Hoffler 1998; Buckles 1999; Anderson 1999), a lack of enabling freedom (Sen 1999) or a lack of harmony (Junne and Verhoken 2004). The emerging field of conflict resolution and peace studies has its natural place in the context of Eurasia towards, among others, exploring the suppressed tensions which burst forth in the post-Soviet space.

In his pioneering study on peace, Johan Galtung argues that peace is not mere absence of war and violence as the traditional understanding might imply. The problem, as he formulated, is under what conditions can different states, and nations within states, not only handle conflicts without violence – negative peace – but engage in cooperative projects for mutual benefit – positive peace. The concept of positive peace aims at influencing parties to the conflict to view the situation from a wider perspective: not only how to prevent conflict from turning violent but also how to resolve contentious issues before they turn violent and result in death and destruction. Its focus is far away from a winner-vs-defeated analysis to an exploration of conflict and its management in a non-zero sum framework. Such an approach also views violent wars as pathways to destruction rather than a means for conflict settlement. As Shirin Akiner (2012: 149) rightly argues, there are no perfect solutions to the complex challenges, but the pooling of experiences and resources helps to find better ways of tackling common concerns. It is also necessary that for inclusive peace stereotypes and preconceived notions about 'the others' should be abandoned.

In this volume, Galtung (Chapter 1) makes the case for peace by understanding the issue from a broader perspective. He cautions that conciliation without conflict resolution is pacification, which may buy time before violence returns because all roads to peace pass through 'deep conflict resolution'. The conflict resolution process must involve both state and non-state actors, including civil society groups. The conciliation process involves acknowledging 'past wrongs, elaborating how and why, and then defining a future together'. Galtung contends that dignity in a conflict situation can be achieved by a process in which parties to the conflict acknowledge, elaborate and design new ways of entering the future together. He argues that 'mediation means mapping conflicts, parties–goals–clashes, testing goals for legitimacy, bridging legitimate goals', and calls for 'empathy, non-violence and creativity'. Citing the case of the EU, he emphasises that third parties like the EU can play an effective role in conflicts. However, the third party must not factor their selfish interests in the calculus of conflict resolution. The recent EU role to broker peace in the aftermath of the war in the Caucasus in 2008 adds substance to his argument.

Emanuela Del Re (Chapter 2) analyses 'paradoxes' and 'levels' of conflict with implications at local, regional and international levels by focusing on Kosovo, South Ossetia and Abkhazia. She draws parallels between these conflicts to juxtapose whether the Kosovo model of conflict resolution can be an ideal one to be replicated elsewhere. She does so by analysing various formulations, such as 'The danger is that if NATO sides with Azerbaijan and Russia sides with Armenia' and 'Is South Ossetia the Kosovo of Russia?', 'Was it the case of a Russia that having been humiliated by the case of Kosovo was looking for revenge?'. The crises in Georgia and Kyrgyzstan, she argues, have been related to the conflict in Kosovo in speculative ways, but such a formulation rarely takes into account the possible effect that such conflicts could have been on Kosovo had they preceded the later. From a wider perspective, there is a certain degree of interdependence among the forces that shape conflicts in the new global scenario, where 'rhetorical conflict resolution techniques do not always prove to be adequate and unexpected interconnections and interests come into play'. Del Re points out that there are many violent truths in a conflict region that may be difficult to counter unless parties rise above their partisan approaches.

Andrew Foxall (Chapter 3) puts forward the significance of cartography for conflict resolution. Placing his study in the North Caucasus, with a particular focus on Stavropol' krai, the largest ethnic Russian territory in the North Caucasus, he presents a critical question: what is the role of maps in conflict management? By elevating Stavropol' krai as a prototype of a conflict-prone zone in the North Caucasus, he emphasises that the cartographical approach to conflict analysis can help policy-makers understand the region and craft policies accordingly so that the ethnic dimensions of the conflict can be comprehended and worked upon. Foxall highlights the role played by educational institutions in conflict management, arguing that 'educational tools, such as the Atlas, are an important part of the process of conflict management', as 'education provides an important neutral platform to address fundamental obstacles to peace because education is universally valued'. Such an approach, he points out, can motivate the parties to the conflict towards collaborative action. This is essential for social justice and human security, and hence for conflict resolution.

The role of external players in fuelling local conflicts is the focus of two chapters. In her chapter on Nagorno-Karabakh (Chapter 4), Françoise Companjen argues that the conflict is exacerbated by clashing interests of regional and external powers. She has brought into focus how players such as Russia, Georgia, Turkey and Iran perceive the issue, and how their different equations with Armenia and Azerbaijan affect the peace process. Besides explaining the origin of the dispute and factors shaping it, she explores the ongoing peace process and its future prospects. Making the case for a people-centric peace process, Companjen emphasises that though conflict resolution may not be imminent, it is crucial to focus on the process of resolution. There is a need to deal with practical issues such as how to involve the inhabitants of Nagorno-Karabakh in a public debate on the future of the region, how to create a fair and just method for gauging public perception and how to involve various parties in the conflict resolution process. Continuing Companjen's focus on the role of external factors, Companjen and Abel Polese (Chapter 5) elaborate the 2008 war between Georgia and Russia and conflicting perceptions of space and power in the Caucasus. The authors argue that the war could have been avoided. They analyse the role of human agency, in this case the role of the Russian and Georgian leaders, towards the escalation of events leading to violent conflict. They argue that 'the use of violence created more problems than it solved'. The war, instead of reducing the tense atmosphere in the region, further protracted it, exacting heavy damage in terms of human and natural resources. Abkhazia and South Ossetia may have different destinies ahead but, the authors argue, their fate may not be absolutely their choice. The 2008 war, Companjen and Polese contend, will likely goad other disgruntled regions in Eurasia to seek violent resolution to conflicts. They argue that for conflict resolution to be successful it is crucial to move away from the state-centred approach towards a more culturally and socially embedded understanding of the conflict.

When the involvement of parties in a complicated conflict is half-hearted the results are disappointing. When parties involved are not genuinely committed to peace and develop ad hoc mechanisms to foster peace, the result is continuation rather than containment of conflict. For the case of the Chechnya conflict, Dmitry Shlapentokh argues that the Chechen aspirations could have been 'nationalised' and 'parochialised' to suit the ideological element of the movement, but that did not succeed as the movement was swept over by the forces of fundamentalism and terrorism. It was also accentuated partly due to the lost opportunity provided by the Kashavyurt Accord (Chapter 6). The accord of 1996 between the Chechen rebels and Russia could have ushered peace in the region, but it failed as different parties harboured contrasting aspirations. This failure contributed to the protracted nature of the conflict. The establishment of the Caucasian Emirate in 2007 by Chechen rebel leaders further contributed to the radicalisation and internationalisation of the Chechnya movement for independence and included it in the map of global jihad.

Sébastien Peyrouse and Marlène Laruelle focus on the 2010 Osh events as a symptom of deeper malaise afflicting Kyrgyzstan. They analyse the issues confronting the post-Soviet state of Kyrgyzstan, which broadly mirror the conflicts in other parts of Central Asia (Chapter 7). The authors argue that the developments in 2010 represented a watershed not only for Kyrgyzstan but also for the whole of post-Soviet Central Asia as they bring into focus the 'major role of social transformations and the lack of economic prospects in fostering tensions'. Expressing doubt over whether the second 'revolution' that overthrew the Bakiyev regime could cater to the needs of state- and nation-building, the authors argue that the issues of underdevelopment, conflicting identity narratives and marginalisation of minorities, coupled with contested interests of players, pose enormous challenges for the fragile nation. They contend that 'the supposed merging of internal and external enemies constitutes a powerful driver of nationalist radicalisation, rallying diverging milieux'. The chapter also points out the ineffectiveness of state machinery to prevent ethnic tensions because it is involved in actions which cannot be considered neutral.

While arguing that regional integration can play an effective role for conflict resolution, Jason Strakes (Chapter 8) explores the prospects and pitfalls of a greater Kurdistan and the perception of the major parties – Turkey, Iraq and Iran – on the issue. He emphasises that subregional economic integration initiatives and agreements have led to relative peace in the region. The Kurdistan issue in the post-Saddam period offers insight into how the players have attempted to offer autonomy to the Kurdish people spread across the countries without actually conceding absolute freedom. Strakes presents a conceptual framework that links the evolution of sub-state diplomacy in Iraqi Kurdistan with conflict and cooperation in the region. He identifies the factors that have contributed to negative security conditions in the Kurdistan regional government territories during the past decade, and investigates the prospects for and evidence of subregional integration between Kurdistani, Syrian, Turkish and Iranian provincial governments

The challenges and prospects of involvement of stakeholders in conflict transformation in Afghanistan is the primary focus of my chapter (Chapter 9). I argue that instability in the country and its implications for the world necessitate a nuanced approach for conflict transformation in the war-torn country. The strategic location of the region, its rich resources and clashing interests of players enhanced Afghanistan's significance as a crucial factor in securing peace and stability at home as well as abroad. The attempts of the international security forces mandated to establish stability and order on Afghan soil and craft peace in a cooperative framework have not succeeded so far. Failed attempts to moderate the Taliban position are a reminder that peace in Afghanistan will be a very complex process. The chapter also focuses on perception of various players and their roles in the conflict, which are mostly shaped by rival interests. The problems of and in Afghanistan cannot be resolved by a sectarian or narrow regional approach, but rather through an overarching peace framework in which all the local, regional and international stakeholders are involved.

Conflict resolution involves creativity, and the case studies on Xinjiang and Kashmir have argued for innovative people-oriented approaches. Peace and development can be intertwined in the conflict zones by involving people, though the process is a difficult and complicated one. In his study of Xinjiang, Henryk Szadziewski focuses on a participatory development model, which can be adapted and applied to the conflict-torn region of Xinjiang (Chapter 10). The author makes an attempt to understand 'how non-governmental Uyghur actors in Xinjiang can operate in an authoritarian and repressive context to operationalise a participatory rights-based approach to development', besides exploring 'the opportunities for leverage that exist for marginalised Uyghur people and [assessing] whether a rights-based approach can at all exist in such repressive environments'. The Kashmir case is well known in international politics due to its protracted nature and nuclear dimension. Seema Shekhawat has focused on its internal dimension in terms of the ongoing separatist movement in the Indian part of Kashmir (Chapter 11). While conceding a holistic view of peace encompasses more than economic development, the chapter mainly deals with the issue of development and its linkage to conflict transformation in Kashmir. The situation in Kashmir has improved in recent years, mainly due to the parties' realisation of the futility of violence and its heavy costs. Though this realisation has not yet dawned in its full import, the peace overtures and negotiations (on-and-off after 2000) indicate that despite the troublesome pace of peace in the region, violence is unlikely to return. This period of thaw needs to be used to foster peace through people-centric development measures.

Conclusion

Exploration of Eurasia brings forth the crucial significance of conflicts in the region. Conflict study in Eurasia is a complex and multi-dimensional endeavour, which suggests that a priori assumptions about the conflicts and their peace prospects are likely to founder when confronted with empirical data. Far from being an analytical given that can be applied regardless of context, 'conflict' must be interrogated for its subtle and sometimes not so subtle shifts in meaning and form. Conflict potentials in the Eurasia region as an emerging theme of analysis cannot be ignored. The emergence of the region from a socialist-controlled economy to a developing market economy has set the stage for an intricacy, not only in terms of theory-building but more crucially in terms of nation-building, to enable a smooth transformation of conflicts while accommodating divergent aspirations. While arguing that each conflict has its locale, situation and dynamics that make it distinct from other conflicts, there are factors such as clash of interests, elements of discontent based on identity, religion, underdevelopment and legacies of the past which have shaped conflicts in the region to varying degrees.

The prevailing volatility, the rising menace of extremism and intermittent violence, the crisis of underdevelopment and poor governance, the competing influence and rich resources in the region in shaping the conflicts in Eurasia cannot be ignored. However, the divergent conflicts and their potential for peace are not on the same pedestal. Different conflicts in the region can be classified as, for example: frozen, such as Nagorno-Karabakh; simmering, such as Chechnya; or highly volatile, as in Afghanistan. But this classification does not minimise the prospect for their flaring up and engulfing the entire region. The prediction that a war in Nagorno-Karabakh may lead to a third world war (noted in Chapter 2) may appear far-fetched; however, it does animate the potential of the vast Eurasian landscape, not only as an unexplored zone of resources, but also as a zone of instability and violence with ramifications for the globe. In this age of globalisation and interconnectedness it is hardly possible that conflict in one region can be prevented from having a global effect. This understanding strengthens the peace constituency, in and outside the region, and gears this constituency for action. The issue, then, is not to study Eurasian conflicts as independent variables, but rather to study their hows and whys as a means to understand diverse factors that fuel conflicts in an attempt to widen discourse and include in its ambit the formulation of how to craft peace in the volatile region. The conflicts being studied have seen diverse peace manoeuvres; while volatile conflicts like Afghanistan have witnessed intense involvement of international and regional players, the 'frozen' conflicts have lacked such involvement. However, in all these cases the common element has been the failure of ad hoc peace mechanisms, as witnessed in the situation of Nagorno-Karabakh, Abkhazia, South Ossetia and Chechnya. As many of these conflicts have been suspended by ad hoc peace mechanisms, 'violence, terrorism and instability can reemerge' in the future. The priority is to move beyond identifying and studying actors in conflicts, or factors behind these conflicts, towards transforming them in a framework based on an inclusive peace. As the imperative of positive peace beckons, it is not a single factor, but rather an array of factors and in varying fashions that need to be addressed while crafting peace. Peace demands a multi-vector approach in which stakeholders must comprehend events individually, regionally and globally – simultaneously – towards resolving conflicts.

Note

I am thankful to anonymous referees for their helpful comments on an earlier version of this introduction.

References

Akiner, Shirin (2012) 'Civil Society in Uzbekistan: Continuity and Innovation', in Anita Sengupta, Suchandana Chatterjee and Sushmita Bhattacharya (eds) *Eurasia Twenty Years After*, New Delhi: Shipra Publications, pp. 129–152.

Allison, Roy (2004) 'Strategic Reassertion in Russia's Central Asia Policy', *International Affairs*, 80 (2): 277–293.

Anderson, M.B. (1999) *Do No Harm: How Aid Supports Peace – Or War*, London: Lynne Rienner.

Bahgat, Gawdat (2002) 'Pipeline Diplomacy: The Geopolitics of the Caspian Sea Region', *International Studies Perspectives*, 3 (3): 310–327.

Barash, David P. (1991) *Introduction to Peace Studies*, Belmont: Wadsworth.

Bassin, Mark (2008) 'Eurasianism "Classical" and "Neo": The Lines of Continuity', *Slavic Eurasian Studies*, 17: 279–294.

Berdal, M. and Malone, D. (eds) (2000) *Greed and Grievance: Economic Agendas in Civil Wars*, Boulder, CO: Lynne Rienner.

Black, Jeremy (1997) *Maps and History: Constructing Images of the Past*, New Haven, CT: Yale University Press.

Brook, Stephen (1992) *Claws of the Crab: Georgia and Armenia in Crisis*, London: Sinclair-Stevenson.

Brzezinski, Zbigniew (1997) 'A Geostrategy for Eurasia', *Foreign Affairs*, 76 (5): 50–64.

Buckles, Daniel (ed.) (1999) *Cultivating Peace: Conflict and Collaboration in Natural Resource Management*, Washington, DC: World Bank Institute.

Cohen, Stephen F. (1985) *Rethinking the Soviet Experience: Politics and History since 1917*, London: Oxford University Press.

Collier, Paul and Hoffler, A. (1998) 'On Economic Causes of Civil War', *Oxford Economic Papers*, 50 (4): 563–573.

Coser, Lewis A. (1956) *The Functions of Social Conflict*, New York, NY: Free Press.

Dawisha, Adeed and Dawisha, Karen (eds) (1995) *The Making of Foreign Policy in Russia and the New States of Eurasia*, New York, NY: M.E. Sharpe.

Dessler, G. (1980) *Organization Theory: Integrating Structure and Behaviour*, Englewood Cliffs, NJ: Prentice Hall.

Diamond, Jared (1997) *Guns, Germs and Steel*, London: Vintage.

Dugin, Aleksandr (1997) *The Foundations of Geopolitics: The Geopolitical Future of Russia*, Moscow: Arktogeya.

Dunlop, John B. (2004) 'Aleksandr Dugin's Foundations of Geopolitics', *Democratizatsiya: The Journal of Post-Soviet Democratization*, 12 (1): 1–35.

Fowkes, Ben (ed.) (1998) *Russia and Chechnya: The Permanent Crisis*, London: Macmillan.

Galtung, Johan (1996) *Peace by Peaceful Means: Peace and Conflict, Development and Civilization*, Thousand Oaks, CA: Sage.

Garnett, Sherman W. (1998) 'Europe's Crossroads: Russia and the West in the New Borderlands', in Michael Mandelbaum (ed.) *The New Russian Foreign Policy*, New York, NY: Council of Foreign Relations, pp. 64–99.

George, Dev (1992) 'Redefining the Middle East: New Countries, New Politics and New Activity', *The Offshore Middle East Report*, March: 25–27.

Goldenberg, Suzanne (1994) *Pride of Small Nations: The Caucasus and Post-Soviet Disorder*, London: Zed Books.

Hagen, Mark von (2004) 'Empires, Borderlands, and Diasporas: Eurasia as Anti-Paradigm for the Post-Soviet Era', *The American Historical Review*, 109 (2): 445–468.

Heathershaw, John (2009) *Post-Conflict Tajikistan: The Politics of Peacebuilding and the Emergence of Legitimate Order*, London: Routledge.

Horowitz, Donald L. (1985) *Ethnic Groups in Conflict*, Berkeley, CA: University of California Press.

Hunter, Shireen T. (1996) 'Forging Chains across Eurasia', *The World Today*, 52 (12): 313–316.

Jongman, Berto J. (2003) 'Mapping the Dimensions of Contemporary Conflicts and Human Rights Violations', in Monique Mekenkamp, Paul van Tongreen and Hans van de Veen (eds) *Searching for Peace in Central and South Asia: An Overview of Conflict Prevention and Peacebuilding Activities*, Boulder, CO: Lynne Rienner, pp. 17–27.

Junne, Gerd and Verkoren, Willemijn (2004) *Postconflict Development: Meeting New Challenges*, London: Lynne Rienner.

Kearns, Gerry (2009) *Geopolitics and Empire: The Legacy of Halford Mackinder*, New York, NY: Oxford University Press.

Khidirbekughli, Doulatbek (2004) 'Mysterious Eurasia: Thoughts in Response to Dr. Schoeberlein', *Central Eurasian Studies Review*, 3 (1): 4–5.

Kleveman, Lutz (2003) 'The New Great Game', *Guardian*, 20 October.

Kupchan, Charles A. (1994) 'Strategic Visions', *World Policy Journal*, 11 (3): 112–122.

Labban, Mazen (2009) 'The Struggle for the Heartland: Hybrid Geopolitics in the Transcaspian', *Geopolitics*, 14 (1): 1–25.

Lederach, John Paul (2003) 'Making our Way Back to Humanity: Beyond 11 September', in Monique Mekenkamp, Paul van Tongreen and Hans van de Veen (eds) *Searching for Peace in Central and South Asia: An Overview of Conflict Prevention and Peacebuilding Activities*, Boulder, CO: Lynne Rienner, pp. 9–13.

Lehrman, Alexander (2004) 'The Distinctive Factors of Central Eurasia: A Response to Professor Gleason', *Central Eurasian Studies Review*, 3 (1): 5–6.

Mackinder, H.J. (1904) 'The Geographical Pivot of History', *The Geographical Journal*, 23 (4): 421–437.

Mackinder, H.J. (1919) *Democratic Ideals and Reality: A Study in the Politics of Reconstruction*, London: Constable and Company Ltd.

Mahapatra, Debidatta Aurobinda (2008) *Central Eurasia: Geopolitics, Compulsions and Connections*, New Delhi: Lancers Publishers.

Mandelbaum, Michael (ed.) (1998) *The New Russian Foreign Policy*, New York, NY: Council of Foreign Relations.

Miall, Hugh, Ramsobotham, Oliver and Woodhouse, Tom (2003) 'Calling for a Broad Approach to Conflict Resolution', in Monique Mekenkamp, Paul van Tongreen and

Hans van de Veen (eds) *Searching for Peace in Central and South Asia: An Overview of Conflict Prevention and Peacebuilding Activities*, Boulder, CO: Lynne Rienner, pp. 29–34.

Moore, C.W. (1986) *The Mediation Process: Practical Strategies for Resolving Conflict*, San Francisco, CA: Jossey-Bass.

Palat, Madhavan K. (1993) 'Eurasianism as an Ideology for Russia's Future', *Economic and Political Weekly*, 28 (51): 2799–2809.

Parrott, Bruce (ed.) (1995) *State-Building and Military Power in Russia and the New States of Eurasia*, New York, NY: M.E. Sharpe.

Pruitt, D.G. and Rubin, J.Z. (1986) *Social Conflict: Escalation, Stalemate, and Settlement*, New York, NY: Random House.

Radio Free Europe/Radio Liberty (2009) 'SCO Summit: "Beast of The East" Appears to have Lost its Teeth', *Radio Free Europe/Radio Liberty*, 16 June.

Rakhimov, Mirzoid (2010) 'Writing Histories in Central Asia: Contemporary Dilemmas', in Maulana Abul Kalam Azad Institute of Asian Studies (ed.) *Writing History in Eurasia: The Soviet State and After*, Kolkata: Towards Freedom, pp. 34–39.

Rapoport, Anatol (1992) *Peace: An Idea Whose Time has Come*, Ann Arbor, MI: University of Michigan Press.

Roy, Olivier (2003) 'Islamic Militancy: Religion and Conflict in Central Asia', in Monique Mekenkamp, Paul van Tongreen and Hans van de Veen (ed.) *Searching for Peace in Central and South Asia: An Overview of Conflict Prevention and Peacebuilding Activities*, Boulder, CO: Lynne Rienner, pp. 97–108.

Sandole, Dennis J.D. and Merwe, Hugo van der (eds) (1993) *Conflict Resolution: Theory and Practice*, New York: St. Martin's Press.

Schoeberlein, John (2002) 'Setting the Stakes of a New Society', *Central Eurasian Studies Review*, 1 (1): 4–9.

—— (2003) 'Regional Introduction: A Host of Preventable Conflicts', in Monique Mekenkamp, Paul van Tongreen and Hans van de Veen (ed.) *Searching for Peace in Central and South Asia: An Overview of Conflict Prevention and Peacebuilding Activities*, Boulder, CO: Lynne Rienner, pp. 66–75.

Seely, Robert (2001) *Russo-Chechen Conflict, 1800–2000: A Deadly Embrace*, London: Frank Cass Publishers.

Sen, Amartya (1999) *Development as Freedom*, New York, NY: Random House.

Shenfield, Stephen D. (2001) *Russian Fascism: Traditions, Tendencies, Movements*, Armonk, NY: M.E. Sharpe.

Shlapentokh, Dmitry (ed.) (2007) *Russia between East and West: Scholarly Debates on Eurasianism*, Leiden: Brill.

SIPRI Yearbook 2002 (2003) Oxford: Oxford University Press, Appendix 1B.

Skelsbaek, Inger and Smith, Dan (2001) *Gender, Peace and Conflict*, New Delhi: Sage Publications.

Smoker, Paul, Davies, Ruth and Munske, Barbara (1990) (eds) *A Reader in Peace Studies*, New York, NY: Pergamon.

Souders, Brian V. and Kanet, Roger E. (1994) 'An Emerging Inter-State System: Russia and the Other Former Republics of the USSR', in P.L. Dash (ed.) *Russian Dilemma: The Ethnic Aftermath*, Cuttack: Aryan Prakashan.

Starr, S. Frederick (ed.) (1994) *The Legacy of History in Russia and the New States of Eurasia*, New York, NY: M.E. Sharpe.

Suny, Ronald Grigor (1999–2000) 'Provisional Stabilities: The Politics of Identities in Post-Soviet Eurasia', *International Security*, 24 (3): 139–178.

Tismaneanu, Vladimir (1995) *Political Culture and Civil Society in Russia and the New States of Eurasia*, New York, NY: M.E. Sharpe.

Trubetskoi, Nikolai S. (1952) *The Common Slavic Element in Russian Culture*, New York, NY: Columbia University.

Waal, Thomas de (2003) *Black Garden: Armenia and Azerbaijan through Peace and War*, New York, NY: New York University Press.

Weisbrode, Kenneth (2001) *Central Eurasia: Prize or Quicksand?*, New York, NY: Oxford University Press.

World Bank (2003) 'Breaking the Conflict Trap: Civil War and Development Policy', *A World Bank Policy Research Report*, Washington, DC: World Bank.

1 A perspective on conflict and peace[1]

Johan Galtung

Dilemmas of conflict and peace

In 1967, in a project for the Council of Europe, a theory was developed for positive peace, inspired by what at that time was the European Economic Community (EEC), the Nordic Community, the beginnings of what became the Association of South East Asian Nations (ASEAN), the Panchsheel[2] between China and India, and above all by Switzerland. The aim of the project was to resolve under what conditions different states, and nations within states, could not only handle conflicts without violence-negative peace, but engage in cooperative projects for mutual benefit-positive peace. Diplomacy was needed; as an institution, diplomacy had evolved from ad hoc envoys via resident bilateral diplomacy and multilateral ad hoc conferences to multilateral permanent organisations, with the United Nations (UN) as the crowning achievement so far. Conflict theory points to multilateralism rather than bilateralism, since a two-party situation has a built-in polarisation less open to deals that can lead to resolution.

Five necessary conditions have been identified for positive peace (Galtung and Lodgaard 1970):

1 symbiosis – mutual benefit;
2 equity – equal benefit;
3 homology – same structure, 'opposite numbers' easily identified;
4 entropy – cooperation mass well distributed between:

- government with government
- government with non-government
- within one state
- between states
- non-government with non-government;

5 transcendence – something more than the sum of states or nations, in practice a multilateral organisation-secretariat.

Diplomacy had been at that stage since the League of Nations, but the states were so different that the conditions of homology and entropy were not satisfied. According to this theory, much more was expected from the six-party multilateral Treaty of Rome EEC of January 1958 than from the German–French bilateralism of May 1950, which centred on two issues: coal and steel. The rest is history, both as broadening of the domain from six to 27 members, and as deepening of the scope from two to diverse cooperation items today. The European Union (EU) story is a success both from a negative and positive peace point of view, capable of handling a rolling agenda of issues, but with such glaring exceptions as the democracy deficit and the euro zone crisis, among other things.

The project for Council of Europe went beyond the Western European countries to the area spanned by NATO–Warsaw Pact–neutral non-aligned (NN) countries. Research was carried out in 19 of those countries, from Washington, DC to Moscow, from Norway to Greece. The most critical conflicts were, of course, over borders, human rights, arms races and deployment, particularly of nuclear arms; the most promising project was economic cooperation under the institutional umbrella of the UN Economic Commission for Europe in Geneva. By simple extrapolation, a UN Security Commission for Europe was among the proposals, with links to what became the Conference-Organization for Security and Cooperation in Europe (C(O)SCE) in Helsinki/Vienna.

During the Cold War (1949–1989) four conditions were identified for a more modest goal – survival of a hot war (Galtung 1984):

- being neutral non-aligned – not being a member of military alliances;
- using defensive defence as the military doctrine;
- self-reliance, so not going to war for resources;
- usefulness to others if kept intact.

This singled out Switzerland, Albania and Yugoslavia, and then Finland, Sweden and Austria as the most likely survivors. More geared towards negative peace, we can only celebrate that the theory was not tested.

In 2010, 20 years away from the Cold War, and the perspective is no longer North Atlantic and Europe-centred, but the era of globalisation. The Warsaw Pact has been dissolved and NATO has expanded eastward, breaking the promises to Gorbachev. The Soviet empire has collapsed, along with communism. In the view of the author the US hegemony is also collapsing (Galtung 2010), and the brand of capitalism it stands for is in deep crisis. These deep and very quick processes – forgetting the accelerating effect of living globally in real time, with ultra-quick communication – lead to a number of key questions, including some about the status and influence of the EU.

On its long march from community-confederation to federation-superstate, the EU has for a long time been 'a superpower in the making' (Galtung 1973). The joint foreign policy and joint security policy of a federation are lagging, but probably emerging; the euro zone with 17 of the 27 goes far towards a joint financial policy, the present problems notwithstanding. How far the system has moved towards a joint army, joint arms production, joint command, control, communications and intelligence (C3I) and access to nuclear arms of member states is difficult to judge. There is a joint passport, an anthem, a day of celebration. But is there really a joint enemy? The situation is ambiguous. The capability, like for a rapid deployment force (RDF) with a global reach, is approaching that of other superpowers, be they fallen or falling. With 11 former colonial powers there is much tradition to be re-enacted, and a 'joint foreign policy' of the 'I'll accept your activity in your former area if you accept mine in mine' variety is needed. But what is the intention? Is it for security for the Council of Ministers and peace for the Commission, or both for both, but with different weighting, military for one, civilian for the other? Or is it towards filling a possible gap when the US hegemony falls and China is unwilling to or incapable of doing so?

We live in a context of two major and related processes. First is regionalisation, based on high-speed transportation and communication, which comes up against cultural borders. Four regions exist – the EU; the African Union (AU); the South Asian Association for Regional Cooperation (SAARC); and the ASEAN – and four are yet to come – Estados Unidos de America Latina y el Caribe (ALC); a Russian Union (RU), with autonomy for all non-Russians; an East Asian community like the Shanghai Cooperation Organization (SCO), with 50 per cent of humanity; and the Organization of Islamic Community (OIC), the ummah from Morocco to Mindanao. Second, the rapid decline and fall of the United States, which, if handled well, may be a blessing for the US Republic as it was for the 11 EU member colonial countries liberated from empires.

The successor system to the present state system with a hegemon will not be a state system with China or the EU as hegemon; nor will it be a globalisation with that much cultural diversity. Quick transportation and real-time communication transcend state borders, but because cultural vicinities and affinities prevent globalisation with a single state – The World – and one nation – humanity – these will not emerge onto the scene until later. We have to make do with waxing regionalisation between the fading state system and a future globalisation. The successor to the present system will be regionalisation, and the EU – being the most mature region – will/can play a major role. There are four regions containing more than 90 of the 192 UN member states: the EU (27 states); the AU (53 states); the SAARC (eight states); and the ASEAN (ten states). Further, three areas seem likely to undergo regionalisation processes: the SCO (six members), Latin America (LA) and the Caribbean (35 countries) and the OIC (as a deepening of the present Organization of Islamic Conference, with 56 members from Morocco to Mindanao; also seen as a struggle for a new caliphate). Russia may one day become region number 8 (the RU), granting Chechnya as much autonomy as the Netherlands has inside the EU. Of the eight regions, the EU, LA, OIC, SAARC and Russia are mono-civilisational, with huge minorities, and AU, ASEAN and SCO are multi-civilisational, more typical of a globalised world.

Some countries are not clearly included in these eight regions: the United Kingdom, United States, Australia and Japan. Will they one day form their own region? Or will younger people in the UK prefer the EU, in Japan the SCO, in Israel some Middle East community, in Australia (with New Zealand) also the SCO, leaving the United States with MEXUSCAN,[3] with Mexico as a bridge to Latin

America? From the history of an interventionist United States it follows that a successor system is neither peaceful nor the opposite. What follows? Let us project the seven most likely regions with seven relations within, and 21 bilateral relations between them – altogether 28 – into a future where there will still be states and nations around, but losing in salience to regions and civilisations (Table 1.1).

The regional, multilateral world shown in Table 1.1, with seven 'no relation', 14 'okay relations', six 'problematic relations' (EU penetrating AU and LA, and intra-regional problems), and only one 'gross problematic relation' (SAARC–OIC) actually does not look that bad at all (Table 1.2).

The most isolated region is LA. The region relating best to all the others is the SCO, closely followed by the ASEAN and EU. The region with most problems with others is the AU (lack of stability within, structural violence from the EU and direct violence from the OIC). The worst problem is between the SAARC and OIC. Looking at the list of the three postulated coming regions, the SCO, Latin America–Caribbean and the OIC are on the way, provoking US counter-forces. An East Asian Community with the two Chinas, the two Koreas and the two Japans (with the Northern Territories) is also taking shape, without Russia and four of the Central Asian republics. The SCO is a reaction to the United States encircling the Russia–China land mass, and may disappear with that encircling, paving the way for East Asia.

Table 1.1 Probable inter-regional relations

	EU	*AU*	*SAARC*	*ASEAN*	*SCO*	*LA*	*OIC*
EU	OK	?	OK	OK	OK	?	OK
AU		?	0	0	OK	0	?
SAARC			?	OK	OK	0	!!!
ASEAN				OK	OK*	0	OK
SCO					OK	0	OK
LA						OK	0
OIC							?

Notes

In Table 1.1 '0' means no relation, 'OK' means exactly that, '?' means that there are problems and '!!!' means gross problems.

* The ASEAN initiative to establish an ASEAN+3 (China, Japan and South Korea), an East Asian Economic Community like the Asia Pacific Economic Community, the United States–Pacific rim, paralleling US Atlanticism with Europe, may coexist with those highlighted here because they are more cohesive, less artificial. But the intra-bloc trade ratio is impressive for ASEAN+3 (60 per cent), even if beaten by the EU (70 per cent).

Table 1.2 Regional relations profiles

	EU	*AU*	*SAARC*	*ASEAN*	*SCO*	*LA*	*OIC*
0s		3	2	2	1	5	1
OKs	5	1	3	5	6	1	3
?s	2	3	1			1	2
!!!s			1				1

What would be the status and influence of the EU in a world of regions? Considerable, if the EU lives up to the challenge. The EU will have enormous status and influence as the model region, having achieved so much inner positive peace, directly, structurally and culturally. The others are all lining up to learn the tricks, to ask the EU to open the boxes of successes and failures. The world relatively recently having been colonised by the 11 colonial powers, many in the other regions speak their colonial languages, even if the colonisers never bothered to learn theirs, putting them at an enormous advantage in a one-way learning process.

There are some regions in crisis areas where the EU could be a particularly useful conflict resolution formula: a Middle East Community consisting of Israel with its 1967 territorial limit and its neighbouring five Arab states including internationally recognised Palestine: a Central Asian Community of Afghanistan and the regions bordering on Afghanistan, all Muslim, absorbing much of the SCO; a West Asian Community, Turkey–Iran–Pakistan–Afghanistan, all Muslim, possibly via Iraq–Iran–Armenia–Azerbaijan; and a Caucasian Community, Georgia–Armenia–Azerbaijan, with Abkhazia, South Ossetia and Nagorno-Karabakh. More than mediation, the model function of the EU – inter-state and inter-function – becomes a positive peace factor, based as it is on the five conditions offered earlier as a general theory.

The crucial point, however, is how the EU will relate to the other six or seven regions. The five-point model could be used again, but this time at a higher level of complexity, for regions rather than for states. However, as a starter, look at the later four points that are related to negative peace. The idea would be that the EU could play a very positive role if it were non-aligned, basing its security more on defensive defence – 'homeland security' – than on, say, RDF. Leave that kind of activity to a level higher up, to something more global. The EU should give up old habits of direct interventionist violence, and the structural violence of extracting resources. The EU would have to do what China may be steering towards: self-sufficiency in resources, such as by becoming less oil and gas dependent, which is close to mandatory anyhow, given the need to reduce carbon emission. And the EU has to be useful, which comes easily for such a resourceful region that through colonialism has stimulated demand for its resources and culture.

The big question is how to relate for mutual (symbiosis) and equal (equity) benefit. Any effort to squeeze resources out of the five Third World regions – LA, AU, OIC, SAARC and ASEAN – should be abandoned in favour of exchange at the same level of processing, giving up all protective tariffs against processed products from the Third World. The EU will have to adjust to a decreasing role in total world trade, as South–South trade among the five regions mentioned is bound to increase in relative significance. The same goes for culture: a regional system based on mutual and equal benefit would demand dialogue, mutual respect and curiosity, not one-way culture traffic.

How about homology and entropy – could they be carried over into a regionalised world? One of the gifts of the EU to other regions and subregions would be the division of power between a council for the states (territorial) and a commission for the departments (functional). If that is acceptable a basic condition for inter-regional homology is satisfied, which allows for the possibility of seven or eight commissions working for peace by peaceful means. With the rapid growth of the civil society both regionally and globally, other regions are now approaching the 'underbrush' condition so fruitful when the EEC came into being. African, Latin American and Asian non-governmental organisations (NGOs) are already lobbying in Brussels, so are European NGOs in East Africa and Addis Ababa. Thus, there is nothing utopian in what is written in these pages; rather, it is amazing how quickly the world is evolving.

But the real test would be the fifth factor on that list: transcendence. What would be the multilateral organisation at the centre of a regional world? It will be a United Regions, of course. Not a United Nations, whose members are in a waning state system – except for the big ones like the United States, Russia, China and India. The regional system is waxing. There would be no veto power given to one or two regions, but maybe decisions by consensus to start with. There would be a United Regions People's Assembly, maybe based on regional parliaments where they exist and in the future on direct elections. The secretariat could rotate from one region to the other, as has been done successfully in the European Community/Union. There is no need to repeat key errors like the UN veto power, no parliament with a popular mandate or a permanent location.

Building peace

The problems confronting human society are located in the past, in the present and in the future, or two of them, or in all three. The traumas of the past can be addressed by the method of conciliation (Galtung 2008). There are traumas going back days, months, years, decades, centuries. They are festering wounds deep down in the social bodies, to be cleaned up through acknowledgment, preparing the ground for a cooperative future. There are the conflicts of the present, for which the method is mediation, for conflict resolution. They are Gordian Knots, not to be cut by brutal violence, but to be unravelled and used for new tissue. There are the challenges of the future, for which the method is peacebuilding, cooperative, symbiotic-equitable projects producing harmony. One must see the world more from above and less from a particularistic angle.

Peace has to be built. Webs of togetherness must be woven; humanising where there has been dehumanisation; depolarising where there has been polarisation. Further, peace has to be kept, by non-violent peace forces, numerous, competent, inserting themselves so densely between violent parties that there is not enough space left for battle. Strengthening capacities to respond to crises and security threats by engaging a variety of actors, including NGOs, women and young people, can be fruitful. These groups could become bandages and tranquilisers, lowering the temperature rather than getting at the root causes. To contribute something to solving big problems one must think big thoughts. Small thoughts will do for small problems, like standardisation of car bumpers. Check your thoughts, let them grow with the people concerned and with those who work in the field rather than with diplomats in sterile rooms with linear agendas. The Track 1 government vs Track 2 civil society with NGOs, local authorities, the young and the women is problematic because Track 1 often becomes Track –1, hoping that Track 2 can weigh in at +1.

The strength of civil society is direct contact, high on empathy and less inclined to violence. If you have no hammer, the world looks less like a nail. But creativity remains a crucial commodity. Its scarcity among diplomats geared towards correct process does not guarantee its presence in civil society – except for artists, engineers, architects, etc. The civil society can do all three – peace-making, peace-building and peace-keeping. The non-governments can probably do it better than the governments. Thus, civil society can make 10,000 dialogues blossom, within and among conflict parties, find out where the shoes pinch and what future society, region or world they want to live in: which Middle East? Which Kosovo? They can let all that information flow together and watch the GNIP – the gross national idea product – grow.

How about reinforcing the role of gender and generation in peace and security? It is very important because in general men are more deductive, from grand principles, and women more compassionate, though there are apprehensions that their conflict-solving and peace-building edge may erode as women move up in male-dominated society, with expertise in fields like law and economics, shaped by male logic – an argument for reshaping them. In general, the older generation is more closed, and the younger more open to discourse, more sensitive to new aspects and new ideas. Thus, in a conflict women should meet the women on the other side(s) and the young the young on the other side(s).

The crucial aspect of conflict resolution is building cooperation. In this context the following points need emphasis.

Resolution orientation: the root cause of violence is usually unresolved conflict. Identification of the underlying conflict is crucial to finding a solution. It is indeed a different approach which needs to be explained. For example, the piracy crisis off the Somalian coast and beyond is an unacceptable crime. But so are more than 200 trawlers from EU countries like Denmark and Spain, off the coast of a failed state, depriving Somalia of seafood export products and food, in addition dropping toxic waste, possibly nuclear. Operation Atalanta will not solve this, but will displace mutual aggression to worse places. Hence the need is to listen to the other side and find a solution that can accommodate all viewpoints. Unresolved and underlying conflict is the fire, violence is the smoke. Conflict is as human as body, mind and spirit. 'Conflict prevention' is meaningless, but 'violence prevention' certainly is not. There is no 'post-conflict', but hopefully there is 'post-violence'. One needs to get out of the Anglo-American view of conflict as a clash of people, groups or parties, and into conflict as a clash of goals. Seeing conflict as a clash of goals makes it a problem to be solved, by creating a reality where legitimate goals can be accommodated and become compatible. Seeing conflict as a clash of parties, the implication is usually to see one or more of them as parties to be controlled, often violently. Concepts and approaches to conflicts matter towards their resolution.

Incompatible goals and means: we tend to judge ourselves by our best intentions – goals – and adversaries by their worst behaviour – means. Identify their best intentions (goals) and look at your own behaviour (means). These are two indispensable jobs, often best done by an outside mediator.

Mapping the conflict: view the actors, their goals/means and their clashes and incompatibilities with empathy.

Legitimising: testing the goals/means for legitimacy, using law, human rights and basic needs as standards. This must be done with impartiality.

Bridging: exploring new social realities under which legitimate goals of all parties may be reasonably satisfied, and do so with creativity.

Cooperating in a post-disaster situation: conciliation, acknowledging the past, concretising, changing into projects for a future together.

Hierarchies produce intractable conflicts. This is true about both international and internal conflicts. There are early warnings, with three components:

1 *Direct violence*: beyond throwing a first stone; capability and intention are proven by a general tendency to participate in wars, among other reasons to create hierarchies and hegemonies.
2 *Structural violence*: a position higher up or lower down in a hierarchy of exploitation–repression–alienation, used to preserve the hierarchy or to destroy it; high up or low down in pyramids of structural violence inspires a culture to make use of violence legitimate, often by divine mandate. A small incident may ignite massive direct violence, upward or downward.
3 *Cultural violence*: the cultural justification of (1) and (2).

A War Participation Index, based on the number of wars a state has participated is divided by the number of years of existence of the state seems to confirm this. The top four in this index are: United States – 3,040; Israel (1947–1985) – 1,842; Ottoman empire and Turkey – 1,552; and England and Great Britain – 1,277. What do these four have in common? Structural violence, both in the sense of settler colonialism within, and of world and regional empire-building without. Also, cultural violence based on hard readings of abrahamitic religions, hard Protestantism for the United States and United Kingdom, hard (not Sufi!) Islam for the Ottoman empire, and hard zionism (not Buber!) for Israel. In all three we find Dualism with Manichean overtones, seeing oneself as good and opponents as evil, and Armageddon as the final arbiter; the DMA syndrome. Add to that the idea of being Chosen by the Eternal, a sense of past and future Glory and the significance of past Trauma suffered on the road, and we have the CGT syndrome. Both syndromes are important building blocks for deep violence. Of course, dialectically they also inspire the same syndromes in the other side. Today, one witnesses that spiralling cultural confrontation. To prevent flaring of conflicts there is a need to enhance early warnings. The remedy is to flatten the pyramid through equitable, symmetric relations of parity; stimulate softer readings of the religions. Peace assumes a high level of equity, an 'equiarchy'; and the road to peace is paved with the acceptance of the other(s) as an equal partner in negotiation and dialogue. But if one or more of them are informed by a highly inequitable deep structure sustained by a deep culture, peace by peaceful means becomes more difficult.

A cornerstone in the global approach towards peace is to promote cultures of human rights and structures of democracy. But the assumption that in their wake follows peace is based on a logical fallacy with serious consequences. Violence in general, and war in particular, is a relation, for example, between two or more states. So is peace. But democracy and human rights may be properties of none, one or more of them, and may be very good for inner peace. Make democracy a relation, like in a regional, or even global parliament, based on free and fair elections, and we are in the interstate and inter-nation peace business. That democracy does not steer major parties to crisis and violence today.

Mediation and conciliation

Mainstreaming mediation is an important aspect of peace building. There are many schools. I stand for dialogue, one-on-one, with all parties for conflict resolution. Mediation means mapping conflicts, parties–goals–clashes, testing goals for legitimacy (I have never encountered a party totally devoid of legitimate goals on which to build), bridging legitimate goals. That calls for empathy, nonviolence and creativity. The danger is the frequent mistake of engaging only two parties (there are always more, and those excluded will sabotage), 'getting them to the table' (they are usually not ready, and feel unfree to talk with other parties listening) and negotiation (continuation of war by verbal means). The method is dialogue: mutual search, first with mediators, then together. The absence of conflict handling in thought, speech and action has to be overcome through a civilian culture of solving conflict rather than winning wars. Conciliation means acknowledging past wrongs, elaborating on how and why, and then defining a future together. One has to act in the present, envisage with the parties a vision of a compelling future, and sensitive to traumas and glories of the past. One has to be creative, though it is more easily said than done. In this context, I explore five cases of mediation and five of conciliation, based on my own experiences in the process.[4]

What does peace in the Middle East look like, between Israel and its neighbours? Much like the European Community imagined by two French statesmen we honour for their creativity. Nazi Germany was so atrocious that it had to be a member of the family – few saw it that way; moreover, the family did not exist except as a wartime alliance. They painted a compelling future on the wall, a community of six, invoking the future to overcome the past and even the present. It was an astounding success.

A Middle East Community (MEC) of six – Lebanon, Syria, Jordan, Palestine (fully recognised), Egypt and Israel – willing to contract to something like 4 June 1967 in exchange for security through peace. The opposite is a non-starter. Others, like Turkey and Cyprus, may join in an Eastern Mediterranean Community. Israel may develop very tight EU relations and Arab countries may join the OIC. And yet there could be an MEC with open borders, rights and obligations. It can be a regional organisation with not one nor two, but six, states, using the six states of the Treaty of Rome European Community as a model, not only a mediator. Open the archives, invite the countries concerned to share the process and its tensions at the same time as NGOs are all over, stimulating dialogues. Work both from the bottom and the top, with dialogues all over. Western Europe managed to moderate Germany. Western Asia and the eastern Mediterranean can manage the same with a more reasonable, more modest Israel.

Imagine the world's biggest oil consumer and potentially biggest oil producer joining to carry out large-scale, non-fossil fuel projects together – maybe financed by little Norway's big oil fund? Unrealistic? Just to the contrary, lack of realism is with the so-called realists. The world would rejoice. But it would take moral courage. And it might take some history/textbook revisionism, maybe on both sides; building on the masters, the Germans, some ten years after the conflict resolution built into the Treaty of Rome.

How about Iraq? Build on past successes. The European Community was an internal interstate success. So was German textbook revision, creating good relations to the 25 invaded countries by today's map and three of the cultures exposed to genocide: Jews, Cinta-Roma and Russians. And so was the Helsinki Conference on Security and Cooperation in Europe. So, make a Conference for Security and Cooperation in West Asia, financed by the EU! Kurdistan would also be on the agenda, as a confederation of four autonomies, without drawing new borders. I have cited here instances of Western aggression against Muslim countries, names, years, particularly traumatic events. Like France attacking Egypt, and England attacking Mysore in 1798, like Italy bombing oases in Libya in 1911 and Spain attacking Xauen in 1925. The perpetrator suffers from amnesia; the victim never forgets. The motives are no doubt resources with well-rewarded autocracies to guarantee delivery; these also include the Crusades to subvert and convert Islam. Maybe, some serious signs of acknowledgement could have salvaged the situation – not to stay out of trouble, but because it is the right thing to do.

True greatness also includes acknowledgement of one's own smallness. That leads to the US/West War on Terror, a complex conflict with acts of war like 9/11, 7/7 in London and 11 March 2004 in Madrid, and attacks on Iraq and Afghanistan. Spain under Zapatero handled 11 March masterfully. Morocco's ambassador was not expelled, nor was Rabat bombed as somebody might have done. He travelled to Rabat for top-level dialogue, no doubt also about Ceuta-Melilla, for which a Hong Kong solution might be useful; legalised almost 500,000 illegal Moroccans in Spain; pulled Spanish troops out of Iraq; and launched an Alliance of Civilizations in Madrid in October 2005. That brings up Sykes–Picot, the foreign ministers of the United Kingdom and France, who in 1916 promised the Arabs independence if they killed and overthrew the Ottoman Turks. They did so and were colonised: Iraq and Palestine for England; Syria and Lebanon for France. Rulers used rulers to define their artificial entities. Maybe an Anglo–French–Arab history book about 1916 is overdue? It is never too late; Arab school children live that trauma even if English and French ones do not. Not all wrongs come from Washington.

Regarding Kosovo, its status as a part of Serbia or its independence as a unitary state are clearly untenable and will lead to endless violence. Division is untenable for at least two reasons: viability and the right of all to consider Kosovo theirs, with free travel and interaction. The following solution can be worked out for peace in the region. For Kosovo, independence as a Swiss-style federation with very high autonomy for the Serbian cantons; a confederation of Serbia, Kosovo and Albania may be acceptable and sustainable. Of course, majority-based self-determination for Kosovo sets a precedent for Bosnia-Herzegovina and elsewhere. For Bosnia, probably self-determination for the three communities, pointing to the Croat part joining Croatia, the Serbian part becoming a Republika srbska, and the Bosniak part a city-state around Sarajevo. And so on. For anything to work the day after tomorrow it has to be aired the day before yesterday so that somebody in due course can say 'It has always been my conviction.'

There is an Ottoman shadow over the region, which brings us to Turkey–Armenia and the question of conciliation. The conflict seems to be trilateral, with Kurds being promised freedom if they would do the dirty job. They did, and got no freedom. The UK–France/Sykes–Picot formula, a part of the zeitgeist, probably passed as the art of statesmanship. Does that exonerate the Turks? No, but it provides a context. Imagine that unconditional acknowledgement implies unconditional compensation – could that stand in the way? Of course. How about building the joint future of neighbours around the contested mountain Ararat? How about making Ararat a Mountain of World Peace, not only for the three abrahamitic religions, but for humanity? Under joint Turkish–Armenian administration, UN aegis and paid for by the EU? Could approaching the past via the future also be for Myanmar? And open the EU for Turkey and Armenia and the Caucasian community. There is conciliation work to be done for many EU charter members, as for formerly colonial countries.

But conciliation without conflict resolution – shake hands, be good friends – is pacification. Like a ceasefire or money for development, it may buy time before violence erupts again. All roads to peace pass through deep conflict resolution. The East Asia formula was industrialisation with tariff protection and a welfare state. In fact, deeper transformation is needed. The EU–ACP structural conflict has an important dimension: who plans whom? Most developed countries love to plan least developed countries, and the EU plans the ACP down to micro-management as a part of Official Development Assistance. Imagine the EU inviting the ACP or the whole former Third World – AU, OIC, SAARC, ASEAN, SCO, ALC – to advise the EU and half a billion EUians? Inviting experts, having dialogues with their nationals in EU diaspora, eliciting good ideas is necessary for symmetry as well as reciprocity.

The EU is facing a very important dilemma: the civilian peacekeeping favoured by the Commission or the military version with rapid deployment favoured by the Council? The latter might like to fill the gap left behind when the United States withdraws its troops, like the British did east of Suez in 1965. The Third World, the chosen battlefield like Orwell's Malabar Coast, might have some advice to offer about taming the forces favouring interventions and enhancing those favouring creative solutions. And maybe the Chinese could offer some advice from the great amount addressed to themselves at the seventeenth congress of the Chinese Communist Party? And can India offer something about high electoral participation in a country with well above one billion people to guide one with less than half of that? The world does not need a new empire, but inter-regional structures for joint planning. As then South African Foreign Minister Dlamini Zuma expressed at a conference in 2001, this is not about money or compensation, but about dignity. How is dignity promoted? It is mainly by perpetrators acknowledging, elaborating and designing new ways of entering the future together. Dignity is a relation with symmetry, reciprocity and equity.

There are global challenges that cut across the regions and countries. The road to safety passes through dialogue and mutual learning of civilisations, with the courage to say 'You have a Truth I miss, may I borrow that one and maybe you want one of mine?' Energy security is another issue of concern. There are associated problems with phasing out carbons in favour of environmentally sound alternatives, such as cutting transportation emissions through local conversion – many conversion profiles are geared to local resources for energy equality, and are not waiting for markets to catch up. There is a need for global maritime security, which needs dense and joint patrolling of the coastal waters off the Horn of Africa to stop illegal fishing, dropping of waste and piracy, with apologies and compensation both ways, and efforts at massive reconciliation. In the context of climate change, not knowing how much is due to change in the solar system – with glaciers melting for the last 10,000–15,000 years – and how much is human-made is no excuse for doing nothing. But we should be aware of such gains as the Northwest Passage, the greening of Iceland and Greenland and the Siberian coast in calculating costs and benefits. All of them, and many others, need global and humane solutions. They need global cooperation. We cannot afford to be divided and fighting. Hence conflicts, international or internal, have to be resolved all over the globe in favour of a positive peace. Let us start with Eurasia.

Notes

1 This chapter is a modified compilation of three unpublished papers. The presentations include the keynote address 'From Early Warning to Early Action: Developing the EU's Response to Crisis and Longer Term Threats', at EU Commission, Brussels, 12 November 2007; the concluding remarks 'Wrapping Up, the Road Ahead, Strengthening the Capacities to Respond to Crises and Security Threats', at EU Commission, Brussels, 4 May 2009; and the keynote address, 'The Status and Influences of the European Union in the Era of Globalization', EU Parliament, 10 May 2010.

2 Panchsheel, also called five principles of peaceful coexistence, was signed between China and India in 1954. The principles are: (1) mutual respect for each other's

territorial integrity and sovereignty; (2) mutual non-aggression against anyone; (3) mutual non-interference in each other's internal affairs; (4) equality and mutual benefit; and (5) peaceful coexistence.

3 With North America (United States plus Canada), connecting what was colonised by the Spanish, the French and the English in one huge area.

4 See www.transcend-nordic.org and UN manuals for Transcend and Sabona approaches.

References

Galtung, Johan (1973) *The European Community: A Superpower in the Making*, London: Allen & Unwin.

—— (1984) *There are Alternatives! Four Roads to Peace and Security*, Nottingham: Spokesman.

—— (2008) *50 Years: 100 Peace & Conflict Perspectives*, Basel: Transcend University Press.

—— (2010) *The Fall of the US Empire: And then What?*, Basel: Transcend University Press.

Galtung, Johan and Lodgaard, Sverre (eds) (1970) *Cooperation in Europe*, Oslo: Norwegian Universities Press.

2 From the Balkans to the Caucasus

Paradoxes of the precedents in a post-Balkan perspective

Emanuela C. Del Re

Introduction

The conflicts in the Balkans, and the case of Kosovo in particular, have become for many a model in conflict analysis, evoked when a crisis bursts out in which specific 'Balkan' variables are identifiable. Defining the current status of the conflicts in the Balkans, with a focus on Kosovo, is essential to explore the challenges ahead and potential future scenarios, and to understand what renders the region so significant. Can Kosovo be truly considered a model for analysis of other conflicts, such as those in the Caucasus? Many questions arise relating to interpretations of Kosovo as, for example, Serbia's 'frozen conflict', and South Ossetia as Russia's 'Kosovo'. Based on years of field research, this chapter offers an in-depth analysis of these (and other) questions. It seeks to identify the features of a new 'post-Balkan' conflict model adaptable to new geo-political scenarios. The analysis develops from attempts to find convergences or divergences between the crisis in Kosovo and the crises in the Caucasus. After an examination of the narratives of conflicts, this chapter considers the role of peacekeeping in conflict situations and then explores different views on whether the experience of the Balkans can be a reference point. The chapter proposes a new approach towards conflict resolution that emerges from the 'Balkan experience'.

The echoes of a conflict

The conflicts in the Balkans have become a model in conflict analysis. The recent crises in Georgia and Kyrgyzstan, for instance, have been compared to the conflict in Kosovo. Kosovo is simply taken as a precedent. What emerges is a certain degree of interdependence among the forces that create conflicts nowadays, as a consequence of the dynamics of the new global scenario where rhetorical conflict resolution techniques do not always prove to be adequate, and unexpected interconnections and interests come into play. The main issue is whether the 'Balkan model' does still constitute a valid description of a process incorporating aspects of conflict resolution strategies. It may be more appropriate to talk about a 'Kosovo model', given that the dissolution of the former

Yugoslavia was formally completed by the Dayton Agreement of 1995, and all the states of the former Yugoslavia are in a new EU-oriented phase.

Comparison with cases that are taken as models is a very complex issue, provoking reactions and criticism. For example, speaking in 2006 (well before the Russia–Georgia conflict of 2008) Vladimir Voronin, the president of Moldova, reacted vehemently to the suggestion that the Kosovo model could be applied to Moldova. The uniqueness of individual conflicts notwithstanding, in political terms a 'Kosovo model' exists, and that is used in different contexts. In November 2010, Eisikovits and Eiran (2010) suggested that the 'Kosovo model' should be applied to the Middle East. Frida Ghitis (2010) cautions against this, arguing that 'No matter how appealing Pristina's new modern cafés look today, anyone who thinks the Middle East should travel the road of the war-scarred Balkans is choosing a path that cannot lead to permanent peace.'

In the game of conflict models, in fact, one of the most relevant issues is who identifies with whom. Despite the recognition of the independence of Kosovo, as well as the July 2010 ruling by the International Court of Justice (ICJ) that Kosovo's 2008 declaration of independence from Serbia did not violate general international law, the country has not been universally recognised (86 out of 193 UN members as of September 2011), foreign troops are still deployed there, the economy relies on international assistance and remittances (it has the highest unemployment rate in Europe – 45 per cent in 2009 (UNDP 2011)) and part of the country (northern Kosovo) is still in a political and social limbo (ibid.). The costs of all this can be high (Del Re 2007). Besides, there is a risk of misinterpretation of the ICJ decision. Stefan Wolff emphasises that what the ICJ did was not to make Abkhazia and South Ossetia assume that their declarations of independence would automatically resolve into statehood. He argues:

> it [the decision of the ICJ] demonstrated that 'general international law contains no applicable prohibition of declarations of independence'; argued that the authors of the Declaration of Independence were not the Provisional Institutions of Self-Government of Kosovo, but rather that they 'acted together in their capacity as representatives of the people of Kosovo outside the framework of the interim administration'; it found that Security Council Resolution 1244 (1999), which established the UN Mission in Kosovo (UNMIK) and thus the UN's interim administration of Kosovo, was not violated by the Declaration of Independence.
>
> (Wolff 2010)

Since the verdict of the ICJ, many analysts have pointed out that despite its juridical grounds, the decision appears to be unbalanced when the same arguments about Kosovo are applied to cases in the Caucasus. Mahir Zeynalov refers to Kosovo in the context of Nagorno-Karabakh after the ICJ decision and observes that 'due to the political nature of the ruling, difference in statuses of Kosovo and Nagorno Karabakh at the time of secession and the existence of violence with the involvement of the third state make Kosovo case not applicable to Nagorno-Karabakh (Zeynalov 2010; for the conflict in Nagorno-Karabakh, see also Krüger 2010).

However, the parallel with Kosovo continues. Bhadrakumar (2010) refers to Kosovo while analysing the crisis in Kyrgyzstan, and then argues that in addition to the three main future 'hot spots' of conflict (Sri Lanka; Chechnya, where a nascent nationalist movement fell prey to Islamist networks; and Uzbekistan, which reacted to Andijan with overwhelming repression), a fourth must be considered – Kosovo. He argues that the strategy employed by the United States in the region uses the induction of the Organization for Security and Cooperation in Europe (OSCE) policemen in Kyrgyzstan as a 'first step' that closely follows the strategy applied in Kosovo: in the event that those policemen were targeted there would be the need to deploy armed forces from the NATO bases in neighbouring countries. Bhadrakumar argues that 'OSCE deployment may be designed to soothe tensions, but its downstream impact could be quite to the contrary. It could well turn out that the presence of international observers might embolden ethnic Uzbeks in southern Kyrgyzstan to pursue autonomy' (ibid.).

Moses Kumar has argued that the United States wants to apply the 'Kosovo model' to Sri Lanka. He explains what he means by the 'Kosovo model':

> Following the brutal war in former Yugoslavia, NATO troops occupied the area. The conflict ended and Bosnia-Herzegovina gained freedom. However, things didn't end here for the Americans. They wanted more. That was how Kosovo was separated a decade after the conflict ceased. At first a bogus reconciliation process was initiated by the US. Strangely, it was more about keeping people separated based on ethnicity than integration. Occupying US troops made it difficult for Serbia to carry out any integration with Kosovo (Kosovo was and still is a part of Serbia according to Serbia and most countries). It is this same twisted reconciliation model the US follows on Lanka. Interestingly, Tamil groups in the US highlighted the need for a two state 'reconciliation' model.... In short, most groundwork in the second Kosovo project has been already commenced.
>
> (Kumar 2010)

This indicates that any interpretation of the 'Kosovo model' can become highly ideological and difficult to apply to different contexts. Despite this, the fascination with the 'Kosovo model' is contagious. Levon Zurabyan, the coordinator of the Armenian National Congress (HAK), said in July 2010 that Kosovo's model of independence is applicable to Nagorno-Karabakh: 'There are serious justifications for Kosovo's independence, and those serious justifications are applicable also for Nagorno-Karabakh' (Tert.am 2010). Ethnic Hungarians in Romania have followed the same logic, with Antal Árpád András, Deputy of the Democratic Union of Hungarians in Romania (UDMR), stating in 2008 that 'for Hungarians, the greatest challenge this year is to use efficiently the solution that will be found for Kosovo province', adding that 'Kosovo is not the perfect model because the Hungarian community in Romania wants to obtain autonomy for

Szeklers' County through democratic means … the Hungarian community must discuss its autonomy and seek support from great international powers' (Sznt.com 2008).

It is important to explore precisely what a 'Kosovo model' might represent for those who are involved in ongoing conflicts influenced by separatist aspirations. According to Bruno Coppieters, 'There is no Kosovo model on international recognition' because the Kosovo case presents such unique features that 'external actors have not the capacity to follow this particular Kosovo model'. He refers to the fact that one special aspect of the Kosovo case is the degree of external support it receives from external actors, which made the international recognition of its unilateral declaration of independence a feasible option: 'in no other part of the world, external support to a secessionist movement is sufficiently powerful to achieve such a result' (Michels and Coppieters 2008). Nevertheless, the fact that the 'international community' supported Kosovo to a great extent makes it feasible for others to think that getting support from powerful external actors is the right strategy (Brown 1996).

A perfect case study

In 2008, after the crisis erupted in Georgia, the internet blossomed with messages, manifestos and videos on the issue. These postings were analysed in all possible ways not only by Russians and Georgians, but also by spectators who felt involved in the crisis at various levels and with different degrees of intensity. Emblematic of this is the example of a video circulating on YouTube, entitled 'Freedom for Ossetia. Serbia is with you!'. In the approximately nine-minute video, a Serbian nicknamed 3Frontline3 launches a clear message (3Frontline3 2008), very similar in substance and form to many other videos that were posted on the internet around the same time. The flag of South Ossetia, with its coat of arms (a leopard in a golden field with silver mountains in the background), appears on screen and slowly dissolves into a black background. Large writing appears containing the message 'Let the truth be known', telling viewers that in the coming days and weeks there would be a media campaign against Russia and the Ossetian population. This was followed by a discussion of the political and strategic moves of the United States, which armed and trained the Georgian military, and on the idea that when Russia defends its citizens (such as in Chechnya and Beslan) it is accused of brutality. The video underlined the Islamic aspect of Russia's actions in the North Caucasus, and emphasised that the global situation, in which the possession of nuclear warheads (12,000 for the United States and 7,000 for Russia) should caution others from provoking these countries. The video ended with an appeal: leave the Russians and Ossetians alone – they have a lot to grant a better life to their children. A Serbian flag then appeared, which transformed first into an Ossetian flag, then into the Ossetian emblem, and finally back into the Serbian flag, displaying the text 'You are not alone, my orthodox sisters and brothers. Serbia is 100 per cent with you.' A crowd waving Serbian flags, an image of three fingers on a hand (symbolising the Holy Trinity), the writing 'Kosovo' and 'Frontline', the signature of the person who posted the video online, also appeared in the video. The religious sense is strong, unifying many paradoxes accompanying this game of opportune empathy, implying the question of who must feel close to the Caucasus? It is not the Albanians of Kosovo, who feel united to a South Ossetia that aspires for formal independence, but the orthodox Serbs. Yet, many compare Kosovo to Georgia. But, in the game based on association of ideas, there are also those who would instead hazard a parallel between Kosovo and South Ossetia and Serbia and Georgia. The problem lies in the fact that if similarities have to be seen once the actors have been identified, then they must be paired, with a constant adjustment to the changing international scenario. In the case of the internet, the discussion on who is what, where, how and when, is still raging. It is not by chance that an international symposium, 'The Balkans and Caucasus: parallel processes on the opposite sides of the Black Sea, past, present, and prospects', organised by the New Europe College and the Institute for Advanced Study, took place in April 2010 in Bucharest.

Parallels between the Balkans and the Caucasus

Kosovo is an independent state with its own borders; therefore, it cannot be compared to South Ossetia or Abkhazia. This is one of the most recurring arguments in discussions over possible parallels. The dimension of the population – minority/majority – is strongly perceived as an important indicator in the process of identifying parallels with Kosovo (Albanians in Kosovo constituted the majority in the specific territory; Abkhazians and Ossetians do not). Even more refined is the attempt to pair Kosovo with Georgia, and North Mitrovica with South Ossetia (Mitrovica is a divided city where the Albanian and Serb community live in the south and in the north of the city territory, respectively, the borders of which are demarcated by the river Ibar). There can be parallels between the two populations: both are minorities (in Kosovo Serbs are about 130,000 and the Albanians two million (De Quetteville 2008)). A response based on this parallel comes from Bluerose799 who, in a comment on the article by De Quetteville on the website of the British newspaper the *Telegraph*, argues that if Kosovo decided to invade north Mitrovica, it would have to confront the mighty Serbian army, and the Albanians of Kosovo would not make such a mistake, because they know themselves and the enemy well; the Georgians did not know themselves and the enemy well and succumbed.

Those who argue that Kosovo is more like Georgia than South Ossetia emphasise that the parallel lies in the use of a minority population with the aim of carving out a small piece of land (referring to the Serbs of Kosovo, who could be used as a pretext by Serbia to carve out the territory of Mitrovica, just as Russia did in Georgia with the excuse of the Ossetian minority) (Dobrouna 2008). Those who instead compare Georgia to Serbia underline that Georgia oppresses the internal minority just like Serbia in the past oppressed the Albanians of Kosovo. Russia, then, should be paired with the United States as an interested third party that intervenes to defend the offended minority. There can be one more similarity between Georgia and Serbia that lies in the parallel drawn between Milošević and Saakashvili. The Serbs threw out Milošević a year after the 'defeat' of Kosovo to free themselves of his iron hand; and what can be said of the Georgian leader, democratically elected but too impulsive to calculate the consequences of his military actions? Others contend that it is absurd to compare the two, considering that the Serbian leader committed atrocities that the democratic Georgian, educated to American-style democracy, has never committed (Battista 2008). Yet, as early as 2006 de Waal and Baran (Baran and de Waal 2006; Baran 2006; de Waal 2006) stressed that the winds of war were ready to blow in that part of the Caucasus. The moderate voices in the negotiation process in South Ossetia and Abhkazia (Iraki Alasania and Giorgi Khaindrava) were ousted in favour of the bellicose minister of defence, Iraki Okruashvili, just when an armed crisis was breaking out in the region of Kodori Gorge in Abkhazia. In this context, the parallel with Kosovo might appear tenuous as Kosovo can be construed as a case on its own, *sui generis*.

It is probably because of its stabilising potential in the Balkans, but not as a precedent, which is seen by many as dangerous. According to Dusan Janjić (Tasić 2008), the commonality between the cases of Kosovo and South Ossetia is that they are the result of a disintegration of former federal states on ethnic lines and that both clash with the interests of Russia and NATO. This might be the reason why the then NATO secretary general Jaap de Hoop Scheffer affirmed in 2008 that he did not find any similarity between the two cases. However, according to Oliver Ivanović, in 2008 the Serbian state secretary for Kosovo and Metohija, the conflict in South Ossetia was directly linked with the unilateral independence of Kosovo and this should caution those who support the separatism of Albanians in Kosovo, especially the EU, because there are separatist movements everywhere in the world (ibid.). On the other hand, in Moldova, for example, the day after the declaration of independence of Kosovo, EUTV television in Chisinau (EUTV 2008) reported the declarations of Alexei Ostrovsky, president of the Duma Committee for the Commonwealth of Independent States (CIS) Affairs. He affirmed that the independence constituted a precedent for South Ossetia, Abkhazia and Trasnistria. Similarly, the BBC reported that Russia compared Kosovo with Georgia in affirming that it would change its policies towards the separatist regions in Georgia if the West recognised the independence of Kosovo.

The so-called *frozen* conflicts – conflicts on the territory of the former Soviet republics that have become de facto independent in the last 15 years, while remaining juridically within these republics – have thus re-surfaced (Bancheli *et al.* 2004; Lynch 2004). For example, the crisis in Georgia made the so called 'frozen' conflict in Nagorno-Karabakh re-emerge: the tombstones portraits of the Azeri who died in the conflict, lying in the *Shehidler Khiyabani*, the Martyrs' Lane cemetery and memorial overlooking Baku from a hill, must have smiled then (Scaglione 2008).

The connection with the Caucasus also lies in the argument that Kosovo can be considered Serbia's *frozen conflict* (or even that of Yugoslavia and/or of the

EU, and for some even Russia (Socor 2007)). If one thinks that the *frozen conflict* of Kosovo has been unilaterally resolved by independence without the approval of Serbia, then a parallel can be drawn with territories within the former Soviet Union whose claims for independence might be recognised internationally but not by the states from which they cede. In the case of the former Soviet Union, however, the message from the international community is that Kosovo is a unique case and it has nothing to do with aspirations of other disgruntled regions. As Olcott (2005) argues in her book *Central Asia's Second Chance*, the transformations in these areas can and must spring from the internal dynamics, not from the policies of the West. The West arrived late to the scene of Kosovo. It arrived late in the sense that it simply let independence happen, given that the enormous negotiating effort had not given the expected results and had led to a stalemate, when the stake was the delicate equilibrium between Russia, the EU and the United States. An *exploit* resulted, being preferable to prolonging the process. The *exploit* was the unilateral declaration of independence.

In March 2008 there were fresh clashes between Armenia and Azerbaijan, leading to the death of 16 people. The United States immediately affirmed that it was certainly not a consequence of the recognition of the independence of Kosovo. Göran Lennmarker, the OSCE Parliamentary Assembly's special representative for the South Caucasus, stated at a meeting with the Azerbaijani delegation on the sidelines of the nineteenth session of the OSCE in Oslo that the term 'frozen' used about the Nagorno-Karabakh conflict is a deceptive one (News.am 2010). Commenting on developments in early 2011, Anatoly Tsiganok, a Russian expert, argued that the conflict in Nagorno-Karabakh may cause a third world war if peace does not come out of the stalemate (News.am 2011).

Is South Ossetia the Kosovo of Russia? There were Russian peacekeepers in South Ossetia, to inhabitants of which Russia had extended its citizenship. Russia has not hidden its territorial ambitions (Dobruna 2008). Was Russia, being humiliated by Kosovo's independence, looking for revenge? Maria Lipman, a Carnegie Foundation analyst in Moscow, argues that the attack on Georgia was a clear demonstration of strength by Russia to all those who thought that Russia could be ignored, with clear reference to the humiliation from the diplomatic recognition of the independence of Kosovo by many states. The prospects of NATO enlargement to the post-Soviet space, which Russia saw as its natural sphere of influence, also contributed to such a perception of humiliation. Russia had for a long time sent signals about its discontent at the developments in Kosovo. Sergei Lavrov, the Russian foreign minister, had since 2006 repeatedly and openly told Condoleeza Rice and European diplomats that the recognition of Kosovo would have constituted a precedent for the Caucasus (Torbakov 2006). Perhaps Putin wanted to save face after the humiliation suffered in Kosovo. Russia also criticised NATO, which had brought Serbia, the faithful ally of Russia, under pressure with 78 days of bombing raids. (Barry 2010).

Putin had already started to reaffirm his policy of regaining control over the enterprises that deal with natural resources in Russia by placing his supporters in high positions, while punishing the oligarchs who challenged his power. Reasserting itself as an oil power, it has become apparent that Russia can regulate the flow of energy in Eurasia. A consequence of the recognition of Kosovo, given that Russia had signed agreements with Serbia for a Moscow-led South Stream, was to render Serbia an enormous gas stockpile resource, transforming the country into a key base for energy supply to Europe (Zarakhovich 2008). It is not by chance that the energy issue emerged as fundamental in the game (Auty and De Soysa 2006), given that the crucial oil pipeline Baku–Tblisi–Cheyan (BTC) remained closed two days before the Russian incursion into Abkhazia, South Ossetia and Georgia (Gismatullin and Yackley 2008).

The 'narrative' of conflicts is very important, particularly when parallels are made. This is because out of the many layers of conflict, one that often inspires comparison is related to the most delicate aspect – the loss of lives. A frequently asked question relates to genocide: how do you identify a case of genocide? A diachronic (ideological) parallel recurs, not as much with Milošević or the NATO bombing, but with the so-called Operation Storm (Operacija Oluja) that on 4 August 1995, in a little over 36 hours, witnessed the Croat army and airforce, with the support of the Bosnian-Herzegovina army, re-conquering Krajina for Croatia. Between 150,000 and 200,000 people fled the region. The operation was defined by Carl Bildt as the most efficient example of ethnic cleansing ever seen in the Balkans (Pearl 2002: 224). Many analysts refer to that operation and even compare Saakashvili in Ossetia with Tudjman in Srpska-Krajina because both were inspired by the aim of creating an ethnically pure and loyal state. It is to Operacija Oluja that Ljubinka Miličić refers in an article in *Politika* (quoted in Zanoni 2008), the main Serb newspaper. The journalist wonders 'how many deaths are needed to talk about a genocide?', underlining that the arguments used by NATO in Kosovo in the past are the same that are used by Russia in South Ossetia, with the difference that Russia feels it is the legitimate protector of the region because, according to international agreement, Moscow is the guarantor of peace in South Ossetia. According to Miličić, what some analysts have defined as an attempt by Georgia to repeat Operacija Oluja in South Ossetia was prevented by Russia resorting to the 'war for peace' narrative promoted by NATO and the United States in Kosovo. Miličić also questioned the historian Natalija Naročnicka (president of the Foundation for the Historical Perspective of Moscow) on whether it is legitimate to draw a parallel with Operacija Oluja. Naročnicka replied

> the parallel exists in the moment in which in Georgia there are instructors that train the Georgian army in contemporary war tactics, and transmit the experience they have acquired during the aggression of NATO forces in Kosovo; the Georgian President Saakashvili wanted, as well as Croatia did with Operation *Oluja*, to conquer Tskhinvali in a short time, and demonstrate to the world that Georgia controls the Ossetian territory. But he did not succeed.
>
> (Ibid.)

Nevertheless, the school of thought that denies the parallel between the Kosovo issue and the crisis in the Caucasus contend that there are no massacres that have been witnessed by international observers in Ossetia. But there are some who argue that if Milošević has been unjustly compared to Hitler, what could be said about Saashkavili (Graziosi 2008)? Moreover, according to some experts, it should be remembered that Serbia had proposed several options to resolve the issue of Kosovo to the contact group that includes Russia (besides the United States, United Kingdom, Italy, France, Germany), but its proposals were not accepted. Yet, reply others, Serbia did not respect the NATO ultimatum. According to these interpretations, Kosovo is very different to what happened in South Ossetia.

Caucasus and Kosovo in the mirror

The recognition of Kosovo in 2008 led even charismatic politicians like Lech Wałesa to express some qualm, saying that what has divided Europe can only be the harbinger of troubles (Serbianna 2008). Further, the then president of the Czech Republic Vaclav Klaus affirmed that with the recognition of the independence of Kosovo, Western powers had given Russia a strong justification for its actions in Georgia (*International Herald Tribune* 2008). Whatever the truth, attempts to draw parallels between Kosovo, Georgia, South Ossetia and Serbia seem to be an exercise in acrobatics. For instance, if one draws a parallel between Kosovo and South Ossetia then, according to this logic, Russia should recognise the independence of Kosovo (Vini 2008). However, as the Russian nationalist jurist Narochnitskaja argues, this is only a paradox, as Abkhazians and Ossetians do not need the example of Kosovo because Kosovo is just a contingency, a political precedent.

Is Kosovo a precedent? A pretext? There is no doubt that Kosovo and South Ossetia constitute a chessboard on which the pieces and their roles are played at a high level. What can and must be said is that much of the unclearness in the situation can be attributed to the so-called international community. The ruling by the ICJ that Kosovo's declaration of independence was legal has opened, according to many, a 'Pandora's box' (Ohanian *et al.* 2010), recalling Hesiod's myth in which Pandora was so curious that she opened one of the vases that had been donated to her by the gods, releasing all the evils of mankind, including plagues and diseases, and then closed the vase again, leaving only hope inside. Is there a 'Kosovo model'? This is the question that must be dealt with in order to offer plausible explanation of the complex image created by reactions to the unilateral declaration of independence in 2008, followed by the ICJ ruling in 2010. The analysis will also offer insights into the UN 1244 resolution, which came after the NATO intervention in 1999, which was never accepted by Russia and Serbia. It will cast light on the prominent role assigned to Milošević by the great powers during the process that led to the Dayton Agreements, though later he was put under arrest warrant by the International Criminal Tribunal for the former Yugoslavia.

If a 'Kosovo model' exists, which is capable of inspiring new conflicts based on separatism, then the model must be explained in causal terms. The definition of causality is very difficult in a context where even the actors and their roles are hard to identify. The reverse is also very important for consideration: what effects could the events in Caucasus have on Kosovo if they has preceded the later? At the time of the crisis in Georgia (2008), the president of Kosovo, Fatmir Sejdiu, affirmed immediately that the conflict in Georgia would not have slowed down the process of recognition of independence. Vuk Jeremic, foreign minister of Serbia, flew to New York to request the UN General Assembly to ask the ICJ's opinion on the independence of Kosovo. The opinion in a ruling form in 2010 left a number of issues open, such as the chain of causality connections between different conflicts in the world.

Towards identification of similarities and differences between Kosovo, South Ossetia and Abkhazia, Vladimir Đorđević (2010) outlines the following elements:

Similarities: there is an ethno-territorial dimension in the conflicts of Kosovo, South Ossetia and Abkhazia, and in fact there is an ongoing dispute over the historical right (who was the first inhabiting the area), which is also strongly connected with a symbolic view of the territory as 'sacred land'; the conflicts in Kosovo and Abkhazia in particular were predominantly influenced by major demographic shifts, while on the other hand all three conflicts produced further demographic shifts; the dissolution of the federal states has had a domino effect on smaller areas in both Serbia and Georgia; the ethno-nationalist narrative and ideologies have been used or misused as a political programme, together with the affirmation and consequent influence of charismatic leaders.

Differences: the different use of military force in Serbia and Georgia by the United States, NATO and Russia, based on very divergent (opposite, according to Đorđević) motivations and ideational roots (Đorđević: 'the Russian military engagement of 2008 was intended to be a specific response to the increasingly aggressive Georgian attitude and consequent attack against South Ossetia'); the issue was related to sovereignty in one case and integrity in the other (Đorđević says that 'it has been consistently reiterated on numerous occasions not only by US officials but their NATO partners as well that sovereignty as a principle guaranteeing the inviolability and integrity of international borders should not and cannot be used as a pretext for major violations of humanitarian law; reality, both Abkhazia and South Ossetia were de facto independent territories after their respective disputes with Tbilisi began; Kosovo, on the other hand, was not independent before February 2008' (ibid. 32)); the distinct nature of peacekeeping missions in the two regions; and the difference in the recognition of the independence of the states, as Russia recognised Abkhazia and South Ossetia as independent states (together with Nauru, Nicaragua and Venezuela) but not Kosovo (which has been so far recognised by 86 UN members).

Peacekeeping is particularly relevant because, beyond the undeniable positive outcome of such operations, there is always a strong political side to the way the 'peacekeeping' strategy is defined. According to Đorđević, 'Moscow is using

Abkhazian/South Ossetian territory to gain a more stable footing and establish stronger influence in the whole region.' Analysing the organisation of the peace-keeping operation in Ossetia, Abkhazia and Kosovo, it emerges that 'the Russian forces that have been acting unilaterally in their own interest on many accounts, and thus in direct opposition to the endeavours of the international community' (ibid.: 33). The UN and Commonwealth of Independent States Joint Peace-Keeping Force operate in tandem in the region, with a minor participation by OSCE and others. But the case of Kosovo is different because the basis was that peacekeepers should be neutral and deployed for security and protection reasons, although since 1999 the situation has often been tense and the peacekeeping strategy has been rearranged to face the new challenges (Del Re 2003).

In terms of peacekeeping, it is interesting to see how the countries of the western Balkans, the Caucasus and Central Asia have been ranked in the Global Peace Index for 2010 (Global Peace Index 2010) in a rank from 1 (most peaceful) to 149 (least peaceful): Bosnia-Herzegovina 60; FYR Macedonia 83; Serbia 90; Uzbekistan 110; Armenia 113; Turkmenistan 117; Azerbaijan 119; Turkey 128; Russian Federation 143 and Georgia 142. It is interesting to note that the United States ranked 85 (by comparison, Germany was ranked 16, Italy 40 and India 128). Nevertheless, the issue of potential violent conflicts in the western Balkans cyclically re-emerges, especially coinciding with the withdrawal of international troops. Drawing parallels of the region with the Caucasus, Gerald Knaus argues:

> One of the most interesting developments in the Western Balkans in recent years has, in fact, been the *demobilisation* of formerly highly mobilised societies. Let us not refer to trends as hard to measure as better neighbourly relations or a decline in interethnic tensions. Let us focus instead on hard facts concerning military spending and serious violent crime.... The last five years have seen *growing* military spending in the Caucasus. At the same time this period has seen a decline in defense spending and in the number of men under arms in the Western Balkans. As a result there are today, proportionately to the population, *two and a half times* (!) more men under arms in the South Caucasus than in the Balkans. Western Balkan countries have also decided to have considerably smaller armies than either Turkey or Greece, their regional neighbours. And although they are richer than the countries of the South Caucasus, their military budgets are significantly smaller. This means that they can allocate more of their public spending to other things, from education and health spending to public infrastructure.
>
> (Knaus 2010)

The other issue raised by Đorđević is sovereignty, posing the dilemma between two formulations: 'we should move a step forward' and 'let the capable take their destiny in their hands' (see also the interesting views of Kingston and Spears 2004). There is yet a constructive way of interpreting the 'Kosovo' or 'Balkan' model: the EU acquired enough experience in the western Balkans, such as the regional free trade area and the visa lifting for Serbia, Montenegro and FYR Macedonia at the end of 2009 – a true epoch-making event – to establish the 'Eastern Partnership' with Georgia, Ukraine, Moldova, Armenia, Azerbaijan and Belarus. Gunnar Wiegand, director for Eastern Europe, Southern Caucasus and Central Asia within the European Commission, argued:

> We might be inspired by the experience with the Western Balkans that countries which perhaps didn't work so well together in the past, will do so in specific areas like energy or transport. We should put forward the idea of creating a free trade area between these countries – something which worked quite well in the Balkans.
>
> (Quoted in Pop 2008)

Other elements should be taken into account, which strongly influence the policies in the area, such as Islam and energy routes. Moreover, the geopolitical dimension of the conflicts, where countries play roles to suit their national interests, must also be taken into account. For example, Dominique Wolton, research director at the CNRS, said at the beginning of 2010, 'Balkans and Caucasus have much in common because Turkey is involved in both conflicts' (Panarmenian.net 2010).

Model, precedent, pretext

Kosovo has not yet ascended to the status of a clearly structured conflict resolution model, although it is often defined as such on many occasions. When, as discussed above, Kosovo is referred to as a 'model' by country representatives, whether directly involved in conflicts at various levels, playing different roles, or as external observers, they all give a different interpretation of the concept of 'model', thus posing the question: which aspect of the so-called 'model' do they refer to? Glenda Eoyang and Lois Yellowthunder use Kosovo as a case study within the area of human systems dynamics (HSD), and apply a model called CDE (containers, differences and exchanges) to the process. Containers, differences and exchanges are three conditions posed by the model, and interact with one another in non-linear ways. They argue that conflict resolution and peace building methods are

> usually based on linear causal models of human systems dynamics and thematic categories of behavior, have not resolved issues in ways that are reliable, generalizable, or sustainable. Where theory seems reliable, practice is unpredictable; and where practice is effective, theory is weak, if present at all. The sciences of nonlinear dynamics – chaos and complexity – offer a new approach to these age-old issues of peace and conflict.
>
> (Eoyang and Yellowthunder 2010: 99)

This suggestion is interesting in the case of Kosovo, not only because Kosovo can be used to test the CDE model, but because, as Eoyang and Yellowthunder argue, in order to find common denominators in different conflicts – even when there are similarities – one has to re-arrange variables on every specific case. They have applied the conditions for self-organising – containers, differences and exchanges – to describe how peace-building activities in the region of Kosovo influenced emergent dynamics there. This approach can help understand whether it is possible to define a Kosovo model or not.

In defining the model of Kosovo, there are many variables to be taken into account, such as the temporal dimension, as there have been many phases in the conflict, each of which is fundamental in the development of new strategies of conflict resolution. Regarding the phase of NATO intervention, for instance, one of the effects as pointed out by Eliot A. Cohen is that the conflict in Kosovo helped crystallise a fundamentally new 'American way of war', and 'the maintenance of a coalition became something of an objective in itself', stemming from the desire for political legitimacy abroad and at home (Cohen 2001).

Another important element is the impact of the international community (military, civilian, international organisations, NGOs and other) deriving from the implementation of UN Resolution 1244 (Del Re 2003). The impacts of external intervention in the economy and other aspects of life are also crucial. The concept of 'model' in the case of the Kosovo changes according to perceptions, role, prejudices and contingent elements. In this sense, the comments made by young people from the region and from Western Europe who participated in a visit to Kosovo organised by Pax Christi's Peace Work in the Caucasus, one of the many experiments of conflict resolution through dialogue (Cinta 2010), are interesting. For example,

> Another similarity is that the inhabitants of the Balkans and the Caucasus have been brain-washed with ethno-nationalist propaganda in the past 10–20 years, and that this propaganda now shows consequences especially in the last years marked by the EU accession process

or

> I am not accustomed to the representatives of partly recognized states or entities leaving marks in my passports, and have to reassure myself with the thought that, on that scale, Kosovo is much more recognized than the territories I am usually dealing with [South Ossetia, Abkhazia, Nagorno-Karabakh].

A post-Balkan perspective

The very moment a concept seems to have become a reference point in the analytical process in conflict studies it can crumble. The precise moment in which the conflicts in the Balkans, and the case of Kosovo in particular, have become a model in conflict analysis, evoked when a crisis erupts elsewhere in which specific 'Balkan' variables are believed to be easily identifiable (the local/regional/international dimension of the conflict and the involvement of the great powers;

the multi-level development of the conflict; the issues related to identity and ethnicity and the high symbolic level; the historical/perpetual dimension of the conflict; and the apparent resistance to negotiations by the parties), is questioned. The model itself is nowadays criticised as being outmoded, not only by thinkers from different domains, but by the natural evolution of things.

While elaborating the concept of a 'Balkan' or 'Kosovo' conflict model, I have searched for a new concept that would have the property of including in a prismatic manner all the salient features of the 'Balkan model' in relation to conflict resolution intended in the classic way, and at the same time adding the property of being projected into the future, readjusting the properties to the new challenges. The concept of 'post-Balkan' has emerged as most appropriate.

'Balkanisation' is a classic term, invoked to explain the disintegration of some multiethnic states and their devolution into dictatorship, ethnic cleansing and civil wars. Transient is the concept of the 'Balkan model' – later the 'Kosovo model' – which transcends the aspects of Balkanisation, focusing directly on the process and outcomes of conflict resolution, leaving open options and hypotheses rather than providing definite conclusions. In the future, the concept of post-Balkan will most likely be prominent.

In his acute – although ideologically influenced – and rare analysis, Ugričić (2010) explains the essence of a definition of what constitutes post-Balkan. In his article, Ugričić quotes Adela Peeva's 2003 film, *Whose is this Song?* (Del Re 2010a, 2010b). In the film, the Bulgarian director travels through the Balkans asking people which country/culture a famous song belongs to. In each country people say it belongs to them, reacting very emotionally when Peeva says that other Balkan people affirm that it belongs to their national patrimony. The importance of the documentary lies in the fact that it touches on the concept of national identity and common historical past, aiming at reconciliation with a common cultural heritage. It is a perfect example of post-Balkan self-representation. As Ugričić notes, the film shows that even music represents what he calls 'a symbolic infrastructure' in the Balkans. The problem lies in how this symbolic infrastructure is used and what effects it has (taking into account what effects it has had). Ugričić explains what he means by 'symbolic post-Balkan infrastructure':

> *Post-Balkans*: Balkans after Balkans; troubled Balkans resolved; European Balkans regenerated. *Symbolic*: The dominant vision of and narrative about the world and times defines the dominant experience of the world and times. *Infrastructure*: Arts and culture are a semantic and performative infrastructure of integrated, radiant and viable public domains and societies.
>
> (Ugričić 2010: 1)

What importance does a post-Balkan approach lend to a given issue? It is the identification of a unifying element springing out of the awareness of the common denominators in past experiences. Does 'post-Balkan' lie in the EU? Sabine Friezer points out that in order to get conflict prevention right in the

Balkans and Caucasus, given the risk of new armed clashes in Georgia, Azerbaijan, Armenia and Bosnia-Herzegovina, what is needed is the EU. The EU should take the lead in Bosnia-Herzegovina and in the Caucasus:

> The EU cannot project its interest in peace simply with EU delegations. The EU needs a regional representative to address South Ossetia, Abkhazia and Nagorno-Karabakh, where people continue to die on the line of contact,' she says, and the solution would start simply by naming a regional envoy: 'the EU clearly needs to streamline its conflict prevention and resolution capabilities to be more effective. In the Balkans, countries have a clear EU membership perspective, the Commission is well implanted, large funds are being disbursed, and the conflicts are internal, and reinforced EU delegations can take the political lead. But among the more distant Caucasus neighbours, where conflicts are regional, financial resources fewer, and EU membership a distant hope, a regional envoy, backed with an agile political team, is still needed
>
> (Friezer 2010)

Are the Balkans ready for this new concept? Are we all ready for it? The 'Balkan' and 'Kosovo' models have been quite comfortable reference points so far, and to move beyond them would mean to elaborate complete new strategies and overcome well-rooted axioms and consolidated stigmas. If the post-Balkan Balkans contend that 'post-Balkan' is the EU, then they must work more on the concept. Post-Balkan is the time and the situation in which the Balkans overcome the constriction of the past in all domains – political, economic, social, cultural – and become aware of the unifying elements within the region and become aware of being a region, starting to act consequently. The unifying element of the post-Balkan period is the Balkans themselves, Kosovo included.

References

3Frontline3 (alias) (2008), 'Freedom for Ossetia. Serbia is With You!', 16 August. www.youtube.com/watch?v=H3MotspJOAc (accessed 16 August 2008).

Auty, Richard and Soysa, Indra De (eds) (2006) *Energy, Wealth and Governance in the Caucasus and Central Asia: Lessons not Learned*, Abingdon: Routledge.

Bancheli, T., Bartmann, B. and Srebrnik, H.F. (2004) De facto *States: the Quest for Sovereignty*, Abingdon: Routledge.

Baran, Z. (2006) 'Kosovo Precedent No Solution for Caucasus Region', *Financial Times*, 17 May.

Baran, Z. and de Waal, T. (2006) 'Abkhazia–Georgia, Kosovo–Serbia: Parallel Worlds?', 1 August. www.opendemocracy.net/democracy-caucasus/abkhazia_serbia_3787.jsp (accessed 12 January 2011).

Barry, E. (2010) 'Russia: Ex-Premier Accuses Putin in Tycoon's Trial', 25 May. http://query.nytimes.com/gst/fullpage.html?res=9403E7DD1438F936A15756C0A9669D8B63&n=Top%2fReference%2fTimes%20Topics%2fSubjects%2fT%2fTax%20Evasion (accessed 13 December 2010).

Battista, P. (2008) 'I rischi dell'assolutismo etico', 8 August. www.corriere.it/editoriali/08_agosto_15/rischi_assolutismo_etico_d7bcf4de-6a9e-11dd-86d0-00144f02aabc.shtml (accessed 12 December 2010).

Bhadrakumar, M.K. (2010) 'Kosovo on the Central Asian Steppes', *Asia Times*, 6 August. www.atimes.com/atimes/Central_Asia/LHo7Ag01.html (accessed 6 January 2011).

Brown, M. (1996) *The International Dimension of Internal Conflict*, Cambridge, MA: MIT Press.

Cinta (alias) (2010) 'Looking Back on a Productive, Successful Working Meeting with the Georgian-Ossetian Civil Forum', *Caucasica*, 2 December. http://caucasica.wordpress.com (accessed 4 January 2011).

Cohen, E.A. (2001) 'Kosovo and the New American Way of War', in A.J. Bacevich and E.A. Cohen (eds) *War over Kosovo: Politics and Strategy in a Global Age*, New York, NY: Columbia University Press, pp. 38–62.

De Quetteville, H. (2008) 'Georgia Comparing Kosovo with South Ossetia', *Telegraph*, 11 August.

de Waal, T. (2006) 'The Kosovo Talks are Much More Than About Kosovo', *Financial Times*, 10 May.

Del Re, E.C. (2003) 'When Our Men Arrive: Unmik's Post-Conflict Administration of Kosovo', in P. Siani-Davies (ed.) *Post-conflict Kosovo*, London: Routledge, pp. 88–104.

—— (2007) 'How Much Does the Status Cost', *Est-Ovest*, 6: 21–33. Also available at www.est-ovest.eu/archivio/dettaglio.aspx?a=331 (accessed 23 January 2011).

—— (2010a) 'Frammenti di Kosovo nel caleidoscopio europeo', *Limes*, Special Issue: 159–170.

—— (2010b) 'Balcani: lingue come armi', *Limes*, 3: 54–70.

Dobrouna, A. (2008) 'Kosovo is More Like Georgia Not South Ossetia', 11 August. www.newkosovareport.com/200808111115/Arianit-Dobruna/kosovo-is-more-like-georgia-not-s-ossetia.html (accessed 11 December 2010).

Đorđević, V. (2010) 'Regional Conflicts in the Western Balkans and the Caucasus Revisited: Comparison of Kosovo to South Ossetia and Abkhazia', *Středoevropské politické studie*, Brno, Part I, 12: 22–44.

Eisikovits, N. and Eiran, E. (2010) 'The Kosovo Model for Mideast Peace', *The Providence Journal*, 12 November.

Eoyang, G. and Yellowthunder, L. (2010) 'Complexity Models and Conflict: A Case Study from Kosovo', *E.CO*, 12 (3): 97–113.

EUTV (2008) 'Kosovo Precendent Pentru Transnistria?'. www.youtube.com/watch?v=VFIFCP_pAOs (accessed 11 December 2010).

Friezer, S. (2010) 'Getting EU Conflict Prevention Right in the Balkans and Caucasus', 21 July. www.crisisgroup.org/en/regions/europe/Getting%20EU%20Conflict%20Prevention%20Right%20in%20the%20Balkans%20and%20Caucasus.aspx (accessed 7 January 2011).

Ghitis, F. (2010) 'Kosovo Not the Right Model for Palestinians', *Miami Herald*, 5 July. www.miamiherald.com/2010/05/07/1617478/kosovo-not-the-right-model-for.html (accessed 11 January 2011).

Gismatullin, E. and Yackley, Ayla J. (2008) 'BP Halts BTC Oil Loading, Pipe Shutdown to Last Weeks', 7 August. www.bloomberg.com/apps/news?pid=newsarchive&refer=energy&sid=ah7sKNYnEEzY (accessed 3 January 2011).

Global Peace Index 2010 (2010). www.visionofhumanity.org/gpi-data/#/2010/scor (accessed 5 January 2011).

Graziosi, M. (2008) 'Georgia e cattiva coscienza europea', *L'Ernesto*, 15 August. www.pdci-ibarruri.it/exurss.htm (accessed 4 January 2011).

International Herald Tribune (2008) 'Czech President: Kosovo Freed Russia's Hands', 15 August. www.iht.com/articles/ap/2008/08/15/europe/EU-Czech-Russia-Georgia.php (accessed 3 January 2011).

Kingston, P.W.T. and Spears, I. (eds) (2004) *States within States: Incipient Political Entities in the Post-Cold War Era*, Basingstoke: Palgrave Macmillan.

Knaus, G. (2010) 'New Wars? A Comparison of the Balkans and the Caucasus', 6 February. www.esiweb.org/rumeliobserver/2010/02/06/new-wars-a-comparison-of-the-balkans-and-the-caucasus (accessed 22 December 2010).

Krüger, H. (2010) *The Nagorno-Karabach Conflict: A Legal Analysis*, Heidelberg: Springer-Verlag.

Kumar, M. (2010) 'USA Trying to Impose the Kosovo Model in Sri Lanka', 29 June. www.lankaweb.com/news/items/2010/06/29/usa-trying-to-impose-the-kosovo-model-in-sri-lanka (accessed 2 January 2011).

Lynch, D. (2004) *Engaging Eurasia's Separatist States: Unresolved Conflicts and* De Facto *States*, Washington, DC: US Institute of Peace Press.

Michels, C. and Coppieters, Bruno (2008) 'There is No Kosovo Model on International Recognition', World Security Network, 8 May. www.worldsecuritynetwork.com/showArticle3.cfm?article_id=15631 (accessed 5 January 2011).

News.am (2010) 'Nagorno-Karabakh Conflict not "frozen," Göran Lennmarker says', 9 July. http://news.am/eng/news/24584.html (accessed 12 December 2010).

—— (2011) 'Nagorno-Karabakh Conflict May Cause WWIII, Russian Expert Says', 7 January. http://news.am/eng/news/43875.html (accessed 12 January 2011).

Ohanian, K., Rzayev, S. and Kharadze, N. (2010) 'Kosovo Ruling "Pandora's Box" for Caucasus', Caucasus Reporting Service, Issue 552, Institute for War and Peace Reporting, 30 July. http://iwpr.net/print/report-news/kosovo-ruling-%E2%80%9Cpandora%E2%80%99s-box%E2%80%9D-caucasus (accessed 5 January 2011).

Olcott, M. Brill (2005) *Central Asia's Second Chance*, Washington, DC: The Brookings Institution Press.

Panarmenian.net (2010) 'Dominique Wolton: Conflicts in Balkans and South Caucasus Have Much in Common', 14 June. www.panarmenian.net/.../Dominique_Wolton_conflicts_in_Balkans_and_South_Caucasus_have_much_in_common (accessed 22 December 2010).

Pearl, D. (2002) *At Home in the World: Collected Writings from The Wall Street Journal*, New York, NY: Simon and Schuster.

Peeva, A. (2003) *Chia e tazi pesen?* (Whose is This Song?), Adela Media Film and TV Production Company, Belgium/Bulgaria.

Pop, V. (2008) 'Balkans Model to Underpin EU's "Eastern Partnership"', 18 September. http://euobserver.com/15/26766 (accessed 6 December 2010).

Scaglione, F. (2008) 'Si chiama petrolio il filo rosso tra il Caucaso e il Kosovo', 5 July. www.fulvioscaglione.com/index.php/guerra/116 (accessed 10 January 2011).

Serbianna (2008) 'Kosovo Independence Nothing But Trouble, Walesa', 18 August. www.serbianna.com/news/2008/02911.shtml (accessed 12 January 2011).

Socor, V. (2007) 'Kosovo: Russia's Fifth Frozen Conflict?', *Eurasia Daily Monitor*, 2 April. www.jamestown.org/edm/article.php?article_id=2372067 (accessed 15 January 2011).

Sznt.com (2008) 'Kosovo, a Model for Ethnic Hungarians' Autonomy Drive', 4 January. www.sznt.ro/en/index.php?option=com_content&view=article&catid=16%3Ahirek&id=

188%3Akosovo-a-model-for-ethnic-hungarians-autonomy-drive&Itemid=22&lang=en (accessed 20 December 2010).

Tasić, J. (2008) 'Janjić: Rusija primenjuje model koji je NATO koristio na Kosovu', *Danas*, 11 August.

Tert.am (2010) 'Kosovo's Model is Applicable for Karabakh: Levon Zurabyan', 23 July. www.tert.am/en/news/2010/07/23/zurabyan4 (accessed 12 January 2011).

Torbakov, I. (2006) 'Russia Plays up Kosovo Precedent for Potential Application in the Caucasus', *EurasiaNet*, 4 December. www.eurasianet.org/departments/insight/articles/eav041206a.shtml (accessed 12 December 2010).

Ugričić, S. (2005) 'A Post-Balkan Symbolic Infrastructure', www.eurocult.org/uploads/docs/344.pdf (accessed 1 December 2010).

UNDP (2011) *Sustainability and Equity: a Better Future for All*, Basingstoke: Palgrave Macmillan.

Vini (alias) (2008) Comment to the post by C. Suellentrop, 'Defying the Kosovo logic?', 11 August. http://opinionator.blogs.nytimes.com/2008/08/11/breaking-the-kosovo-rules (accessed 3 January 2011).

Wolff, S. (2010) 'Does the Advisory Opinion of the International Court of Justice on Kosovo's Declaration of Independence Resolve Anything?', 23 July. www.stefanwolff.com/media/does-the-advisory-opinion-of-the-international-court-of-justice-on-kosovo-s-declaration-of-independence-resolve-anything (accessed 2 January 2011).

Zanoni, L. (2008) 'Kosovo e Ossezia del Sud', 14 August. www.balcanicaucaso.org/aree/Serbia/Kosovo-e-Ossezia-del-Sud (accessed 4 January 2011).

Zarakhovich, Y. (2008) 'Russia Cashes on Kosovo Fears', *Time*, 8 March. www.time.com/time/world/article/0,8599,1720718,00.html (accessed 4 January 2011).

Zeynalov, M. (2010) 'Nagorno-Karabakh and Kosovo: Politically Precedent, Legally Different', *Journal of Conflict Transformation*, Caucasus Edition, 15 September. http://caucasusedition.net/analysis/nagorno-karabakh-and-kosovo-politically-precedent-legally-different (accessed 2 January 2011).

3 Mapping ethnic relations

Cartography and conflict management in the North Caucasus, Russia

Andrew Foxall

Introduction

Although it had been visible for at least the last decade, in the aftermath of the bomb attack in May 2010 outside the House of Culture and Sport in Stavropol' it became clear that ethno-nationalist conflict is a reality for people in Stavropol' krai. The attack, responsibility for which is believed to lie with Russian nationalists,[1] took place only moments before a Chechen dance ensemble were due to perform on stage. Three years earlier, in the summer of 2007, six weeks of interethnic rioting in Stavropol' left three students dead (one ethnic Chechen and two ethnic Russians) and numerous others injured (Foxall 2010). And the geopolitics of Russo-North Caucasian relations has been manifest in numerous other examples of interethnic conflict in Stavropol' krai since 1991.

In 2008 and 2009, I visited Stavropol' krai to research the localised geopolitics of interethnic relations in the krai. As I have documented elsewhere (Foxall 2009), I was told that the violent geographies of interethnic relations made visible by the 2007 riots were far removed from the everyday reality lived by residents in Stavropol'. This stands in sharp contrast to the many observers who, based on the violent experience of the two Chechen Wars and broader post-Soviet instability in the North Caucasus republics, have defined the whole North Caucasus region as a tinderbox of interethnic conflict. While interethnic tension among ethnic Russians and ethnic Caucasians does exist in Stavropol' krai, it must be understood in the context of political change, economic liberalisation, military conflict and demographic processes (Zayonchkovskaya 2000). Localised interethnic conflict has, mainly, been due to the large-scale in-migration of ethnic Caucasians over a short time period, roughly coinciding with the two Chechen Wars (1994–1996 and 1999–2002), from the ethnic republics of the North Caucasus into the rural raions in eastern Stavropol' krai. This in-migration occurred at the same time that rising levels of militant Islam and ongoing insecurity in the republics combined with a depressed economy to lead to growing levels of Russian nationalism and xenophobia.

Understanding that interethnic conflict (both violent and non-violent) permeates various aspects of daily life in Stavropol' krai, various mechanisms have been developed by krai authorities to manage interethnic relations. These mechanisms can be dated to the adoption of the krai constitution in 1994. Over the last decade, two mechanisms have been particularly notable, both of which are a result of 'The Complex program of harmonization of interethnic attitudes in Stavropol' krai for 2000–2005' (adopted on 31 December 1999). The first mechanism, in 2005, was the creation of the *Komitet Stavropol'skogo kraya po delam Natsaional'nostei i kazachestva* (Committee of Stavropol' krai for Nationality and Cossack Affairs), which provides a space within regional government for the peaceful resolution of interethnic tension. Together with the Institute of Geography at Stavropol' State University, this committee published, in 2008, an *Ethnic Atlas of Stavropol' Krai* (*Etnicheskii Atlas Stavropol'skogo kraya*). This atlas is the second mechanism, and it is this that I am primarily concerned with in this chapter. The atlas, which maps the changing ethnic geography of Stavropol' krai through successive Soviet and post-Soviet censuses, is an attempt by krai authorities to negotiate interethnic conflict through cartography, and points to an embryonic 'conflict management of cartography'.[2]

This chapter suggests that political-administrative tools, such as the atlas, are an important part of the process of conflict management in Stavropol' krai: they provide an important platform to address fundamental obstacles to interethnic peace because they are ostensibly neutral. At the same time, such tools also function in policy-making, through helping authorities develop appropriate policies in the face of changing daily realities on the ground. In what follows I begin by considering the study of peace in geography. I then discuss the situation in the North Caucasus and the geographic context of Stavropol' krai, briefly detailing the contemporary demographic processes visible in the krai and emphasising the ethnic basis of these processes. I move to explore the various governmental policies and initiatives developed in the post-Soviet period to manage interethnic relations. The more recent of these policies are administered under the umbrella of the 'Stavropol' Krai Committee for Nationality and Cossack Affairs'. For this reason, I detail the origins and activities of the Committee. The substantive empirical material explores the publication of the *Ethnic Atlas of Stavropol' Krai* as an example of what I earlier termed the 'conflict management of cartography'. By way of a conclusion, I highlight the role of the atlas in negotiating interethnic conflict in the krai.

Mapping ethnic relations: geographies of war and peace

Ethnic relations have long been a core theme in conflict management and international relations (IR). In both IR (through the paradigm of 'realism') and conflict management (Horowitz 1990), researchers have seen ethnic conflict in zero-sum terms and as a cause of war. This chapter, though, draws on an alternative corpus of literature related to 'peace'. The establishment of peace has long been a scholarly concern. Peace is a core theme in social science literature, perhaps no more so than in IR, for whom 'The search for peace was a founding preoccupation' (Moore *et al.* 2008: 411). Following the Second World War, 'peace research' (PR) developed as an empirical, comparative science. Yet, contemporary researchers are critical of the manner that 'the initial critical and creative spirit of PR has long disappeared and the subject has turned into a "normal science" that does not reflect on its basic categories or its role in society' (Jutila *et al.* 2008: 625). Nevertheless, the original aim of PR – 'that research should be explicitly value based, i.e. valuing peace over war and other forms of violence, and that research should be politically relevant' (ibid.: 625) – remains relevant today and is manifest in the development of a critical peace research (CPR) agenda. While no explicit connection has yet been made, CPR can also draw useful insights from critical geopolitics (CG), in particular the strand of contemporary research in CG that has called for the development of a 'pacific geopolitics', understood as 'the study of ways of thinking geographically about international relations can promote peaceful and mutually enriching human coexistence' (Megoran 2010: 285). Influenced by critical research agendas, CPR calls for a more reflexive and participatory agenda and considers itself an epistemic community that houses a multitude of approaches, each with a shared focus on critical reflection, dialogue and creativity. Using a medical metaphor, Jutila *et al.* (2008: 634) explain how:

> In a medical context 'the diagnostic task is to *map* the patient ... on a set of diseases described in pathology texts', that is, to compare a patient's symptoms with existing categories of diseases.... In PR one has lived with the promise that something similar in terms of categories could be addressed. (Emphasis added)

The ability to map 'peace' is thus central to the CPR agenda. However, while mapping has long been used in war research, its take up has been slow in peace research. This is indicative of a wider interest in 'war' over 'peace', which has come to dominate recent geographical research. As Megoran (2010) notes, both Kliot and Waterman's (1991) volume, *The Political Geography of Conflict and Peace*, and Flint's (2005) edited book, *The Geography of War and Peace*, are more concerned with 'conflict' and 'war' than with 'peace'. Flint's book, for example, has 11 chapters in the section 'geographies of war' and only three under the section 'geographies of peace'. Yet, as early as 1969, Robert McColl published an article ('The insurgent state: Territorial bases of revolution') in the journal *Annals of the Association of American Geographers* in which he used contemporary insurgencies in China, Indonesia and elsewhere to propose a descriptive geographic model (i.e., map) of rebel strategies as a manifestation of a territorial imperative (O'Loughlin and Wittmer 2010). Since McColl's article, many military-geographic studies published have made extensive use of mapping. This emphasis on war has left a whole raft of potentially useful geopolitical questions unanswered. How can peace be mapped? How can maps be used to promote peace? What is the role of maps in conflict management?

This chapter analyses the *Ethnic Atlas of Stavropol' Krai* as a way to re-focus debate towards the role of mapping in both conflict management and peace studies. In doing so, it extends existing work within these disciplines away from the North American and European contexts in which they were devised towards Russia, and the North Caucasus in particular. Through the geopolitical discourses embedded in the atlas, this chapter also explores the visualisation of Stavropol' krai as it has unfolded in post-Soviet Russian state institutions. In mapping the ethnic geography of multiethnic Stavropol' krai, the atlas serves to reinforce messages contained in the preamble to the Russian Constitution; namely that 'the multinational people of the Russian Federation [are] united by a common fate on our land'.

The North Caucasus

The North Caucasus is located in southern Russia. In a physical sense, southern Russia is usually divided between the plains and mountains. The plains are a continuation of the great plains of Russia: the steppes of the rivers Don and Volga. The mountains, by contrast, rise up to 5,642 m (Mount Elbrus) and form a natural border between Russia and the nation-states of the South Caucasus. This physical geography informs the human geography of the region, whereby many nations of people live in close vicinity, and there are significant regional differences in economic specialisation. For many centuries the North Caucasus has also been a zone of contact between two major religions – Orthodox Christianity and Islam. This can be seen in the contemporary geopolitical narrative of a 'clash of civilizations' (Huntington 1996). In a political-administrative sense, the North Caucasus is traditionally thought of as being composed of seven republics (Adygea, Chechnya, Dagestan, Ingushetia, Kabardino-Balkaria, Karachaevo-Cherkessia and North Ossetia-Alania), two krais (territories) (Krasnodar krai and Stavropol' krai) and one oblast' (region) (Rostov Oblast').

For an area so small (the republics occupy an area of approximately 113,800 km^2, or 0.7 per cent of Russia's total land area), the North Caucasus has exerted a disproportionately strong influence on post-Soviet Russia. As Russia's most volatile region, the North Caucasus republics are linked to the most serious national crises that post-Soviet Russia has faced, including the two Chechen Wars, the Budennovsk hospital siege (1995), the Nord-Ost theatre siege (2002), the Beslan school hostage siege (2004) and the Moscow Metro bombings (2010). While initially located in Chechnya (due to the two Chechen Wars), violence has since spread to neighbouring Ingushetia and Dagestan (where there is latent civil war) and on to Kabardino-Balkaria, Karachaevo-Cherkessia and Adygeya, which are 'increasingly becoming one large battlefield' (Vatchagaev 2009). Occasionally this violence has spread into Stavropol' krai, most notably in the Budennovsk hospital siege in 1995 and the Essentuki train bombing in 2003.

For much of the post-Soviet period, Russia used military force to try to quell instabilities in the North Caucasus. This is visible not only in the First Chechen War, led by President Boris Yeltsin between 1994 and 1996, and the Second Chechen War, launched by President Vladimir Putin in 1999 (until 2002), but also in Russia's counter-terrorist operations (*Kontrterroristicheskaya operatsiya* – KTO) in Chechnya (which officially lasted from 1999 to 2009). This changed when Dmitri Medvedev became president in 2008. In January 2010, as part of his efforts to address the relentless troubles of the North Caucasus, Medvedev re-drew the federal borders of Russia by creating the North Caucasus Federal District (NCFD). The NCFD became the eighth federal district since 2000, when President Vladimir Putin initially reorganised the federal structure of the Russian Federation on the model of Russia's seven military districts. The NCFD is composed of six ethnic republics (Chechnya, Dagestan, Ingushetia, Kabardino-Balkaria, Karachaevo-Cherkessia and North Ossetia-Alania) and one territory (Stavropol' krai).[3] Given that the republics each have majority non-ethnic Russian populations (Table 3.1), Stavropol' krai is in a sense on the 'border' between Russia 'proper' and the North Caucasus (what Malashenko (3 December 2009) has called Russia's 'internal abroad').

Post-Soviet 'transition' since 1991 has had a significant impact on the North Caucasus, with major levels of economic dislocation throughout each of the republics. This was compounded by the two Chechen Wars, which not only destroyed the Chechen economy and much of its infrastructure but also led to a flight of capital and investment from the region. Broader post-Soviet instabilities, notably the rise of militant Islam, have contributed to a contemporary situation characterised by high unemployment, a depressed local economy and widespread poverty. As a result, the North Caucasus republics are net 'receivers' from government subsidies and receive more than half of their budgetary funds from Moscow: in 2010 Chechnya and Ingushetia obtained over 90 per cent of their budget funds from Moscow, compared with Stavropol' krai which received only 35 per cent. Between 2000 and 2010, the Russian government spent a total of 800 billion roubles ($25.7 billion) on the North Caucasus republics (Putin 2010).[4]

While much attention has been paid to military campaigns and other aspects of violence, the impacts of instabilities in the North Caucasus on the republics themselves have been far more wide-ranging (Vendina *et al.* 2007). For example, the United Nations Food and Agriculture Organization (2010) observed that instabilities have undermined the food security of the local population, with the

Table 3.1 Ethnic Russian population in the subjects of the North Caucasus Federal District, 2010 Russian Census

Subjects	*Percentage of population*
Chechnya	1.9
Dagestan	3.6
Ingushetia	0.8
Kabardino-Balkaria	22.5
Karachaevo-Cherkessia	31.6
North Ossetia-Alania	20.8
Stavropol' krai	80.9

Source: 'National composition of the population, by region of the Russian Federation' (Natsional'nii sostav naceleniya po sub'ektam Rossiiskoi Federatsii). www.gks.ru/free_doc/new_site/population/demo/per-itog/tab7.xls (accessed 24 May 2011).

rural poor, internally displaced persons and other marginalised peoples most affected. In a region where approximately 70 per cent of the population partially derive livelihood from agriculture, an estimated 80 per cent of the population live below the Russian national poverty line.

As a result of post-Soviet instabilities in the North Caucasus republics, hundreds of thousands of people (both ethnic Caucasian and ethnic Russian) have migrated away from the region. It is estimated that between 400,000 and 600,000 people fled the North Caucasus due to the First Chechen War, while the Second Chechen War displaced a similar number of people. The impacts of this mass-migration have been felt throughout much of Russia, with the establishment of significant ethnic Caucasian communities in regions previously dominated by ethnic Russians. This is particularly true in southern Russia, especially Rostov Oblast', Krasnodar krai, and Stavropol' krai.

Despite this out-migration, between 1989 and 2010 the population of the North Caucasus republics increased from around 5,310,000 people to 7,082,511 people. At the extreme is Dagestan, where the population increased by over 60 per cent from 1,802,579 in 1989 to 2,910,249 in 2010. Already one of the most densely populated areas of Russia (in 2010 population density was approximately 62.2 people per square kilometre, compared with 8.4 people per square kilometre for Russia), this population growth (due to high levels of natural increase) has increased pressure on the available land in the North Caucasus. As a result, an additional migrant population has left the republics in response to deteriorating economic conditions and employment opportunities there.

The impacts of these processes have been particularly acute in Stavropol' krai, which, owing to its proximity to the republics and attractive urban and rural opportunities for employment, has been the primary destination for migrants fleeing the republics. This is especially true in the eastern raions of the krai, which are sparsely populated and where the availability of land contrasts sharply with the situation in the republics.

Stavropol' krai

Stavropol' krai 'occupies a special place in the strategy for Russia's territorial development because of its contemporary geopolitical position, at the centre of the North Caucasus, contiguous to a majority of the republics of the area' (O'Loughlin *et al.* 2007: 250) (see Map 3.1). Founded in 1777 as an advanced outpost of the Russian empire in the North Caucasus, Stavropol' is the administrative centre of Stavropol' krai. The administrative division of the krai includes: 330 municipal units; nine urban districts; 26 municipal districts; 14 urban settlements; and 281 rural settlements. Aside from Stavropol', other major cities include the industrial centres of Budennovsk and Nevinnomyssk, in the east and west of the krai, respectively, and the Caucasus Mineral Waters region, comprising Pyatigorsk, Essentuki, Kislovodsk and Zheleznovodsk, in the south of the krai. Further south are the ethnic republics of Dagestan (which also borders the krai in the east), Chechnya, Ingushetia, North-Ossetia-Alania, Kabardino-Balkaria

Map 3.1 Stavropol' krai and the North Caucasus.

and Karachaevo-Cherkessia. To the north of the krai is the Republic of Kalmikiya and Rostov Oblast', and to the west is Krasnodar krai.

Because of its proximity to the North Caucasus republics, Stavropol' krai has been affected by the geopolitical instabilities that have characterised the region since 1991. This is visible not only in the number of terrorist attacks on its cities (such as those in Budennovsk and Essentuki) nor, for that matter, the militarisation of its landscape or the periodic damage to key elements of its infrastructure, but also in its changing population geography.

Population change in Stavropol' krai

'The exodus of the ethnic Russians is creating a problem for the whole North Caucasus' (Putin, quoted in Smirnov 2005). According to the 2010 Census, Stavropol' krai had a population of 2,786,281 people. This made Stavropol' krai the fourteenth most populous federal subject in Russia (the krai contained 1.9 per cent of the Russian population) and the second most populous territory in the North Caucasus Federal District (behind Dagestan). Stavropol' krai is one of the most multicultural regions in Russia, and the 2010 Census recorded over 140 different ethnic groups in the krai (Table 3.2). One reason for this is the krai's position as a southern outpost of Russia in the North Caucasus, providing proximate access to the Black Sea, Caspian Sea and South Caucasus nation-states (Armenia, Azerbaijan and Georgia). It is situated between two distinct ethnodemographic regions, on the one hand central Russia and the Ukraine, which are

Table 3.2 Ethnic composition of Stavropol' krai population, 2010 Russian Census

Ethnicity	*Population*	*Percentage of total population*
Russian	2,232,153	80.9
Armenian	161,324	5.9
Dargin	49,302	1.8
Greek	33,573	1.2
Roma	30,879	1.1
Ukrainian	30,373	1.1
Nogay	22,006	0.8
Azeri	17,800	0.6
Karachay	15,598	0.6
Turkmen	15,048	0.5
Chechen	11,980	0.4
Tatar	11,795	0.4
Turk	10,419	0.3
Avar	9,009	0.3

Source: 'National composition of the population, by region of the Russian Federation' (Natsional'nii sostav naceleniya po sub'ektam Rossiiskoi Federatsii). www.gks.ru/free_doc/new_site/population/demo/per-itog/tab7.xls (accessed 24 May 2011).

Note

This table only includes national groups with a population of 9,000 people or more. Thus, it does not show the nationalities of 108,167 people who identified themselves as members of smaller national groups, including significant numbers of Kabardians, Ossetians, Lezgins, Georgians and Belarussians. It should further be noted that 26,855 people refused to indicate their nationality on the census form, and thus are also not included in the figure.

populated predominantly by Slavs, and on the other the mosaic of ethnic groups in the North Caucasus republics, with growing demographic potential.

Currently 80.9 per cent of the population, ethnic Russians previously composed 81.6 per cent of the krai's population in 2002, 84 per cent in 1989, 87.8 per cent in 1979 and 91.3 per cent in 1959. This 'de-Russification' of Stavropol' krai reflects both the out-migration of ethnic Russians and the in-migration of ethnic Caucasians (together with low rates of natural increase for ethnic Russians and high rates of natural increase for ethnic Caucasians), and is part of a process visible in the North Caucasus more broadly. In 1959 ethnic Russians accounted for 38.8 per cent of the population in the seven ethnic republics of the North Caucasus, and by the time of the 2010 Census this figure had decreased to 9.3 per cent. While the out-migration of ethnic Russians is part of a much longer-term process, post-Soviet instabilities in the North Caucasus undoubtedly intensified this. In absolute terms, the ethnic Russian population in the republics decreased by around 575,000 people between 1959 and 1989 and around 465,000 people between 1989 and 2010. As a result, ethnic Russians are a minority in the North Caucasus (Belozerov 2005). This process is seen as politically sensitive in Russia, as 'the retreat of ethnic Russians from this region [the North Caucasus] has long been equated with losing control over it' (Dzutsev 2009).

In Stavropol' krai, the large-scale net in-migration of ethnic Caucasians (particularly Avars and Dargins from Dagestan, and Armenians from Armenia) contrasts sharply with the net out-migration of ethnic Russians and other Slavic peoples. Since 1991 there has been a noticeable shift in the ethnic geography of the krai, with ethnic Russians migrating to raions in the north and west furthest away from the republics, and ethnic Caucasians moving from the republics to raions in the south and east. Not only have ethnic Caucasians moved into traditionally Russian-dominated raions, but, at a more local scale, they also settled in territories inhabited by other ethnic groups. While significant numbers of ethnic Caucasians have settled in Stavropol' krai since the late 1970s, often living and working in villages and other rural settlements close to the borders with the republics, mass-migration from the ethnic republics in the post-Soviet period has intensified these well-established migration flows. As a result, the ethnic Caucasian population in Kurskii raion (which borders Chechnya, Dagestan, North-Ossetia-Alania and Kabardino-Balkaria) increased from 32.9 per cent of the raion's population in 1970 to 48.5 per cent in 2002. In Neftekumskii raion, which borders Dagestan, ethnic Caucasians composed 62.4 per cent of the raion population in 2002, versus 47.3 per cent in 1970. Meanwhile, in Stepnovskii raion, which borders both Kurskii and Neftekumskii raions, the percentage of ethnic Caucasians in the raion population increased from 3.1 per cent in 1970 to 34.9 per cent in 2002.

Interethnic conflict in Stavropol' krai

As the situation has deteriorated in the North Caucasus republics in the post-Soviet period, levels of ethno-nationalism and xenophobia have increased throughout Russia. Amnesty International (2006) reported that, despite having their basic human rights guaranteed under Article 19 of the Russian Constitution, discrimination of ethnic minorities is widespread. This is particularly the case for ethnic groups from the North Caucasus, as since 1991 *Kavkazofobiya* (Caucasus-phobia) has permeated virtually every aspect of Russian society.

In Stavropol' krai, reports from the Moscow-based NGOs SOVA Centre (Kozhevnikova 2009) and EAWARN (Astvatsaturova 2007, 2009) suggest that interethnic conflict is increasing both in frequency and intensity. In 2002, a study conducted jointly by Stavropol' State University and the Russian Academy of Sciences suggested that there was a low level of interethnic conflict in the majority of Stavropol' krai (Kolosov *et al.* 2001). However, the following year research carried out by the Centre for Ethnopolitical Studies in Moscow suggested that ethnic discrimination in Stavropol' krai was widespread. Mariya Astvatsaturova (2005), writing for EAWARN, noted that while there had been a decrease in the level of xenophobia in Stavropol' krai since 2002, there was still a 'dynamic balance in interethnic attitudes' with the 'latent potential' for conflict. Citizens in the krai, she wrote, were becoming increasingly 'anxious due to the variation of the krai's ethnic structure'. By 2007, the 'conflict readiness' of the youth was manifest in the riots of late May and early June when one ethnic Chechen was beaten to death and two ethnic Russians were stabbed to death (Foxall 2010). These riots became central to regional authorities' attempts to manage interethnic relations, as authorities analysed and reviewed existing policies and programmes in light of the riots, and assessed the role of ethnic associations in preventing conflict and maintaining peaceful interethnic relations. While I move to discuss these (and other) mechanisms of conflict management in the next section, it is important to note that interethnic conflict continues in Stavropol' krai.

Astvatsaturova (2009) observed that interethnic tensions in Stavropol' krai had increased, as reflected by increasing instances of household nationalism and xenophobia. In public places, for example, instances of ethno-national violence had become widespread and it was becoming increasingly common to see graffiti like '*Rossiya dlya Russkikh*' ('Russia for (ethnic) Russians'), swastikas and other nationalist inscriptions throughout Stavropol'. While this, she reasoned, did not reflect a strengthening of interethnic intensity, interethnic conflicts did 'still represent a threat'. As such, Astvatsaturova noted, the situation required not only 'constant attention and preventive actions from the state power structures', but was also evidence of the 'underestimation by authorities of conflicts with an ethnic component'. Astvatsaturova's warning proved timely. In the summer of 2009 alone there were high-profile interethnic clashes in: Pelagiade, Izobil'nenskii raion (August 2009); Irgakly, Stepnovskii raion (June 2009); Georgievskii, Predgornii raion (May 2009); and Stavropol' (April 2009). Reflecting on these events, Sergei Markedonov (2009) wrote that the multiethnic composition of the krai population represents a security threat as both individually and collectively these ethnic groups have a 'latent' potential for conflict.

In the years since Astvatsaturova's warning there have been several prominent interethnic clashes in Stavropol' krai, including those in: Stavropol' (May 2010 and November 2010); Makhmud-Mekteb, Neftekumskii raion (September 2011); and Divnom, Apanasenkovskii raion (September 2011). In the aftermath of the 2010 bomb attack in Stavropol', Vladimir Nesterov (head of the Union of Slavic Communities in Stavropol', a Russian neo-nationalist organisation) suggested that one likely reason for the attack was the large-scale in-migration of ethnic Caucasians into the krai since 1991.

Interethnic relations and conflict management

Understanding that interethnic conflict impacts on various aspects of daily life, regional authorities throughout Russia attempt to manage interethnic relations. According to the national and regional policy of Stavropol' krai, authorities recognise the importance of monitoring and managing interethnic relations, suggesting that specific 'national policy' programmes should: pay attention to the experience of ethnic minorities in the labour market; assist in the economic development of national-cultural autonomies; create development programmes for economically 'depressed' areas; create ethnic educational schemes; and develop regional cooperation for the maintenance of peace and stability (www.garant.ru 1999). Questions of ethno-national policy are also implicated in other policies, such as those concerning migration. The policy 'About measures on improvement of work with refugees and the compelled immigrants and their social adaptation in Stavropol' krai' (adopted 14 July 1999, Decree No. 421) specified that it was necessary to develop a nationalities policy in view of contemporary migration patterns. At the same time as being economic and sociocultural concerns, interethnic relations also impact on traditional conceptions of security; the ethno-national policy for Stavropol' krai for 2006–2010 recognises the importance of proactivity (rather than reactivity) in the prevention and settlement of interethnic conflicts.

Since 1996, authorities in Stavropol' krai, in line with the Federal Law 'About national-cultural autonomy' (adopted by the State Duma on 22 May 1996, No. 74-F3),[5] have allowed national-cultural autonomies to develop in the krai. National-cultural autonomy is seen as a means to satisfy varying ethnopolitical demands from ethnic minorities, and as a way to achieve interethnic stability and prevent interethnic conflict. At the beginning of 2003, there were 20 national-cultural autonomies in Stavropol' krai, representing ethnic minorities including Dargins, Armenians, Greeks, Germans and Turkmen. At the same time, there were over 70 national-cultural organisations, including Slavic organisations, registered in the krai.

Over the last decade, the two main policy documents in the sphere of interethnic relations in Stavropol' krai were 'The basic directions of national and regional policy of Stavropol' krai' and 'The Complex program of harmonization of interethnic attitudes in Stavropol' krai for 2000–2005' (both adopted on 31 December 1999) (Astvatsaturov 2007). Reminiscent of the Soviet-era process of 'folklorisation' of ethnic minorities (see Zaslavsky 1994), the Complex programme focused on the construction of an atmosphere of interethnic harmony and emphasised, for example, the role of festivals and seminars, days of national cultures, cultural societies and policy-oriented academic conferences. The Complex programme also paid attention to: studying the interethnic situation in the krai; introducing a system of monitoring of interethnic attitudes; and forecasting and prevention of interethnic conflicts. To realise each of these, krai authorities awarded three contracts to Stavropol' State University (approved on 26 December 2001, Decree No. 320) for projects entitled: 'The creation of system of monitoring and forecasting of ethnopolitical and ethnosocial processes in Stavropol' krai'; 'Ethnic migration in Stavropol' krai: problems of adaptation and migratory behaviour of ethnoses'; and 'The formation of modern skills of interethnic interaction in Stavropol' krai'. Another project approved by krai authorities in this period (in early 2002) was the *Ethnic Atlas of Stavropol' Krai*. More recently, on 26 March 2007, a programme for the 'Development of ethno-social and ethnoconfessional relations in Stavropol' krai between 2007–2009' (*Razvitie etnosotsial'nikh i etnokonfessional'nikh otnoshenii v Stavropol'skom Krae na 2007–2009 godi*) was adopted by Decree No. 163 of the Governor of Stavropol' krai.[6] The primary objective of this programme was to create conditions that guarantee equality for all citizens. The programme also emphasised the use of culture as a means to integrate ethnic populations, and foresaw greater influence for mass media in reporting ethno-social processes and ethno-confessional attitudes.

An important part of the Complex programme was the creation, in 2005, of the 'Committee of Stavropol' krai for National and Cossack affairs' (*Komitet Stavropol'skogo Krai no delam natsional'nostei i kazachestva).*[7] This committee complements two other organisations, both of which were created in Stavropol' city in 2007 as a direct outcome of the riots in the summer of that year: the 'Advisory Council for questions of national-ethnic relations under the administration of Stavropol' city' ('*Konsul'tativnii Sovet po voprosam natsional'no-etnicheskikh otnoshenii pri administratsii goroda Stavropolya'*);[8] and the 'Stavropol' city department for questions of national-ethnic relations, public communications, religious organisations and Cossacks' (*Otdel po voprosam natsional'no-etnicheskikh otnoshenii, svyazyam s obshestvenimi, religioznimi organizatsiyami i kazachestvom administratsii goroda Stavropolya*). The committee is responsible, according to federal law and the legislation of Stavropol' krai, for: developing policies in the area of national attitudes; maintaining state support of Cossacks; maintaining relations between religious organisations and enforcement authorities; and participating in state policy concerning compatriots abroad. This is manifest most recently in the regional programme, 'Development of ethnic and ethno-confessional attitudes in Stavropol' krai for 2007–2009' (*Razvitie etnicheskikh i etnokonfessional'nikh otnoshenii v Stavropol'skom krae na 2007–2009*). The committee, acting within federal law, also coordinates the activities of krai authorities to counteract national and religious extremism. More broadly, the committee is responsible for: responding to interethnic tension and interethnic conflicts; developing conflict warning and prevention measures; the long-term monitoring of interethnic attitudes; and cooperating with academics, policy-makers, politicians and leaders of ethnic and religious communities. Initially headed by Vasili Shnukov (2005–2009), Boris Aleksandrovich Kalinin became the current chairman of the committee in July 2009. One of Kalinin's first acts upon becoming chairman was to visit, in August 2009, the rural raions in eastern Stavropol' krai, where interethnic relations are particularly tense.[9]

'*Etnicheskii Atlas Stavropol'skogo Kraya*'

Published in October 2008, the *Etnicheskii Atlas Stavropol'skogo kraya* (*Ethnic Atlas of Stavropol' Krai*) is key to authorities' attempts to manage interethnic relations in Stavropol' krai. An outcome of 'The Complex program of harmonization of interethnic attitudes in Stavropol' krai for 2000–2005', the atlas originally appeared in policy discussions in 2002 under the title *Ethnic Atlas of the Population of Stavropol' Krai* (*Etnicheskii atlas naseleniya Stavropol'skogo kraya*). The atlas represents a clear attempt by authorities to create a 'conflict management of cartography'.

Authored by Vitali Belozerov, Alexander Panin and Vasili Chichin, all of whom are based in the Institute of Geography at Stavropol' State University (SGU), the atlas analyses the changing ethnic geography of Stavropol' krai through drawing on statistical data from Soviet and post-Soviet censuses between 1926 and 2002. This is supplemented by data from the regional Statistics Office

(*Statisticheski Upravlenie*) and successive editions of the *Demographic Yearbook of Russia* (*Demografecheskii Ezhegodnik Rossii*). Over the course of 208 pages, the atlas makes use of more than 150 maps to analyse the ethnic character of demographic process and migration patterns.

The atlas is split into five chapters. Chapters 1–4 analyse demographic processes in Stavropol' krai at the macro- and meso-scales, outlining, respectively: the position of Stavropol' krai within Russia; the ethnic basis of demographic processes in Stavropol' krai; migration processes and ethnic migration; and the ethnic composition of the krai population. Chapter 5 is entitled 'Cities and Areas: An Ethnic Portrait' and analyses the micro-scale of demography within Stavropol' krai, detailing the ethnic structure of the population of not only all the cities and areas of Stavropol' krai, but also the 107 villages in the krai with a population of more than 1,000 inhabitants. Throughout the atlas, data are shown not only statistically, but also cartographically. It is notable, in this context, that Chapter 3 (on 'migration processes and ethnic migration') includes a map of the major terrorist attacks in Stavropol' krai since 1991 (pp. 48–49).

Writing the foreword to the atlas, Vladimir Shapovalov (Rector of SGU) explained that the work was designed to aid the 'development and realization of regional policy and to develop effective measures in the area of harmonization of interethnic attitudes' (p. 6). In an interview with *Stavropol'skaya Pravda*, Vitali Belozerov argued that by analysing existing demographic processes in Stavropol' krai, the atlas was central to any understanding of the ethno-political situation in contemporary Russia, and that it should inform policy in this area. Belozerov explained:

> Our krai is not typical for Russia in terms of its geopolitical position and the ethnic structure of the population, but, having been created in history as an advanced Russian post [in the North Caucasus], Stavropol' remains this today. And consequently, the processes of migration occurring within the North Caucasus, and the frequent change in the ethnic balance [of the population], are part of the all-Russian 'resonance'. In the nineteenth century, for example, there was both the peaceful and military colonisation of the North Caucasus, with the resettlement in the south not only of Cossacks, but also inhabitants of Central Russia and Ukraine. And at the end of the twentieth century and beginning of the twenty-first century, all of this has been repeated but in reverse: the mass out-migration of Slavs from 'hot' points of the south to the north.
>
> (*Stavropol'skaya Pravda* 2008)

Stavropol'skaya Pravda, reporting on the publication of the Atlas, emphasised the importance of the atlas for policy-makers through drawing attention to the 'demographic explosion' of North Caucasian ethnic groups:

> Since 1960, the North Caucasian people have gone through a population explosion: their number has doubled every ten years. Yet, the territory

where they live has not changed size. [Because of this] residents of some republics have ... become seasonal migrants, living on earnings from Central Russia, Siberia, to the Far East, or they have moved to the closest available work, in particular to Stavropol'. And it continues today ... Dargins already compose 1.5% of the krai population, and this is growing.... The objective reality of this is not pleasant for anyone. The fraction of the [ethnic] Russian population has decreased: in 1959, they made 91.3% of the krai population, and in 2002 only 81.6%.... The tendency is clear: the fraction of Russians in the ethnic structure of the krai population is decreasing. What will the situation be in the future and how will it threaten Stavropol'? Researchers have posed these questions to society and authorities [with the publication of the atlas].

(Ibid.)

The atlas, Shapovalov explained, was not published 'by accident', but rather was related to:

[the] features of region in which we live, a region where hundreds of people have coexisted for centuries with neighbourly attitudes. For a long time, the university [Stavropol' State University] has been seriously engaged with research in this area. But not only this. Besides us, we would like the professional competence of biologists, computer scientists, doctors, and teachers to form ethno-cultural consciousness in youth. Moreover, I believe, that today when the government of the krai defines priority directions of strategy of development till 2030, our scientific research can appear extremely important and useful.

(Ibid.)

The Atlas, thus, is an important part of the conflict management architecture in the krai. Together with other educational tools, the Atlas provides an important platform to address fundamental obstacles (not least, the changing ethnic structure of the krai population) to interethnic peace. The need to create an 'ethno-cultural consciousness' (about which Shapovalov spoke) is also apparent in other krai-level authorities, most immediately the 'Development of ethnic and ethno-confessional attitudes in Stavropol' krai for 2007–2009' policy. At the same time, the atlas also functions in policy-making, through helping authorities develop appropriate policies in the face of changing daily realities on the ground. Reviewing the atlas, Vasili Shnukov (former chairman of the Stavropol' krai Committee for Nationality and Cossack Affairs) alluded to this dual education–policy-making purpose, when he explained:

The work of scientists at SGU deserves the highest estimation. In our difficult daily work, we constantly feel the necessity of strict scientific analysis and generalisation that allow us to competently solve questions of interethnic attitudes, which are especially significant today in the North Caucasus.

> There is, alas, the regular phenomenon of violent conflicts involving different ethnic groups, in which the 'nationality card' is played, as a result of the changes of the ethnic structure of the population. In particular, experience shows that the transformation of [ethnic] Russians into the minority populations in multi-ethnic regions increases the probability that different sort of conflicts, including interethnic, will occur. Though today Slavs are still the majority population of Stavropol'skii krai, the migration streams of last years, the military conflict in the Chechen Republic, the closure of tens of factories where people earlier had work, have all led to an outflow of the Slavic population. Certainly, it could break the ethnic balance [of the population] that has developed historically, and demands steadfast attention so that the further transformation of natural migratory processes does not result in tensions and even conflict. And if we speak about the urgency of harmonisation of interethnic attitudes, and about the restoration of mutual trust (between ethnic groups) … then it is necessary to speak about authorities, public organizations, and national diasporas. And the contribution of scientists is useful for us [as politicians].
>
> (Ibid.)

Conclusion

In this chapter I have argued that the publication of the *Ethnic Atlas of Stavropol' Krai* points to an embryonic 'cartography of conflict management'. Through mapping ethnic populations over time and space, the atlas is integral to the krai authorities' efforts at managing interethnic relations and negotiating interethnic conflicts. These efforts are also visible in the creation of the Stavropol' krai Committee for Nationality and Cossack Affairs, and wider attempts to integrate a 'nationalities' policy into krai administration and institutions. In Stavropol' krai, authorities 'celebrate' the multiethnic population through festivals (for example, *Den' Stavropol'skogo kraya* (Day of Stavropol'skii krai)), days of national cultures, cultural societies, and other initiatives which are outcomes of the 'Complex program of harmonization of interethnic attitudes in Stavropol' krai for 2000–2005'. While Horowitz (1990), writing on 'ethnic conflict management for policymakers', suggests that ethnic conflict is intractable, partly because ethnicity has an ascriptive character (it relates to birth) and therefore is 'non-negotiable', the evidence from Stavropol' krai appears to dispute this.

The low-level of economic development in the North Caucasus, I have argued, plays a significant role in interethnic conflict. This is particularly true in Stavropol' krai where, Avksentiev and Lobova (2004: 530) note, 'there is a definite tendency both in the opinion of experts as well as in mass opinion to view ethnic conflicts as results of economical problems and hazards'. In this respect, Stavropol' krai authorities' efforts to manage ethnic relations were boosted on 2 July 2010 when Aleksandr Khloponin announced a new strategy for the NCFD. Intended to boost its economic development and stem the cause of rising ethnic and religious violence in the region, the 'Development of the North Caucasus, 2010–2012' (*Razvitie Severnogo Kavkaza, 2010–2012*) policy represents one of the first serious attempts by Russia to address the problems of the region. At the beginning of 2010, the NCFD comprised 6.5 per cent of the population of the Russian Federation, while supplying only 1.18 per cent of the country's tax revenues. With no correlation between the economic development of a region and the amount of federal money it receives, Khloponin's programme aims to improve the investment climate in the North Caucasus between 2010 and 2012 before starting an 'active growth phase' in the period 2013–2025. Vladimir Putin set an ambitious growth rate for the NCFD of 10 per cent per year, and called for the creation of at least 400,000 new jobs over the next ten years.

As well as economic development, Airat Aklaev, writing in 1996 for the Berghof Research Centre for Constructive Conflict Management, noted that 'negotiations over power-sharing institutions and democratized federalism in Russia are the main avenues of constructive conflict management in Russia's ethnopolitics' (1996: 74). Clearly, any long-term interethnic 'peace' (understood as more than simply the absence of violence – or what Galtung (1964) called 'negative peace') in Stavropol' krai cannot successfully avoid ethnic minorities' questions either. Indeed, it might be reasonable to think that the population of Stavropol' krai, with its newly acquired democracy, might exert a positive influence on interethnic issues. However, while political institutions in Stavropol' krai are designed on the principle of power-sharing to ensure that minorities' rights and concerns – political, economic, cultural – are heeded, scholarly research that has been undertaken on the topic (Popov and Kuznetsov 2008) suggests that institutional ethnic discrimination and *Kavkazofobiya* throughout Russian society undercuts these attempts.

Cartography has been used far more in the study of war than peace. The project of a 'cartography of conflict management' as outlined in this chapter is a productive approach to 'develop tools to identify and explore transformative possibilities for peace' (Megoran 2010: 395). By itself, however, the atlas is not enough, and more must be done to improve interethnic relations not only in Stavropol' krai but also in Russia as a whole.

Notes

1 Although investigators opened a criminal case under Russia's terrorism laws in the aftermath of the attack, nobody has yet been charged with the attack, let alone convicted.
2 In March 2010, Mikhail Solomentsev, chairman of the Moscow City Committee for Interregional Relations and National Policy, announced that authorities in the capital had created a map showing the main areas of ethnic tension in the city. Solomentsev explained that a variety of people, including representatives from the police and security services, and culture, education, social and sport departments, had collaborated on the project to highlight 'race-hate hot spots'. See RIANovosti (2010).
3 The centre of the NCFD is Pyatigorsk in southern Stavropol' krai.
4 The amount of financial assistance increased over this period – from $500 million per year in 2000 to $6 billion in 2009. It should also be noted that particular assistance is

targeted and thus not counted within these figures: for example, between 2009 and 2015 Ingushetia will receive a unique assistance package from Moscow worth $1 billion as a part of a federal programme to develop the North Caucasus republics.

5 This law was amended on 29 June 2004 (No. 58-FZ). The amendment gives the regions of the Russian Federation the right to render financial support to national cultural autonomies 'for the purpose of preserving the national identity, developing the national language [mother tongue] and national culture and implementing national and cultural rights of citizens of the Russian Federation, identifying themselves with certain ethnic communities.'

6 The policy is available in its entirety at www.stavinvest.ru/docs/kzp_etnic.doc.

7 The committee has a website; see www.stavkomnat.ru.

8 The advisory board has a website; see http://stavropol.stavkray.ru/bezop/pksovet.

9 Two months before Kalinin's visit, in June 2009, there had been a large-scale interethnic riot in Stepnovksii raion.

References

Aklaev, Airat (1996) *Ethnopolitical Legitimacy and Ethnic Conflict Management: The Case of the Russian Federation in the early 1990s*, Occasional paper no. 9, Berghof Research Centre for Constructive Conflict Management, Berlin.

Amnesty International (2006) 'Russian Federation: Violent Racism Out Of Control'. www.amnesty.org/en/library/info/EUR46/022/2006 (accessed 21 May 2010).

Astvatsaturova, Mariya (2005) 'Stavropol'skii krai: Ideologiya mezhnatsional'nikh otnoshenii na regional'nom urovne – printsipi, napravleniya, tekhniki i tekhnologi', (Stavropol' Krai: The Ideology of International Relations at the Regional Level – Principles, Directions, Technicians, and Technologies), EAWARN, no. 61. www.eawarn.ru/pub/Bull/WebHome/61_33.htm (accessed 4 January 2009).

—— (2007) 'Stavropol'skii krai: mezhetnicheskie otnosheniya v etnopoliticheskom landshafte', (Stavropol' Krai: Interethnic Relations in an Ethnopolitical Landscape), *Kazan Federalist*, no. 3–4. www.kazanfed.ru/publications/kazanfederalist/n23–24/10 (accessed 22 May 2009).

—— (2009) 'Problemi etnicheskikh otnoshenii na Stavropol'e' (Problems of Ethnic Relations in Stavropol'), EAWARN, 21 July. http://eawarn.ru/index.php?option=com_content&task=view&id=283&Itemid=40 (accessed 21 July 2009).

Avksentiev, Viktor and Lobova, Ludmilla (2004) 'Ethnopolitical Problems of Post-Soviet Russia: The Case of Northern Caucasus', in Gerald Hinteregger and Hans-Georg Heinrich (eds) *Russia: Continuity and Change*, Wien: Springer-Verlag, pp. 527–546.

Belozerov, Vitali S. (2005) *Russifikatsiya i derussifikatsiya: Ethnicheskaya karta Severnogo Kavkaza vchera i segodnya* (*Russification and Derussification: The Ethnic Map of the North Caucasus Yesterday and Today*), Moscow: Haugs.

Belozerov, Vitali S., Panin, Alexander N. and Chichin, Vitali V. (2008) *Etnicheskii Atlas Stavropol'skogo kraya* (*Ethnic Atlas of Stavropol' krai*), Stavropol': Stavropol' State University Press.

Centre for Ethnopolitical Studies (2009) 'Stavropol'skii krai: Diskriminatsiya ntsional'nikh men'sheinstv v sotsial'no-economicheskoi sfere (Stavropol' Krai: Discrimination of National Minorities in the Social-economic Sphere)'. www.indem.ru/Ceprs/Minorities/Sta/Sta13.htm (accessed 8 August 2009).

Dzutsev, Valeri (2009) 'North Caucasus' Ethnic Russian Population Shrinks as Indigenous Populations Grow', *Eurasian Daily Monitor*, 6 (120). www.jamestown.org/single/?no_cache=1&tx_ttnews%5Btt_news%5D=35730 (accessed 7 March 2012).

Flint, Colin (ed.) (2005) *The Geography of War and Peace: From Death Camps to Diplomats*, Oxford: Oxford University Press.

Foxall, Andrew (2009) 'Stavropol' Two Years On: Positive Developments in Ethnic Relations', Central Asia-Caucasus Institute, Johns Hopkins University, 1 September.

—— (2010) 'Discourses of Demonisation: Chechens, Russians, and the Stavropol' riots of 2007', *Geopolitics*, 14 (4): 684–704.

Galtung, Johan (1964) 'An Editorial', *Journal of Peace Research*, 1 (1): 1–4.

Horowitz, Donald (1990) 'Ethnic Conflict Management for Policymakers', in Joseph V. Montville (ed.) *Conflict and Peacemaking in Multiethnic Societies*, Lexington, KY: Lexington Books.

Huntington, Samuel P. (1996) *The Clash of Civilisations and the Remaking of World Order*, New York, NY: Simon & Schuster.

Jutila, Matti, Pehkonen, Samu and Väyrynen, Tarya (2008) 'Resuscitating a Discipline: An Agenda for Critical Peace Research', *Millennium: Journal of International Studies*, 36 (3): 623–640.

Kliot, Nurit and Waterman, Stanley (eds) (1991) *The Political Geography of Conflict and Peace*, London: Belhaven.

Kolosov, Vladimir A., Galkina, Tamara A. and Krindach, Alexei D. (2001) 'Territorial'naya identichnost' i mezhetnicheskie otnosheniya, na primere vostochnikh raionov Stavropol'skogo kraya' (Territorial Identity and Interethnic Relations, the Example of the Eastern Raions of Stavropol' Krai), *Polis (Politicheskie Issledovaniya)*, 2: 61–77.

Kozhevnikova, Galina (2009) 'Radical Nationalism in Russia, and Efforts to Counteract it in 2008', Sova Centre for Information and Analysis. http://xeno.sova-center.ru/6BA2468/6BB4208/CCD6D21 (accessed 8 June 2010).

Malashenko, Alexei (2009) 'U nikh tut portreti Putina, Medvedeva, no oni za shariat' (They have Portraits of Putin and Medvdev, but they are for Sharia), Slon, 3 December. www.slon.ru/articles/203931 (accessed 3 December 2009).

Markedonov, Sergei M. (2009) 'Na Stike Mirov Stavropol'skii Krai: fornost russkikh ili zone integratsii?' (Stavropol' Territory On a Join of Worlds: An Advanced Post of Russia or a Zone of Integration?), *Chastnii Korrespondent*. www.chaskor.ru/p.php?id=7827 (accessed 4 January 2010).

Megoran, Nick (2010) 'Towards a Geography of Peace: Pacific Geopolitics and Evangelical Christian Crusade Apologies', *Transactions of the Institute of British Geographers*, 35 (3): 382–398.

Moore, Cerwyn, Radice, Hugo and Sharma, Serena (2008) 'Introduction', *Millennium: Journal of International Studies*, 36 (3): 411–412.

O'Loughlin, John and Wittmer, Frank (2010) 'The Localized Geographies of Violence in the North Caucasus of Russia, 1999–2007', *Annals of the Association of American Geographers*, 101 (1): 178–201.

O'Loughlin, John, Panin, Alexander and Wittmer, Frank (2007) 'Population Change and Migration in Stavropol' Kray: The Effects of Regional Conflicts and Economic Restructuring', *Eurasian Geography and Economics*, 48 (2): 249–267.

Popov, Anton and Kuznetsov, Igor (2008) 'Ethnic Discrimination and the Discourse of "Indigenization": The Regional Regime, "Indigenous Majority" and Ethnic Minorities in Krasnodar Krai in Russia', *Nationalities Papers*, 36 (2): 223–252.

Putin, Vladimir Vladimirovich (2010) 'Prime Minister Vladimir Putin Visits North Caucasus Federal District and Attends United Russia Interregional Conference to Discuss the Strategy for Social and Economic Development of the North Caucasus Through

2020, in Particular the Programme for the Years 2010, 2011 and 2012', 6 July. http://premier.gov.ru/eng/events/news/11301 (accessed 3 December 2009).

RIANovosti (2010) 'Moscow Authorities Create Map of Ethnic Tension Sites', 22 March. http://en.rian.ru/russia/20100322/158275719.html (accessed 21 May 2010).

Smirnov, Andrei (2005) 'Ethnic Russians in the North Caucasus Face Decision to Emigrate', *Eurasia Daily Monitor*, 2 (17). www.jamestown.org/single/?no_cache=1&tx_ttnews[tt_news]=30543 (accessed 21 April 2010).

Stavropol'skaya Pravda (2008) 'Etnicheskii atlas Stavropol'skogo kraya podgotovlen so trudnikami SGU' (Ethnic Atlas of Stavropol' Krai is Prepared by Employees of SGU), 24 October. www.stapravda.ru/20081024/Etnicheskij_atlas_Stavropolskogo_kraya_podgotovlen_sotrudnikami_33756.html (accessed 24 October 2008).

United Nations Food and Agriculture Organization (2010) *Russian Federation: North Caucasus*. www.fao.org/emergencies/country_information/list/europe/russianfederation/en (accessed 11 November 2010).

Vatchagaev, Mairbek (2009) 'Kabardino-Balkaria: Another North Caucsaus Hot Spot?', *Eurasian Daily Monitor*, 6 (132). www.jamestown.org/single/?no_cache=1&tx_ttnews[tt_news]=35250 (accessed 10 November 2010).

Vendina, Olga, Belozerov, Vitatli S. and Gustafson, Andrew (2007) 'The Wars in Chechnya and Their Effects on Neighbouring Regions', *Eurasian Geography and Economics*, 48 (2): 178–201.

www.garant.ru (1999) 'Osnovnie napravleniya natsional'noi i regional'noi politiki Stavropol'skogo kraya, yablyayushchiesya Prilozheniem No. 1 k Postanovleniyu Gubernator kraya ot 31 dekabrya 1999', no. 798. www.garant.ru/hotlaw/stav_real (accessed 21 May 2010).

Zaslavsky, Viktor (1994) *The Neo-Stalinist State: Class, Ethnicity, and Consensus in Soviet Society*, New York, NY: M.E. Sharpe.

Zayonchkovskaya, Zhanna A. (2000) *Migratsii: Naseleniye Rossii 1999 (Migrations: The Russian Population 1999)*, Moscow: Knizhniy dom Universitet.

4 Complexities of the peace process in Nagorno-Karabakh

Françoise Companjen

Introduction

On 5 March 2011 Russian President Dmitry Medvedev, Armenian President Serzh Sargsyan and Azerbaijani President Ilham Aliyev met in Sochi to further deliberate on peace negotiations, underway since 1992, on Nagorno-Karabakh. The most important achievement so far is the adherence by the two main parties, Armenia and Azerbaijan, to the principle of settling the conflict through peaceful means. The repeated commitment to peace needs support by the international community against the background of intermittent violence in the region. Despite commitment to peace, the irreconcilable positions of the two main rival parties complicate the peace process. While Azerbaijan wants to secure its territorial integrity, demanding that Armenia withdraws its armed forces from occupied Azerbaijani territory, Armenia argues that it protects the interests of the breakaway republic Nagorno-Karabakh. The representatives of the self-proclaimed independent Nagorno-Karabakh Republic (NKR) are not included in the negotiations, thus leading to an exclusive peace process with its inherent weakness affecting the conflict resolution process in NKR.

Nagorno-Karabakh is little larger than inhabited Israel without the Negev desert, or almost twice the size of South Ossetia. It has a predominantly Armenian population of about 140,000 people, mostly Apostolic Christian. During the fights and upheavals, both Armenians and Azerbaijanis fled from each other's territories. In total, over 500,000[1] Azeris have been living as internally displaced persons (IDPs) in Azerbaijan as they fled from Armenia, the provinces around the disputed area, and from Nagorno-Karabakh itself. With the support of regional and international players such as Russia and the United States,[2] the conflict could be solved sooner rather than later, as relations between the White House and the Kremlin have improved. Such a complex situation involving many different parties and different issues such as energy politics needs a collaborative approach for its resolution. The EU can play a proactive role towards finding a settlement for this vexed problem so close to its borders and potentially explosive in terms of territorial arrangements (the South Ossetia incident in August 2008 is a case in point).

The politics in the region in the context of energy and also relations of the countries in the region with other countries are also significant, impinging on the peace process. The EU is dependent on energy imports from Russia, Azerbaijan and Turkey. The relations of the EU members with the South Caucasian countries are diverse. Germany is interested in Armenia for trade purposes. Its relations with Georgia are significantly determined by then Georgian President Eduard Shevarnadze's efforts in reuniting East and West Germany during the last years of the Cold War. France, on the other hand, is especially interested in Armenia in view of the large Armenian diaspora living in France. The British are oriented towards Azerbaijan in view of oil giant BP's large financial interest in the Baku–Tbilisi–Ceyhan oil pipeline and the South Caucasus gas line. Almost two decades of negotiations call for a recapitulation of the situation, unpicking various issues and interests at stake.

In this chapter I will first give a short summary of theory relevant to this conflict and its resolution in the South Caucasus before explaining the historical origins of the dispute, discerning specific elements in it (genocide, oil and gas pipelines) and elaborating the role of regional (Turkey and Iran) and international (Russia, the United States, EU and UN) players and their geopolitical interests in the region. Finally, I will provide an account of the peace process and its future prospects.

Conflict in South Caucasus

Conflicts in the Caucasus have been presented in different ways, either in the context of a clash of civilisations between Orthodox and Muslim people (Huntington 1993), as interethnic conflicts (Tishkov 1999), in historical terms with an analysis of events (de Waal 2003; Chervonnaya 1994) or in judicial terms (Waters 2005, 2011). Many writings focus on a geopolitical analysis (Companjen *et al.* 2010) combined with a peace- and dialogue-oriented approach (Cohen 2002; Matveeva 2002; see also various NGOs in Azerbaijan, Armenia and the United Kingdom).[3] Each perspective influences the conceptualisation and analysis of the problem. The literature mentioned above reflects four basic strategies to conflict resolution. These are: (1) alternative dispute resolution (ADR) with formal state negotiations generally reinforcing the socio-political status quo; (2) public policy, based on the idea of social engineering and involving all stakeholders in the decision-making process; (3) the analytical school concentrating on the origin of the conflict and jointly formulating solutions; and, finally (4) the most difficult, an active effort to gain peace through forgiveness and reconciliation. This last strategy is only possible if Galtung's notion of 'positive peace' is followed, meaning that 'all goals are pursued simultaneously and conjunctively' (Clements 2002: 80). Thus there are basically two schools in peacekeeping activities: the formal and informal ones. The first school is official, diplomatic and governmental; the second is fuelled by informal, voluntary efforts made mainly by NGOs (ibid.: 77). I will take both views into account while discussing the case of Nagorno-Karabakh and summarise these as peace building. Long-term peace building has a preventive character. Support through economic prosperity is very important for success. Many peace building models consider socio-economic development an important motivation to discourage fighting and to express differences in non-violent ways. According to Collier and Hoeffler (2004), the key characteristics that lengthen conflict are low per capita income, high inequality and a moderate degree of ethnic division. While consensus exists on the importance of economic growth in peace-building activities, the role of elites and corruption are still subject to debate. Clements (2002: 82) argues that elite corruption and 'minimal attention to the role of the public sector in rectifying horizontal and vertical inequalities' can subvert peace-building efforts. On the other hand, Hanne Fjelde (2009) contends that political corruption is not necessarily associated with a higher risk of civil war, especially in oil states. Since one of the two main parties in the Nagorno-Karabakh conflict, Azerbaijan, is a rich oil state, this point of reference is also relevant.

It is crucial in the context of Nagorno-Karabakh to analyse the conflict from a historical perspective, as it will bring into focus the historical antecedents of the conflict and the perspectives of parties, particularly Armenia and Azerbaijan, and factor their divergent claims. These claims revolve around historical arguments (ancient and Soviet history), constitutional claims (Nagorno-Karabakh was an autonomous oblast within the Soviet Socialist Republic (SSR) of Azerbaijan), various legal documents or lack thereof (just before the Soviet occupation) and attributions of motives to the young Stalin when he was running the Kavkaz Bureau. According to Armenians, based, for example, on ancient texts of Strabo and Plinius the second, the Nagorno-Karabakh area from times immemorial was Armenian. Azeris point to the city of Shusha in the Karabakh khanate, founded by Panah Ali khan in the 1750s, to stake claim to this territory. The khanate was a big, predominantly Azeri cultural-political centre (Azerbaijan National Commission for UNESCO 2001). In the nineteenth century the Karabakh area came under Russian control during Russian expansion into the South Caucasus after winning the Russo-Persian war (1826–1828). From the 1830s onward, Shusha split into an Azeri Muslim part and an Armenian Christian part of the city.

More recent points of argument go back to the Bolshevik revolution in 1917. The three trans-Caucasus countries of Georgia, Armenia and Azerbaijan had united briefly as a federation before becoming independent republics, thereby managing to postpone their incorporation into the Soviet Union between 1918 and 1921. But by 1920 the intervention from Bolshevik Moscow was increasing: part of the population was against the Bolsheviks, but others were helping them. It was a time of relative confusion, with decisions being made and retracted on the making of new Soviet borders. It was not always clear who was formally and legally in charge of these regions during that period. Very few people were involved in the hammering out of the Soviet South Caucasus region: first and foremost J. Stalin, but also G. Chicherin, S. Ordzhonikidze[4] and, to a lesser extent, Lenin. According to Ilqar Niftaliyev (2010):

> It was Ordzhonikidze who proposed, for the first time in a telegram sent to Stalin and Chicherin in mid-1920, separating Nagornyy Karabakh out as an autonomous region within the existing Azerbaijani SSR.... For his part,

> Stalin first laid out his position on the Armenian–Azerbaijani territorial conflict in a telegram to Ordzhonikidze on 8 July 1920: 'My opinion is that one cannot endlessly manoeuvre between the sides. One should back one of the sides, in this case – Azerbaijan and Turkey. I have spoken to Lenin, he doesn't mind.

There are several views circulating on what exactly happened in those scantily documented days. One Armenia-oriented view claims that during this period of change and ambiguity Nagorno-Karabakh and Nakhichevan were given to Armenia by an Azerbaijani communist leader,[5] but this decision was retracted by Stalin's intervention (Manasyan 2007). One of the issues here is referring to 'Karabakh' instead of 'Nagorno-Karabakh' in a motion presented for voting. As Alexander Manasyan explains it:

> Nariman Narimanov, the leader of Azeri National-Communists, substituting the question, raised the following proposal for voting: 'To leave Karabakh within the borders of Azerbaijan's Soviet Socialist Republic', whilst according to the agenda of the meeting the question to be discussed was not about Karabakh but Nagorno Karabakh. At the time, this substitution of the subject of the question did not pass. In the course of the meeting and during the open voting the proposal did not pass, i.e. it was rejected. Nevertheless, the next day during the repeated discussion of the issue Stalin took the word 'to leave' from Narimanov's proposal and included it into the decision of CBRCP [Caucasus Bureau of the Russian Communist Party], which, under Stalin's pressure, 'adopted' the decision without any discussion or voting. The decision states: 'to leave Nagorno Karabakh within the borders of Azerbaijan's Soviet Socialist Republic,' despite the fact that Nagorno Karabakh never before was a part of AzSSR, and moreover, at the time was already declared as an integral part of Soviet Armenia.
>
> (Ibid.)

As to reasons why Stalin would have pressured the CBRCP into adopting this decision, some argue it was Stalin's paranoia of Armenians and a secret deal between him and Atatürk (Hareya 2008) that led him to give Nagorno-Karabakh to Azerbaijan. A variation on this story is that Stalin thought it strategically better vis-à-vis bargaining with Turkey. Defending an Azeri view, Ilqar Niftaliyev refutes the argument that Stalin gave away Nagorno-Karabakh and Nachkhivan to Azerbaijan on the basis of some particular liking. Rather, he argues that:

> For Stalin, the … territories were a bargaining chip in a wider strategic game, the essence of which was the speedy creation of Soviet republics in the South Caucasus with the prospect of their subsequent inclusion into a single, multi-ethnic and effectively unitary Soviet state.
>
> (Niftaliyev 2010)

Manasyan and Niftaliyev also offer insightful accounts of developments in the region during the mid-1920s. What these discussions show is that the Soviets developed an ethnic-territorial policy giving different (ethnic) regions various degrees of autonomy. Nagorno-Karabakh was given a formal place along with Nakhichevan and Zanzegur, the first of which came under control of Azerbaijan and the second of which went to Armenia. Thus the origin of 'ownership' of Nagorno-Karabakh is defined differently in different points in time. The Armenians can refer to ancient history, to the Russian pre-Soviet period and to the first decision of the Kavkaz Bureau, before it reversed its decision. The Azeri can refer to the eighteenth-century khanate and the twentieth-century Soviet period: Nagorno-Karabakh was part of the AzSSR confirmed in both Soviet Constitutions of 1936 and 1977 until unrest grew during *glasnost* and *perestroika* policy of the late 1980s.

In February 1988, the Assembly of Nagorno-Karabakh asked the authorities in Moscow to be unified with the SSR Armenia.[6] This request was not granted because the Soviet Constitution had forbidden redrawing of borders. The request in itself, however, was enough to trigger violence between Armenia and Azerbaijan, with Azeris being expelled from Karabakh and pogroms on Armenians living in Baku and Sumgait. The Soviet army managed to restore order but failed to restore a feeling of justice (all the more so because some claim Russia had an active role in creating agitation in the first place) as the unrest spread. But after the bloody war between Azerbaijan and Armenia it has become a self-proclaimed independent republic not recognised by any state, not even by Armenia. It is protected by and connected to Armenia through a corridor on Azerbaijan soil. The occupied zone involves seven districts of Azerbaijan, including the better-known Lachin and Kelbajar provinces. In the run-up to independence from the Soviet Union in 1991, upheavals in Nagorno-Karabakh began in 1988, escalating into vicious fights and ending in the Armenian occupation of territory around Nagorno-Karabakh. This lasted till a ceasefire was signed in 1994 between Azerbaijan and Armenia.

Azerbaijan declared itself independent from the Soviet Union in August 1991. Nagorno-Karabakh did the same the following month. Before the end of 1991 a referendum was held in Nagorno-Karabakh for independence, which was formalised on 6 January 1992. Violence broke out in the two regions, leading to massacres of civilians and forcing thousands of ethnic Azeris and Armenians to flee. According to Human Rights Watch the Khojaly Massacre on 26 February 1992 was one of the ghastly scenes of violence, in which about 200 Azeri villagers, including women and children, were killed. It is considered the largest massacre to date in this conflict. Armenia gained the upper hand with the assistance of the Russian 366th Rifle Regiment. A zone connecting Nagorno-Karabakh to Armenia was also conquered in the course of the violence.

Post-Soviet phase: negotiations

It can be argued that since the ceasefire of 12 May 1994, various leaders from both sides moderated their erstwhile rigid positions over Nagorno-Karabakh. The leaders were prepared to make concessions, while the voters back home, imbued with feelings of nationalism, were not. Since the ceasefire was signed between Azerbaijan and Armenia in 1994, little tangible progress has been made following many meetings that took place between the Armenian and Azeri presidents. In agreement with theory, the formal negotiations between states have mainly reinforced the socio-political status quo. At least these formal negotiations have achieved long-term non-violence (1992–2011), with repeated confirmation of the principle of resolution of the conflict through non-violent means. It is ironic that Nagorno-Karabakh was not represented at the negotiation table in any dialogue process.

Various phases and principles can be distinguished in the peace process: the Paris, Prague and Madrid Principles. The 1993–1997 negotiations focused on confidence building, thus postponing legal status issues. In this phase confidentiality was also considered important. The 1998–2003 negotiations were focused on the return of refugees and IDPs, and withdrawal of blockades, formulated in one single agreement on status, security and consequences of the conflict ('package' agreement). After 2003 the package approach was rejected, and Ilham Aliyev set Armenian withdrawal from occupied territories as a precondition for status negotiations (International Crisis Group 2007).

The OSCE mediators presented the Madrid Principles on 10 July 2009 and called on the leaders of Armenia and Azerbaijan to endorse and finalise the following basic points:

> 1) the return of the territories surrounding Nagorno-Karabakh to Azerbaijani control; 2) an interim status for Nagorno-Karabakh providing guarantees for security and self-governance; 3) a corridor linking Armenia to Nagorno-Karabakh; 4) future determination of the final legal status of Nagorno-Karabakh through a legally binding expression of will; 5) the right of all internally displaced persons and refugees to return to their former places of residence; and 6) international security guarantees that would include a peacekeeping operation.
>
> (Statement by the OSCE Minsk Group co-chair countries 10 July 2009)

These principles were generally agreed to by both parties. Then a shift became apparent towards the second school of conflict resolution, which emphasises the inclusion of all stakeholders in the decision-making process. In December 2009 and January 2010 the OSCE mediators handed over an 'update' of the Madrid Principles, stating with reference to point 4 that Nagorno-Karabakh should be included in the peace talks. Both presidents discussed this update jointly in Sochi in January 2010 in the presence of the Russian foreign minister. In the meantime, President Aliev claimed to have accepted the updated principles, although his answer implicitly was predicated on a final legal status of Nagorno-Karabakh as a part of Azerbaijan, whereas point 4 did not stipulate this. The Armenian President Sargsyan made it clear earlier that Nagorno-Karabakh could not return to Azerbaijan's control, but he did clarify his position with regard to the Armenian-controlled territories around Nagorno-Karabakh. So far, not even point 1 has been implemented, although more details have been thought out as how to withdraw forces from the districts. Partial withdrawal would allow for borders to open and communications and programmes to be launched – such as the beginning of the return of displaced people to some areas monitored by international observers. The next stage would be to determine the status of Nagorno-Karabakh: for example, a federation or confederation, independent, or a solution inspired by other existing models (Cyprus, Kosovo, Scotland or Aland). Officially, the NKR has three claims, supported by Armenia: (1) no subordination by Azerbaijan; (2) NKR cannot be an enclave within Azerbaijan but must have overland access to the outside world; and (3) NKR must have security guarantees (de Waal 2005).

At this point, it would be important to facilitate people-to-people contact: trade and tourism to normalise everyday life while legal solutions are being sought. In principle this should enhance economic growth, which is an important variable supporting peace processes. Facilitating people-to-people contact would also mean opening the way to additional conflict resolution strategies in the informal sphere. The chances of achieving 'positive peace' and reconciliation are greatest when both formal and informal strategies can be applied.

Different parties and issues involved

The Nagorno-Karabakh conflict is one of the protracted conflicts in the post-Soviet space, with four major parties involved in the conflict: two are directly involved – Armenia and Azerbaijan – and two are indirectly involved – Russia and Turkey (and to a much lesser extent Iran). Finally, there are the international organisations such as the OSCE and the UN. First of all, it is the inhabitants of Nagorno-Karabakh – both the Armenians inside the self-proclaimed independent republic (140,000) and the Azeri IDPs residing outside of it (more than 500,000), who bear the brunt of the conflict directly. It is ironic that these people are *not* present at the OSCE Minsk talks. The two sovereign countries Azerbaijan and Armenia are represented at the negotiations. Russia, the United States and France are involved as OSCE Minsk group mediators and as countries representing their own interests. While Turkey is a staunch supporter of Azerbaijan, Iran appears to have toed the line of Russia in the conflict. Turkey and Azerbaijan share a common heritage engendering mutual solidarity. Both countries closed their borders to Armenia in 1993 as a pressure tactic to resolve the conflict. Armenia, on the other hand, can count on the support of the Russian Federation, which has military bases in its soil. Finally, two issues are also linked to the conflict: the question of the 1915genocide, and the recent rapprochement between Turkey and Armenia about re-opening borders. These two issues will be dealt with later.

Armenia

Since Armenia is land-locked between Georgia to the north, Turkey to the west, Iran to the south and Azerbaijan to the east, the closure of borders in 1993 by Turkey and Azerbaijan, with the exception of recent years, meant slow economic development for Armenia. All goods to Armenia formally have to come in through Georgia or Iran.[7] The BTC (Baku–Tbilisi–Ceyhan) pipeline, which could have followed a more direct line from Baku to Ceyhan through Armenia, was built with a detour through Georgia to avoid the conflict area. Thus both Armenia and Azerbaijan suffer from the frozen conflict: Armenia is relatively isolated and misses out on revenues; Azerbaijan is stuck with about 600,000 IDPs.

As a result of its geographical location, Armenia has preferred to balance its policy between the big regional powers. Consequently, its position has not always been clear to the outside world, with the West underlining Armenia's pro-Russian stance and the Russians on the contrary having a watchful eye on Armenia for its pro-Western attitude.[8] Armenia cannot afford to somehow get enmeshed in the tensions between the United States and Iran or between Russia and Georgia, which were volatile enough to erupt into an actual war in August 2008. Armenia's borders with both Azerbaijan and Turkey being closed, and with either the Georgian or Iranian borders closed, the situation for Armenia would obviously be catastrophic as about two-third of its trade take place via Georgia and about one-third via Iran. Germany is Armenia's largest trade partner and the United States is a great source of income in the form of development aid; there is also private funding from the Armenian diaspora living in the United States and France. Similarly, like Georgia, which stresses its ancient Christian European identity and prefers to call itself Eastern European rather than South Caucasian, Armenia gravitates towards a European identity. A difference of Armenia's foreign policy with that of Georgia's, particularly after the Rose Revolution, is that the foreign policy of the former is characterised as 'complementarian' while that of the latter is 'dichotomous' (Iskandaryan 2011: 54) in terms of Georgia's orientation towards the West (NATO/EU) and away from Russia, though trade between Georgia and Russia has resumed.

Azerbaijan

In Azerbaijan, oil revenues are being used to build an Azerbaijani army which aspires to be independent from NATO and Russia. Billions of dollars are being pumped into the defence budget, although a relatively small amount is being used for equipment and training. In spite of agreements to use peaceful means for problem solving, a military solution is not totally unimaginable after what happened in South Ossetia in August 2008, but it is unlikely in the current scenario. With recent investments and its population of more than eight million, Azerbaijan has a bigger active capability than Armenia, which has a population of almost three million (International Institute for Strategic Studies 2010: 174,

176). However, Armenia has both Russian military (Gyumri) and airforce (Yerevan) presence (ibid.: 231, 174). The lease of this base may be extended until 2044. In 2011 the Armenian parliament also 'ratified a deal to allow Russian troops to remain in the country for more than 30 years, boosting Moscow's military influence in the strategic South Caucasus region' (Agence France-Presse 2011). The Armenian deputy defence minister, Ara Nazarian, explained, 'In addition, according to the amendments, the Russian side will assist Armenia in the provision of armaments and modern military equipment' (ibid.).

The military-geographical situation of Nagorno-Karabakh moreover is a difficult one for military manoeuvring. Karabakh is a small mountain preceded by plains that are easy to monitor and defend. Whereas a sophisticated air attack might be needed, it has been the Azerbaijani navy which has significantly increased its capabilities (Giragosyan 5 May 2008), which would be of little use in Nagorno-Karabakh. In a country with authoritarian rule, a real military force paradoxically remains a threat and a rival to the president. Therefore, one may not underestimate, but also not overestimate the capacity of the Azerbaijani army in the coming decade.

Russia

Russia is important to Armenia in at least two ways, namely for security and investment, especially concerning energy. Gaining independence from the Soviet Union in 1991 was not easy for any of the three trans-Caucasus countries, including Armenia. Russia's influence in Armenia was immense, especially shortly after independence. Moscow proclaimed an emergency situation and even went so far as to jail Armenia's future first president, Levon Ter-Petrosyan. In view of the fact that the Nagorno-Karabakh was an autonomous oblast in Azerbaijan, the Kremlin was at the time supporting Azerbaijan in this conflict. On the other hand, it has military bases in Gyumri, Armenia, close to the Turkish border and has been strengthening its position there. Azerbaijan has also been strengthening its military with oil money. Relations between Russia and Azerbaijan are friendly, with an undertone of competition when it comes to energy pipelines. Azerbaijan's cooperation on the BTC pipeline circumvented Russian territory, but Azerbaijan trades with Russia on other fronts. The Turkish–Armenian 'détente' has been a reason for Azerbaijan to warm up to Russia. Clearly, one should not underestimate the potential influence of Russia in this area, especially because Russia is the only country that has leverage to encourage Armenia to withdraw from the districts so that IDPs may return under the protection of an international peace force. The United States could have some leverage in Azerbaijan. Since relations between Russia and the United States have improved, now would be the time to use this leverage and implement the steps agreed on with safety guarantees for the population.

Turkey

With Turkey's efforts to meet the criteria to join the EU under the zealous leadership of the foreign minister, Ahmet Davutoğlu, it is showing the world it can be a regional power of significance. Turkey and Armenia began doing what was unthinkable during a good dozen years earlier – namely to talk about opening borders. Some of the meetings between Turkish and Armenian officials were arranged informally around football matches, hence the term 'soccer diplomacy'. But under auspices of the Swiss Ministry of Foreign Affairs, the opening of borders was formalised in a protocol which, although signed by both parties in October 2009, has not been ratified yet. The Swiss, realising the complexity and interconnectedness of various issues, purposefully disentangled them: the protocols therefore state no preconditions on either the genocide question or on Nagorno-Karabakh. In this strength lies also its weakness because the issues do influence the process of opening borders and vice versa. Thus, the meeting arranged with President Obama for both prime ministers – Sargsyan of Armenia and Erdogan of Turkey – on 12 April 2010 did not lead to ratification of the border protocol, which could have a stabilising effect in the region.

The normal relations of Turkey with Armenia could help further a peaceful settlement in Nagorno-Karabakh. The protocols could help the parties intensify regional trade and cooperation between the South Caucasus countries. Through peace and prosperity and more people-to-people business and contact, this would diminish at least part of the existing fear and moderate the nationalistic feelings of some groups fuelling the diplomatic stranglehold. In the past, leaders of Armenia and Azerbaijan were prepared to take risks towards a peaceful settlement of Nagorno-Karabakh, which their nationalistic supporters could not accept. If, however, people do business and learn each other's languages, as is happening already,[9] in anticipation of more exchange in the near future, the leaders can once again demonstrate leadership without being punished for it. Once relations are normalised, Turkey could encourage closer relations between the Armenian authorities and the Euro-Atlantic countries. Azerbaijan is of course not too thrilled with this protocol between Turkey and Armenia to open borders. Perhaps Azerbaijan feels betrayed by 'brother' Turkey, because Armenia had not met any conditions on Nagorno-Karabakh, the reason why the borders were closed in the first place.

The United Nations

Some argue that a solution will only be possible when it will be in the interest of external powers, including Russia, to work together with other players more intensively. It must be noted that at the UN level, resolutions were brought to the fore to recognise Nagorno-Karabakh and to allow the return of IDPs to the region. Although not all were accepted, there are positive exceptions such as the UNSC resolutions 822, 853, 874 and 884, which stipulate the immediate withdrawal of Armenian forces from occupied Azerbaijani territories without, however, invoking Chapter VII of the UN Charter.

There are various contentious issues that impact the conflict in and over Nagorno-Karabakh. Armenian pressure groups are lobbying various governments to have the massacre of 1915 recognised as genocide. Besides, 'energy politics' cannot be excluded from the Nagorno-Karabakh's negotiation politics. Armenia is traumatised by the loss of at least one million lives in war and deportations, while fighting the Turks in 1915. The Armenian diaspora has a strong lobby in Washington and in European capitals to have the massacre in 1915 recognised as genocide. About 15–20 countries have recognised the genocide so far. Turkey claims Turkish lives were also lost, and the Turkish government denies genocide, the difference lying in premeditated systematic murder or 'normal' casualties as a result of war.[10] In an effort to conduct rational foreign policy the question of genocide has been delegated to a scientific Turkish–Armenian commission and excluded from the protocols. However, the Armenian diaspora in the United States is relentless and more hawkish in its demands than the Armenian government itself. Barack Obama, during his presidential election campaign in 2008, made promises to the Armenian diaspora on recognising the genocide of Armenians. After Obama's election, in view of important relations with Turkey, the promises were downplayed, using the building up of relations between Turkey and Armenia as a reason. The US Senate, however, in April 2010 has proposed and accepted an amendment with regard to the genocide, thus reintroducing this delicate and painful issue in present day US–South Caucasus politics. As a gesture of protest Turkey temporarily summoned back its ambassador from Washington. The United States does not want to put too much pressure on its relations with its NATO ally Turkey and jeopardise its oil interests in Azerbaijan.

Thus energy politics is also involved in the negotiations around Nagorno-Karabakh. Some changes in energy supply deals can be read as a message of Azerbaijan's discontentment with Turkey's unconditional signing of the protocols. Azerbaijan has signed a deal with Russia and Russia and Turkey have an ongoing gas-line project. If Turkey and Armenia manage to open borders, this will weaken Russian influence in Armenia. But in view of the global economic crisis (from which Russia suffers as well) trade and energy revenues may be more important than politics. In view of the complexity of the situation involving regional politics between Turkey, Armenia and Azerbaijan, embedded in geopolitics with Russia, the United States and the EU, with each party having its own interests, it is not surprising that the protocols have not been ratified yet, nor that the updated Madrid Principles have not been accepted yet. For this to happen, some kind of leverage is needed. The leverage should be sought in cooperation between Russia and the United States and/or through people-to-people contacts towards strongly encouraging Armenia and Azerbaijan to reach an amicable settlement. Trade and tourism should enhance a feeling of security and make it easier to endorse and finalise the settlement instead of looking back.

If perfect solutions are too difficult to find at the negotiating table, as we have seen, it is necessary to focus on all goals simultaneously and conjunctively.

It implies focusing on the process instead of on the result (Gudykunst and Kim 2003: 287) and beginning to work on practical issues such as promotion of economic growth and prosperity and involvement of the inhabitants of Nagorno-Karabakh in a public debate on the future of the territory. Taking into consideration the four conflict resolution strategies discussed earlier in the chapter, the first strategy is covered by the formal negotiations mediated by the OSCE. The second strategy, to involve all the stakeholders – in this case meaning the NKR – has been added to the Madrid Principles; but there are more stakeholders who must be taken into consideration. Also, the Lachin corridor, Azerbaijani territory but strongly associated with the safety aspect of the Armenians living in Nagorno-Karabakh, should be included in the debate, referendum and conflict resolution process. It is important to involve the displaced people originally from Nagorno-Karabakh as well, especially if the future of NKR should come to a vote. The third principle, analysing the origin of the conflict is being applied in great detail by local scholars studying, for example, Stalin's letters and other documents. Retrieving and spreading this and other factual information is important for conducting debates based on truthful and versatile facts. The part which is missing here is not to use this information for digging one's self into a scholarly trench fight, but to use this intelligence to come to dialogue and work on a substantiated solution. This is an important step towards the fourth strategy of forgiveness and reconciliation. For this, more informal and mediated discussions are needed, for example by various professional NGO staff members representing various groups of people involved. It is important that the pro-peace groups in the region (Mikhelidze and Pirozzi 2008: 29–37) are encouraged to do their work so that people at the grass-roots level can consider the various options. Should it come to a vote, it is essential to use a fair and just method for a popular vote on the status of Nagorno-Karabakh, involving the displaced people originally from Nagorno-Karabakh even though this may pose some practical problems such as presenting proof of where one has previously lived.

From other conflicts we have learned that economic prosperity is crucial for enhancing positive peace. Ratification of the protocols between Turkey and Armenia on opening borders should help develop trade and prosperity for all, thereby increasing stability and constructive solutions in the area. The EU can help by giving more support to civil society actors representing the people involved. Finally, the EU should overcome its own differences and formulate one combined policy towards the South Caucasus countries.

Conclusion

The Nagorno-Karabakh conflict displays its complexity in multiple layers, but at the same time it has also, as the past years of negotiations and peace efforts have revealed, evolved various novel mechanisms towards transforming conflict in one of the violent regions in Eurasia. It needs emphasis that parties to the conflict and also other players involved in it must rise above partisan interests and look at the conflict through the prism of the victims and as an opportunity to resolve conflicts in the post-Soviet space in a collaborative framework. Russia has an important role in the negotiations, but it appears to be defending its own interests, whether genuine or perceived, rather than playing the role of a serious broker. If Turkey and Armenia open their borders and enjoy the profits of trade and tourism, Russia may eventually have less influence in the region. On the other hand, various plans are being made for building pipelines, thus impacting energy politics in the region with a bearing on the Nagorno-Karabakh conflict. Whether it is Russia or the EU, they have raised their stakes in the energy politics in the region. After the August 2008 war in South Ossetia, Europe again received a wake-up call about being dependent on Russian gas. The United States has also both strategic and economic interest in the region. Perhaps the 'soft' and 'hard' – the informal and formal – powers better work in tandem on this problem involving almost 600,000 Azerbaijani IDPs living in stressful circumstances for nearly 16 years, not to mention the feelings of insecurity of many citizens in Armenia and Nagorno-Karabakh! It needs emphasis that Azerbaijan does not formally want to lose 15–20 per cent of its territory and that certain Armenian groups still hope for compensation in fiscal or geographical terms should the genocide be formally recognised. The conflict is sometimes used conveniently by both parties as a distraction from national affairs. By stimulating informal debates, the strengthening of civil society and encouraging trade and entrepreneurship, the EU can help raise awareness with the public at large to see through such strategies and to maintain the focus on the peace process. Since it is argued that elite corruption and minimal attention to the public sector can undermine the peace process, more comparative research is needed on the way civil society activities and entrepreneurship can stimulate and enforce peace in a conflict zone.

Notes

1 The United Nations High Commission for Refugees refers to approximately 586,000 IDPs in a total Azeri population of 8.8 million. It is difficult to get exact, verified numbers. *Military Balance 2010*, published by the International Institute for Strategic Studies, for example, mentions a total Azeri population of 8,238,672. Azeri sources mention higher numbers of IDPs, up to 800,000.

2 The US deputy assistant secretary of state, Tina Kaidanow, met with the Azerbaijani foreign minister, Elmar Mammadyarov, in Baku in April 2011. According to the Azerbaijani Ministry of Foreign Affairs, Kaidanow underlined that the United States, as an OSCE Minsk Group co-chair, supported the rapid settlement of the Nagorno-Karabakh conflict.

3 The NGOs include Conciliation Resources, Global Dialogue and the International Centre for Human Development.

4 Chicherin was the People's Commissar for Foreign Affairs of the RSFSR and Ordzhonikidze was Secretary of the Caucasus Territorial Bureau of the Central Committee of the Russian Communist Party (Bolsheviks).

5 According to Armenian sources, the Azerbaijani communist leader Nariman Narimanov declared Nakhichevan, Zangezur and Karabakh to be part of Soviet Armenia. For details, see www.armeniapedia.org.

6 In late March 1988, additional Soviet troops were moved to Yerevan as mass meetings, sit-ins and hunger strikes continued in the city. In Armenia, the Karabakh Committee was formed, soon to be headed by Levon Ter-Petrosian, the future Armenian president. In Karabakh, its counterpart was the Krunk Committee (from the Armenian for 'crane', a symbol of longing for the homeland). On 15 June, the Armenian SSR Supreme Soviet passed a resolution granting the request of the NKAO Oblast Soviet to reunite the NKAO with Armenia. Two days later, its Azerbaijani counterpart refused the NKAO request. Thus the Soviet leaders were faced with a constitutional crisis: litigation between the two union republics. For details, see Zverev (1996).

7 Armenia has an estimated $200 million trade with Turkey – indirectly through Georgia and Iran. The number of Armenians working illegally in Turkey varies from about 12,000 to about 50,000–100,000, depending on sources. The most conservative estimate is based on a report by Eurasia Partnership foundation (Kurt 2009). Javid Valiyev takes the intermediate position of about 50,000 (Valiyev 2010).

8 This became clear when Armenia's minister of foreign affairs, Vartan Oskanian, spoke at the Institute Clingendael in The Hague, 31 January 2007, on 'The Diplomacy of Small States'.

9 Panel discussion at the presentation of Spotlight on Armenia (Hug 2011) on 30 May 2011 at Nieuwspoort in The Hague, which I attended.

10 The term genocide did not exist in 1915 and was introduced by the UN in 1948. The criteria named in 1948 have then been retrospectively applied to the killings in 1915. In the context of 'genocide in the Caucasus' the case of the Circassians (or Adygs) in the North Caucasus should be mentioned. Almost one million were deported and an estimated 400,000 killed in 1864 during the Russo-Caucasian war.

References

Agence France-Presse (2011) 'Armenia Agrees Long-term Russian Army Presence', *Hurriyet Daily News*, 12 April. www.hurriyetdailynews.com/default.aspx?pageid=438&n=armenia-agrees-long-term-russian-army-presence-2011-04-12 (accessed 2 June 2011).

Azerbaijan National Commission for UNESCO (2001) 'Susha Historical and Architectural Reserve', 24 October. http://whc.unesco.org/en/tentativelists/1574 (accessed 3 June 2011).

Chervonnaya, Svetlana (1994) *Conflict in the Caucasus: Georgia, Abkhazia and the Russian Shadow*, Glastonbury: Gothic Image Publications.

Clements, Kevin (2002) 'The State of Art of Conflict Transformation', in Paul van Tongeren, Hans van de Veen and Juliette Verhoeven (eds) *Searching for Peace in Europe and Eurasia: An Overview of Conflict Prevention and Peacebuilding Activities*, Boulder, CO: Lynne Rienner, pp. 77–89.

Cohen, Jonathan (2002) 'Regional Introduction', in Paul van Tongeren, Hans van de Veen and Juliette Verhoeven (eds) *Searching for Peace in Europe and Eurasia: An Overview of Conflict Prevention and Peacebuilding Activities*, Boulder, CO: Lynne Rienner, pp. 404–415.

Collier, Paul and Hoeffler, A. (1998) 'On Economic Causes of Civil War', *Oxford Economic Papers*, 50 (4): 563–573.

Companjen, F.J., Maracz, L.K. and Versteegh, L. (eds) (2010) *Exploring the Caucasus in the 21st Century*, Amsterdam: Pallas.

de Waal, Thomas (2003) *Black Garden: Armenia and Azerbaijan through Peace and War*, New York, NY: New York University Press.

—— (2005) *The Nagorno Karabakh Conflict: Origins, Dynamics and Misperceptions*, London: Conciliation Resources.

Fjelde, Hanne (2009) 'Buying Peace? Oil Wealth, Corruption and Civil War', *Journal of Peace Research*, 46 (2): 199–218.

Giragosyan, Richard (2008) 'Looking to 2020: Azerbaijan's Military Aspirations', 5 May. http://noravank.am/eng/articles/detail.php?ELEMENT_ID=3497 (accessed 4 June 2011).

Gudykunst, W. and Kim, Y.Y. (2003) *Communicating with Strangers: An Approach to Intercultural Communication*, New York, NY: McGraw Hill.

Hareya, Armen (2008) 'Stalin's Annexation of Karabakh to Azerbaijan was Due to His Paranoia of Armenians', 6 October. www.huliq.com/61594/stalin%E2%80%99s-annexation-karabakh-azerbaijan-was-due-his-paranoia-armenians (accessed 2 June 2011).

Hug, Adam (ed.) (2011) *Spotlight on Armenia*, London: Foreign Policy Centre.

Huntington, Samuel (1993) 'The Clash of Civilizations', *Foreign Affairs*, 72 (3): 22–50.

International Crisis Group (2007) 'Nagorno-Karabakh: Risking War', Europe Report no. 187. www.crisisgroup.org/~/media/Files/europe/187_nagorno_karabakh___risking_war.pdf (accessed 2 June 2011).

International Institute for Strategic Studies (2010) *The Military Balance 2010*, London: IISS.

Iskandaryan, Alexander (2011) 'Armenia–Russia Relations: Geography Matters', in Adam Hug (ed.) *Spotlight on Armenia*, London: Foreign Policy Centre, pp. 54–56.

Kurt, Suleyman (2009) 'Report: 12,000 Armenian Citizens Working Illegally in Turkey', 5 December. www.todayszaman.com/news-194672-100-report-12000-armenian-citizens-working-illegally-in-turkey.html (accessed 2 June 2011).

Manasyan, Alexander (2007) 'Nagorno-Karabakh Conflict: On the Frontlines of the Information War, or the Last', 19 February. http://ichd.org/?laid=1&com=module&module=static&id=378 (accessed 2 June 2011).

Matveeva, Anna (2002) 'Nagorno Karabakh', in Paul van Tongeren, Hans van de Veen and Juliette Verhoeven (eds) *Searching for Peace in Europe and Eurasia: An Overview of Conflict Prevention and Peacebuilding Activities*, Boulder, CO: Lynne Rienner, pp. 445–467.

Mikhelidze, N. and Pirozzi, N. (2008) 'Civil Society and Conflict Transformation in Abkhazia, Israel/Palestine, Nagorno-Karabakh, Transnistria and Western Sahara', MICROCON Policy Working Paper 3, Brighton, pp. 29–37.

Niftaliyev, Ilqar (2010) 'Stalin on the Territorial Integrity of the Azerbaijani SSR', Visions of Azerbaijan. www.visions.az/nagorno_karabagh_con,175 (accessed 2 June 2011).

Statement by the OSCE Minsk Group co-chair countries (2009) Press release, 10 July. www.osce.org/item/38731.html (accessed 2 June 2011).

Tishkov, Valery (1999) 'Ethnic Conflicts in the former USSR: The Use and Misuse of Typologies and Data', *Journal of Peace Research*, 36 (5): 571–591.

Valiyev, Javid (2010) 'Turkey–Armenia: Borders and Trade', *Azerbaijan in the World*, 3 (7), 1 April. www.ada.edu.az/uploads/file/bw/pdf331.pdf (accessed 2 June 2011).

Waters, Christopher P.M. (ed.) (2005) *The State of Law in the South Caucasus*, Basingstoke: Palgrave Macmillan.

Zverev, Alexei (1996) 'Ethnic Conflicts in the Caucasus 1988–1994', in Bruno Coppieters (ed.) *Contested Borders in the Caucasus*, Brussels: VUB University Press.

5 Subtle line between self-defence and war

South Ossetia 2008

Françoise Companjen and Abel Polese

Introduction

In the night between 7 and 8 August 2008 Georgia launched a military operation to regain the territory of South Ossetia, de facto under separate rule since 1992. As a first step the Georgian side contacted the Russian peacekeepers to inform them that they were planning a military operation to re-establish 'constitutional order' in the 'Tskhinvali Region' (the Georgian term for South Ossetia) (www.spiegel.de 25 August 2008). Shortly afterwards Georgian troops started bombing several areas of the South Ossetian capital Tskhinvali, allegedly targeting Ossetian militia positions. The attack caused casualties among various people, including the Russian peacekeepers. Within a few hours Russian soldiers started entering South Ossetia through the Roki tunnel, connecting North and South Ossetia. Once deployed, the Russian 58th Army and Russian Airborne Troops in South Ossetia started an offensive, also through Abkhazia, where Russian naval forces blockaded part of the coast to allow some of their forces to land. They then joined with the troops coming from South Ossetia to attack Kodori Gorge and eventually converge in Gori, a few kilometres from South Ossetia. In five days the Russian troops occupied the Georgian cities of Poti, Gori, Senaki and Zugdidi and started marching towards Tbilisi. Only after a ceasefire agreement signed by Georgia and Russia on 15 and 16 August did the parties agreed to suspend hostilities, but Russia retained the right to keep troops in Abkhazia and South Ossetia by virtue of a bilateral agreement with the two governments.

On 26 August Russia, then followed by Nicaragua (and in 2009 Venezuela and Nauru), recognised the independence of Abkhazia and South Ossetia. The United Nations called on members not to recognise the independence of Abkhazia and South Ossetia and so far this call has been respected. Even republics from the Commonwealth of Independent States (CIS)[1] were hesitant to take concrete steps towards recognition of these breakaway republics. The new developments surrounding contested independence of republics, however, were enough to raise the question of whether such a path towards independence could lead to creation of new states in other parts of world. Both South Ossetia and Abkhazia formally met the criteria of the Montevideo Convention: they have a territory, population, government and recognition (Green and Waters 2010). This was not the only legal issue raised by the parties to the conflict. Both Georgia and Russia also submitted a number of claims to the Strasbourg Court of Human Rights against one another (Bigg 2008a). This was the first time ever in history that two members of the Council of Europe entered into an open conflict. Besides, it also remained fuzzy as to how to confront the issue, given that both parties were accused of war crimes (*Der Spiegel* 2009).

Was this conflict avoidable and to what extent? This is a question that arises every time violence escalates in some part of the world. It is legitimate to ask what could have been done to prevent war. When human agency has, or seems to have, a major role, it might be possible to argue that a conflict was avoidable or preventable. Framing the discussion in the social theory of international relations (Wendt 1992), this chapter looks at the conflict from several perspectives and considers it as a synergy of actions that could have been avoided. In our view the role of human agency, and in particular of the Georgian and Russian political leaders, were of primary importance in the evolution of the events. Accordingly, we consider the August 2008 events as certainly embedded in structural factors, but also depending on agency with the (local) perception of space and power being conflictual from the onset. This perception moves away from the neo-realist state-centred approach to provide a more socio-cultural and economically embedded vision of the conflict.

Literature on ethnic conflict tends to rest on the assumption that structural factors such as existence and distribution of ethnic groups in a country or a region underlie a conflict (Fearon and Laitin 2003: 75–90). In addition, economic performances (Collier and Hoeffler 2002: 13–28) and economic and social structures have been deemed important in the escalation of a conflict, especially an interethnic one (Horowitz 2000), which is a different category of conflict (Sambanis 2001: 259–282). What other scholars have pointed out is the idea that conflict is fed by social organisation when inequality is present and increases, so that conflict can be seen as emerging from conflicts of interests (Oberschall 1972). When it comes to international conflicts, a large body of research in international relations (IR) starts from the prisoners' dilemma to construct a rational choice approach to conflict (Schelling 1960), based on state-centred necessities, be they considered consistent or multi-vectoral but still explainable through pressures exerted by international competition. Accordingly, democracy and democratic values are a major determinant of state behaviour and determine the likelihood of getting involved in a conflict (Dixon 1994: 14–28). Although old stable democracies are assumed to be more interested in economy and peace, young democracies, as Mansfield and Snyder (2002) point out, tend to be the initiators of war.

However, after the appearance of a social theory of international relations, conflict can be seen embedded in ideas, culture and agency rather than in material power structures that inform relations between states (Wendt 1992: 391–425). Beliefs and perceptions could influence the way the leaders perceive the information they receive (Jervis 1976), and thus influence decisions that determine the fate of a state, a region or a group. They also rest on critique in 'the false promise of international institutions' (Mearsheimer 1994: 5–49), where the usefulness of international institutions in political decision-making is questioned.

The individual-vs-state discussion is of vital importance if one wants to understand to what extent the Ossetian conflict was avoidable or at least preventable. As Wendt puts it, 'anarchy is what states make of it' (1992: 391–425), but if states are 'peopled' (Jones 2007; Polese 2010: 45–62) and depend on individual decisions that leaders construct from their own perceptions, then the social and interpersonal aspects of a leadership are of utmost importance. In our view this twenty-first-century war at the edge of Europe was about both agency and structure in a context of accumulated mutual aggravation, especially since the election of the new pro-Western President Saakashvili in January 2004. It is about structural factors, personal ambitions and the fact that now not only the Russians but also the Georgians have a trained army.[2]

Conflict? What conflict?

What kind of conflict was the one about and with South Ossetia? The unusual nature of the region, its history and international status make it difficult to determine. The Russian side was talking of ethnic cleansing or even genocide; the Georgian side talked of unlawful separatism; and the international community was looking for the sense of all these arguments. In everyday practice, Georgians and South Ossetians have lived in peaceful coexistence for generations, sometimes in separate villages and sometimes in interethnic marriages. Here again, it is what individual people, ethnic-political entrepreneurs, make of the situation, if need be using history and ethnicity to their advantage: 'The national "histories" and myths created by the opposing sides are often mutually exclusive and evoke strong feelings among the people involved' (Green and Waters 2010: 10). In practice, the Georgian–South Ossetian 'border' was rather open. Before the Rose Revolution, extensive black-market trade took place with people regularly travelling up and down between Tbilisi and Tskhinvali. President Saakashvili of Georgia, as part of his reform efforts, put an end to this illegal trafficking of goods. An unfortunate side-effect was that many South Ossetians were driven into the arms of North Ossetians and Russians for some form of income (International Crisis Group 2010: 4). Closing down the black-market perhaps strengthened the Georgian state in the short term but, paradoxically, restraining one of the few sources of income for South Ossetians in the long run added to the building up of tension and to de facto loss of state territory after the war in 2008. In that sense there is more than one economic side to the conflict.

The '11 September of Europe', as some have called it (Radio Free Europe/Radio Liberty 2008), changed the geopolitics and strategic balance of Europe and possibly of the world. Some countries, including Russia, suggested the events might lead to a new cold war (Traynor 2008). Even more importantly, this separation created a precedent of a de facto state, not recognised by the international community, that by virtue of recognition by Russia and Nicaragua, meets the formal criteria to be considered a state (Ó Beacháin n.d.). Such facts also shed new light on to what extent Kosovo's independence (still unrecognised by a number of states) could be used as a parallel. Similarities to and differences from the Kosovo case are many, and often different actors tend to concentrate on different sides of the question, referring to the differences or the similarities depending on their own convenience. Russia was squeamish about Serbia's territorial integrity and its alteration, but adopted a contrasting approach to similar issues in the context of Georgia and even Chechnya. On its side, Georgia recognised Kosovo's independence but found it harder to accept a similar situation within its borders, an issue that some analysts (Oliker 2008) and scholars have addressed (McCorquodale and Hausler 2010: 26–53), suggesting that Ossetian and Abkhazian claims were legitimate in the frame of a minority within a state, not per se as seeking international recognition.

The role of the international community (and international law and soft power) were also extensively analysed and, while it is believed that it helped contain the conflict a bit, many think it could have done better and made its voice heard more effectively.[3] Paradoxically, the influence of international law is perceived to be greater after the war than before (Green and Waters 2010: 6). International rules were drawn upon *after* the war to justify behaviour and to attribute meaning to what had happened. Under 'reason of state', each side felt it had the right to do what it did. This led to accusations of misconduct and excessive use of force being advanced by both sides, mentioned in international independent reports. Russians (and Abkhazians and Ossetians) accused the Georgians of attempted genocide; Georgians accused Russians of provocation and then unlawfully backing the separatist region, while condemning as illegal the two regions' declarations of independence and subsequent Russian recognition.

An independent International Fact-Finding Mission on the Conflict in Georgia (IIFFMCG) was set up by the Council of the European Union by its decision of 2 December 2008. As the mission report states, it is the first time that the EU has decided to intervene actively in a serious armed conflict. About nine months later in September 2009, the EU report, comprising three volumes, concluded that the Georgians were wrong to attack but Russia reacted disproportionately:

> On the night of 7 to 8 August 2008, a sustained Georgian artillery attack struck the town of Tskhinvali. Other movements of the Georgian armed forces targeting Tskhinvali and the surrounding areas were under way, and soon the fighting involved Russian, South Ossetian and Abkhaz military units and armed elements. It did not take long, however, before the Georgian advance into South Ossetia was stopped. In a counter-movement, Russian armed forces, covered by air strikes and by elements of its Black Sea fleet, penetrated deep into Georgia, cutting across the country's main east–west road, reaching the port of Poti and stopping short of Georgia's capital city, Tbilisi. The confrontation developed into a combined inter-state and intra-state conflict, opposing Georgian and Russian forces at one level of confrontation as well as South Ossetians together with Abkhaz fighters and the Georgians at another.
>
> (IIFFMCG 2009:10)

At any rate, both parties have been accused of war crimes and unfair behaviour (www.spiegel.de 21 September 2009). It might be difficult to understand who is 'right', but it is perhaps appropriate to ask what could have been avoided. To do this we will engage with different accounts of the conflict, while trying to explore the motivations of each of the parties.

Background

The territory now known as North Ossetia became part of the Russian empire in 1774, while South Ossetia was annexed in 1801. Further to the creation of the USSR, North Ossetia became part of the Russian SFSR and South Ossetia part of the Georgian SSR until 1989, when the South Ossetian regional council asked Georgia to grant South Ossetia the status of autonomous republic. Subsequently, Georgia adopted a law on national language and banned regional parties in an attempt to boost national unity. Afraid that this tendency would mean further restrictions, South Ossetia's Supreme Soviet approved a decision to unite with North Ossetia, gain full sovereignty, and held elections in 1990. To oppose this move, the Gamsakhurdia government abolished South Ossetia's autonomous status the same year, a move which eventually led to a war (1991–1992). At the end of the war in 1992, South Ossetia remained formally under Georgian rule although de facto independent. In 2006 a popular referendum in South Ossetia further endorsed independence.

Abkhazia was absorbed into the Russian empire in 1864 as a special military province. Further to the creation of the USSR, Abkhazia was made into an SSR in 1921 and later reconverted into an autonomous republic within Georgia in 1931. At the end of the Soviet Union, an agreement was reached between Georgia and Abkhazia that gave the latter a larger degree of autonomy. When, in 1992, Georgia announced it was about to restore the 1921 constitutions, the fear that this would decrease the Abkhazia's autonomy prompted it to declare independence from Georgia. A war followed in 1992–1993, culminating in the Abkhaz capture of the capital Sukhum(i). Vladislav Ardzinba was elected president by the parliament in 1994. He won the first direct elections in 1999. In 2004 Abkhazia held presidential elections that led to a power coalition by Sergey Bagapsh and Raul Khadjimba.

Legally, the two territories, in contrast to republics of the USSR, display a major difference in the context of assertion of their right to independence. The USSR was divided into Union republics, such as Russia, Ukraine and Georgia, within which some autonomous republics (i.e. Adjara, Crimean ASSR or Karakalpak ASSR) were granted higher autonomy. Lower in the hierarchical scale there were autonomous oblasts (i.e. Nagorno-Karabakh or South Ossetia). According to the USSR Constitution adopted in 1977, the only republics that could legally leave the USSR were the Union republics. All other lower entities needed to settle issues directly with the Union republic they were part of. In spite of this clear judicial distinction, from a Russian perspective there appears to be little difference between Abkhazia and South Ossetia in August 2008, which seems to pinpoint the importance of agency over structure in the frame of this conflict. It was not who had the right to secede according to national and international law, but who was allowed to do so and who was not and how strong was the support to secessionist movements. From a Georgian and legal perspective, of course, there was a difference between Abkhazia and South Ossetia.

The Georgian perspective

Of the three autonomous regions of Georgia, Abkhazia and South Ossetia had claimed independence and Ajara has complied with the central authority in Tbilisi in 2004. According to the Soviet Constitution of 1977, Georgia had the right to separate itself from the Soviet Union, but the three autonomous regions did not have the right to secede from Georgia. Georgia did exactly that in two steps: first, on 31 March 1991 in a referendum for independence from the Soviet Union; then on 26 May 1991 in the first post-Soviet presidential elections in an independent Georgian republic. Zviad Gamsakhurdia, appealing to anti-communist feelings and nationalistic aspirations, won the first Georgian presidential elections with 87 per cent of the vote. When South Ossetia announced its own elections in December 1991, the Georgian president cancelled the autonomy of South Ossetia and sent troops there, a military intervention which he lost. A month later, Gamsakhurdia was ousted from Georgia by militia who invited the ex-foreign minister of the Soviet Union and first secretary of the Communist Party in Georgia, Eduard Shevardnadze, back from Moscow to restore order in Georgia. Gamsakhurdia, however, fought back from exile.

In July 1992, the leader of Abkhazia, Vladislav Ardzinba, wrote a letter to Shevardnadze announcing that Abkhazia wanted to return to the Constitution of 1925, when Abkhazia was an SSR in a joint federation with the SSR Georgia (Companjen *et al.* 2010: 185). About a month later (14–16 August 1992), Georgian troops were shot at in Abkhazia when they crossed the Georgian–Abkhazian border, unannounced, looking for kidnappers (a frequent activity in those days) (Hewitt 1996: 217; Companjen 2004: 52) The Georgians shot back and the fight escalated. In spite of the Abkhazians being outnumbered, they seized Sukhum(i), also thanks to a number of aid troops from neighbouring regions. Atrocities were committed by both sides, and once Abkhazians gained control about 250,000 ethnic Georgians had to flee Abkhazia. From a Georgian state perspective the separation of Abkhazia looked illegitimate and violated Georgian territorial integrity.

To end this war against both Abkhazian troops and against Gamsakhurdia fighting back, Shevardnadze decided to ask for help from the Russians and made a deal with President Yeltsin. All former Soviet Republics (such as Ukraine, Moldova, Armenia, Azerbaijan and the Central Asian republics) had joined the CIS, except Georgia. According to the deal, Georgia would now become a CIS member, Russia would get military bases in Georgia for a certain amount of time and with about 2,000–3,000 CIS troops for a peacekeeping mission under the auspices of the UN and the Organization for Security and Cooperation in Europe

(OSCE). In exchange, the pro-Gamsakhurdian troops would be defeated. The territorial dispute was called 'frozen' to at least avoid further violence and to allow for negotiations. Shevardnadze remained in power until the Rose Revolution in November 2003.

In 2008 Georgian President Mikheil Saakashvili tried to find an agreement with the Abkhazian President Sergey Bagapsh. He offered autonomy, representation in parliament and a free economic zone, among other things, but the Abkhazian government remained cold to this proposal, further fuelling anger and frustration in Georgia, which sees Russia as a main actor in the continuation of the conflict. From a Georgian perspective, Tbilisi offered various far-reaching proposals to Abkhazia and would have come to an agreement had it not been for the Russian Federation exercising power behind the scenes. A main concern was the official presence of Russian citizens in both Abkhazia and South Ossetia, mainly due to Moscow's passport policy that makes it extremely easy for former USSR citizens (and their descendants) to apply for a Russian passport regardless of their country of residence. An analyst noted:

> good neighbourly relations require that states refrain from granting citizenship *en masse* to citizens of another state without that state's explicit consent. Russia violated the above principles by conferring citizenship on residents of Georgia's breakaway regions of South Ossetia and Abkhazia, since Georgia not only did not consent to Russia's handing out passports to its citizens, but also repeatedly objected to it.
>
> (Wild 2008)

From a Georgian perspective, Russians were handing out Russian passports which would give them an excuse to enter South Ossetia in order to defend 'their Russian citizens'. Russians point out that since unemployment was so high in South Ossetia a Russian passport guaranteed some rights to a pension and other benefits. The Russians said they were taking responsibility for these people. In virtue of this passport expansion, the number of Russian passport holders does not necessarily mirror the real ethnic composition of the two regions. Thus the Georgians claim that Russia had little reason to defend its so-called minorities since they were created artificially during a couple of years and months before the war. This point of view is defended by legal analysts (Green and Waters 2010).

It is noteworthy that Georgia has portrayed the conflict as an interstate armed conflict. Since the international community has not recognised the independence of South Ossetia and Abkhazia, Georgia thereby avoids any kind of recognition of these territories other than being Georgian. Portraying this conflict as an interstate rather than intrastate conflict also draws more international attention. It cannot be denied that this short war changed geopolitics. Moreover, especially initially, Georgia as a small state against Russia could count on some sympathy from the international community. The war not only drew everyone's attention to Georgia, the South Caucasus and the issue of Europe's dependency on

Russian gas, but in its aftermath, the Georgian government set up a big legal campaign addressing various courts such as the International Court of Justice and the European Court of Human Rights, which again drew public attention. Various NGO leaders travelled across Europe to spread information about the war, distributing time-lines and correcting media reports. From a humanitarian perspective, Georgia has had to deal with about 240,000[4] internally displaced persons (IDPs) since the civil war of 1992–1993, and about another 10,000 IDPs from South Ossetia after the war in August 2008.

The Russian perspective

The end of the USSR has not only meant a reduction in Moscow-controlled territory; it has also meant loss of many strategic regions and a quick creation of a Russian diaspora in the near abroad. In Georgia, for example, about 6 per cent of the population was Russian and in Abkhazia about 14 per cent. The Abkhaz coast was, and in many respects still is, a major tourist destination for Russians, only a few kilometres away from Sochi and enjoying tropical vegetation and climate.

From a Russian perspective, Moscow has protected Georgia throughout history by incorporating Georgia first in the czarist empire and later into the Soviet Union, thereby helping feudal Georgia to modernise; therefore Georgia could, and should, show some gratitude for the education received from Russia (Grant 2009). Since Georgian intelligentsia often followed their education in St Petersburg until the Russian Revolution, Georgian minds were formed in part by the Russian education system. These students are sometimes referred to as the tergdaleulebi: meaning in Georgian, 'those who have drunk from the River Terek' (Reisner 2010). From a Georgian perspective this meant 'having crossed the River Terek'. Prince Ilia Chavchavadze (1837–1907) was the most influential of these educators, leading the Georgian people to imbibe a sense of national awakening. Notions of the Southern Enlightenment (Diderot) reached Georgia through Russia: Catherine the Great had given support to Diderot even if she thought the ideas were not practical ('anything is possible on paper, but I have to use human skin'). Other ideas reached Georgia (and Armenia) through Lord Byron, who wrote a critique on Russian culture and progress. But it is not only culturally, but politically also that Russians claim Georgia should be grateful to Russia.

Perhaps Russia's intervention in South Ossetia and Abkhazia is justified by ever-increasing numbers of Russian citizens living in the regions, and could be seen as the only logical attitude once Georgia attacked Russian citizens. The Russian presence in the area has been increased tremendously not only by the conflicts that have made a number of ethnic Georgians flee the areas, but also the ease of obtaining a Russian passport, which was much more valuable than a Georgian one for many (it gives the right to legally work in Russia, no questions asked on the border and, after the introduction of a visa for Georgians, allows them to cross the border). The number of Russian passports issued in South

Ossetia increased substantially in the months preceding the war. In this context, one can refer to a process of 'passportisation' and almost to a 'manufacturing' of Russian nationals.

The election of the Western-oriented Mikheil Saakashvili has not improved the situation in the eyes of the Russian government, and issues such as the Baku–Tbilisi–Ceyhan oil and gas pipelines and Georgia's overt plans to join NATO meant that punitive action had to be undertaken against the 'dissident country', at least to show what one would risk by openly challenging Moscow.

Increased tensions meant that Russian diplomats were rather ostentatiously expelled from Georgia on the pretext of being spies; Russia, as a response, boycotted Georgian products from 2006, while increasingly engaging to protect its people in South Ossetia and Abkhazia. In sum, several factors appear to have played roles in the Russian aggression. The NATO expansion eastwards with Georgia (and previously Ukraine) seeking NATO membership posed a threat to Russia – at least it easily might have been perceived this way by Russian authorities. After all, Russia's 'near abroad' or 'trans-Caucasus' as it is called from the Moscow point of view, had for some time belonged to the Russian circle of influence. The recognition of Kosovo by the West in spite of Serbian opposition was irritating to Russia, to say the least. All 11 representatives of the Serb minority in Kosovo boycotted the proceedings in February 2008 on the subject of Kosovo's independence. Russia was strongly opposed to recognition both on the basis of traditional ethnic affinity with the Serbs as well as on grounds of international law. Recognising Kosovo would mean many other enclaves in the world (Macedonia, Tibet, Nagorno-Karabakh, South Ossetia, Chechnya) would have a precedent to claim independence. When the West recognised the independence of Kosovo, recognising South Ossetia and Abkhazia was discussed in the Russian Duma not long afterwards. In May 2008, three months after Kosovo's declaration of independence, Russia, China and India released a joint statement calling for fresh negotiations between the authorities of Belgrade and Pristina.

There were other reasons for irritation on the Russian side. The competition going on in building pipelines circumventing Russian energy supplies to Europe had to be discouraged. The Winter Olympic games coming up in Sochi at the border with Abkhazia called for stability in the area. For this occasion, but also more in general, Russia was in need of ports on the Black Sea. Controlling Abkhazia adds more points of access (harbours) to the Black Sea. Finally, much Russian money has been invested in real estate on the Abkhaz coastline.

Immediately after the war, Russia claimed before the UN Security Council that it was acting in self-defence, protecting people with Russian passports and that the military intervention was a unilateral humanitarian intervention because of the 'genocide' and 'ethnic cleansing'. However, as Green and Waters claim (2010: 56), 'Russia did *not* in fact invoke the *legal* claim of unilateral humanitarian intervention'. A death toll on the Russian and Ossetian side of around 150 (BBC News 2008) (with the total number of deaths mentioned in the EU mission report (IIFFMCG 2009) being 850) can hardly be called a genocide. Publications are appearing from international law experts, arguing that the Russian claim to self-defence is hardly valid and that the military intervention in Georgia was unlawful. However, it is also pointed out that Georgia had signed the 1992 Sochi agreement not to change the status quo through force and violence. The EU report also concludes that Georgia was the first to strike; therefore, Georgia cannot claim self-defence either.

Forgotten voices: Ossetian and Abkhazian perspectives

South Ossetia has about 60,000 inhabitants, one-third of which were Georgian. The area was characterised by a mixture of Georgian and South Ossetian villages with inhabitants from mixed marriages. Many of these inhabitants were assimilated into Georgian culture. The border areas east and west were largely under the control of Tbilisi. From 2006 onwards, South Ossetia had two governments: one from the separatist government with Eduard Kokoiti (Kokoyty, or in Russian Kokoyev) and another loyal to Tbilisi, with Sanakov, located in Kurta. The South Ossetians, akin to the North Ossetians in language, race and culture (descendants from the Alans), at various moments have indicated a desire to merge with North Ossetia, which is part of the Russian Federation. Also, during the Russian revolution South Ossetians felt closer to Bolshevik Moscow than to Menshevik Tbilisi. As an autonomous oblast they were entitled to their own language and culture, but not to sovereignty as per the provisions of the Soviet Constitution.

When the leaders from South Ossetia wanted to have their own elections in December 1991, the Georgian President Gamsakhurdia retracted the autonomous status of this region and sent in Georgian troops: thousands of people were killed and many South Ossetians fled to North Ossetia. However, this military intervention ended in failure. The fighting ended formally in July 1992 under the guidance of Russian President Boris Yeltsin. A peacekeeping operation was started under the responsibility of the OSCE, with troops from CIS countries; in practice, these were mainly Russian soldiers. In 1993 and 1994, after the election of South Ossetian leaders, they repeated their wish to join North Ossetia. The main sources of subsistence for South Ossetians are small-scale farming and trade in black-markets. There is little employment. The central government in Tbilisi closed down the large *ergneti* market in an effort to restructure its own economy and ban the black-market. South Ossetians were pushed into the arms of Russia (passports, financial security) and North Ossetia due to these measures. In 2006 a referendum was held among the people of South Ossetia, in which the majority wished for association with North Ossetia. However, the results of this referendum have not been recognised by any international organisation.

The South Ossetians claim that the Georgian army ravished Tskhinvali, not making much distinction between civil and military targets. South Ossetians from a Georgian background claim that Ossetian soldiers attacked mainly people from Georgian villages, thereby committing 'ethnic cleansing'. They allege that the South Ossetians and North Caucasian voluntary militia plundered during the August 2008 war. In the first few days after the war, the people expressed their wish to connect with North Ossetia, but President Edward Kokoiti of South Ossetia had to shelve this idea and exchange it for independence. If South Ossetia joined North Ossetia it would appear like military annexation by Russia. Russia recognised South Ossetia as an independent state, but the vast majority of the international community has not.

The population of Abkhazia was 525,061 according to the 1989 census: 17.8 per cent Abkhazian, 45.7 per cent Georgian, about 14 per cent Russian and a few more Armenians. By 2003 the population was reduced by half: most of the Georgians had fled in September 1993. In 2009 there were 30,000 to 55,000 ethnic Georgians in Abkhazia, especially in the Gali region. The exact number is hard to obtain because at least 10,000 mainly elderly ethnic Georgians are seasonal workers, farming in the Gali region, but spending the winter months back across the border close to Zugdidi. Between the civil war of 1992–1993 and the August war of 2008, the central Georgian authorities still had control over 'Upper' Abkhazia, an area around the Kodori valley. The same applies to the region around Gali, a small town in southern Abkhazia close to the Georgian city of Zugdidi.

The Abkhazians deny any kind of separation through violence. From their perspective they were still negotiating with Tbilisi about their status when the then Georgian minister of defence, Kitovani, crossed the border close to Zugdidi without prior announcement. Allegedly he was looking for a kidnapped minister with 11 staff members. The Abkhazians then opened fire when they found these people illegally present on Abkhazian territory. This was the beginning of what turned into a (civil) war. Moreover, they refer to a 'cultural genocide' by the Georgian army because their national archives and cultural monuments were specifically targeted during the war in 1992–1993. Abkhazia declared independence not straight after the war in 1993, but only after the population had opted for an independent state in a referendum held on 3 October 1999. The Abkhazians want recognition of their independence before they let any IDPs return to Abkhazia. One of the discouraging factors for Abkhazians is that they would be a minority again in their own country if all the IDPs were to return. In spite of a lot of good work done by various NGOs[5] to promote people-to-people contact, resentment and fear remain after the atrocities committed against each other as fellow citizens and neighbours.

In March 2008, Georgia published a peace proposal much akin to the previous one from 2006. The document provides unlimited autonomy for Abkhazia (right to its constitution, government and laws, except matters of foreign policy and sovereignty) but is slightly less advantageous than the 2006 proposal. The previous proposal suggested a federal state which Abkhazia would be part of, with an Abkhazian vice president and Abkhaz as one of the formal languages of Georgia. Abkhazia came close to accepting both the 2006 and 2008 proposals, but a treaty was not signed.[6] Although Abkhazia was not directly involved in the war, the peace enforcer Russia occupied buffer zones around Abkhazia. Many people fled from that region, thus increasing the number of IDPs. With help from the Russian airforce, Abkhazia was also able to reclaim the last bits of territory (Kodori valley and the Gali region) from the central authority in Tbilisi. Russia recognised Abkhazia as an independent state. Contrary to South Ossetia, Abkhazian infrastructure has not been damaged. With the Winter Olympics planned for 2014 right across the Abkhaz border at the Russian Sochi, there are quite a number of financial interests along the coastline in that region.

Conclusion

Looking back at the theoretical notions brought to the fore, varying from more agency-driven, socio-cultural and economic hypotheses to more neo-liberal state-centred propositions, this case shows that economic motives played an important role both in South Ossetia (high unemployment, living at subsistence level) and Russia (secure its financial investments along the coast of Abkhazia; securing ports for trade and security; stabilising the region for the Winter Olympics in Sochi). The role of ethnicity appears less important than practical economic motives. Russia's recognition of the independence of both Abkhazia and South Ossetia even though both territories had a different legal status shows agency was involved. Also, perhaps the misinterpretation of photos indicating the Russian 58th army preparing to enter the Roki tunnel, whereas the Russians claim the army was simply executing routine movements, involves agency above state-centred theory. The idea that conflict is fed by social organisation when inequality is present and increases is contradicted in so far that during the Shevardnadze period, Georgia hardly had a functioning army. It became an option to strike out only after the Georgian army had been carefully trained and equipped by the Americans.

From Moscow's perspective, the August 2008 events were a way to set some people free and defend Russian citizens in the 'near abroad', a claim which does not hold in view of the artificial 'passportisation' that had been going on. From a Georgian perspective it was the (failed) attempt to re-establish the rule of law on separatist territories. The EU fact-finding mission led by Swiss diplomat Heidi Tagliavini suggested that, although Georgia started the attack on Tskhinvali, South Ossetia, both parties – Georgia and Russia – are to blame for the build-up of tension. Russia is blamed for using military force to reshape borders, something which had become almost unthinkable in post-Second World War Europe, and for using disproportionate force to do so. The EU report brought into focus the human tragedy involved in the war: the lives lost and the people displaced.

The amount of force Russia used seems to be motivated by the desire to set an example for all those defying the Kremlin as overtly as Saakashvili did. Still, many questions remain unanswered. The first one is what the Georgian president expected from the international community and from Georgia when he made the decision to attack Tskhinvali. He might just have misinterpreted signals, not only from the Russian military exercising at the other end of the Roki tunnel, but also from the West. Perhaps he expected more support from the West. Given the failure of the operation, it might even seem that the attack was not patiently planned and tested but was an impulsive action, which would confirm even more the role of agency in the conflict. Perhaps, in this the West could have given Georgia clearer signals, preventing the first shots on 7 August.

Russia has claimed to act in self-defence, a claim which is difficult to argue as a valid one. To claim the intervention was a unilateral humanitarian one is definitely legally dubious. Russia has recognised the independence of South Ossetia and of Abkhazia, but the UN has asked the international community not to recognise these states and so far most of the members of the international community have not. Georgia considers Abkhazia and South Ossetia as occupied territory by Russia. As often happens, the use of violence created more problems than it solved. From a Russian perspective, the advantages of having two more states as allies still need to be assessed against the risk that such a development implies – namely to have provided Chechnya and other Federation republics with a (relatively) legal precedent in the Caucasus on how independence of small republics can be supported, at least in theory. In due course Abkhazia will perhaps want real independence instead of being incorporated into the Russian Federation, as is now informally the case. South Ossetia might prefer to join North Ossetia, which is part of the Russian Federation. This will give rise to questions on the legitimacy of other entities in the region and beyond, not only Chechnya but also, among others, Nagorno-Karabakh.

Notes

1 The CIS is a loosely associated regional organisation composed of former Soviet republics coordinating efforts in the sphere of economy, law-making, security, crime prevention and participating in UN peacekeeping forces. It should be noted that Georgia was the only former Soviet country not to join the CIS in the immediate aftermath of its independence under the leadership of President Gamsakhurdia. It joined the CIS under President Shevardnadze. Furthermore, although formally the peacekeeping forces were CIS forces and thus should have been composed of soldiers from different ex-Soviet countries, in practice the forces were Russian. This was one more problem in the conflict because peacekeeping forces should be neutral and not predominantly representative of one of the parties involved.

2 The Americans first started training the border security forces after 9/11, but later also started training the Georgian military. Georgia sent about 2,000 of these trained men to Iraq and later a smaller number to Afghanistan.

3 This has been as a result of the EU inability to react promptly. However, it has also been perceived as the difficulty of responding to Russia when it shows little concern about its reputation in the West (Bigg 2008b; also see Lobjakas 2008). The result is a long diplomatic struggle that has mainly shown EU weakness (Yasmann 2008).

4 Numbers are approximate; some 10,000 mainly elderly were seasonal workers commuting between Zugdidi and the Gali region, staying in Gali in the summer and autumn for harvesting and returning to Zugdidi in the winter.

5 For example: the London-based Conciliation Resources; Tbilisi-based NGO Studio Re (documentaries by Mamuka Kuparadze); Paata Zakhareishvili, Centre for Development and Cooperation, who as an expert on this conflict is involved in various NGOs, human rights committees and in publishing (with Arda Inal-Ipa and Paula Garb) a dialogue series: *Aspects of the Abkhaz–Georgian Conflict* (Zakhareishvili *et al.* 2001–2006).

6 Sometimes the Russians are blamed for influence behind the scenes of negotiations. Sometimes it is pointed out that the central government in Tbilisi made questionable moves such as transferring the trusted Georgian former envoy for peace talks with Abkhazia at a crucial moment in 2006, or not meeting the Abkhazian representatives who had come to Tbilisi to negotiate.

References

BBC News (2008) 'Russia Scales Down Georgia Toll', 20 August. http://newsbbc.co.uk/1/hi/world/europe/7572635.stm (accessed 3 July 2011).

Ó Beacháin, Donnacha (n.d.) 'The EU and OSCE Involvement in Post-Soviet Frozen Conflicts', unpublished manuscript, resulting from the research project 'Resolution of Frozen Conflicts in the Former Soviet space: The Role of the OSCE and EU', funded by Irish Research Council for the Humanities and Social Sciences.

Bigg, Claire (2008) 'Russia, Georgia Take War To Rights Court, Radio Free Europe/Radio Liberty', 23 October. www.rferl.org/content/Russia_Georgia_War_Rights_Court/1332240.html (accessed 3 July 2011).

—— (2008) 'Does Russia Care What the West Thinks?', 29 August. www.rferl.org/content/Does_Russia_Care_What_The_West_Thinks/1194876.html (accessed 3 July 2011).

Collier, Paul and Hoeffler, Anke (2002) 'On the Incidence of Civil War in Africa', *Journal of Conflict Resolution*, 46 (1): 13–28.

Companjen, F.J. (2004) 'Between Tradition and Modernity', PhD Thesis, VU University Amsterdam, Amsterdam.

Companjen, Françoise, Marácz, László and Versteegh, Lia (2010) *Exploring the Caucasus in the 21st Century*, Amsterdam: Pallas.

Der Spiegel (2009) 'Georgia Not a Victim of "Russian Aggression" ', 17 June. http://rt.com/politics/der-spiegel-georgia-not-a-victim-of-russian-aggression (accessed 3 July 2011).

Dixon, William (1994) 'Democracy and the Peaceful Settlement of International Conflict', *American Political Science Review*, 88 (1): 14–28.

Fearon, James and Laitin, David (2003) 'Ethnicity, Insurgency, and Civil War', *American Political Science Review*, 97 (1): 75–90.

Grant, Bruce (2009) *The Captive and the Gift: Cultural Histories of Sovereignty in Russia and the Caucasus*, Ithaca, NY: Cornell University Press.

Green, James and Waters, Christopher (2010) *Conflict in the Caucasus: Implications for International Legal Order*, Houndmills: Palgrave Macmillan.

Hewitt, G. (1996) 'Abkhazia: A Problem of Identity and Ownership', in J. Wright, S. Goldenberg and R. Schofield (eds) *Transcaucasian Boundaries*, London: UCL.

Horowitz, Donald (2000) *Ethnic Groups in Conflict*, Berkeley and Los Angeles, CA: University of California Press.

Independent International Fact-Finding Mission on the Conflict in Georgia (IIFFMCG) (2009), Brussels, September.

International Crisis Group (2010) 'South Ossetia: The Burden of Recognition', Europe Report no. 205, 7 June. www.crisisgroup.org/en/regions/europe/caucasus/georgia/205-south-ossetia-the-burden-of-recognition.aspx (accessed 10 July 2011).

Jervis, Robert (1976) *Perception and Misperception in International Politics*, Princeton, NJ: Princeton University Press.

Jones, Rhys (2007) *Peoples, States, Territories*, Oxford: Wiley-Blackwell.

Lobjakas, Ahto (2008) 'EU Overwhelmed by Russian Cut and Thrust in Georgia', Radio Free Europe, 16 August. www.rferl.org/content/EU_Overwhelmed_By_Russian_CutAndThrust_In_Georgia/1194068.html (accessed 20 August 2008).

McCorquodale, Robert and Hausler, Kristin (2010) 'Caucuses in the Caucasus: The Application of the Right of Self Determination', in James Green and Christopher Waters (eds) *Conflict in the Caucasus: Implications for International Legal Order*, Houndmills: Palgrave Macmillan, pp. 26–53.

Mansfield, Edward D. and Snyder, Jack L. (2002) 'Democratic Transitions, Institutional Strength, and War', *International Organization*, 56 (2): 297–337.

Mearsheimer, John (1994) 'The False Promise of International Institutions', *International Security*, 19 (3): 5–49.

Oberschall, Anthony (1972) *Social Conflicts and Social Movements*, Englewood Cliffs, NJ: Prentice Hall.

Oliker, Olga (2008) 'Kosovo and South Ossetia More Different Than Similar', Commentary, Radio Free Europe/Radio Liberty, 25 August. www.rferl.org/content/Kosovo_And_South_Ossetia_More_Different_Than_Similar/1193663.html (accessed 3 July 2010).

Polese, Abel (2010) 'The Formal and the Informal: Exploring 'Ukrainian' Education in Ukraine, Scenes from Odessa', *Comparative Education*, 46 (1): 45–62.

Radio Free Europe/Radio Liberty (2008) 'Pasternak Could Not Imagine What Vladimir Vladimirovich Imagines', interview with Giya Kancheli, Radio Free Europe/Radio Liberty, 14 September. www.rferl.org/content/Pasternak_Could_Not_Imagine_What_Vladimir_Vladimirovich_Imagines/1199851.html (accessed 3 July 2011).

Reisner, O. (2010) 'Travelling Between Two Worlds: The Tergdaleulebi, Their Identity Conflict and National Life', *Identity Studies*, 2 (1): 36–49.

Sambanis, Nicholas (2001) 'Do Ethnic and Nonethnic Civil Wars Have the Same Causes?', *Journal of Conflict Resolution*, 45 (3): 259–282.

Schelling, Thomas (1960) *The Strategy of Conflict*, Cambridge, MA: Harvard University Press.

Traynor, Ian (2008) 'Russia: We are Ready for a New Cold War', *Guardian*, 26 August.

Wendt, Alexander (1992) 'Anarchy is What States Make of It: The Social Construction of Power Politics', *International Organization*, 46: 391–425.

Wild, Natalie (2008) 'Does a State Have the Right to Protect Its Citizens Abroad?', Radio Free Europe/Radio Liberty, 22 August. www.rferl.org/content/Does_A_State_Have_The_Right_To_Protect_Its_Citizens_Abroad/1193050.html (accessed 10 January 2012).

www.spiegel.de (2008) 'Road to War in Georgia: The Chronicle of a Caucasian Tragedy', 25 August. www.spiegel.de/international/world/0,1518,574812,00.html (accessed 4 June 2011).

—— (2009) 'Independent Experts Blame Georgia for South Ossetia War', 21 September. www.spiegel.de/international/topic/georgia (accessed 3 July 2011).

Yasmann, Victor (2008) 'The Looming Diplomatic War Between Russia and the West', Radio Free Europe/Radio Liberty, 26 August. www.rferl.org/content/The_Looming_Diplomatic_War_Between_Russia_And_The_West/1193904.html (accessed 3 July 2011).

Zakhareishvili, Paata, Inal-Ipa, Arda and Garb, Paula (2001–2006) *Aspects of the Abkhaz–Georgian Conflict*, Dialogue Series, Irvine, CA: University of California.

6 Chechen conflict viewed through the prism of National Bolshevism

Parallels and incongruities

Dmitry V. Shlapentokh

Introduction

The study of the law of historical process and an attempt to 'objectivise' reasons for the changes could be traced back to fifteenth-century European thought; this attempt to find the single model for the changes had been finally shaped up in the twentieth century. This approach implies not just the attempt to find out the single reason for the changes, but also affirms that the historical process has just one avenue to move along. Here the historical process is seen as being quite similar to that of the process in nature – both the biological process and, of course, the laws of cosmology that have clearly defined patterns of development. One could clearly see such a view of history in the grand theories of Marx, Hegel and many others. In Marx's theory the triumph of communism is as inevitable as the rise of the human being after millions of years of evolution. The approach also implied the attempt to find the fixed patterns for the development of particular phenomena such as revolutions. Still, as the recent theories prove, there is no fixed pattern in the development process. The diverse revolutions can follow different patterns and their ideological frameworks change accordingly. Some move from internationalist millenarianism to traditional nationalism into which early revolutionary creed is incorporated. This is indeed the usual model and could be seen in the Russian, Chinese and Iranian revolutions. Still, there is the other possible scenario. In this case the original nationalistic animus is transformed into internationalist revolutionary ideology and practice. As this chapter shows, the developments in the post-Soviet Chechnya are amply instructive of this phenomenon, further adding another crucial dimension to conflict discourse. Though parallels could be drawn between conflicts across time and space, the differences in socio-political and cultural setting significantly impact the process, as well as the outcome.

National Bolshevism and its influence

Revolutionary movements evolve, as does any other social phenomenon. Their relationship with nationalism also evolves and is complicated and has been studied for a long time. The researchers have mostly paid attention to the absorption of revolutionary and, implicitly, internationalist drives by nationalistic animas. The Russian experience could be a good example in this context. The Bolsheviks came to power under the slogans of the worldwide proletarian revolution and preaching Marx's dictum: 'Proletarians of all countries unite!' They were also keen to reject nationalism as a 'bourgeois' ideology that separated the workers and prevented them from achieving their final liberation. It is true that almost from the very beginning of their existence, the Bolsheviks had maintained their rule through terror and did their best to increase the power of the state. In their actions – fighting against those who wanted to create their own states – the Bolsheviks also emerged as people whose goal was to create Russia as 'one and indivisible'. This was one of the major, if not *the* major, shibboleths of the Whites, the Bolsheviks' enemy and the very reason why some of the Bolsheviks' enemies had finally decided to accept them as the country's legitimate rulers. Still, while the logic of the events had made the Bolsheviks statists and imperialists of a sort, their ideological framework was entirely different.

The thrust of their ideology – at least in the first years of their rule – was worldwide revolution. Yet, soon after the end of the civil war, the Bolshevik elite came to the conclusion that the capitalist world had entered what they called 'temporary stabilisation'. And they increasingly emphasised the importance of building socialism 'in our country'. The translation of this slogan into concrete action implied an increasing emphasis on the state, and by the early 1930s Russian nationalism had been fully resurrected in its idiosyncratic form and had become a functional ideology of the regime. Nationalism was mixed with Marxism-Leninism, and later Stalinism, and produced what is usually known as 'National Bolshevism' (Brandenberger 2005).

Similar events can be traced to Red China and contemporary Iran. In all of these cases, the internationalist/cosmopolitan and, actually, anti-state, early creed had been increasingly marginalised by native nationalism and concern with the power and glory of the state. The ideological transformation had led to changes in the approach to foreign experience. In the beginning of the revolutionary process, interest was mostly focused on foreign revolutionary traditions, and, consequently, on foreign history. The early Bolsheviks were more interested in the French Revolution and the Paris Commune than in their native Russian revolutionary past. And, of course, any positive notions about the Russian czars in their capacity of strengthening the state were out of the question. However, by the 1930s, Russian history was fully integrated into the regime's ideology and had become a dominant frame of reference (Schaefer 2011; Smith 2001). The Russian czars in their role as builders of the empire were praised. This could also be seen in China, where the ideology of the First Sovereign Emperor of Qin, the brutal unifier of China, had been incorporated in the ideological discourse of the late Maoist China, and in Iran, where Cyrus the Great, founder of the grand Achaemenid Empire, became increasingly popular among Iranian officials.

Thus the various modifications of 'National Bolshevism' were quite common and were widely known and studied. Still, National Bolshevism was not the only form of evolution of the revolutionary movement. Indeed, an opposite trend emerged: the transition from nationalism to universalistic revolutionism, which corresponded with the increasing interest in foreign revolutionary experiences. The case of the Chechen – actually North Caucasian – resistance is an example of this evolutionary path. At first, the North Caucasian resistance was under the nationalist banner. In Chechnya, for example, nationalists under Dzhokhar Dudaev were the leading force. Their only goal was to create an independent state. Islam was an important building block in the ideological arrangements of the Chechen resistance from the very beginning of the fight against Moscow. Still, at that point it was in a way a part of nationalistic discourse and was accepted for the very reason that the Chechens, similar to many other communities in the Northern Caucasus, were historically Muslims. Consequently, Islam, in its particular form, was integrated in the ideology of the resistance in a rather 'National Bolshevistic' fashion.

The peculiar form of 'National Bolshevism', i.e. the mixture of Islam and Chechen traditions, could well be a dominant ideology in Chechnya if Moscow and Grozny had found a way to achieve a *modus vivendi* of a sort. The chance for such a development was not excluded if the Khasavyurt Agreement of 1996 held. The agreement stipulated ceasefire, demilitarisation of the Chechen capital and Russian–Chechen cooperation to stop permanent looting. All decisions on the final status of Chechnya would be postponed until 2001. Chechnya in such a case would have enjoyed practically complete autonomy. This sort of model could have been viable if one would remember that the Kadyrov clan would receive the same sort of arrangements in the future. Still, neither the Russian elite nor many of the people of the Northern Caucasus were ready for compromise. Moscow definitely did not want Chechnya's complete independence, which would have had the most far-reaching implications for the very existence of the Russian Federation. Indeed, Yeltsin's regime was seen as being weak and unstable by the local elite. The further erosion of the Kremlin's authority would have sent a clear signal to the local elite. Its members would have come to the conclusion that the Kremlin could bow under pressure and the local elites could well get either complete independence or at least wide autonomy from the centre. This would be an incentive to fight not just for the elites of the ethnic republics – both in the North Caucasus and the Russian heartland, e.g. Tatarstan and Bashkiria (Crosston 2004), but even for the elites in purely Russian regions. Indeed, the local elites and what seems to be a considerable amount of the local population would rather see themselves as residents of an independent state than under the rule of a governor who depended on the Kremlin's whims. They also assumed that they would get a much better deal in a close relationship with foreign countries rather than with Moscow. This was, for example, the case with Eduard Rossel, the governor (1995–2009) of the Svedlovsk Oblast region with its capital in Yekaterinburg. During Yeltsin's presidency, he seriously contemplated becoming the independent ruler of the 'Ural Republic' if not de jure then de facto. He even produced a considerable amount of new currency, 'Urals francs'. He believed that as the leader of a new state he would rather move closer to Europe, i.e. Germany (he was an ethnic German, descendent of those Russian

Germans who were deported to the Urals by Stalin during the Second World War), than to Moscow. The people in the Kremlin were pretty much aware of these scenarios and how the elites all over Russia would interpret the Khasavyurt Agreement. It would be seen not as a sign of peacefulness but, rather, a sign of weakness, as a prelude to the disintegration of the Russian Federation in the fashion of the USSR a few years earlier. Thus, Moscow had no desire for compromise; the same could be said of their counterpart. This set in motion a second war in 1999, which, in one form or another, has continued up to the present, despite Moscow's assertion that it had ended the same year.

As time progressed, the resistance movement started attracting not just Chechens but also considerable numbers of people of other ethnic origins. In this arrangement, nationalism does not work. Consequently, the emphasis was increasingly on Islam as the trans-ethnic and trans-cultural force; here, Islam was separated from its ethno-centric peculiar form. The Islamic puritanical movements known as Salafiyya and Wahhabism became increasingly popular. Interest in Islam as an internationalist doctrine also led the Chechen movement away from national history and tradition to foreign traditions and know-how. This process had already started at the beginning of Putin's presidency in 2000 and had accelerated by the end of it, finally leading in 2007 to an open split between nationalistic and universalistic jihadists. By that time, political and ideological connections between North Caucasian jihadists and foreign jihadists, who had had a strong interest in the Russian North Caucasus since the 1990s, had been strengthened; and their works were either translated into Russian, which emerged as the *lingua franca* of the resistance, or works in Russian had been composed on the basis of the work of foreign jihadists. Jihadisation/universalisation of the resistance had also broadened the outlook of the members in a more general way. They had turned to the experience of the revolutionary movements, and the totalitarian regime that emerged in their wake shaped their own strategy and gauged what sort of society they needed to build in case of their victory.

Nationalists and the jihadist alternative

Jihadist internationalists had emerged among the members of the North Caucasus resistance already in the 1990s. By 2006–2007, their ideological disagreement with nationalists had become fully crystallised. Indeed, the stress on internationalism and integration in the global jihad increasingly alienated jihadists from nationalist-minded members of the Chechen resistance who thought mostly about independence from Russia. For some members of the jihadist resistance, the division between Chechens and Russians has become pretty much meaningless. Amir Magas, a commander of the forces of North Caucasians in the Republic of Ingushetia, pointed out that it would be wrong to regard the present conflict in the North Caucasus as a 'Russian–Caucasian War', i.e. as a conflict between Russians and the various ethnic groups in the Caucasus. It is actually a war between infidels and Islam; and the ethnicity of the participants plays a very minor role. As a matter of fact, there are a number of traitors to

Islam from the ranks of the various people of the Caucasus, who are traditionally good Muslims. At the same time, on the side of the Islamists are 'quite a few Russian Muslims and representatives of other people taken by Russia' (Magas 2006). While ethnic Russians could be good Muslims, not only ordinary Chechens but even Muslim clergy could actually be quite similar to kafirs (non-believers). Indeed, the muftis of the North Caucasus who have become incorporated in officialdom are actually indistinguishable from the infidels (a-Dagestani 2007). Because of this, it is implied that they could be targeted by jihadists. In fact, all those who work for the Russian government are infidels and are legitimate targets for attack. If these people are wounded, no one should help them (*Chechenpress* 2007). The participants of jihadist internet sites are absolutely convinced that nationalism is the mortal enemy of true Islam and, consequently, of jihad. They proclaim that the enemies of Islam try to divide Muslims along ethnic and national lines. Muslims should fight this (Kavkaz Centre 2007a). In this peculiar internationalism, they appeal to the authorities of modern Islamic intellectuals like Sayiid Qutb, who proclaimed that it would be a great mistake to regard Islam as a sort of parochial teaching. The goal of Islam is to liberate not just Arabs, not even just Muslims, but actually all of humanity (Qutb 2007).

This grand goal of Islam could hardly be achieved if narrow nationalism is the ideological framework. The international audience has also been drawn into these polemics against nationalists. Certain jihadists expressed their frustrations with nationalist-minded members of the North Caucasian resistance in a letter sent to fellow jihadists in Waziristan, the region in Pakistan infested by the extremist Taliban, in response to their correspondence.

In May 2007, a 'Mudzhakhid Sag' wrote on the internet to a friend in Waziristan, stating that he and similar-minded people had a disagreement with nationalist-minded Chechens who believed that the mujahideen (plural of mujahid, meaning warriors) are fighting for the creation of an independent Chechnya. The point is that he, the author of the article, and similar-thinking people fight not for a national state but for the creation of Islamic khalifat (the Islamic system of governance) all over the Caucasus. In fact, among the fighters, there are people of various ethnic origin, including ethnic Russians. The very fact that the fighting rank-and-file included not just people from the Caucasus but also ethnic Russians and recent converts indicated that not only did fighters discard the narrow goals of nationalists – e.g. the creation of independent Muslim states in the Northern Caucasus – but even discarded the notion of an Islamic khalifat in the Caucasus as being too narrow. It was just a springboard, or at least one of the springboards, for a much greater enterprise. Elaborating on this, he noted that the place where he, the author of the article, is fighting is small. Still, he believes that from there the flame of jihad would spread all over the world and that the victorious armies of various jihadists would reach Waziristan and Iraq and would liberate Jerusalem (Sag 2007).

The liberation of Jerusalem is seen in this case not as a purely political act but as an act of religious/metaphysical implication. It should signify the end of the domination of the infidels and the transformation of humanity into a universal

Islamic umma (community). Global jihad here looks like a worldwide proletarian revolution as Marx and protagonists of Marxism interpreted it in the first years of the Soviet regime. Here, the collapse of the global capitalist order would mean not just a new stage in the development of humanity, but a leap to another dimension. The metaphysical implications of letters directly connected with the preaching of internationalism were well received by addressees in Waziristan. In fact, the quoted North Caucasian jihadist received a response from an individual who proclaimed himself to be a mujahid from Waziristan. He pointed out that the Chechens should fight for the glory of Allah, not for the creation of a national state. In fact, they should completely disregard nationalism as had been done in Waziristan by true mujahideen. One should not hate Russians just because they are Russians. Those who hate Russians just because they are a people of different ethnicity and who believe that they are better than their enemies just because they have a different bloodline are guilty of nationalism. This hardly makes them good Muslims or dedicated fighters for the cause of Allah. They are cowards, love women and actually hate the heroic mujahideen, such as Ayman Al-Zawahiri. It is the sins of nationalists that cause Chechens to suffer so much. These nationalists – and their influence could be recorded, as the author implied, among many – are not just the bad Muslims but actually are not Muslims at all, and from this perspective are not much different than their enemies. The way these nationalists explain their victories indicates clearly that they are not true Muslims. These Chechen nationalists believe that they won the first war with the Russians only because of their military valour, not because of Allah. At present, by sending Russians against those who crushed them, Allah is showing them that without him they are defenceless.

The author of the article complained that he sent his objections to Kavkaz Centre, but they were not published. In fact, Kavkaz Centre did not respond to his letter at all. He also noticed that Kavkaz Centre had placed on its site songs with music that is explicitly prohibited by Islam (Sag 2007). The very fact that complaints were laid against Kavkaz Centre is worth noting. The point is that Kavkaz Centre, which is the major internet vehicle of the jihadists, did not publish the letter, which could well indicate that the leaders of the resistance were still uncertain about the future and possibly are trying to avoid an open split and trying to find common ground for both nationalists and jihadists. This attempt on the part of at least some of the editors of Kavkaz Centre to find a compromise can be understood. Indeed, the attempt to move Chechens from nationalism to universalistic jihadism has faced growing resistance from increasing numbers of Chechen fighters. While some fighters reject jihadism outright, others tried to find a compromise of some sorts.

Attempting compromise

While Chechen jihadists – in fact, Muslim extremists of various ethnic origins – have presented their idiosyncratic image of the past and present, their nationalistic opponents have their alternative vision of the past and the present. For jihadists – as for the early eschatological Marxists and early Christians – ethnicity/nationality is anathematised as the greatest heresy that divides the fighters for a better life in what Marxists would define as their 'national quarters'. The true Muslims should be united and fight together for universal communism, the Kingdom of God, or the perfect society that would transcend what Marx defined as 'pre-history' – written history from the time of the pharaohs to the present, the era of social division, suffering and wars. While for radical jihadists nationalism/ethnicity is quite a dangerous heresy, this is not the case with Chechen nationalists who dream about the creation of an independent Chechen state. For universalist jihadists the global victory of Islamic umma would create the ideal society, actually a sort of futuristic community outside of the confinement of human history, as it is usually understood. Chechen nationalists have the same, albeit modified, vision of the future. They are not much concerned with the universal Islamic umma, but rather with their kin. Still, in their presentation, independent Chechnya should emerge as the almost ideal society; and Chechens, the residents of this independent state, should be a beacon for humanity.

While the jihadists try to marginalise, ignore or even curse their nation's history, especially if its legacy leads them away from what they regard as true Islam, the story is quite different for Chechen nationalists. For them, Chechen greatness is a subject of utmost importance. They are quite eager to present Chechen history as being of the greatest importance for humanity. In this vision, Chechens – as true superhumans – become the founders of human civilisation. This assumption that Chechens belong to a sort of chosen people – those who not only create the very foundation of civilisation but actually are destined to lead humanity to salvation – provides a sort of ideological bridge for compromise. At least, this was the case for some Chechen intellectuals. Indeed, for them, Chechen nationalism and respect for Chechen history does not preclude internationalist appeal, the drive for worldwide jihadist revolution, but actually reinforces it.

Abdurakhman Avtorkhanov has presented Chechen history in such a way. According to him, the people from the Caucasus are one of the most ancient civilisations on the earth and created the entire human civilisation, including the Russian state. The Chechens' extraordinary abilities manifested in their illustrious history do not preclude them from being a major force in universal jihad. Chechens, as the author of the article implies, could well be compared with the Bolsheviks who were able to mobilise the masses for revolution. Indeed, the Chechens would now create a 'party of a new type', which, in a way, would be similar to that of the Bolshevik party created by Lenin. This party would embrace all active people with extraordinary talents, who, of course, would be converted to Islam. Here, Avtorkhanov implies that these people would be quite similar to the active and talented people at the beginning of the twentieth century who joined the Bolsheviks in droves for they understood that it was the party of the future. Nationalistic prejudices were absolutely foreign to the Bolsheviks. Their ranks embraced people of all ethnic backgrounds, including Jews. This could also be the case, as Avtorkhanov suggested, with a new Islamic party, with the Chechens as its backbone. Indeed, it is not surprising that Boris Berezovsky, the exiled tycoon and Putin's sworn enemy, is ready to embrace Islam and join this party. This party would change humanity in the most radical way and would prepare the way for the triumph of the really harmonious society that would be created after the coming of Mahhdi (the 'Guided One', the promised saviour of Islam, according to Shia Islamists) (Avtorkhanov 2007).

Avtorkhanov tries to reconcile nationalism with universalistic jihadism but his design does not work. His discussions about converts are telling. While Berezovsky's conversion to Islam became a manifestation of the author's wild imagination,[1] the conversion of Slavs, mostly ethnic Russians, to Islam is a well-recorded phenomenon in post-Soviet Russia. It should also be noted that conversion to Islam by people whose ancestors had never been Muslims and who themselves could be atheists is not just a Russian phenomenon as it can be found all over the world. These conversions are the result of global changes. Here, Islam started to play a role that had been played by the internationalist communist movement and other forms of non-religious radicalism, and which virtually came to extinction after the collapse of the USSR. In the case of Russia, the conversion to Islam is also deeply connected with the fact that the collapse of the USSR was not just the end of a particular socio-economic and ideological system, but actually a collapse of the Russian state and its cultural/ideological framework as known in history. Converts could be easily accepted only in the context of a universalistic, denationalised version of Islam. It is not surprising that some of them, albeit not all, joined the jihadists. This trend demonstrates the increasingly dominant role of the jihadists in the Islamic resistance in the North Caucasus, as well as beyond.

Good and bad converts

The collapse of the USSR had been a catastrophe for Russians and, in a way, much more serious than the 1917 Bolshevik Revolution and civil war. First, the events of 1991 destroyed the Russian state/empire as it had been known for centuries. As a matter of fact, Russia's current western borders are the same as they were at the beginning of the seventeenth century. It is true that after the 1917 revolution Russia had completely fallen apart. Still, the Bolsheviks were able to re-conquer most of it during the civil war, and, needless to say, after 1945 the Red Army – seen by the majority of Russians as the Russian army – was in the middle of Europe. Nothing of this is in store for Russia's future. It is clear that not only is Russia's imperial heritage lost for good, but that even the present-day Russian Federation could well fall apart, and the continuous immigration of non-Slavic people could put a big question mark on the very existence of Russians as an ethnic group. Indeed, Russians could well be dissolved in a sea of mostly Muslims of various ethnic origins, as well as of Chinese. The fear of ethnic Russians' marginalisation and final disappearance is raised endlessly by various Russian national-minded intellectuals as well as the general masses who believe that the Chinese, for example, would rather assimilate Russia than vice versa

(Nyiri and Breidenbach 2005: 79; Dugin 1996). This feeling is quite widespread among average Russians and feeds the violent ethnic riots that erupted not just in provincial cities – Kondopoga (2006) and Stavropol' (2007) – but even in downtown Moscow (2010).

In this situation, the views of some of the dreamers of the resurrection of the grand Russian empire – like that of Alexandr Dugin, the prominent neo-Eurasianist – are viewed as not just irrelevant to Russia's future, but plainly ridiculous. One might add that Dugin himself, while dreaming about the grand Eurasian empire based on the happy symbiosis of Orthodox Russians, Muslims of various origins and West/Central Europeans at the beginning of his intellectual career, increasingly viewed Russia's future with apprehension. He might grudgingly accept the notion that the chances for building a great Eurasian empire are lost for good and Russia should not expect to possess much imperial splendour in the future but, rather, most likely continuous marginalisation and, possibly, disintegration.

Second, Russians not only lost their state and dominant position as an ethnic group, but also their cultural/spiritual backbone, what is usually called the 'Russian idea', and which emphasised Russia's special messianic role in history. This notion emerged during the dawn of Russia's modern history and, as had been noted by Nikolai Berdiaev, a seminal Russian émigré philosopher, had been blended with a Soviet variation of Marxism. As a matter of fact, it became the essential ingredient of 'National Bolshevism', the major ideological fodder for most of Soviet history. This notion of the country's special mission or even of the moral superiority of the Russian orthodox civilisation, the notion propagandised recently by such diverse people as Archimandrite Tikhon and Nataliya Narotchnitskaya, a prominent Russian politician, historian and diplomat, is facing increasing scepticism. As a matter of fact, many of today's ethnic Russians look at the Orthodox Church and orthodoxy as replacing the official 'National Bolshevism' of the Soviet era as the major ideological props of the regime, with indifference, scepticism and even hostility. The sense of a dead end for Russia as a state is reinforced by another feeling. The end of Russia as a powerful state signifies the end of Slavic civilisation in which Russia/the USSR had played the central and, in a way, cementing role, even for those Slavs who, like the Poles, regarded Russians as their historical enemy. Indeed, not just the Poles but even the 'brotherly' Ukrainians and Belorussians have rather guarded views on Russia. In this sense of an ideological/spiritual vacuum, universalist Islam, with its messianic and quasi-socialistic streak – and its more than one-billion-strong umma – has become a magnet for increasing numbers of ethnic Russians. Some of them join the resistance, becoming indispensable practitioners of terror in Russia. This is the case with Pavel Kosolapov.

Kosolapov was close to Shamil Basaev, the deceased leader of the Chechen resistance (www.islam.ru 2007). Basaev was one of the most implacable Chechen terrorists. He was engaged in dreaded terrorist attacks, and Kosolapov has apparently followed in his footsteps. He was engaged in a variety of terrorist enterprises (Tumakova 2007) and was a valuable asset for jihadists (DPNI 2007).

Kosolapov, an ethnic Russian, was born in the Volga region in 1980. He studied at a military college (although he was dismissed from the school for theft). Returning to the Volgograd region, he became a friend of the local Chechens. He converted to Islam and went to Chechnya to join the resistance. Some observers, such as Russian prosecutors, believe that he was responsible for quite a few terrorist attempts across the country. According to some observers (Jeffries 2011: 456), Kosolapov was engaged in terrorist attacks on the Moscow Metro, the bus station in Voronezh, the market in Samara and other places. Some reports claim (*Izvestiya* 2007) he was responsible for blowing up the gas pipelines in Torzhok and in close proximity to Moscow. He was also a prime suspect in the attempt to derail the Nevsky Express train in 2007. The Nevsky Express, the elite train that connected St Petersburg and Moscow, was presumably well guarded; while Kosolapov derailed the train, no human life was lost. The other attacks that took place in the same year were, however, deadly; many people were killed. During the attack on the Moscow Metro, 42 people were killed and 250 wounded. In the Samara attack, 22 people died and seven were wounded. Later, in 2010, Kosolapov would also be credited with the successful and deadly train wreck of the same Nevsky Express. This time the result was more serious. Indeed, the 2010 wreck led to the death and injury of many, including several highly positioned Russian officials. While Kosolapov was possibly the most known among those ethnic Russians who converted to Islam and became jihadists, he was hardly the only one. There was evidence of quite a few converts who joined the North Caucasian jihadists and who later, along with others, spread all over the world. Ethnic Russians' conversion to Islam and active participation of converts in jihad is not a peculiar Russian phenomenon. Conversion to Islam and participation in jihad also became rather common in the West (Pipes 2005). As a matter of fact, these converts – together with other members of the North Caucasian resistance – could be found as far away as Afghanistan, engaged in fighting US-led NATO forces (Weir 2002).

Although some converts joined the jihadists, others have a different approach to the world around them. Some are not proponents of jihadism; some believe that Russians could be peacefully transformed into Muslims even under the present regime. Others fully support the Islamised version of Eurasianism, where, in a healthy symbiosis of Orthodox Russians and Muslims of various ethnic origins, Muslims would take the lead. The number of these people is growing, and there are a considerable number of ethnic Russian converts to Islam who proclaim that they could live peacefully with the present-day regime in Moscow. They even have their own organisation, the National Organization of Russian Muslims (NORM). These converts and Eurasianism-inclined Muslims evoke nothing but disquiet among those converts and non-converts who engage in a mortal struggle not just with Putin's Russia, but who regard themselves as a part of a global jihad. Contributors to Kavkaz Centre derided NORM for including prominent convert Ali Viacheslav Polosin, who started his career as an Orthodox priest. The author of the article regards all of them as agents of the FSB, the Russian secret police (Kavkaz Centre 2007a).

Other contributors to North Caucasian jihadists publications have followed suit. This is, for example, the case with a contributor to *Jamat Shariat*, Ali Bekkhan. Bekkhan pointed out that there are quite a few ethnic Russians who have converted to Islam and supposedly became good Muslims. They created the organisation NORM, led by such individuals as Abu Talib (Anatoly Stepchenko), Polosin and Kharun ar-Rusi (Vadim Sidorov). Close to them are other well-known intellectuals and politicians, such as Geidar Dzhemal' and Shamil Sultanov. These people could have some knowledge of Islam, as was the case with Polosin, 'the leader of these troublemakers'. Still, they could hardly be real Muslims. What concerns them is not the spread of Islam but the power of the Russian state, and the might of the Russian empire. They approach Islam from this perspective. They believe that it is only the unity of Orthodox Russians and Muslims inside Russia and Russia's alliance with Muslim countries that would make Russia once again a global power. It is clear, the author of the quoted article states, that here are just pure Russian imperialists with an instrumental view of Islam. He also mocked the people who believe that discord between the Russian state and Muslims of various ethnic origins is just the result of a sinister plot of Jews and Americans (Bekkhan 2002). But while pro-Kremlin converts evoke nothing but disgust from jihadists, the proponents of various forms of Islamicised Eurasianism evoke virtual paroxysms of hatred from jihadists who believe that jihad is the only way of dealing with the Putin regime. Thus, converts who decide to fight would be jihadists and hardly be accepted as full-fledged members of the resistance by the nationalists because of their ethnicity. It is also clear that discarding ethnicity not only helps jihadists to receive a stream of new recruits, including converts, but also to plug them well into the global jihad with a change of their outlook.

North Caucasian jihad and global jihad

While positioning themselves in opposition to nationalists, jihadists still – at least in the beginning of their intellectual and political evolution – were nurtured by the traditions of native Chechnya and, of course, their Soviet experience. However, with the development of their universalism, they became less and less parochial in their intellectual outlook and were increasingly influenced by foreign ideas. This process was encouraged by movements from the opposite side. Indeed, global jihadists, including Al Qaeda, had expressed a keen interest in the development in the Russian North Caucasus earlier. While they would bring their own ideas and experience to the North Caucasian jihadists, these foreign jihadists would not make the North Caucasian jihadists their intellectual clones. The foreign experience would be accepted, reworked, reinterpreted, integrated with both Russian and European traditions/experiences of totalitarian movements and only then emerge as a finished product, an operational model.

While Russian jihadist-Bolshevism has its own dynamics and native cultural/historical base, as time progresses, it becomes more and more influenced by foreign Islamists, including a number of Islamists who belong to Al Qaeda, a visible influence since mid-1996. In December 1996, Osama bin Laden's deputy, Ayman Al Zawahiri, attempted clandestinely to enter Chechnya and develop a new base for the organisation after Sudan expelled the Al Qaeda leadership. Arrested in Dagestan, which borders Chechnya in the east, Zawahiri spent six months in prison in Makhachkala, the capital. He was found guilty of entering Russia without a visa and was released in May 1997. In a handwritten statement in Arabic made public by the Russian authorities five years later, Zawahiri claimed to be a 'businessman' who had entered Dagestan 'to study the local market and to build contacts for our business'. In a file stored on a laptop computer found in an Al Qaeda safehouse in Kabul after the fall of the Taliban, Zawahiri wrote that 'God blinded the Dagestani authorities to our identities' (Aron 2007). As Al Qaeda was pondering expanding Islamic revolution worldwide, Russia and Chechnya emerged in the mind of Al Qaeda ideologists and practitioners, if not as Lenin's proverbial 'weakest link', at least as an important front of global jihad.

According to testimonies in 2002 at the trial in Hamburg of Mounir El Motassadeq, a Moroccan accused of assisting the 11 September hijackers, his friends and co-conspirators – who were 'obsessed with jihad' and 'cheerfully' sang songs about martyrdom – 'always talked about Kosovo, Afghanistan, and Chechnya'. In the autumn of 1999, three of the 11 September pilots left Hamburg for the Al Qaeda training camp near Kandahar in Afghanistan, with the intention of 'fighting the Russians in Chechnya'. They were informed that there were 'enough fighters' in Chechnya. Instead, according to German investigators, the Al Qaeda leadership ordered the three to 'begin laying plans' for what became the 11 September attack (ibid.: 69). They were hardly alone in perceiving Chechnya as an important place for jihad. Jose Padilla, who was accused of planning terrorist attacks in the United States, claimed he went abroad 'just to help Muslims who were under attack in the 1990s in places like Kosovo and Chechnya' (Goodnough 2007). Leon Aron, whose review of Gordon Hahn's book *Counsel Legal and Illegal* is quoted, stated that the 'prospect of an all-Russian jihad, with which Hahn opens his book, is a very remote eventuality today' (ibid.). The dream of some members of Al Qaeda that Chechnya and other regions of the former USSR would be the launching pad of the global jihadist revolution might not materialise. Still, all of these foreign jihadists have a strong influence on followers in Russia; and their views have been integrated in the local intellectual discourse. Each revolutionary group of modern history is aware of their predecessors and looks at them as examples. It is well-known that the protagonists of the French Revolution were much aware of classical antiquity and of people of the Enlightenment, which was saturated in the traditions of ancient Rome and Greece, and tried to imitate the heroes from that period of European history. Later, more than a century after the French Revolution, this was also done by the Bolsheviks in their appeal to the French Revolution, quite a popular subject in Russian intellectual life at the end of the nineteenth century and the beginning of the twentieth century. The Bolsheviks were interested in the French Revolution for a variety of reasons. First, as was the case with the protagonists of the French Revolution, the Bolsheviks tried to find in it the justification for their actions, i.e. their 'Reign of Terror'. Second, in contrast to the protagonists of the French Revolution, they tried to find in the events of the past the appropriate details, know-how and tools for solving the political task. None of this interested the protagonists of the French Revolution when they turned to ancient Greece and Rome. The Bolsheviks were different from the protagonists of the French Revolution in another aspect as well. The French revolutionaries looked at Greek and Roman history as part of their historical patrimony; Greek and Roman history was a part of the historical tradition of the West, including France. For the Bolsheviks, the French Revolution was a part of the foreign historical experience. Still, this did not deter them. Moreover, they were anxious to look to the experiences of their Western contemporaries and the work of contemporary intellectuals in search of a solution for their practical tasks.

Increasingly, assertive jihadists from the North Caucasus have followed the same path; they do not just rely on indigenous Russian revolutionary traditions, but also look to foreign jihadists. In their work they find practical advice and general political/philosophical outlooks that they incorporate in their daily life. A jihadist member of the North Caucasian resistance translated the book of Abu Mus'ab al-Suri, or, at least, he claimed that it was a translation, not his original work. Arguing that al-Suri's thoughts are quite important as he spent 25 years engaging in jihad, he stated that the work is an important compendium of know-how and a general outlook for Russian jihadists, and for this reason it should be analysed in detail (al-Suri 2007). The work had several important and related themes. First, it provided justification for indiscriminate acts of terror against infidels, as well as those the author regarded as pseudo-Muslims. Second, the work provided the major outlines for terrorist/military operations against the enemy. Finally, the work deals with the description/image of the ideal society that would emerge after victory.

The ideas of the foreign jihadists were accepted not word-by-word but in a reworked form and integrated with other intellectual traditions, many of them of local origin. However, the exposure to ideas outside the North Caucasus, the former USSR, internationalised the view of the North Caucasian jihadists. This not only made them more efficient in their terrorist activities but also made their integration into the worldwide jihad easier. The movement of North Caucasian resistance from nationalism to universalistic jihadism does not mean that the nationalists lost ground completely. To start with, a considerable number of Chechens, as well as other people from the North Caucasus, became weary of the war, and the perspective of open-ended, practically endless conflict was hardly appealing for them. Many of them would opt for some modicum of autonomy from Russia, but not necessarily for complete independence if it would entail a debilitating war. Moscow clearly understood this feeling and approximately by the end of Putin's first term had provided considerable autonomy to Ramzan Kadyrov, the ex-rebel who became Moscow's anointed ruler of Chechnya. Kadyrov had enjoyed practically complete independence from Moscow, if not de jure at least de facto. His formal acknowledgement of Moscow's supremacy was rewarded by a generous subsidy that looks like tribute. He also incorporated a considerable number of rebels in his paramilitary units, which are formally controlled by Moscow but actually are at his full disposal. Still, one cannot return to the early 1990s when jihadism could be marginalised and dissolved in the 'National Bolshevism' of the sort of independent/semi-independent Chechen state. North Caucasian jihadism continues to exist, with potential for further proliferation. The problem could emerge not from the North Caucasians, but from the Russian side. The source of the problem is the rise of Russian nationalism and even semi-fascist feelings among a considerable number of the Russian population, especially the underprivileged youth. Their views have become quite similar to that of the nationalists and neo-fascists in Europe, which should be made known to avoid the possible misunderstanding of the phenomenon.

Traditionally, fascism/Nazism is related in the people's mind with the experience of the Second World War, when the Nazi and fascist armies engaged in a war of conquest. Nazism is implicitly connected not just with the notion of racial supremacy but also with ideology and the practice of empire-building. The story is quite different with the present-day racists/neo-Nazis in Europe. Their concern is not empire but the presence of what they regard as racially and culturally alien bodies in the midst of white and historically Christian Europe. British racists, for example, did not want the conquest of India or Pakistan, but the 'cleansing' of Britain of the people from that part of the former British empire, and here British nationalists are quite similar to other European nationalists regarding their strong anti-immigrant feelings (Piper 1998: 91). They are not imperialists but actually parochial isolationists. This could also be said about Russian nationalists; they regard Russia as invaded by Muslims of various ethnic origins who change the cultural/demographic balance of the country and who also engage in crime. The Russian nationalists regard these minorities as one of the regime's major problems. In their view, the regime represents the minorities but not ethnic Russians. The desire of these nationalists is not the re-conquest of the North Caucasus and establishment of Moscow's full control over all parts of it, but rather quite the opposite. They want the deportation of all North Caucasians back to their 'historical motherland', and Russia's complete separation from the North Caucasus. They should be fully independent and receive no Russian subsidies. In any case, these nationalists believe the North Caucasians should receive no money when a considerable number of ethnic Russians live in poverty and the government is increasingly destroying the safety net, a remnant from the Soviet era. They also point out that most of the subsidies are actually stolen by the North Caucasian elites, including those close to Kadyrov. Many Russians believe that subsidies to Chechnya will end soon. If this idea is implemented in one or other form, the economic situation in the North Caucasus would be aggravated even more and jihadists would receive increasing numbers of recruits. Indeed, in this case, for many residents of the North Caucasus the job of 'professional revolutionaries' or, to be precise, 'professional jihadists' would be the only available employment option. The nationalists might well be integrated in jihadism, creating a new and, possibly, bizarre combination.

Conclusion

The revolutionary movements, if one would interpret the term broadly, often follow a well-defined model. In the case of victory, the messianic and internationalist overtones become duly incorporated into the primordial native nationalism, creating what is known in Russia as 'National Bolshevism' which upholds the importance of not the messianic trans-ethnic early Bolshevism but the importance of the Russian state/empire in the form of the USSR. The Chechen resistance could well have followed the same track if the Khasavyurt Agreement had held; some elements of Chechen statehood would have emerged. In such a case, trans-ethnic Islam would be fully incorporated in local nationalism, the basic framework for the existence of a Chechen semi-independent/independent state. However, the agreement did not hold, and the prospect of the creation of an absolutely independent Chechen state became bleak. In addition, the Chechen resistance became increasingly blended with the resistance of other ethnicities, historically Muslim. At that point, nationalism became increasingly unworkable and internationalist jihadism provided the ideological framework of the movement. Jihadism was not just the outcome of the internal evolution of the North Caucasian resistance, but also facilitated its spread. It proceeded to include not just the Muslims from the North Caucasus and other parts of the world, but even Russian converts for whom Islam in its jihadist form became the ideological alternative to the spiritual void created by the collapse of the USSR. Jihadism not only helped the North Caucasian resistance to swell in numbers, but also helped them to be plugged into the global jihadist movement. The people in the Kremlin started to understand the danger of universalistic jihadism and attempted to return to a modified Khasavyurt Agreement. Moscow installed Ramzan Kadyrov as the virtually independent ruler of Chechnya, de facto if not de jure, and provided him with generous subsidies. However, jihadism has its own momentum.

Note

1 Berezovsky, similar to other members of the Russian elite of various ethnic origins, was hardly a man hobbled by principles. He was a man of mixed ethnic heritage with a Jewish father, at least from an ethnic point of view. It was ethnicity that had actually mattered in the Soviet and post-Soviet Russia. Later, he found a religion he thought more appropriate to his interests, becoming an Orthodox Christian. One could assume that he could well have converted to Islam or any other creed if this would have helped to promote his interests.

References

a-Dagestani, Guliam Mukhammad (2007) 'Obradui litsemerov vestiu vilikoi kazni' (You Shall Please Hypocrites with News of Great Execution), *Chechen Times*, 3 May.

al-Suri, Abu Mus'ab (2007) 'Boevaia ideologia: Politika i ee granitsy' (Combat Ideology: Politics and Its Limits), 22 August. http://www.jamaatshariat.com/ru/content/view/405/34 (accessed 22 August 2007).

Aron, Leon (2007) 'Jihadi Murat', *The New Republic*, 5 November.

Avtorkhanov, Z. (2007) 'Griadet Kavkaz!' (Caucasus is Coming!), *Chechen Times*, 3 May.

Bekkhan, Ali (2002) 'Litso Predatelia ile Sataniskii Pisk Russkikh Genov' (The Face of the Traitor or Satanic Squeaking of Russian Genes), 4 April, www.jamaatshariat.com (accessed 9 April 2002).

Brandenberger, David (2005) *National Bolshevism: Stalinist Mass Culture and the Formation of Modern Russian National Identity, 1931–1956*, Cambridge, MA: Harvard University Press.

Chechenpress (2007) 'Obrashchenie mudzhakhidov Kabardy i Balkarii' (The Appeal of Mujahideen of Kabarda and Balkaria), 26 July.

Crosston, Matthew (2004) *Shadow Separation: Implication for Democratic Consolidation*, Aldershot and Burlington, VT: Ashgate.

DPNI (Dvizhenie Protiv Nelegal'noi Imigratsii) (2007) 'Ekspert: Eto uzhe tretia avariia primerno na tom zhe uchastke', 16 August.

Dugin, Aleksandr (1996) *Misterii Evrazii*, Moscow: Arktogeia.

Goodnough, Aby (2007) 'Jose Padilla Convicted on All Counts in Terror Trial', *New York Times*, 16 August.

Izvestiya (2007) 'Former Basayev 'Right Hand' Kosolapov Key Suspect in Neva Express Bombing', 29 October.

Jeffries, Ian (2011) *Political Developments in Contemporary Russia*, New York, NY: Routledge.

Kavkaz Centre (2007a) 'NORMirovannye munafiki' (Measured False Muslims), 21 May (accessed 21 May 2007, no longer available).

—— (2007b) 'Reshenie Shariata otnositel' no natsionalizma i patriotzma' (Decisions of Sharia Law in Regard of Nationalism and Patriotism), 28 July (accessed 28 July 2007, no longer available).

Magas, Amir (2006) 'Eto voina mezhdu Islamom i Kufrom' (This is the War Between Islam and World of Infidels), *Chechen Times*, 2 November.

Nyiri, Pal and Breidenbach, Joana (2005) *China Inside Out: Contemporary Chinese Nationalism and Transnationalism*, Budapest: Central European University Press.

Piper, Nicola (1998) *Racism, Nationalism and Citizenship: Ethnic Minorities in Britain and Germany*, London: Ashgate.

Pipes, Daniel (2005) 'Converts to Terrorism!', *New York Sun*, 6 December.

Qutb, Sayyid (2007) 'Dizhikhadi na puti Allakha' (Jihad Along the Way to Allah), 16 August. www.kavkaz-news.info. (accessed 16 August 2007).

Sag, Mudzhakhid (2007) 'Privetstvie mudzhakhedu iz Viziristana ot chechenskogo mudzhakheda' (Greeting to Mujahidin's of Waziristan from Chechen Mujahidin), 23 May. www.jamatshariat.com (accessed 23 May 2007).

Schaefer, Robert W. (2011) *The Insurgency in Chechnya and the North Caucasus: From Gazavat to Jihad*, Santa Barbara, CA: Praeger Security International.

Sebastian, Smith (2001) *Allah's Mountains: The Battle for Chechnya*, London: I.R. Tauris.

Tumakova, Irina (2007) 'Nevski ekspress podorval "russkii bin Laden"' (Nevskii Express Train was Blown up by 'Russian Bin Laden'), *Izvestiia*, 30 October.

Weir, Fred (2002) 'Chechnya's Warrior Tradition', *Christian Science Monitor*, 26 March.

www.islam.ru (2007) 'Novosti v strane: Pavel Kosolapov "russkii Ben Laden" i "islamskii terrorist"' (Pavel Kosolapov 'Russian Bin Laden' and 'Islamic Terrorist'), 31 October. www.islam.ru (accessed 31 October 2007).

7 Kyrgyzstan

Conflict and prospects of peace

Sébastien Peyrouse and Marléne Laruelle

Introduction

The year 2010 represents a watershed not only for the history of Kyrgyzstan, but also for that of post-Soviet Central Asia as a whole. In Kyrgyzstan, a second 'revolution' led to the overthrow of President Kurmanbek Bakiyev and to the country's transformation – in theory at least – into the first parliamentary democracy in the Commonwealth of Independent States (CIS). In themselves, these were unique events. But the pogroms in Osh in June 2010 added an additional effect to the signals of destabilisation that the country has been emitting for many years. They reveal the failure of Kyrgyzstan in terms of statehood. The trauma of the Osh events has enabled new political forces to cohere around nationalist claims, which are now going to play a key role in the modes of political legitimisation in Kyrgyzstan. However, it is the deep transformations of the social fabric that constitute the essential background of Kyrgyz developments, and attempts to rebuild the political consensus in the country will have to take them as their point of departure. This chapter places the Osh events in the Kyrgyz political context, and discusses the major role of social transformations and the lack of economic prospects in fostering tensions.

2010: a quickly changing political context

There is a limit to the parallel between the 'Tulip Revolution' of March 2005 and the events of 7 April 2010, for the differences are more numerous than the similarities (Temirkulov 2010). The reasons for discontent are largely similar, however. With both Akayev and Bakiyev presidential families the patrimonial drift had been steadily growing.[1] The dissatisfaction of the opposition and of some regional leaders (mostly from the south in 2005 and from the north in 2010) was on the increase. The grave social crisis concerning the recurrent impoverishment of rural areas had apparently been left unresolved. Yet, the first 'revolution' took off around a highly political event, namely the rigging of parliamentary elections in February–March 2005 (Cummings and Ryabkov 2008; Radnitz 2006; Hale 2005; Olcott 2005), whereas the second was more akin to a social outburst. Among the reasons for this popular discontent, one should note Bakiyev's exclusion of several leaders from the *kurultay* (the traditional meeting of leaders) in March, the decrease of migrant remittances due to the global economic crisis and Moscow's removal of tax exemptions for Kyrgyzstan's oil imports, an act that led to a surge in gasoline prices, which also affected the prices of basic goods (Trilling and Umetov 2010).

The first revolution was part of the wave of 'colour revolutions' that took place in Serbia, Georgia and Ukraine, in the sense that it was partly orchestrated by opposition groups (political parties, civic groups and NGOs) seeking to challenge the results of rigged elections; the second seems to have been much more popular in origin, a part of localised protests without the opposition parties as the source of dissent.[2] The first began in the south, while the second came from the poorest regions of the north, Talas and Naryn. After violent clashes between police and demonstrators in Talas on 6 April 2010, the country erupted within a single day. On 7 April, demonstrators in the capital stormed and ransacked the presidential palace and government buildings, and the president fled with his family. The reaction of the administration is another distinguishing feature. The security forces serving Bakiyev unhesitatingly fired on the demonstrators, killing nearly 90 people (Lillis 2010) (it seems that snipers had been enlisted on the side of the government forces (Marat 2010b)), while Askar Akayev had refused to resort to violence.

The international context also differed. While the events of 2005 had surprised Moscow, which tried to support Akayev before resolving to recognise the legitimacy of the revolutionary government, in 2010 Moscow was at the forefront of the movement against Bakiyev's clan and seemed to welcome the change of regime. The Kremlin nonetheless remained sceptical about the government of Roza Otunbayeva, a former minister of foreign affairs and ambassador to Washington (Marat 2010a). Although the Kyrgyz army did not attempt to resist this change of power and immediately endorsed the new government – a positive sign about its neutrality, which is not true of the militia forces and security services – the difficulty that the ruling classes had in controlling the demonstrators became quite apparent. The first 'revolution' had required nearly a month, the second took only two days; the feeling that governments are appointed and removed by the street protests increased.

While the first 'revolution' did not change the nature of the political system, Bakiyev revealing himself to be more authoritarian and despotic than Akayev, the second 'revolution' was proclaimed as being about regime change. Indeed, the interim government has succeeded in adopting a new constitution by referendum (with more than 90 per cent of votes in favour) for the transition to a parliamentary system. However, these positive results must be qualified. About 500,000 Kyrgyz labour migrants in Russia and Kazakhstan did not vote (Interview: 2 July 2010) and one can only wonder about the voting conditions provided for the hundreds of thousands of refugees in the southern part of the country. The electoral rolls were tampered with and the participation rates in some northern areas, such as Chui and Issyk-Kul, were unusually high (Interviews: 27 June 2010, 3 July 2010). Further, the electorate actually voted primarily for a return to stability, not for a new political system. Finally, the establishment of a parliamentary system does not necessarily mean a change in political practices (Luong 2010), as parties are poorly organised, often having no clear ideological platform, and some of which call for order and the return to a presidential and authoritarian system.

More than a change of regime, the second 'revolution' signalled a new phase in the destabilisation of Kyrgyzstan. Shortly after the events, and before leaving the country, the former president, taking refuge at his home in Jalalabad, rekindled the conflict between the northern elites, themselves newly in power, and the southern ones. This exacerbated interethnic relations. On 13–14 May, Bakiyev's supporters stormed the regional administrations of the three major southern cities, Jalalabad, Osh and Batken. This led to clashes with pro-government security forces, leaving dozens injured and some dead. Groups loyal to the interim government, and composed largely of Uzbeks, were able to take power back. The Uzbeks' involvement alongside Roza Otunbayeva angered many Kyrgyz people. Moreover, Uzbek groups burned the house of Kurmanbek Bakiyev and those of his brothers in the village of Teiit, near Jalalabad, an event that the International Crisis Group rightly called a 'Rubicon' in ethnic tensions (International Crisis Group 2010: 9). This act caused violent reactions among the supporters of the former Kyrgyz president, who in turn raided the private 'Friendship of the Peoples' university, which conducts its courses in Uzbek (Ianovskaia 17 May 2010). Between April and June the small, confined riots continued, impacting all the minorities – Russian, Meskhetian Turks and Dungans. On 7 June, the car of mafia boss Oybek Mirsidikov, also known as Black Oybek, was caught in an ambush at the entrance to the city of Jalalabad and he was assassinated. Oybek Mirsidikov was a leading figure in the criminal networks of southern Kyrgyzstan. He was close to the two relatives of the deposed president, Zhanysh and Akmat Bakiyev, and suspected of managing a share of the drug traffic on their behalf, from Afghanistan through the Tajik Pamirs (Vasilyev 2010).

Deciphering the 'Osh events'

After a fight between some Kyrgyz and Uzbeks in a casino, a large crowd of Uzbeks gathered in the centre of the city of Osh on the evening of 10 June and clashed with Kyrgyz groups during the night. Over 11–14 June, crowds of ethnic Kyrgyz, alarmed by rumours about Uzbek aggression, descended on Uzbek neighbourhoods. Shops were looted, houses set on fire and people assassinated.[3] While the city was supposed to be under control, thousands of Kyrgyz from neighbouring villages and remote provinces – especially Alay, one of the poorest regions of the country, famous for its warrior traditions – arrived as reinforcements to continue the killings and the looting of Uzbek neighbourhoods (International Crisis Group 2010). The conflict spread to Jalalabad and Bazar-Kurgan. With security forces unable to regain control of the city, Roza Otunbayeva declared the situation unmanageable, requested (unsuccessfully) military assistance from Russia and announced a partial mobilisation of the army, not so much to send it in as reinforcements, but in order to detain many thousands of men in the barracks, men who might otherwise have joined the Kyrgyz insurgents. Official reports count around 300 dead (probably more), and 2,600 totally destroyed buildings.[4] At least 120,000 refugees fled to the Uzbek border, which accepted only women and children, before being sent back home two weeks later (Volosevich 2010). By this time the capital had managed to regain control of cities and its suburbs; local religious leaders and 'aksakals' (male elders from the community) played facilitating roles and invited the parties in conflict to make peace.[5] However, the situation so far remains very volatile and ethnic tensions continue today.

The 2010 events will remain subject to conflicting interpretations. The government states that the riots were organised by the Bakiyev clan, and also sees in them the hand of the Islamic Movement of Uzbekistan, Hizb ut-Tahrir, Al Qaeda and the Islamic Party of Rebirth of Tajikistan – though this is a very unlikely argument (www.ferghana.ru 2010). It also more discreetly mentions the ambiguous role of Uzbek leaders, mainly Kadyrzhan Batyrov, a successful businessman, vice-chairman of the Uzbek national cultural centre of the Jalalabad region and founder of the private Uzbek University. For several months, Batyrov has been calling the traditionally apolitical Uzbek minority to become politicised. He demanded autonomous status for the Uzbeks in the south, recognition of Uzbek as a state language alongside Kyrgyz and Russian, a 30 per cent quota of administrative positions for Uzbeks and the appointment of an Uzbek as vice-governor in the southern regions of the country (Khamidov n.d.; Osmonov 2006). The majority opinion in Kyrgyzstan, among the media and the intellectual and political elites of the country, is very clearly anti-Uzbek. Uzbeks stand accused of being heavily armed, of organising popular uprisings to gain independence, and of initiating ethnic killings in order to generate a spontaneous defensive reaction by the Kyrgyz (Interview: 2 July 2010). The Uzbeks, for their part, speak of an ethnic conflict organised by the state organs in which they would have been the victims, with some even talking of genocide.[6]

Although the ethnic factor did not trigger the riots, it obviously functioned as a political resource for violence. More than 700,000 Uzbeks live in the south, where they represent between one-quarter and one-third of the population. They are the majority in the cities of Osh and Uzgen, as well as in the rural district of Aravan (Ferrando 2009). Uzbeks are under-represented in local administrations and at the national level, but not in the private sector. While they dominate the economy of the bazaars, the Kyrgyz control the state structures, especially the power ministries. Criminal groups from both communities share the shadow economy, especially drug trafficking, although the Kyrgyz are dominant. The old resentment of the herders and former nomads against the plains farmers and urban traders functions as a driver of violence. Anti-Uzbek slogans ('Death to the Sarts', where Sarts is a pejorative term to designate Uzbeks and more generally urbanites accused of enriching themselves at the expense of rural dwellers by speculating on prices in the bazaar) have revealed that ancient cultural tensions are easily reactivated (Robert 2010: 7–12). The massive looting meanwhile confirmed the weight of social tensions. The unemployed youth who came from the poorest rural areas such as Alay were openly exploited to conduct anti-Uzbek pogroms. Finally, a long history of ethnic tensions must be taken into account. The events occurred almost 20 years to the day after the Uzgen riots of June 1990, riots that saw Uzbeks and Kyrgyz compete for control of arable land. Alleged reports that Kyrgyz were trying to build houses on an Uzbek collective farm served as the spark, and the riots continued until interventions by the Soviet army (TASS 1990).

In light of these events, it seems that the project of a multinational Kyrgyz state has failed. The militia and force structures, the vast majority of which are Kyrgyz, were unable to stop the violence against the Uzbeks and sometimes participated in it. Although police stations and military barracks were indeed plundered, some voluntarily gave their guns or let the Kyrgyz brigades drive around in their armoured vehicles.[7] In this context, the interim government showed that it lacked control over the power structures, which remained largely sympathetic to Bakiyev. In addition to the rivalry between Kyrgyz groups from the north and south, often presented as one of the drivers of local political life, there is now the further ethnic split between the Kyrgyz majority and Uzbek minority. The latter find themselves caught between the Kyrgyz, who regard Kyrgyzstan as their ethnic state where minorities are merely 'guests', and Uzbekistan, which seeks above all to preserve the stability of the Islam Karimov regime and thus refused to play an interventionist role in the crisis. Some of the Uzbek community thus sought protectors from among the proliferating Islamic groups.

Struggling for development prospects

Upon the collapse of the Soviet Union, Kyrgyzstan was presented in the West as the 'Switzerland of Central Asia', an allusion not only to its geography, but further still to its rapid democratisation and to the unprecedented liberalisation of its economy. Bishkek quickly became the good student of the post-Soviet class for international donors like the World Bank and the International Monetary Fund (IMF), and it joined the World Trade Organization (WTO) in 1998. On the political level, Kyrgyzstan obtained privileged financing from American and European foundations in order to build a 'civil society' and to facilitate the introduction of principles of the 'rule of law' and of 'good governance' into their administration. Kyrgyz society opened up to international influence, the NGOs multiplied, opposition parties formed and its press was (and still is) the most free in all of Central Asia (Petric 2006: 287–301).

The country's ensuing path turned out to be more complex. During the Soviet Union's last years about one-third of the republic lived below the poverty line, a high figure comparable to Tajikistan's. Within a few years of its collapse, this figure rose to more than 50 per cent, as Kyrgyzstan came, during the first transitional years, to hold the sad record of the largest increase in inequalities in all of

Central Asia. As elsewhere in the region, the corruption of state employees is an endemic problem. All administrative posts must be bought, not only in key fields such as justice and the police, but also in public services, education, agriculture and industry (Engvall 2011). The population can be charged for even the smallest administrative procedure; the financial demands of the police are particularly feared. The privatisation of the country's wealth and the nepotism of the successive presidential families deeply infiltrate the country. Under Akayev – and even more under Bakiyev's regimes – mafia and criminal groups were placed under state supervision (Marat 2006), with the effect of quickly delegitimising the state in the eyes of the population.

Given the very high overall levels of unemployment and poverty in the country, the agricultural sector is still a vital source of income for the population. Kyrgyzstan has become the largest agricultural producer in terms of percentage of GDP, but it has the smallest amount of arable land (Jones 2003: 262). The area of irrigated land is limited to 10,700 km^2. In agricultural terms, regional disparities are extremely high. The north has 887,000 ha of arable land, used mainly for growing wheat, but the south has less than half that area, only 415,000 ha, for more than half of the population. The ratio of land per person is 0.19 ha in the south, compared to 0.53 ha in the north (www.rdiland.org n.d.). Kyrgyzstan is the only country in the region that has resolutely embarked on the conversion of large Soviet farms, guaranteeing the right to private property and creating the legal conditions for an open land market. In the 1990s, rural communities were confronted with economic devastation. The living conditions had significantly worsened in a process of 'reagrarianisation' marked by agricultural infrastructure, dilapidating capital stock, great loss of livestock and dwindling harvest outputs (Jaquesson 2010). The role of agriculture for securing one's livelihood became more important. These difficult situations contributed to the strengthening of rural domestic economies: patriarchal social functioning, withdrawal into the family (a growth of endogamy), subsistence production centred on working a plot of land, and partially demonetarised economies. The only cash resources available come from the sale of products in the markets, and remittances from labour migrations, with the rest of the local economy operating on systems of subsistence and barter.

Further, the energy shortfall is disrupting the functioning of the national economy. The explanations for this situation are many. Some are structural – natural aridity, mountainous areas, difficulty in irrigation and limited natural resources other than water – while others are contingent – the Soviet heritage of water sharing and the focus on the cultivation of cotton, the need to rebuild hydroelectric infrastructure that dates from the Soviet era, the absence of regional cooperation between states, large-scale corruption and the need to train populations on responsible water usage. With the fall of the Soviet Union and the rupture in relations between the republics, electricity production in Central Asia fell dramatically. Although they were theoretically compatible with three gas- and oil-producing states (Kazakhstan, Uzbekistan and Turkmenistan) and two hydroelectric-producing ones (Kyrgyzstan and Tajikistan), cooperation on energy issues between Central Asian states has proved more than difficult. Negotiations to exchange water for oil and gas regularly break down, with each of the participants undermining the terms of engagement (Wegerich 2011: 27–31).

The Kyrgyz electricity supply system thus is not only obsolete, but also structurally in deficit (Dadabaev 2005: 169–184; Asian Development Bank 2005; Eurasian Development Bank 2008). Electricity has become a rare commodity, and each winter the country experiences an energy crisis forcing it to cut off the electricity for long periods, even in the capital, disrupting households and the functioning of industries. While the winter of 2007–2008 was very difficult in terms of harsh weather, the winter of 2008–2009, despite its milder temperatures, was accompanied by further worsening of the energy situation. The water levels in the reservoirs of Toktogul in Kyrgyzstan fell drastically (Juraev 2009). The hydroelectric plants were heavily affected, and some industries were hampered in their production. The impact on agriculture was particularly visible: 30 per cent less water, even irregularly, caused 40 per cent less crops.

Kyrgyzstan possesses an immense capacity for electricity production of 3,786 MW (Botpaev *et al.* 2011). The country is still very dependent on the Central Asia Electricity Grid, which enables border regions to benefit from the electricity produced in Kazakhstan, Uzbekistan and Tajikistan. However, the progressive disappearance of, and will of producer countries to leave, the grid make the problem more acute for the Kyrgyz authorities. All the power plants were built under the Soviet regime and require considerable maintenance and upgrading works, the costs of which are estimated to be about 180 million dollars. More than half of the country's electricity system is considered to have massively deteriorated. The lines and the substations are almost permanently overloaded, with demand far outstripping supply. Losses due to financial default, diverted funds or negligent management may be as high as 25 per cent of production (Zozulinsky 2010). The Kyrgyz electricity companies operate mostly at a loss, and close to half of the electricity produced generates no revenue. Indeed, in order to make production profitable, the price of a kilowatt-hour would have to be a minimum of 2.25¢, whereas the current rate is only 1.57¢ (Botpaev *et al.* 2011). The government prefers operating at a loss to the social discontent that a price rise would provoke.

The Kyrgyz authorities have put all their hopes in the two hydroelectric stations of Kambarata 1 and 2, despite the tensions this creates with Uzbekistan, and Russia's exasperation at the speed of construction and frequent reluctance to provide the necessary funds. The first turbine of Kambarata 2, which was delivered by Moscow, was put into operation in November 2010. While the second and third turbines are still pending, the real issue is that of the future realisation or otherwise of Kambarata 1. The rather high construction costs have put the viability of this dam into question: 2009 estimates projected a budget of $1.7 billion, but this was revised markedly upwards in 2011 to as much as $3–4 billion, owing to the need for building to be done with reinforced concrete instead of ballast. This cost will considerably increase the cost price of a kilowatt-hour to as much as 14¢, whereas current market cost price is only 2–3¢

(Karybekov 2011). The future of Kambarata 1 is therefore far from assured if its profitability is not certain, and the production of Kambarata 2 will remain limited if Kambarata 1 does not operate upstream. In any case, Kyrgyzstan will find it hard to avoid the reality of making electricity increasingly expensive. But an increase in prices will by no means translate into better efficiency of the system. The real stake is thus that of operational efficiency, and of transaction transparency, which seem difficult to achieve given that successive governments have constantly manipulated the water–energy nexus, a real arm of foreign policy and of domestic political legitimacy.

Until the mid-2000s, the Kyrgyz state budget was chiefly buffered by the gold mine of Kumtor (Laruelle and Peyrouse 2010). In recent years additional revenue has been provided by the re-export of Chinese products to Uzbekistan and Kazakhstan, but also, to a lesser extent, Russia and Afghanistan (Raballand and Kaminski 2009: 581–590). According to World Bank calculations, in 2009 Bishkek re-exported close to three-quarters of incoming Chinese products, enabling it to generate substantial revenues. China accounts for 60–70 per cent of Kyrgyz imports and largely overshadows trade with Russia or the EU, but Bishkek's trade deficit with Beijing in 2008 is alleged to be more than 250 per cent of its GDP. Kyrgyzstan offers a very advantageous system for the payment of customs taxes, which are calculated on the basis of product volume rather than value. Chinese traders, preferring to negotiate with the easily corruptible Kyrgyz customs officers rather than with the Kazakh authorities, who are much stricter on imports, thus see the country as a particularly attractive but unstable option (Interviews: February 2008, September 2010). Yet this does not suffice to escape the schema of foreign financial aid: financial backers have contradictory expectations and debt reimbursements thwart public investment capacity. Moreover, this profitable situation has been challenged since 2010 by the Russia–Kazakhstan–Belarus Customs Union, which limits the prospects of economic growth for Kyrgyzstan. Bishkek cannot afford to be excluded from the Russian and Kazakh markets as rising prices for fuel and food coming from these two countries have been particularly destabilising. By joining the Customs Union, Bishkek would benefit from lower fuel prices, but would need to increase tariffs, making it harder to re-export Chinese goods (*Oxford Analytica* 2011).

Brutal transformation of the social fabric

In two decades, the Kyrgyz social fabric has been brutally reshaped: agriculture and industry now each involve only one-quarter of the active population, whereas the services sector has taken off, and employs half of the 2.5 million working-age people. Everyday small services comprise the vertebral column of the Kyrgyz economy: selling at bazaars, transporting Chinese products, catering, private transportation (taxi, collective buses) and so on (Laruelle and Peyrouse 2008: 13–23). With a GDP of about $2,200 per capita, Kyrgyzstan continues to be one of the poorest countries in the world (185th position). It combines an official unemployment rate of close to 20 per cent and recurrent poverty in rural milieux, whose revenues are largely insufficient to cover daily costs (CIA World Fact Book n.d.; Europa.eu n.d.). The World Food Programme (WFP) reckons that about one million Kyrgyz citizens are regularly affected by food insecurity (Fumagalli 2008; Linn 2008). For the majority of the population, the transition to the market economy meant, above all, the disappearance of the welfare state. Thanks to lack of investment, the Soviet-built infrastructures that it inherited are now run-down. Access to health care has reduced due to its partial privatisation. Public transport was drastically cut; it has now increased but is run by private companies. School has also become inaccessible for some rural milieux, in particular for girls, and the literacy rate has fallen from 99 per cent to 84 per cent (Laruelle 2009).

Internal migration has been rather considerable: populations living at high altitude have been led to migrate towards areas at lower altitudes so they can turn their hands to agriculture, since herding has dramatically collapsed. Demographic pressures on arable lands have therefore risen, and provoked conflicts for access to water, in particular in the Batken region at the Kyrgyz–Tajik border. While some areas are depopulating, others are experiencing agricultural overpopulation, in particular in the plains of the south in the Fergana Valley, which is the demographic heart of Central Asia (World Bank 2007; Ronsijn 2006). This poverty or lack of perspectives provides fertile soil for the growing instabilities. There are, for instance, an increasing number of people taking out classified ads in the hope of becoming a *pikechik* (a sort of professional demonstrator). The recruitment of a few thousand people, in exchange for a modest remuneration and payment for transport costs, food and alcohol makes it possible to organise popular uprisings.

Hundreds of thousands of rural dwellers have also made their way to the provincial towns and, of course, the capital, whose inhabitants have increased by about 20 per cent (Alymbaeva 2012). This massive rural exodus has caused major perturbations in social structures and cultural traditions: the arrival of rural households in the cities has not been well viewed by the urban elites, who are distinctly more Russified, and see it as a sign that augurs insecurity. At the same time, some of the young rural generations, uprooted and without any professional prospects, have entered into the informal economy and underground movements, sometimes of Islamic obedience. Territorial inequalities in terms of wealth have increased. The north is far more prosperous, urban and industrialised than the south. Indeed, poverty sharply affects rural zones (two-thirds as compared with one-third for urban zones), some mountainous regions such as Naryn, the region of Talas, as well as that of Osh in the south of the country (despite being an agricultural area), whereas Bishkek and the region of Chui have more favourable socio-economic conditions (Mogilevskiy n.d.; Slay 2010).

Foreign-bound migration flows have also grown in magnitude since the end of the 1990s. About 500,000 Kyrgyz are emigrating, whether for short or long periods, half to Kazakhstan (where they work on tobacco and cotton plantations and building sites), and half to Russia (construction, public roads and catering) (Dolotkeldieva 2012). As the majority of them work illegally, they experience difficult working conditions, and have minimal legal and medical protection. In total, about 20 per cent of Kyrgyzstan's workforce has left the country. The remittances sent back by these migrants (mainly men, but also a growing number of women) are estimated to represent, depending upon the year, between one-third and one-half of the state budget. More than one million citizens out of five million in the country lives directly on the money sent by emigrated family members (Marat 2009). For the most part, these migrants originally come from the country's southern rural regions. However, the migrations do not only concern the rural milieux: the growing unemployment among new university graduates is just as disturbing, if not more so. Given the attractiveness of the Russian and Kazakh markets, where the working conditions are much better, the salaries more competitive and the environment more dynamic, there is no way Kyrgyzstan can be competitive. This brain drain reduces prospects for the future: the country wins out in terms of social stability thanks to the migrations, which serve as a safety valve as regards the sclerosis of the work market, but the departure of its small qualified urban elite has cast a shadow over the future.

Which road to recovery?

Parliamentary democracy, implemented after the June 2010 referendum and the October legislative elections, still has to prove itself in this weakened country. The population's disillusionment in relation to politics is profound. Criticisms have grown in number against the presence of the American and Russian bases, which played no role in resolving the conflict of 2010 – and besides which, they had no legal capacity to do so. The country's insertion into the international arena and its multiple foreign partnerships are unable to resolve the domestic problems. For Kyrgyzstan, a country that had sought to be the most 'globalised' in Central Asia, the impression of having lost the 'information war' during the Osh events is a supreme failure. The most democratic country of Central Asia, the one most open to the West, and the one in which civil society is supposed to have been most supported is also the most unstable, as well as that with the most widespread feeling that the sovereignty to emerge from independence is but an illusion.

The supposed merging of internal and external enemies constitutes a powerful driver of nationalist radicalisation, rallying diverging milieux. Kyrgyz-language newspapers, in particular *Alibi* and *Apta*, did not hide their radical reading of the Osh events, with articles sometimes almost calling for interethnic hatred, while Russian-language newspapers, although less pointed, almost never gave the floor to the Uzbek version of events. Some of the journalists who criticised the Kyrgyz version of the story have been accused of not being 'patriotic' (Najibullah 2010). Even the opposition media have remained largely silent on Uzbeks being disproportionately targeted by police raids and arbitrary arrests. The government's non-recognition that the post-conflict situation is marked by unjustified detentions, rigged trials, daily violence and land grabs to the clear detriment of the Uzbeks confirms that the state is no longer able to take a neutral role in the ethnic tensions. This impression was corroborated in May 2011 when the Kyrgyz parliament declared persona non grata Kimmo Kiljunen, the head of an international commission that investigated Osh events, saying the report was one-sided, incited racial hatred and threatened national security (RFE/RL 2011).

Paradoxically, Kyrgyzstan is the only country in Central Asia that lacks a state-fostered ideology, but the one where deteriorating socio-economic conditions and unstable political life has created a fertile background for interethnic tensions (Marat 2008). The totally polarised Uzbek and Kyrgyz narratives of victimhood and the politics of grievance will now take years to erase and will hinder any prospect of building a civic identity. The memory of mutual benefits between communities is vanishing to the advantage of that of competition for shared natural resources and economic niches. On the Kyrgyz side, the failure of statehood is therefore interpreted as the failure of nationhood. What thus dominates today is the illusion that the more Kyrgyzstan becomes the state of the Kyrgyz in terms of identity narrative, historical references, language policies and marginalisation of the minorities from decision-making, the more it will be able to succeed in reconstructing itself as a state. Ethnic differentiation will therefore probably be reinforced in the years to come, just as the logics of territorial and socio-economic segregation between communities. But the temptation of monoethnicism goes against the will to build a parliamentary democracy.

The candidatures for the electoral presidential campaign of October 2011 have therefore a difficult political context to manage. Of a total of 19 registered applications, there were few serious and well-known candidates. The main contenders were the prime minister from the Social-Democratic Party, Almazbek Atambayev, the former parliament speaker Adakhan Madumarov, head of Butun Kyrgyzstan, and the leader of the Ata Jurt nationalist party, Kamchybek Tashiyev. As the winner of over 60 per cent of the ballots in the first round, Atambayev was the preferred candidate of Russia, Turkey and the West, while Tashiyev competes with Adakhan Madumarov, as both draw on nationalistic themes and Kyrgyz voters from the country's south. To the traditional north–south divisions, often used to explain the lack of unity among the Kyrgyz elite, one can now add the opposition between 'revolutionary' and 'revanchists' in the events of 2010. Opposition between the Kyrgyz majority and national minorities has not weakened, especially as the various investigative committees for the Osh events failed to assign responsibility, while inhibiting any process of national reconciliation. The nationalist narrative that Madumarov and Tashiyev advance has contributed to shaping public discourse. The campaign has focused on discussions of identity, with controversy over state symbols (Manas, the anthem, flag and school programmes), while most candidates carefully avoid major socio-economic issues. The neo-patrimonial logic that pushes each network to establish control over its portion of resources has also been hidden.

It is on the social level that the greatest efforts are required. Employment prospects have not improved, migration flows have intensified with the departure of tens of thousands of Uzbeks in the wake of the violence last year, and the recession has intensified, affecting agriculture and trade. Foreign investment is falling, the Customs Union of Russia, Belarus and Kazakhstan has slowed Kyrgyz trade with China, and Russia has reduced its economic commitments in the country. Challenges in Kyrgyzstan are therefore not only numerous, but overlapping, and confirm the need for a comprehensive approach to security.

Notes

1 In 2005 the main criticisms were levied against Akayev's wife, Mayram, and their two children Aydar and Bermet. In 2010 the main objects of popular vengeance were Kurmanbek Bakiyev's brothers, in particular Zhanysh and Akmat, as well as his son, Maksim.

2 However, opposition leaders had prepared themselves for the change, in particular following the evolution of Russian criticism towards the government in place, and Roza Otunbayeva had already been seen as a consensus personality able to lead the opposition in the case of Bakiyev's ouster.

3 Much controversy remains over 'who started it'. The different arguments advanced are difficult to analyse in the absence of an international audit. For a chronology of events, see Human Rights Watch (2010).

4 The figures are still difficult to confirm for several reasons: Muslim tradition requires the deceased to be buried before sundown, therefore complicating the administrative record, and at the time of the pogroms collective graves were arranged in order to obscure the exact number of bodies.

5 However, critics have also spoken out about the inability of religious leaders to calm spirits (www.24.kg.org 2010).

6 The blogs and discussions on Facebook and Twitter are filled with accusations of genocide. In the post-Soviet space, the term is largely used to decry any mistreatment of minorities, without regard for its precise legal meaning. For example, the Russians of Kazakhstan complained of genocide at the beginning of the 1990s and the Russian media regularly accuses Tbilisi of perpetrating genocide against South Ossetians.

7 The images captured by participants and observers are eloquent in this regard. The Kyrgyz militia then attempted to confiscate compromising photos and videos, but they were posted online, such as on YouTube.

References

Alymbaeva, Aida (2012) 'Internal Migrations in Kyrgyzstan: The Geographical and Sociological Issues of Rural Migration', in M. Laruelle (ed.) *Labor Migration and Social Upheaval as the Face of Globalization in Central Asia*, Leiden: Brill.

Asian Development Bank (2005) *Electricity Sectors in CAREC Countries: A Diagnostic Review of Regulatory Approaches and Challenges*, Manila: ADB.

Botpaev, Ruslan, Budig, C., Orozaliev, J., *et al.* (2011) 'Renewable Energy in Kyrgyzstan: State, Policy and Educational System', Kassel University. http://solar-publikationen.umwelt-uni-kassel.de/uploads/110923%20SWC%20Paper_Botpaev_RE%20in%20Kyrgyzstan.pdf (accessed 20 November 2011).

CIA World Fact Book (n.d.). https://www.cia.gov/library/publications/the-world-factbook/geos/kg.html (accessed 5 January 2011).

Cummings, Sally and Ryabkov, Maxim (2008) 'Situating the Kyrgyz Revolution', *Central Asian Survey*, 27 (3–4): 241–252.

Dadabaev, Timur (2005) 'Water Politics and Management of Trans-Boundary Water Resources in Post-Soviet Central Asia', in Birgit Schlyter (ed.) *Prospects for Democracy in Central Asia*, Istanbul: Swedish Research Institute in Istanbul, pp. 169–184.

Dolotkeldieva, Asel (2012) 'Kyrgyz Migrants in Moscow: Public Policies, Migratory Strategies, and Associative Networks', in M. Laruelle (ed.) *Labor Migration and Social Upheaval as the Face of Globalization in Central Asia*, Leiden: Brill.

Engvall, Johan (2011) *The State as Investment Market: An Analytical Framework for Interpreting Politics and Bureaucracy in Kyrgyzstan*, Uppsala: Uppsala University Press.

Eurasian Development Bank (2008) *Obshchii elektroenergeticheskii rynok sng*, Almaty: Eurasian Development Bank.

Europea.eu (n.d.). Kyrgyz Republic. http://trade.ec.europa.eu/doclib/docs/2006/september/tradoc_113409.pdf (accessed 5 January 2011).

Ferrando, Olivier (2009) 'Minorités ethniques d'Asie centrale: le destin croisé des Ouzbeks de la vallée du Ferghana', *Études interculturelles*, 2: 33–45.

Fumagalli, Matteo (2008) 'The "Food–Energy–Water" Nexus in Central Asia: Regional Implications of and the International Response to the Crises in Tajikistan', EUCAM Policy Brief, no. 2.

Hale, Henry (2005) 'Regime Cycles: Democracy, Autocracy, and Revolution in Post-Soviet Eurasia', *World Politics*, 58 (1): 133–165.

Human Rights Watch (2010) *Kyrgyzstan: 'Where Is the Justice?', Interethnic Violence in Southern Kyrgyzstan and its Aftermath*, New York, NY: Human Rights Watch.

Ianovskaia, Mariia (2010) 'K chemu privedet "ethnicheskii faktor" v napriazhennoi obstanovke na iuge Kyrgyzstana?', 17 May. www.ferghana.ru/article.php?id=6581 (accessed 3 August 2010).

International Crisis Group (2010) 'The Pogroms In Kyrgyzstan', Asia Report no. 193.

Jaquesson, Svetlana (2010) *Pastoréalismes, Anthropologie historique des processus d'intégration chez les Kirghiz du Tian Shan intérieur*, Wiesbaden: Reichert.

Jones, K.D. (2003) 'Land Privatization and Conflict in Central Asia: Is Kyrgyzstan a Model?', in D.L. Burghart and T. Sabonis-Helf (ed.) *In the Tracks of Tamerlane: Central Asia's Paths to the 21st Century*, Washington, DC: Centre for Technology and National Security Policy.

Juraev, Shaibek (2009) 'Energy Emergency in Kyrgyzstan: Causes and Consequences', EUCAM Policy Brief 5.

Karybekov, Ernest (2011) 'Kyrgyzstanu nevygodno stroitel'stvo GES "Kambarata-1"', 25 May. http://24kg.org/economics/100761-yernest-karybekov-kyrgyzstanu-nevygodno.html (accessed 20 November 2011).

Khamidov, Alisher (n.d.) 'Forging Broken Links: Uzbeks and the State in Kyrgyzstan', Institute for Public Policy. www.ipp.kg/en/analysis/295 (accessed 3 August 2010).

Laruelle, Marlene (2009) 'The Growing Illiteracy in Central Asia: A Challenge for the EU', EUCAM Commentary 6.

Laruelle, Marlene and Peyrouse, Sébastien (2008) 'Impact et enjeux sociaux des évolutions économiques en Asie centrale', *Autrepart*: *Les mondes post-communistes. Quels capitalismes? Quelles sociétés?*, 48 (4): 13–23.

—— (2010) *L'Asie centrale à l'aune de la mondialisation: Une approche géo-économique*, Paris: Armand Colin.

Lillis, Joanna (2010) 'Kyrgyzstan: Bishkek Mourns Victims of Political Violence', 8 April. www.eurasianet.org/departments/insightb/articles/eav040910b.shtml (accessed 3 August 2010).

Linn, Johannes F. (2008) 'The Compound Water–Energy–Food Crisis Risks in Central Asia: Update on an International Response', Brookings Institution Commentary, 12 August. www.brookings.edu/opinions/2008/0812_central_asia_linn.aspx (accessed 28 December 2009).

Luong, Pauline Jones (2010) 'Recurring Referendums: The Struggle for Constitutional "Reform" in Kyrgyzstan', in *Kyrgyzstan: Recovery and Reformation, Policy Perspectives*, Ponars Policy Papers, pp. 18–23.

Marat, Erica (2006) 'The State–Crime Nexus in Central Asia', *Silk Road Papers*, Washington, DC: The Central Asia-Caucasus Institute.

—— (2008) 'National Ideology and Statebuilding in Kyrgyzstan and Tajikistan', *Silk Road Papers*, Washington, DC: The Central Asia-Caucasus Institute.

—— (2009) 'Labor Migration in Central Asia: Implications of the Global Economic Crisis', *Silk Road Papers*, Washington, DC: The Central Asia-Caucasus Institute.

—— (2010a) 'Russian Mass Media Attack Bakiyev', *Eurasia Daily Monitor*, 7 (63), 1 April. www.jamestown.org/programs/edm/single/?tx_ttnews[tt_news]=36226&tx_ttnews[backPid]=27&cHash=5f81ad077b (accessed 3 August 2010).

—— (2010b) 'Bakiyev, the Security Structures, and the April 7 Violence in Kyrgyzstan', *The Central Asia-Caucasus Analyst*, 28 April. www.cacianalyst.org/?q=node/5316 (accessed 3 August 2010).

Mogilevskiy, Roman (n.d.) 'Poverty Indicators and Monitoring in Kyrgyzstan: Case Study', World Bank Paper. http://info.worldbank.org/etools/docs/library/85673/devdebates/ECA/mogilevskiy.pdf> (accessed 8 June 2011).

Najibullah, F. (2010) 'Is Kyrgyz Media Providing the Whole Picture?', 31 July. www.eurasianet.org/node/61648 (accessed 3 August 2010).

Olcott, Martha Brill (2005) 'Lessons of the Tulip Revolution', Testimony Before Commission on Security and Cooperation in Europe, 7 April. www.carnegieendowment.org/publications/index.cfm?fa=view&id=16758 (accessed 3 August 2010).

Osmonov, Joldosh (2006) 'Uzbek Community in Kyrgyzstan Want Uzbek as Official Language', *The Central Asia-Caucasus Analyst*, 14 April. www.cacianalyst.org/?q=node/4020 (accessed 3 August 2010).

Oxford Analytica (2011) 'Customs Union Offers Marginal Benefits to Central Asia', 28 July.

Petric, Boris-Mathieu (2006) 'Le Kirghizstan, royaume des ONG', *Outre-terre*, 3: 287–301.

Raballand, Gaël and Kaminski, Bartłomiej (2009) 'Entrepôt for Chinese Consumer Goods in Central Asia: The Puzzle of Re-exports through Kyrgyz Bazaars', *Eurasian Geography and Economics*, 50 (5): 581–590.

Radnitz, Scott (2006) 'What Really Happened in Kyrgyzstan?', *Journal of Democracy*, 17 (2): 132–146.

RFE/RL (2011) *Head of Commission on Kyrgyz Violence declared Persona Non Grata*, 26 May. www.rferl.org/content/head_of_commission_on_kyrgyz_violence_declared_persona_non_grata/24205930.html (accessed 28 May 2011).

Robert, Seans (2010) 'What's Ethnicity Got To Do With It? Healing the Wounds of Uzbek–Kyrgyz violence in the Ferghana Valley', in *Kyrgyzstan: Recovery and Reformation, Policy Perspectives*, Ponars Policy Papers, pp. 7–12.

Ronsijn, Wouter (2006) 'Coping During Transition in Rural Areas: The Case of Post-Soviet Southern Kyrgyzstan', Ghent University Conflict Research Group Working Paper no. 4.

Slay, Ben (2010) 'Recent Developments in the Poverty/Energy/Vulnerability Nexus in Kyrgyzstan and Tajikistan', UNDP Paper. http://europeandcis.undp.org/uploads/public1/files/vulnerability/Senior%20Economist%20Web%20site/Publications/Slay_PEV_paper_December_2010.pdf> (accessed 6 June 2011)

TASS (1990) Foreign Broadcast Information Service, Moscow, FBIS-SOV-90-108, 5 June.

Temirkulov, Azamat (2010) 'Kyrgyz "Revolutions" in 2005 and 2010: Comparative Analysis of Mass Mobilization', *Nationalities Papers*, 38 (5): 589–600.

Trilling, David and Umetov, Chingis (2010) 'Kyrgyzstan: Is Putin Punishing Bakiyev?', 5 April. www.eurasianet.org/departments/insight/articles/eav040610a.shtml (accessed 3 August 2010).

Vasilyev, Yuri (2010) 'Kirghizia: za chto ubit Chernyi Aybek?', 7 June. www.svobodanews.ru/content/article/2064618.html (accessed 3 August 2010).

Volosevich, Alexei (2010) 'Bezhentsy iz Kyrgyzstana v Uzbekistane. Ukhod i vozvrat', 30 June. www.ferghana.ru/article.php?id=6638 (accessed 3 August 2010).

Wegerich, Kai (2011) 'Politics of Water in Post-Soviet Central Asia', in D. Heaney (ed.) *Eastern Europe, Russia and Central Asia 2010*, London: Routledge, pp. 27–31.

World Bank (2007) 'Kyrgyz Republic Poverty Assessment, Vol. II: Labor Market Dimensions of Poverty', Report no. 40864-KG.

www.24.kg.org (2010) 'Muftii Kyrgyzstana priznal, chto dukhovenstvo strany opozdalo s reagirovaniem na tragicheskie oshskie sobytiia', 6 August. www.24.kg/community/80205-muftij-kyrgyzstana-priznal-chto-duxovenstvo.html (accessed 3 August 2010).

www.ferghana.ru (2010) 'SNB Kyrgyzstana: Pogromy na iuge organizovali Maksim Bakiev, uzbeki i Taliban', 24 June. www.ferghana.ru/article.php?id=6629 (accessed 3 August 2010).

www.rdiland.org (n.d.). www.rdiland.org/OURWORK/OurWork_Kyrgyzstan.html (accessed 3 August 2010).

Zozulinsky, Artyom (2010) 'Kyrgyzstan: Power Generation & Transmission', US Department of State, 2 October. http://photos.state.gov/libraries/kyrgyzrepulic/328656/pdfs/Kyrgyz%20Power%20Industry%20Report%20_2_.pdf (accessed 24 November 2011).

Interviews

Mars Sariyev, Political scientist at the headquarters of Zamandash, Bishkek, 2 July 2010.

Experts in Chinese business, Bishkek, February, Almaty, September 2008 and 2010.

Members of the OSCE who observed the election on 27 June 2010 and 3 July 2010.

Members of Zamandash, the political party advocating for Kyrgyz migrants, Bishkek, 2 July 2010.

8 Southern Kurdistan

From conflict zone to subregional integration in Greater Eurasia

Jason E. Strakes

Introduction

In the near-decade since the removal of the Ba'athist regime of Saddam Hussein, Iraqi Kurdistan – or Southern Kurdistan – has emerged as an epicentre of both conflict and cooperation in the Near East and Subcaucasus.[1] The Kurdish-majority region of northern Iraq has traditionally been regarded by foreign observers as a 'prisoner of geopolitics', in that it is simultaneously landlocked, encircled by rugged mountainous landscapes and surrounded by states whose governments have often maintained hostile relationships with their respective Kurdish minority populations (O'Shea 2004: 61; Dahlman 2002: 271–274; Stansfield 2003b: 26; Zhigalina 2003; Gunter 2008: 237). At the same time, the highly strategic location of the territories controlled by the Kurdistan Regional Government (KRG) has granted it the position of a virtual crossroads between the Al-Jazirah plain and Al-Hasakah governorate (*muhafaza*) of northeast Syria, the Eastern Anatolia region of Turkey and the northwest provinces (*ostānhā*) of Iran.

Yet, while the evolution of the KRG since 2003 is often examined in the context of its variably symbiotic and competitive relationship with the Arab-dominant central government of Iraq (GoI), as well as its role in Ankara's ongoing struggle with guerrilla forces of the Kurdistan Workers' Party (*Partiya Karkerên Kurdistan*/PKK), it has seldom been considered in terms of its international interactions and growing diplomatic engagements with the subregions of neighbouring countries. Though foreign relations between the KRG and its neighbour states have become the norm, this process is particularly represented by the increased pursuit of cross-border cooperation and integration between the provincial governments of Iraqi Kurdistan (Erbil, Dohuk and As Sulaymaniyah), the Southeast Anatolia (Diyarbakır and Gaziantep), Eastern Anatolia (Malatya and Hakkâri) and Mediterranean (Adana) regions of Turkey, Iranian Azerbaijan and Kurdistan (West Azerbaijan, Kordestan and Kermanshah) and central and northern Iran (Isfahan and Mazandaran).

Further, these arrangements have progressed despite continued internal and external security problems related to unresolved societal conflicts, insurgent activities and combined incursions and bombardments by Turkish and Iranian military forces in the northern and eastern boundary zones of the KRG, which have resulted in civilian casualties and displacement from border settlements. On a secondary level, such relationships have contributed to the establishment of political and economic connections between Northern (Turkish), Southern (Iraqi) and Eastern (Iranian) Kurdistan, in spite of the virtual abandonment of the traditional nationalist objective of uniting Kurdish populations across the boundaries of their respective host states, or 'Greater Kurdistan' (O'Leary and Salih 2005: 8–15; Chorev 2007: 3). Conversely, despite the precedent of strategic associations between the Syrian leadership and the Iraqi Kurdish movement, the recurrently volatile relationship between the Kurdish inhabitants of northeast Syria and the Damascus regime, combined with Baghdad's preparations against external security threats since 2003, has prevented significant cross-border interactions between the Al-Hasakah subregion and the KRG.

The present study therefore examines the patterns of tension and accommodation that have developed among the three northern provinces of Iraq that comprise the KRG and its neighbouring states from the immediate pre-Iraq War period to present. The analysis proceeds in three stages: (1) it presents a conceptual framework that links the evolution of sub-state diplomacy in Iraqi Kurdistan with levels of conflict and cooperation in the region; (2) it identifies and reviews the factors that have contributed to negative security conditions in the KRG territories during the past decade; and (3) it investigates the prospects for and evidence of subregional integration between Kurdistani,[2] Syrian, Turkish and Iranian provincial governments during this period.

Historical background of the KRG

The foundations of a de facto Iraqi Kurdish polity were first laid with the negotiation of the Autonomy Agreement by Mullah Mustafa Barzani and then Vice-President Saddam Hussein al-Tikriti in March 1970 (MERIP 1974). An effort followed to demarcate and defend a separate but equally legitimate realm of political representation in northern Iraq, supported by tribal authorities and the Peshmerga guerrilla resistance that began in 1961. While this allowed the Kurds to define and occupy a territorial space for the first time in the history of the Iraqi republic, the 1975 Algiers Agreement between Baghdad and Tehran ended outside military support, leading to their subsequent defeat by the Iraqi armed forces (Stansfield and Resool 2006). The imposition of the 'no-fly zone' at the 36th parallel by UN Security Council Resolution 688 after the Persian Gulf War in April 1991 was followed by the withdrawal of the Baghdad administration. With the election of the Kurdistan National Assembly (*Civata Nîştimanî Kurdistan*) in May 1992, the leading Kurdistan Democratic Party (*Partîya Demokrata Kurdistan*/PDK) and Patriotic Union of Kurdistan (*Yeketî Niştîmanî Kurdistan*/YNK) consolidated their control over the three northernmost provinces. In October of the same year the Assembly released a declaration for the establishment of both a federal region of Iraqi Kurdistan, and a federated state of Iraq (Gunter 1993: 309).

However, beginning in mid-1993, these arrangements gradually collapsed as a combined result of institutional changes and the economic activities of Kurdish leaders and their political factions. The merging of three independent Kurdish parties with the ruling PDK altered the delicate 50/50 power division in the legislature, while the unregulated influx of international aid from foreign governments and donor agencies intensified conflicts of interest between the clientelist networks managed by either wing (Chorev 2007: 4). By the end of 1993, ensuing tensions escalated into an internal civil war directly involving party militias.

As a result of these recurrent conflicts, in August 1996 the administrative structure of the KRG separated into two geographic jurisdictions: the PDK executive centred in Erbil and exerting control over Dohuk, and the YNK presiding over Sulaymaniyah (Stansfield 2005: 198–203). The Washington Agreement that formally resolved the Kurdish civil war in 1998 solidified this arrangement (Khalil 2009: 22–23). Each jurisdiction thus maintained separate cabinets and an independent security apparatus, unified only by two structures: the Assembly and the court. The resolution of this quarrel with the assistance of the Turkish and US governments returned Kurdish leaders to the task of accumulating resources fuelled by a combination of international aid flows, control of illicit trade, state-managed companies and foreign investment. The period between the internal KRG conflict and the 2003 coalition invasion is thus identified as the 'golden era' of Iraqi Kurdistan, in which regional ruling elites were provided with a window of opportunity to pursue autonomy, accumulate wealth and develop its institutions (Stansfield 2003a).

Conceptual framework

The past decade has witnessed the growing phenomenon of the pursuit of international relations by subnational governments, sometimes in accordance with constitutional allocations of decision-making powers, and in other cases in conflict with central state authorities (Criekemans 2010: 1). While this issue initially focused on the diplomatic competencies of federated democracies in northwest Europe, it has since expanded to include the foreign relations of developing and non-democratic states in which autonomous republics, subregions or provinces have established relationships with foreign governments, industries or international organisations (Cornago 2010: 16–18). This process of 'normalisation' has become particularly pertinent as the increasing presence of quasi-independent states like Kosovo since 2008 and unrecognised 'de facto', 'para' or 'semi' states (e.g. Somaliland and Puntland in Somalia, Transnistria in Moldova, Abkhazia and South Ossetia in Georgia and Nagorno-Karabakh in Azerbaijan) in global politics has fostered an ongoing debate: do they constitute a direct threat to the territorial integrity of their host states, or are they emerging diplomatic players which must ultimately be engaged as a necessary aspect of conflict management and resolution?

Such controversies might be interpreted according to the concept of 'contentious regulation', in which the external legitimacy of diplomatic activities engaged in by a sub-state unit is inherently affected by the institutional and legal approaches of national governments in either accommodating or constraining their foreign policy prerogatives (Cornago 2010: 28–34). The application of this analytical perspective is especially relevant in the context of the KRG's role in a nascent or nominal Iraqi federal system. Despite the constitutional delegation of certain sovereign powers to the Kurdish leadership in Erbil, in recent years the administration of Prime Minister Nouri al-Maliki has sought to reimpose limits upon its independent activities (Stansfield and Anderson 2009; Gunter 2010).

Sub-state diplomacy in the KRG

Each of the ruling parties of the KRG has introduced administrative structures for the conduct of external relations since their respective inception in 1946 and 1975. The Politburo of the PDK governs its provincial jurisdictions through a system of 24 regional branches (*liqs*), the sixth, seventh and eighth of which have maintained representative offices in Europe (London), the United States (Washington, DC) and Iran, while the Office of Public Relations conducts its foreign affairs (Stansfield 2003b: 230n55; Kurdistan Democratic Party-Iraq 2008). The YNK also maintains a Bureau of International Relations which provides information for and coordinates the activities of its overseas party representatives, and reports directly to the Secretary General, Politburo and Leadership Council regarding diplomacy with foreign governments (Stansfield 2003a: 113, 164; Patriotic Union of Kurdistan 2008). After its establishment by Law No. 20 of the Kurdistan National Assembly in 1993, the KRG Ministry of Humanitarian Affairs and Cooperation, which initially acted as a liaison with NGOs and UN agencies operating in the region, also served as a virtual foreign ministry in the absence of de jure international recognition (Stansfield 2003b: 164, 205, 230n55).

However, the contemporary phase of diplomatic practice in Iraqi Kurdistan was initiated with the creation of the KRG Department of Foreign Relations (DFR) in September 2006. The structure and functions of the DFR are articulated in Official Order No. 143, signed by then Prime Minister Nechirwan Barzani, pursuant to the powers relegated to the KRG under Paragraph 4, Article 121 of the 2005 Iraqi Constitution (Kurdistan Regional Government 2009b). This document designates seven Directorates (including International Relations in the Region; Foreign Offices Abroad; International Organizations; and Protocol and Delegations) which carry out essential tasks such as supervision and assessment of the KRG representative offices maintained in the United States, United Kingdom, Brussels (EU), Germany, France, Italy, Spain, Portugal, Australia and Iran, organising visits by foreign delegations, facilitating contacts with foreign missions and offices in the KRG, and, importantly, coordinating with the Kurdistan Region Board of Investment to arrange visits by foreign businesses and company representatives (Kurdistan Regional Government 2009a, 2009b). While the DFR is formally identified as operating in tandem with the Iraqi Ministry of Foreign Affairs – as Hoshyar Zebari has served as foreign representative of both the PDK since 1992 and Iraq since 2003 – in reality, it performs multiple functions directed at consolidating the federal autonomy of the KRG, as well as increasing its international profile and legitimacy (Chorev 2007: 7).

Theoretical linkages

The process model displayed in Figure 8.1 presents the main factors involved in the transition from conflictive to cooperative interactions between the contemporary KRG and external polities since 2003. The theoretical structure is composed of four variables: one independent (IV), two intervening (INTV), and one dependent (DV), while the plus (+) and minus (–) symbols indicate a positive or negative relationship between them. In the first instance, the continued pursuit of international relations and diplomatic recognition by both the PDK (Erbil and Dohuk) and YNK (Sulaymaniyah) authorities of the KRG since its establishment in 1992 (IV) exerts a positive effect upon the outcome (DV), or the development of cooperative relations with the provincial governments of neighbouring states (i.e. Syria, Turkey and Iran). However, the overall strength of this relationship is at the same time influenced by two intervening variables. At the level of Iraqi domestic politics, the often contentious relationship between the KRG and GoI, as well as the residual effects of continued insurgent and terror activities, have a potential constraining influence on the ability of the Kurdish leadership to engage in cooperative external relations (INTV1).

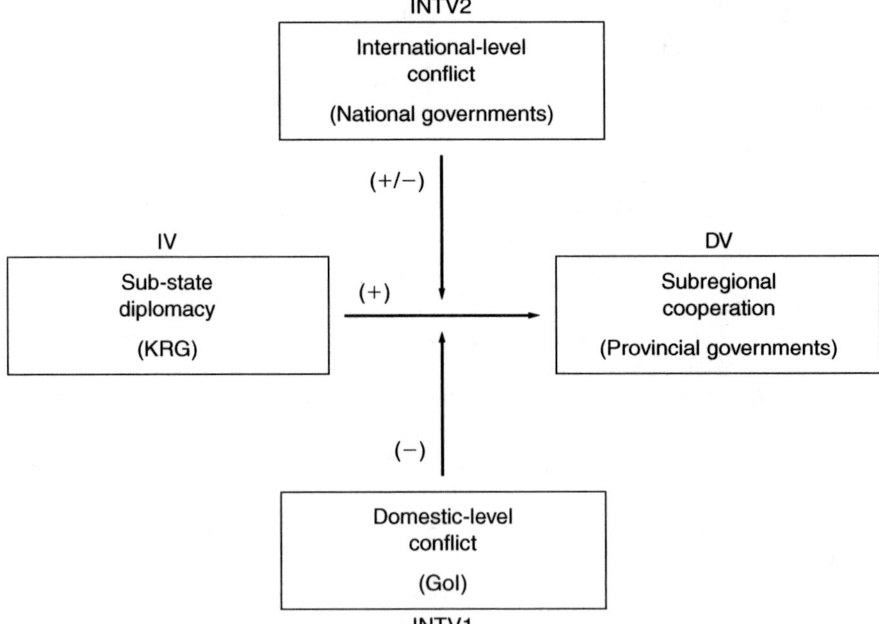

Figure 8.1 Model of conflict and cooperation in Iraqi Kurdistan, 2003–present.

Conversely, at the international level, the degree of tensions or conflicts of interest with the national governments of neighbouring countries is expected to increase the incentives to seek further cooperation with provincial-level authorities in these states (INTV2). These effects are assumed to occur simultaneously and are therefore combined with one another.

The main hypothesis extended in this study is therefore that the respective provincial administrations of Iraqi Kurdistan have pursued integrative efforts with local governments of neighbouring states as a type of 'back door' strategy to bypass or override its ongoing security disagreements or acute tensions with their national leaderships. The supporting evidence which demonstrates the existence of these relationships is drawn from five primary types of empirical data, each representing relative degrees of integration: (1) state visits or meetings involving provincial, ministerial or industrial officials; (2) the conclusion of protocols, memoranda of understanding or agreements between government or industry representatives; (3) the opening of trade centres, fairs and exhibitions; (4) the establishment of customs checkpoints, border crossings and terminals, and (5) infrastructural arrangements such as communications, fuel and power supply or transportation networks. This information is derived from a content analysis of English language and translated open-source media reports (including newspapers, transcripts of television broadcasts and websites) from 2002 to present. In sum, this provides a means of mapping the patterns of cooperation between the KRG and its neighbouring polities according to geographic location in the surrounding region.

The role of the KRG in regional conflicts

Accurate estimates of the total Kurdish population in Iraq and neighbouring countries have often been difficult to determine due to a combination of suppression, lack of reliable census data and changes due to migration and fertility rates. It is generally accepted that the largest number of ethnic Kurds reside in Turkey, followed by Iraq, Iran and Syria. While there was an ethnic dimension to the historic enmity between the central government of Iraq and the Kurdish movement, this has also occurred in interaction with geography and territory, as its leadership originally sought to establish an autonomous political entity within national boundaries rather than an independent state (Romano 2006: 305). Yet, the perception among regional governments that their respective Kurdish minorities seek to establish a 'Greater Kurdistan' uniting the Kurdish populations of the Near East is a longstanding one. A declassified Central Intelligence Agency (CIA) document dated 13 June 1963 states that 'Kurdish irredentism has been a problem to Iraqi regimes ever since the country was formed in 1921' (CIA 1963). This understanding of Kurdish ambitions has endured in the contemporary period, remaining highly influential in assessments of the Kurds' relationship with their host governments.

However, in reality the unifying goal of establishing a Kurdish state has been constrained and altered by both external and internal forces. First, communication between Kurdish populations has been relatively limited, while rivalries have developed between political parties seeking to represent and attract the support of Kurds in their respective countries. Second, Kurdish cultural traits are highly diverse and fractionalised, as evidenced by religious and linguistic cleavages within the territories inhabited by Kurds (Bonine 2002: 301–302). Further, the ideological objectives of traditional Kurdish nationalism (*Kurdayetî*) have been defined differently within the Kurdish societies of Turkey, Iran and Iraq as a result of political conditions (Natali 2005: 160). Lastly, despite the concentration of Kurdish populations in contiguous regions of Iraq and Turkey and mountainous and forested topography conducive to the pursuit of insurgent strategies, the varying policies of assimilation pursued by each of these states have had a diversifying effect upon the Kurdish diaspora (O'Leary and Salih 2005: 8–15). While Shi'a and Sunni Kurds in Turkey and Iran have been subject to cultural repression by religious and linguistic majorities, the Ba'athist movements in Iraq and Syria have subjected their respective Kurdish populations to Arabisation policies that sought to reengineer the demographics of ethnic and sectarian minority communities.

Domestic-level conflicts

KRG and GoI

Domestic constraints on the pursuit of international cooperation by the KRG are generated by several unresolved tensions within the post-war Iraqi political environment. These are composed of three interrelated issues: (1) continued instability caused by residual effects of the civil conflict of 2005–2008; (2) the contentions between Erbil and Baghdad regarding oil exploration rights and the conclusion of production-sharing contracts (PSCs) with foreign prospecting companies; and (3) the delayed implementation of the referendum process to determine the future status of Kirkuk. Actions taken by the KRG leadership to establish legal and organisational foundations for an independent petroleum industry have provoked retaliation by the GoI, including exclusion of companies from bids, cancellation of deals and memoranda of understanding, and reduction of oil shipments (Khalil 2009: 6–7). Observers have also suggested that the objective of increasing the economic development of Iraqi Kurdistan through foreign investment in the oil sector threatens to disrupt its sensitive relationship with neighbouring states, whose governments perceive a linkage between energy self-sufficiency and territorial independence (Khalil 2009: 9). Other accounts allege similar reservations among the leaderships of Syria, Turkey and Iran regarding the potential annexation of Kirkuk and the resultant control of its oil reserves by the KRG (Barkey 2009: 16).

International-level conflicts

KRG and Syria

From the mid-1970s until after the 2003 Iraq War, the al-Assad regimes of Syria pursued a policy of expedient sponsorship of both the Iraqi Kurdish parties and the PKK in order to challenge their regional opponents in Baghdad and Ankara. In return, the Iraqi Kurdish leaderships maintained a policy of silence regarding the internal situation of Syrian Kurds (Lowe 2006a: 301–302). Perhaps the most significant factor affecting the relationship between Western and Southern Kurdistan in recent years was the 12 March 2004 riots in the district capital of Al-Qamishli in Al-Hasakah, in which tensions between Kurdish and Arab spectators at a football stadium escalated into open violence that was suppressed by security forces armed with live ammunition. Similar crackdowns in response to public funeral processions in the following days provoked mass unrest among Syrian Kurds, which spread to the cities of Jazirah, Afrin, Ayn al-Arab, Al-Hasakah and Aleppo, resulting in hundreds of arrests and reprisals (Lowe 2006b: 5; KurdWatch 2009: 3).

The ensuing instability served as a catalyst to alter the orientation of Kurdistanis towards their Syrian brethren, as well as the al-Assad leadership. In response to these events, major student demonstrations were held at Sulaymaniyah and Salahaddin universities, as well as by student unions in Erbil, which petitioned the Kurdistan National Assembly to request that the UN condemn the actions of the Syrian government (KurdSat TV 2004). In Sulaymaniyah, thousands of protestors entered the streets, while a large group, including students, clerics and political activists, gathered at the building housing the KRG Council of Ministers as well as representatives of the Coalition Provisional Authority (CPA) to demand US intervention in Syria on behalf of the Kurdish population (Associated Press Worldstream 2004). These public expressions of solidarity were swiftly reciprocated by KRG officials, when on 17 March 2004 Assembly Speaker Adnan Mufti released a statement condemning the violent actions against Syrian Kurds and urging the legal investigation and prosecution of those responsible (*Kurdistani Nuwe* 2004). On the same day, while meeting a delegation of Syrian Kurdish political and tribal representatives to observe ceremonies commemorating the Days of Halabja and Anfal Martyrs Remembrance in Salah-al-Din, KRG President Massoud Barzani issued a statement echoing the one given by the parliament.

The Syrian government and state-controlled media during this period identified the incidents as being instigated by foreign forces, while the US State Department extended public criticism of its domestic policies, which produced further sensitivity towards interference in Syria's internal affairs (Gambil 2004: 6; Tejel 2009: 117). The United States and Iraq have also asserted that Al Qaeda in Iraq (AQI) fighters have infiltrated into Kurdish-controlled districts of Mosul province through the eastern Syrian border, later resulting in the closure of the Rabiah border point by Coalition forces (Cagaptay 2008: 16; Knights 2008: 21).

In May, a PDK newspaper asserted that the pressures exerted against Syrian Kurds by Damascus, in addition to the earlier violence in Al Qamishli (allegedly incited by former Saddam regime elements in collaboration with Syrian security forces), had resulted in an inflow of internally displaced families from Western Kurdistan into the KRG (*Khabat* 2004). Finally, in the following month, it was reported by a Baghdad-based PDK press outlet that Syrian authorities had closed the border gate and crossing point at Faysh Khabur in Dohuk without formal announcement, thus barring passage of private citizens into Iraqi Kurdistan (Al-Ta'akhi 2004).

The KRG, Turkey and Iran

The primary international dynamics which affect the cooperative external relations of the KRG are the periodic artillery strikes, air raids and cross-border incursions by the Turkish Armed Forces (*Türk Silahlı Kuvvetleri*/TSK) and Iranian Revolutionary Guard (*Sepāh*) since the resumption of armed struggle by the PKK and the formation of its Iranian auxiliary Party for a Free Life in Kurdistan (*Partiya Jiyana Azad a Kurdistanê*/PJAK) in 2004. These are partially driven by the presence of PKK and PJAK encampments in the Qandil mountain range between Zakho in Dohuk and Qanqil in Erbil, through which they have established an informal zone of control. Further, since concluding an agreement with the former regime in 1996, Turkish forces have maintained several installations inside the boundaries of Dohuk province, including a base at al-Amadiya, a tank depot and a military airstrip at Bamernê in Zakho subdistrict (Stansfield *et al.* 2007: 4–5; Knights 2008: 24). Beginning in 1997, Ankara had introduced a moratorium on direct offensive actions or incursions into the territory of northern Iraq. However, between December 2007 and February 2008 the TSK pursued a two-month air campaign followed by an eight-day land operation in Zab in retaliation against PKK attacks in Şirna and Hakkari provinces in October, which killed nearly 30 troops (Jenkins 2008). These were reportedly successful in temporarily suppressing PKK activities, but failed to effectively curtail the insurgency. In addition, evidence exists of intelligence sharing and coordinated operations between Turkish and Iranian forces (Barkey 2009: 6). Together these have continued to result in the destruction of land and property, civilian deaths and displacement.

One of the most significant events to have affected KRG–Iran relations was the September 2007 incident in which a US commando unit arrested Kermanshah provincial government representative Mahmoud Farhadi during a visit to Sulaymaniyah as part of a trade delegation, on the suspicion that he was an operative of the Iranian Revolutionary Guard Corps (Quds Force). In response, Tehran announced its intention to close each of its border crossings with Iraq until its citizen was released. Iraqi media reported that the border closures resulted in a drastic increase in market prices of imported Iranian foodstuffs and primary goods, as well as threatening the livelihoods of transporters (Aswat al Iraq 2007).

Subregional cooperation

The process of integration between the KRG provinces and their neighbours began in the years immediately prior to the Iraq War. After 2003 this development was further stimulated by a unique situation in which provincial governments in Iraq were able to pursue greater initiative in conducting political and economic relations than ever before. While these policies have often evolved as a pragmatic means of gaining access to necessary resources in circumstances of deprivation, it has been bolstered in some cases by previously existing associations and dependencies.

KRG and Syria

Diplomatic interactions between KRG representatives and the Syrian government date to the period long preceding the March 2003 coalition invasion. Given the origins of the YNK in Damascus in June 1975 and its subsequent hosting by the Syrian Ba'athists as a strategy of undermining their rivals in Baghdad (Lowe 2006a: 301–302), state visits were often conducted to promote ideological solidarity (*Kurdistani Nuwe* 2001). In October 2002, during a delegation to Syria by YNK officials led by Prime Minister Barham Ahmed Saleh, a meeting was held with the heads of the economics ministry and the national chamber of commerce in Damascus. The discussion focused on inviting Syrian companies to support village rehabilitation and to provide construction and health services in the KRG under the auspices of the UN Resolution 986 Oil-for-Food Programme (Agence France Presse 2002). It was also reported that a policy had been introduced in the previous month, for unrestricted travel for Syrian traders to the KRG. However, there is little evidence that these plans were actually brought to fruition. High-level KRG–Syrian contacts conducted by both PDK and YNK leaderships in the following months concentrated upon their respective positions regarding the impending US invasion of Iraq, as well as assuaging concerns for its potential encouragement of Kurdish aspirations for independence. Thus, the development of more substantial cooperation between neighbouring polities has been prevented by wartime security practices, periodically unstable conditions in Syrian Kurdistan and the consequent sealing of the border between Al-Hasakah and Dohuk governorates.

The KRG and provinces of Turkey

Turkey has gradually evolved into the KRG's leading trade partner over the past decade, in spite of serious persisting security-related disagreements between Ankara and Erbil. As of 2007, roughly 70 per cent of all private and state contracts concluded by the KRG were with Turkish companies, while Turkish goods are prevalent in Erbil retail shops due to exports at a value of $5 billion (Karlsson 2009). Yet the US observers have asserted that the Anatolia region has largely been excluded from these developments. Cross-border commerce has largely been dominated by companies with ties to Ankara-based political and national security elites, while few provincial firms are active in investment in northern Iraq or have employed local labour in construction projects (Phillips 2009: 13).

There is evidence that this condition has begun to change, particularly due to increasing economic cooperation between the KRG and Diyarbakır province, which is traditionally regarded as the political centre of Turkish Kurdistan. The first major contact was initiated during September 2003, when a group of industry and trade officials from Erbil, Dohuk and Sulaymaniah participated in the Middle East 2003: Second International Industrial Fair, and engaged with their counterparts in Diyarbakır on pending bids for reconstruction projects (*Turkish Daily News* 2003). In October 2005, a delegation of 350 officials representing the chambers of commerce of the three KRG provinces and Kirkuk attended a seven-day international trade fair in response to a formal invitation from the Turkish government (*Khabat* 2005). On 15 May 2008, a cooperation protocol was signed between the Chambers of Commerce and Industry of Erbil, Dohuk and Diyarbakır to improve conditions for Turkish business activity and foreign investment in the KRG (Anatolia News Agency 2008). Turkish media described these diplomatic activities as forming a 'strategic triangle' between provincial capitals (Internet Haber 2008). According to statements by the chairman of the Diyarbakır Chamber of Commerce, Mehmet Kaya, the protocol was necessary to reverse the decline in Turkish–Iraqi trade as a result of bilateral tensions since 2005, as well as to take advantage of recent advances in the Diyarbakır construction, marble and foodstuff sectors (ibid.).

In spring 2009, a second protocol for the expansion of economic cooperation was signed between the Erbil and Diyarbakır Chambers of Commerce, followed by a delegation to attend the Erbil Regional Countries Trade Fair held from 28 April to 2 May (*Kurdish Globe* 2009). The event profiled products and technologies from several major regional economic sectors, including agriculture and food processing, clothing, furniture and building and construction (Pyramids International 2009).[3]

The industrial leaders of Dohuk have also pursued commercial diplomacy in Adana province on the Mediterranean coast, where an international business fair was held in March 2008.[4] In Malatya province, immediately west of Diyarbakır, the deputy chair of the Chamber of Commerce and an Iraqi business group met with their Turkish counterparts in July to extend invitations to invest in Iraq in order to aid post-war reconstruction, and to participate in a Dohuk electronics fair to be held the following month (UPI Energy 2008a; Anatolia News Agency 2008).

A major international trade fair held in Gaziantep on 9–12 October 2008 featured products from 150 regional companies, and was attended by a delegation from the Sulaymaniyah Chamber of Industry and Commerce as part of a series of Turkish business engagements initially planned for late summer. In June 2009, the Erbil Chamber of Industry and Commerce sought to expand its Turkish associations by inviting officials from Adana to address the decline in national production of fruits and vegetables, by increasing imports from the produce sector in south central Turkey (Anatolia News Agency 2009). In October the representatives of Hakkâri and Batman provinces in the Grand National Assembly of Turkey (*Türkiye Büyük Millet Meclisi*) and the head of the Ankara-based Yüksel construction company led an official delegation to Erbil to conduct talks with DFR director Falah Mustafa Bakir and the KRG deputy prime minister. Another meeting in the spring of 2010 initiated discussions with representatives of Hakkâri regarding the construction of a new border crossing between Southeast Anatolia and the KRG, which would be assisted by the Chamber of Commerce (Aswat al Iraq 2010). These contacts were intended as part of a policy to further facilitate trade and investment in the region.

The KRG and provinces of Iran

While Iran has received much attention in recent years regarding its influence and suspected interference in post-Ba'ath Iraq, its geographic position has also made it a hub of increased economic cooperation between subregions of the Near East. In particular, those provinces that comprise the southwestern frontier of the Caucasus region (Eastern Kurdistan and Southern Azerbaijan) are both heavily populated (a total of over 13,000,000 people) and contain major agricultural, industrial processing and manufacturing centres, which by 2005 constituted over 13 per cent of Iran's national GDP (Ismailov and Papava 2006: 71–74). The recent establishment of formal trade relations and infrastructural ties between Erbil and West Azerbaijan exemplifies this trend. A particularly important dimension of this process has been the continuance of commercial diplomacy despite recurrent security problems in the KRG–Iranian border areas.

In January and March 2005, the commerce department and International Fairs Company of West Azerbaijan organised an exhibition in Dohuk, while the governor general of the province visited both Dohuk and Erbil to arrange labour visits for engineers and plan sales of electrical power to the KRG (Mehr News Agency 2005; IPR Strategic Business Information Database 2008). The trend accelerated on 15 June 2006, when Tehran officially recognised the Haji Omaran International Border Crossing as the second major transit point (next to Khosrawi/Al-Muntheria) between Iran and Iraq (Radio Free Europe/Radio Liberty 2006). The crossing contains several important administrative structures, including a customs office, a tourism visa and stay department, a centre for residence and travel and a foodstuff inspection unit (*Khabat* 2007). This decision was followed by the initiation of a project to provide electrical power supplies to communities within the border zone that had been deprived of regular services (*Kurdish Globe* 2006a). In September a negotiating team – including the Erbil governor, Nawzad Hazdi, and the governor of Choman district – signed an agreement with Iranian officials in Piranshahr county (shahrestān) to provide electricity for a total of 400 village residences in Haji Omaran subdistrict (*Kurdish Globe* 2006b). During October 2006 an additional meeting was convened between officials of the KRG Ministry of Electricity, the accounting manager of Haji Omaran township and the governor of East Azerbaijan province regarding integrating Erbil into the northwest Iranian power grid. The KRG provided the equivalent of $455,000 to finance the purchase and operation of the local power plant, which was completed within a few months.

In April 2008, provincial government officials of Erbil and West Azerbaijan signed a series of trade and anti-smuggling agreements. A ceremony was later held to commemorate the opening of the Haji Omaran-Tamarchin border gate and announce its conversion from an informal marketplace to an officially recognised trade zone (Soma 2008). From 27–31 May, the Third Iranian Trade Exhibition and Product Fair was held at the Erbil International Fairground, and was jointly sponsored by the Erbil Chamber of Commerce, the KRG Ministry of Trade and the West Azerbaijan International Exhibition Company (Kurdistan Regional Government 2008; Murad 2008; UPI Energy 2008b). Over 160 Iranian firms from the construction, food processing and agricultural sectors participated and concluded contracts with KRG trade representatives. Most significantly, the convention was held despite the concurrent shelling and incursion by Iranian security forces into Haji Omaran in pursuit of PJAK insurgents. In November of the same year, a five-day exhibition coordinated by the West Azerbaijan Chamber of Commerce was held in Dohuk to promote increased investment by Iranian state-owned firms in the province (Thai Press Reports 2008).

On 5 August 2008, an official agreement was concluded between KRG and Iranian officials to reopen the Haji Omaran border point after its closure due to security incidents earlier in the year. The KRG-licensed Federal and Iranian Nil Cheshm Gustar transportation companies later began regular bus services through the border gate (Khidir 2008; *Kurdish Globe* 2008). On the same day, a new bus terminal linking Urmia, the provincial capital of West Azerbaijan and Erbil was inaugurated in a public ceremony at Piranshahr (Islamic Republic News Agency 2008). The deputy governor of West Azerbaijan province announced additional plans to introduce commercial air travel between the provincial capitals of Urmia and Erbil, which commenced in February 2010 (PUK-media 2010). These operations were generally expected to increase cross-border trade activity, which according to KRG Ministry of Trade statistics had already reached a total of $1 billion in 2007 (Fars News Agency 2008b). On 3–6 September, managers of the Erbil postal and communications departments met with the West Azerbaijan deputy governor general of political and security affairs to initiate cooperation in delivery services and conclude an agreement on a common postal code system and mail exchange (Vision TV of Islamic Republic of Iran 2009). In November, Sulaymaiyah representatives and the governor of Sardasht in West Azerbaijan conducted a meeting at the Kileh market near the international boundary (described as the main historic trade route into Iraqi Kurdistan) on its conversion into an official crossing (Vision TV of Islamic Republic of Iran 2008).

The establishment of the Haji Omaran Customs Complex, which was formally recognised in April 2008, has also facilitated the rapid expansion of commercial exchange, official traffic and tourism between the KRG and Iran (AK

News 2010). As a result, bilateral trade has increased by a reported 70 per cent, contributing to an overall trade volume of $4.5 billion between Iraq and Iran in 2009. An additionally significant customs and transit facility directly adjacent to Haji Omaran is the Tamarchin terminal and checkpoint located in Piranshahr, which was officially inaugurated on 15 April 2008 (Vision TV 2008a). The opening ceremony featured the signing of an agreement by the governors of Erbil and West Azerbaijan, which included provisions for cooperation in transportation of goods, increasing exports, imports and passenger exchange, construction of border markets, prevention of smuggling and education and health services. This was followed by a stated commitment by the West Azerbaijan governor, General Rahim Qorbani, to provide development assistance and poverty relief to Erbil (Vision TV 2008b). During November additional agreements were concluded which eliminated visa requirements for Iranian citizens and customs duties for road transportation (Fars News Agency 2008a). In June 2009, a seven-point memorandum was signed by the KRG and West Azerbaijan customs departments, which initiated a plan to upgrade the Tamarchin facility (Vision TV 2009). Finally, the KRG leadership has also pursued integration efforts at the Bashmakh border point with Kordestan province. In March 2010, a meeting was held between Kordestan Governor-General Esmail Najjar and KRG Deputy Prime Minister Salih to discuss the establishment of a joint industrial zone to promote enhanced ties (Press TV 2010)

The most recent efforts at expanding the economic relations of the KRG have penetrated into northern and central Iran, beyond the contiguous areas populated by the Iranian Kurdish minority. In September 2009 KRG Trade Minister Abubkair Ali received a delegation from Mazandaran province to discuss increasing the volume of Iraq–Iran commercial exchange, as well as to arrange a fair and plans for establishing a trade centre in the provincial capital (Kurdistan Ministry of Trade 2009). In April 2010 this was reciprocated by a meeting of industrial and mining experts in Amol to discuss measures for increasing the province's comparatively marginal level of trade with the KRG (Thai Press Reports 2010). Also in April, the presidents of Erbil and Isfahan Chambers of Commerce, Jalil al-Khayyat and Mahmoud Eslamian, concluded an agreement on increasing trade and commercial exchange. Al-Khayyat later led a visit to the Mobarakeh Steel Complex (the largest national heavy metals facility) with his Dohuk and Sulaymaniyah counterparts, to discuss information sharing in production and transport between Iran and the KRG (Fars News Agency 2010a; Right Vision News 2010).

One of the earliest developments in commercial diplomacy between Southern and Eastern Kurdistan dates to May 2002, when a YNK trade delegation composed of representatives of the industry and finance ministries and the head of the Sulaymaniyah cigarette factory made an official visit to the capital city of Sanandaj in central Kordestan province. The visit focused upon preparations for an upcoming trade fair featuring local firms to be held in Sulaymaniyah, and resulted in the signing of agreements to facilitate transit through the border point at Bashmakh in Penjwin district (*Kurdistani Nuwe* 2002a). In subsequent years these would serve as a foundation for a major commercial and transportation route between provinces. Another promising interaction took place later the same month, in which the governors of Sulaymaniyah and Kirkuk and directors of the finance and security ministries convened a meeting with officials from Kermanshah to discuss trade facilitation, customs and border controls and increased cooperation in the fields of sports, culture and education (*Kurdistani Nuwe* 2002b). Continued contacts with industrial leaders of Sanandaj culminated in December 2003 with the opening of an Iranian trade centre in Sulaymaniyah for the sale of locally produced goods. The centre was endorsed by YNK Secretary General Jalal Talabani and governor of Kordestan Asadullah Razani as emblematic of the strong 'cultural, commercial and political relations' between the KRG and Iran, as well as of the potential for expansion of regional commerce and trade (*Kurdistani Nuwe* 2003).

Bilateral relations between Sulaymaniyah and Kemanshah were further consolidated by an August 2006 engagement that established administrative committees to coordinate customs, service projects, fuel, education and health policies, and negotiated the importation of electrical power from Iran. An agreement was signed by the respective provincial governors on cooperation in a wide range of policy areas, including services, educational exchanges between provincial universities and transport of Iranian fuel to the KRG via Basra in southern Iraq, which was also observed by the governors of Erbil and Kirkuk (KurdSat 2006a, 2006b). As part of a draft memorandum of understanding to counter smuggling, the export of oil products to Sulaymaniyah was finalised during a reciprocal visit to Kermanshah in September (IPR Strategic Business Information Database 2006). Under this agreement, shipments of kerosene to Sulaymaniyah totalling 30,000 litres commenced in December for a three-month period, in order to circumvent the shortage of adequate supplies from Turkey and the Al-Bayji refinery in Kirkuk (Agence France Presse 2006; KurdSat TV 2006c).

The border-crossing point at Bashmakh–Marivan was inaugurated as an official international point of entry on 26 July 2007, and was endorsed by Iranian President Mahmoud Ahmadinejad as a means to facilitate importation of nationally produced goods into Sulaymaniyah.[5] In addition, Kermanshah Governor Dana Ahmad Majid suggested that it would improve regulation of trade and prevent the passage of expired produce and foodstuffs to markets in the KRG. In May 2010, Kordestan Governor Najjar announced the recent signing of several memoranda of understanding with Sulaymaniyah on measures to promote commercial relations, including a 24-hour trade exchange at Bashmakh–Marivan, establishment of a joint industrial town, exhibitions and construction of border bridges and infrastructure (Fars News Agency 2010b). The Iranian Katoush Tunnel and Water Works Construction Company has been contracted to launch the Bashmakh Bridge project, which is pending completion (Katoush Construction 2007).

An additional meeting was held in June 2010 between the head of the Sulaymaniyah provincial power department and the managing director of Kordestan Power Distribution Company, Mohammad Najafian. An agreement was announced to increase electricity supplies to Bashmakh from 240 to 500 kilowatts per hour (Fars News Agency 2010c). In the following week, a major trade exhibition was held in Sulaymaniyah that reportedly hosted 185 firms from 21 Iranian provinces. The director of the Kordestan branch of the Telecommunications Company of Iran also advertised an agenda to upgrade the KRG communications infrastructure (Fars News Agency 2010d).

Subregional integration patterns

Tables 8.1, 8.2 and 8.3 present a summary of data on cooperative activity between the provincial authorities of the KRG, Turkey and Iran from 2002 to present. These outcomes are also affected by geographic factors such as contiguity or proximity between subdivisions in each country. The results in Table 8.1 indicate that as both the administrative seat of the contemporary KRG and the historic sphere of influence of the Iraqi Kurdish movement, Erbil has played a leading role in establishing cooperative relations with Diyarbakır and the contiguous Iranian province of West Azerbaijan, with the majority of activity concentrated in the latter. This suggests strong motivations to acquire access to the considerable economic resources of Southeast Anatolia and northwest Iran, as well as to capitalise upon the ethnic and cultural affinities between Iraqi and Iranian Kurds.

In Table 8.2, Dohuk province exhibits the most minimal level of participation in subregional interactions, which are equally concentrated in Diyarbakır and West Azerbaijan. These outcomes may be explained by the fact that Dohuk is physically removed from the Iranian provinces that border the KRG, while its subordinate position within the PDK-dominated ruling apparatus may have limited its degree of initiative in cross-border diplomacy. At the same time, the lack of significant cooperation with the contiguous Turkish provinces of Şırnak and Hakkâri, despite the reliance of Dohuk on revenues from commercial transit through the Habur/Ibrahim Khalil border gate at Zakho, may reflect the continued PKK and Turkish security operations on both sides of the border. These have fostered unrest and refugee flows among their mutual domestic populations comparable to the situation in Syria (Phillips 2009: 11; Barkey 2010: 3).

Finally, in Table 8.3, Sulaymaniyah displays the highest level of interaction with Iranian authorities, with the majority of activity concentrated in Kordestan and Kermanshah provinces. This pattern is possibly reflective of the intimate political and security cooperation between the YNK leadership and Iranian government that dates to the mid-1990s, as well as the dependence of the provincial capital on Iranian electrical power supplies (Bahcheli and Fragiskatos 2008: 69; Cagaptay 2008: 16).

Table 8.1 Level of subregional integration in Erbil province

Level of integration	*Turkish provinces*					*Iranian provinces*				
	Diyarbakır	*Gaziantep*	*Malatya*	*Adana*	*Hakkâri*	*West Azerbaijan*	*Kordestan*	*Kermanshah*	*Isfahan*	*Mazandaran*
State visits	1	0	0	1	2	4	1	0	1	2
Signed agreements	2	0	0	0	0	6	0	0	1	0
Trade centres and exhibitions	2	1	0	0	0	2	0	0	0	0
Customs checkpoints and border crossings	0	0	0	0	0	4	0	0	0	0
Infrastructural arrangements	0	0	0	0	0	2	1	0	0	0
Total	5	1	0	1	2	17	2	0	2	2

Table 8.2 Level of subregional integration in Dohuk province

Level of integration	*Turkish provinces*					*Iranian provinces*				
	Diyarbakır	*Gaziantep*	*Malatya*	*Adana*	*Hakkâri*	*West Azerbaijan*	*Kordestan*	*Kermanshah*	*Isfahan*	*Mazandaran*
State visits	1	0	1	0	0	1	0	0	1	0
Signed agreements	1	0	0	0	0	0	0	0	0	0
Trade centres and exhibitions	2	0	1	1	0	3	0	0	0	0
Customs checkpoints and border crossings	0	0	0	0	0	0	0	0	0	0
Infrastructural arrangements	0	0	0	0	0	0	0	0	0	0
Total	4	0	2	1	0	4	0	0	1	0

Table 8.3 Level of subregional integration in Sulaymaniyah province

Level of integration	*Turkish provinces*					*Iranian provinces*				
	Diyarbakır	*Gaziantep*	*Malatya*	*Adana*	*Hakkâri*	*West Azerbaijan*	*Kordestan*	*Kermanshah*	*Isfahan*	*Mazandaran*
State visits	1	0	0	0	0	1	3	3	1	0
Signed agreements	0	0	0	0	0	0	7	3	0	0
Trade centres and exhibitions	2	1	0	0	0	0	2	0	0	0
Customs checkpoints and border crossings	0	0	0	0	0	0	3	0	0	0
Infrastructural arrangements	0	0	0	0	0	0	3	1	0	0
Total	3	1	0	0	0	1	18	7	1	0

Conclusion

This study has sought to examine a significant emerging trend in the Near East and Subcaucasus region, in which territories traditionally associated with political and military conflict have gradually begun a process of cross-border integration. External threats posed by national governments may therefore motivate increased cooperation at the subnational level. This suggests a need to move beyond standard geopolitical and ethnic conflict explanations of relations between Iraqi Kurdistan and its neighbours, towards recognising the diplomatic strategies pursued by local governments as a means of gaining access to necessary political and economic resources. In this manner, otherwise small, isolated statelets that are commonly viewed as 'hot spots' of intractable problems may potentially evolve into hubs of productivity. The larger significance is that units that occupy a particularly unusual position in the international system – de jure autonomous yet de facto unrecognised – can become catalysts for change in how neighbouring states conduct business. At the same time, geographic location and levels of domestic and international tensions are shown to have affected the extent of interaction and cooperation between different subnational jurisdictions. Several conclusions may be drawn from the data and analysis presented in the preceding sections. First, despite previous ties and the absence of direct conflict with Damascus, integration with Syria remains unfeasible due to the sensitivity of its own Kurdish situation. Second, despite formal decisions to unify the KRG administrations in recent years, the enduring regional dominance of the PDK and Erbil are represented by its high level of activity with proximate centres of commerce in Northern Kurdistan and to a much greater extent, northwest Iran. Third, the province of Dohuk has been marginalised in the integration process due to its reliance upon transit fees and exposure to border tensions with southeastern Turkey. Finally, the intimate relationship forged in previous years between the YNK and western Iranian officials endures in a more advanced series of mutual agreements and exchanges. As the independent foreign policy agenda of the KRG will proceed as long as it retains its autonomous status, and the conflicts on its frontiers continue to be unresolved, one can only expect the dynamics assessed above to continue into the foreseeable future.

Notes

1 This term describes the wider region encompassing Anatolian Turkey, the upper Euphrates Valley, northern Mesopotamia and northwest Iran, in addition to the former Soviet republics of Georgia, Armenia and Azerbaijan.

2 The term 'Kurdistani' is used here to refer to the evolving national consciousness of Iraqi Kurdistan, represented by the increasing self-identification of citizens of the KRG as 'Kurdistanis' (Stansfield and Ahmedzadeh 2008).

3 Importantly, all import customs in Erbil are waived for the agriculture, food and stationery sectors, while rates for all other industries are limited to 5 per cent (Pyramids International 2009).

4 The head of the Dohuk Chamber of Commerce also stated in an interview that solely representatives from the provincial government were able to attend the event due to security conditions elsewhere in Iraq.

5 The facilities at the Bashmakh POE were built between January 2005 and January 2006 by the Turkish Biltek Construction Company, which was contracted for the project by the US Army Corps of Engineers.

References

Agence France Presse (2002) 'Iraqi Kurds Aim to Build Economic Ties with Syria', 15 October. Lexis Nexis Academic.

—— (2006) 'First Iranian Kerosene Arrives in Iraqi City', 14 December. www.kurdishinstitute.eu/en/info/latest/first-iranian-kerosene-arrives-in-iraqi-city-517.html (accessed 6 June 2010).

AK News (2010) 'Iran Eyeing Second Place in Exchange Volume with Kurdistan', 6 January. www.aknews.com/en/aknews/2/100654 (accessed 4 February 2010).

Al-Ta'akhi (2004) 'Syria Loses Iraq's Kurdish Border Crossing Point', 15 June. Lexis Nexis Academic.

Anatolia News Agency (2008) 'Iraqi Businessmen Call for Turkish Investments', 19 July. Lexis Nexis Academic.

—— (2009) 'Iraqi, Turkish Businessmen Urge Boost in Trading', 24 June. Lexis Nexis Academic.

Associated Press Worldstream (2004) 'Iraqi Kurds Protest Clashes Involving Fellow Kurds in Syria; Demand Kurdish Rights', 18 March.

Aswat al Iraq (2007) 'Prices Increase in Arbil Markets after Iranian Borders' Closure', 24 September.

—— (2010) 'Erbil Governor Discusses with Turkish Officials Opening of New Border Crossing', 26 April.

Bahcheli, Tozun and Fragiskatos, Peter (2008) 'Iraqi Kurdistan: Fending off Uneasy Neighbors', *International Journal of Contemporary Iraqi Studies*, 2 (1): 67–82.

Barkey, Henri J. (2009) 'Preventing Conflict Over Kurdistan', Carnegie Endowment for International Peace. http://carnegieendowment.org/files/preventing_conflict_kurdistan.pdf (accessed 6 June 2010).

—— (2010) 'Turkey's New Engagement in Iraq: Embracing Iraqi Kurdistan', United States Institute of Peace Special Report 237. www.usip.org/files/resources/SR237_Turkey's%20New%20Engagement%20in%20Iraq.pdf (accessed 6 June 2010).

Bonine, Michael E. (2002) 'The Kurds and Kurdistan: A Commentary', *Eurasian Geography and Economics*, 43 (4): 300–304.

Cagaptay, Soner (2008) '360 Degrees from Irbil: The KRG's Views of Its Neighborhood', in Soner Cagaptay (ed.) (2008) *The Future of the Iraqi Kurds*, Washington, DC: Washington Institute for Near East Policy, pp. 12–20.

Chorev, Matan (2007) 'Iraqi Kurdistan: The Internal Dynamics and Statecraft of a Semi-state', *Al Nakhlah: The Fletcher School Online Journal for Issues Related to Southwest Asia and Islamic Civilization*, autumn: 25–35. http://fletcher.tufts.edu/al_nakhlah/archives/Fall2007/Matan_Chorev_AN.pdf (accessed 6 June 2010).

Cornago, Noé (2010) 'On the Normalization of Sub-State Diplomacy', in David Criekemans (ed.) *Regional Sub-State Diplomacy Today*, Leiden: Martinus Nijhoff Publishers, pp. 11–36.

CIA, Office of Current Intelligence (1963) Current Intelligence Memorandum, Subject: Iraqi-Kurdish Rebellion, 13 June. www.c-span.org/PresidentialLibraries/Content/Kennedy/NSF-CO-IRAQ-19630613.pdf (accessed 6 June 2010).

Criekemans, David (2010), 'Introduction', in David Criekemans (ed.) *Regional Sub-State Diplomacy Today*, Leiden: Martinus Nijhoff Publishers, pp. 1–10.

Dahlman, Carl T. (2002) 'The Political Geography of Kurdistan', *Eurasian Geography and Economics*, 43 (4): 271–299.

Fars News Agency (2008a) 'Iran, Iraq Abolish Customs Duties on Road Transportation – agency', 19 November. (accessed 6 June 2010 via Lexis Nexis).

—— (2008b) 'Iran, Iraqi Kurdistan Promote Ties', 21 November. http://english.farsnews.com/newstext.php?nn=8708300930 (accessed 6 June 2010).

—— (2010a) 'Iran Ready to Invest in Iraq's Telecommunication Infrastructure', 28 June. http://english.farsnews.com/newstext.php?nn=8904071093 (accessed 30 June 2010).

—— (2010b) 'Iran Ready to Supply Electricity to Northern Iraq', 23 June. http://english.farsnews.com/newstext.php?nn=8904021492 (accessed 23 June 2010).

—— (2010c) 'Iraq Keen to Use Iran's Experience in Steel Production', 26 April. http://english.farsnews.com/newstext.php?nn=8902061426 (accessed 23 June 2010).

—— (2010d), 'Iranian Official Stresses Expansion of Trade Ties with Iraqi Kurdistan', 10 May. http://english.farsnews.com/newstext.php?nn=8902181264 (accessed 23 June 2010).

Gambil, Gary C. (2004) 'The Kurdish Reawakening in Syria', YASA e.V., Kurdish Centre for Legal Studies & Consultancy. www.yasa-online.org/reports/The_Kurdish_reawakening%20_in_Syria.pdf (accessed 6 June 2010).

Gunter, Michael M. (1993) 'A De Facto Kurdish State in Northern Iraq', *Third World Quarterly*, 14 (2): 295–301.

—— (2008) 'The Permanent and New Realities Facing the Kurdistan Regional Government: Options and Prospects', *Journal of Muslim Minority Affairs*, 28 (2): 237–249.

—— (2010) 'Kurdish–Arab Tensions and Irbil–Baghdad Relations', 26 March. www.jamestown.org/single/?no_cache=1&tx_ttnews%5Btt_news%5D=36197&tx_ttnews%5BbackPid%5D=7&cHash=c28c42af72 (accessed 6 June 2010).

Internet Haber (2008) 'Diyarbakır, Erbil, Dohuk Üçgenii', 16 May. www.internethaber.com/news_detail.php?id=141151 (accessed 9 February 2010).

IPR Strategic Business Information Database (2006) 'Kermanshah Oil Exports to Sulaymaniyah: Overview', 7 September.

Islamic Republic News Agency (2008) 'New Bus Terminal Opened on Iran–Iraq Border', 6 August.

Ismailov, Eldar and Papava, Vladimir (2006) *The Central Caucasus: Essays on Geopolitical Economy*, Stockholm: CA & CC Press.

Jenkins, Gareth (2008) 'A Military Analysis of Turkey's Incursion into Northern Iraq', 7 March. www.jamestown.org/programs/gta/single/?tx_ttnews%5Btt_news%5D=4774&tx_ttnews%5BbackPid%5D=167&no_cache=1 (accessed 6 June 2010).

Karlsson, Ingmar (2009) 'Northern Iraq: A Kurdish Piemonte?'. www.cmes.lu.se/wp-content/uploads/2009/07/northern-iraq-e28093-a-kurdish-piemonte.pdf (accessed 8 February 2010).

Katoush Construction (2007) http://katoushco.com/Current%20Project.htm (accessed 6 June 2010).

*Khabat (*2004) 'Syrian Kurds Reportedly Flee to Iraqi Kurdistan', 11 May, Lexis Nexis Academic.

—— (2005) 'Iraqi Kurdish Delegation Visits International Trade Fair in Turkey', 2 October, Lexis Nexis Academic.

—— (2007) 'Iraqi Kurdish Paper Describes Key Border Point with Iran', 8 March, Lexis Nexis Academic.

Khalil, Lydia (2009) 'Stability in Iraqi Kurdistan: Reality or Mirage?' Saban Center for Middle East Policy, Brookings Institution, Working Paper no. 2. www.brookings.edu/~/media/Files/rc/papers/2009/06_kurdistan_khalil/06_kurdistan_khalil.pdf (accessed 6 June 2010).

Khidhir, Qassim (2008) 'Bus Service Opens Between Hajji Omaran and Iran: Daily Service Begins for Travelers Coming to Erbil or Going to Iran', *The Kurdish Globe*, 14 August. www.kurdishglobe.net/servlet/WritePDFServlet?ID=143 (accessed 8 February 2010).

Knights, Michael (2008) 'Guiding the Kurdish Role in Securing Northern Iraq', in Soner Cagaptay (ed.) *The Future of the Iraqi Kurds*, Washington, DC: Washington Institute for Near East Policy, pp. 21–30.

Kurdish Globe (2006a) 'Electricity to Reach Haji Omaran Border Crossing in Less than 3 Months and a Half', 17 October. www.kurdishglobe.net/servlet/WritePDFServlet?ID=15 (accessed 6 June 2010).

—— (2006b) 'KRG Team Visits Iran to Secure Electricity Supply', 11 September. www.kurdishglobe.net/displayArticle.jsp?id=1780FA949F8A25DF71324B634D64388 (accessed 6 June 2010).

—— (2008) 'Erbil and Western Azerbaijan Province to Cooperate: Historic Trade Relations Further the Region Ties to Iran's Western Province', 11 September. www.kurdishglobe.net/servlet/WritePDFServlet?ID=148 (accessed 4 February 2010).

—— (2009) 'Turkey's Trade in Iraq Amounted to 6 Billion USD in 2008', 2 May. www.kurdishglobe.net/displayArticle.jsp?id=18F90A249EF76D2674A343447D64BF37 (accessed 8 February 2010).

Kurdistan Democratic Party-Iraq (2008) 'Organization'. http://www.kdp.se (accessed 6 June 2010).

Kurdistan Ministry of Trade (2009) 'An Iranian Delegation was Received by the KRG Acting Minister of Trade'. http://kurdistanmot.com/en/chalaki/index.php?page=2 (accessed 6 June 2010).

Kurdistan Regional Government (2008) 'Kurdistan Region Enters Trade Show Season', 12 May. http://krg.org/articles/detail.asp?smap=02010100&lngnr=12&rnr=223&anr=24177 (accessed 6 June 2010).

—— (2009a) 'The Department of Foreign Relations: Kurdistan Regional Government', 7 December. www.krg.org/articles/detail.asp?lngnr=12&smap=04080000&rnr=267&anr=19906 (accessed 6 June 2010).

—— (2009b) Official Order No: 143, 25 January. www.krg.org/uploads/documents/Official_order_25_Jan_09__2009_06_04_h19m0s19.pdf (accessed 6 June 2010).

Kurdistani Nuwe (2001) 'Kurdish PUK Official in Syria, Says His Party Opposes "Plots" Against Iraq', 29 December, Lexis Nexis Academic.

—— (2002a) 'Iraq: Iranian Trade Fair to be Held in Sulaymaniyah 18 May', 11 May, Lexis Nexis Academic.

—— (2002b) 'Iraqi Kurdish, Iranian Delegations, Discuss Drug Smuggling, Cooperation', 27 May, Lexis Nexis Academic.

—— (2003) 'Iranian Trade Centre Opened in Iraqi Kurdish City of Sulaymaniyah', 8 December, Lexis Nexis Academic.

—— (2004) 'Iraqi Kurdistan Parliament Condemns Attacks on Kurds in Syria', 18 March, Lexis Nexis Academic.

KurdSat TV (2004) 'Iraqi Kurdish Students Protest Against Attacks on Kurds in Syria', 16 March, Lexis Nexis Academic.

—— (2006a) 'Iraq's Sulaymaniyah, Iranian Kermanshah Delegations Discuss Cooperation', 18 August, Lexis Nexis Academic.

—— (2006b) 'Iraqi Kurdish, Iranian Officials Sign Agreement on Commercial, Education Ties', 20 August, Lexis Nexis Academic.

—— (2006c) 'Sulaymaniyah Governorate is to Receive Iranian Fuel', 14 December, Lexis Nexis Academic.

KurdWatch (2009) 'The Al-Qamishli Uprising: The Beginning of a "New Era" for Syrian Kurds?'. www.internaldisplacement.org/8025708F004CE90B/(httpDocuments)/17DB441867D20170C12577280033ECCB/$file/kurdwatch_qamischli_en.pdf (accessed 6 June 2010).

Lowe, Robert (2006a) 'Kurdish Nationalism in Syria', in Mohammed M.A Ahmed and Michael Gunter (eds) *The Evolution of Kurdish Nationalism*, Costa Mesa, CA: Mazda Publishers, pp. 287–308.

—— (2006b) 'The Syrian Kurds: A People Discovered', Chatham House Middle East Programme. www.chathamhouse.org.uk/files/3297_bpsyriankurds.pdf (accessed 6 June 2010).

Mehr News Agency (2005) 'Iran to Hold Specialized Exhibition in Dahuk of Iraq', 8 January. www.mehrnews.com/en/NewsDetail.aspx?NewsID=146557 (accessed 6 June 2010).

MERIP Reports (1974) 'Iraq and Kurdish Autonomy', no. 27, pp. 26–30.

Murad, Ali S. (2008) 'Iran Finds Two Methods of Entrance into Kurdistan', *Kurdish Globe*, 6 June. www.kurdishglobe.net/displayArticle.jsp?id=541B476D9746E24C3349F0732DC3CC72 (accessed 4 February 2010).

Natali, Denise (2005) *The Kurds and the State: Evolving National Identity in Iraq, Turkey, and Iran*, Syracuse, NY: Syracuse University Press.

O'Leary, Brendan and Salih, Khaled (2005) 'The Denial, Resurrection and Affirmation of Kurdistan', in Brendan O'Leary, John McGarry and Khaled Salih (eds) *The Future of Kurdistan in Iraq*, Philadelphia, PA: University of Pennsylvania Press, pp. 3–46.

—— (2004) *Trapped Between the Map and Reality: Geography and Perceptions of Kurdistan*, New York, NY: Routledge.

Patriotic Union of Kurdistan (2008) 'About the YNK: Structure'. www.YNK.org/web/htm/about/struct.html (accessed 6 June 2010).

Philips, David L. (2009) *Confidence Building Between Turks and Iraqi Kurds*, Atlantic Council of the United States. www.acus.org/files/publication_pdfs/65/Confidence-BuildingBetweenTurksandIraqiKurds.pdf (accessed 6 June 2010).

Press TV (2010) 'Iran, Iraq to Build Joint Industrial Town', 30 March. www.presstv.ir/detail.aspx?id=122014§ionid=3510213 (accessed 6 June 2010).

PUKmedia (2010) '1st Iranian Plane Landed in Iraqi Kurdistan', 28 February. http://pukmedia.com/english/index.php?option=com_content&view=article&id=1516:1st-iranian-plane-landed-in-iraqi-kurdistan&catid=1:economy&Itemid=389 (accessed 6 June 2010).

Pyramids International (2009) Regional Countries Trade Fair, 28 April–2 May. www.pyramidsfaireg.com/exhibitions_l.htm (accessed 9 February 2010).

Radio Free Europe/Radio Liberty Newsline (2006) 'Formal Border Crossing Opened Between Iraq and Iran in Kurdistan'. www.hri.org/news/balkans/rferl/2006/06-06-16.rferl.html#42 (accessed 6 June 2010).

Right Vision News (2010) 'Iran: Isfahan and Iraqi Kurdistan to Boost Trade Exchange', 23 April, Lexis Nexis Academic.

Romano, David (2006) *The Kurdish Nationalist Movement: Opportunity, Mobilization and Identity*, Cambridge, MA: Cambridge University Press.

Soma (2008) 'Haji Omaran open for trade', *Soma* 39, April 29–May 8. http://soma-digest.com/PDFs/soma-digest-39.pdf (accessed 6 June 2010).

Stansfield, Gareth (2003a) 'The Kurdish Dilemma: The Golden Age Threatened', in Toby Dodge and Steven Simon (eds) *Iraq at the Crossroads: State and Society in the Shadow of Regime Change*, Oxford: Oxford University Press, pp. 131–148.

—— (2003b) *Iraqi Kurdistan: Political Development and Emerging Democracy*, London and New York, NY: Routledge Curzon.

—— (2005) 'Governing Kurdistan: The Strengths of Division', in Brendan O'Leary, John McGarry and Khaled Salih (eds) *The Future of Kurdistan in Iraq*, Philadelphia, PA: University of Pennsylvania Press, pp. 195–215.

Stansfield, Gareth and Ahmadzadeh, Hashem (2008) 'Kurds or Kurdistanis? Conceptualizing Regionalism in the North of Iraq', in Reidar Visser and Gareth Stansfield (eds) *An Iraq of its Regions: Cornerstones of a Federal Democracy?*, New York, NY: Columbia University Press, pp. 123–150.

Stansfield, Gareth and Anderson, Liam (2009) 'Kurds in Iraq: The Struggle between Baghdad and Erbil', *Middle East Policy*, 16 (1): 134–145.

Stansfield, Gareth and Resool, Shorsh Haji (2006) 'The Tortured Resurgence of Kurdish Nationalism in Iraq, 1975–1991', in Mohammed Ahmed and Michael Gunter (eds) *The Evolution of Kurdish Nationalism*, Costa Mesa, CA: Mazda Publishers, pp. 98–122.

Stansfield, Gareth, Lowe, Robert and Ahmadzadeh, Hashem (2007) 'The Kurdish Policy Imperative', Chatham House Middle East Programme. www.chathamhouse.org.uk/files/10685_bp1207kurds.pdf (accessed 6 June 2010).

Tejel, Jordi (2009) *Syria's Kurds: History, Politics and Society*, New York, NY: Routledge.

Thai Press Reports (2010) 'Iran, Iraqi Kurdistan to Boost Trade Exchanges', 20 April. http://english.farsnews.com/newstext.php?nn=8901301380 (accessed 6 June 2010).

Turkish Daily News (2003) 'Iraqi Businessmen Show Great Interest in Fair to be Held in Diyarbakir', 24 September. www.hurriyetdailynews.com/default.aspx?pageid=438&n=iraqi-businessmen-show-great-interest-in-fair-to-be-held-in-diyarbakir-2003-09-24 (accessed 6 June 2010).

United Press International Energy (2008a) 'Iran Reaches Trade Deal with Iraq', 18 April.

—— (2008b) 'Iraqi Delegates Prepare for Business Expo', 19 March. www.upi.com/Top_News/Special/2008/03/19/Iraqi-delegates-prepare-for-business-expo/UPI-12861205975314 (accessed 6 June 2010).

Vision TV of Islamic Republic of Iran (2008) 'New Border Checkpoint Opens Between Iran, Iraq', 16 April, Lexis Nexis Academic.

—— (2009) 'Iran's West Azerbayjan, Iraqi Kurdistan Customs Sign Memo', 26 June, Lexis Nexis Academic.

Zhigalina, Olga (2003) 'The Kurds of Western Asia: Geopolitics Today', *Central Asia-Caucasus Journal*, 1 (19): 18–22.

9 Prospects of inclusive peace, perception of players and stakes involved in post-9/11 Afghanistan

Debidatta Aurobinda Mahapatra

Introduction

This chapter focuses on post-9/11 Afghanistan, where there are no apparent Cold War era dynamics and associated conflict paradigms; however, the instability in the war-ravaged strategic region, its ramifications and the efforts of national, regional and international players to foster peace and stability in the region are crucial for study from a conflict and peace perspective. The location of the region as a crossroad of cultures and civilisations, as well as the resources and interests of players, have enhanced the importance of the region as a crucible for international peace and security. While the earlier conflicts in the region, whether during the Cold War or pre-Cold War eras, were mostly confined to empires, such as the British or Russian empires, or between the forces of ideology or internecine rivalry, post-9/11 circumstances present a scenario which has global ramifications. The task of international forces that are mandated to establish stability and order in Afghanistan and craft peace in a new cooperative framework without radicalism, remains arduous.

The conflict in Afghanistan is perhaps one of the most fragile ones, with high tangible and intangible costs. Fragile state apparatus plagued by corruption and criminalisation further make the task of conflict transformation a difficult one. Instead of weakening of fundamentalist forces, the recent trends indicate that these forces thrive, despite some success in eliminating sections of them, and despite efforts to wedge a dividing line between radical and moderate Taliban. As the scheduled departure of the International Security Assistance Force (ISAF) draws near, there are renewed efforts to eliminate radical elements amidst stiff resistance. While players and negotiators have divergent perceptions about how to craft peace, and while some of them advocate a regional format for conflict transformation in the region, the intransigence of the parties has made the solution a difficult goal. The Taliban, referred to as Talibjan as a newly constructed mechanism to draw the radical group into the orbit of the peace process, has not moderated its format of engagement as it clings to its old policies. However, the attempts at London and Kabul conferences in 2010 held promise for conflict resolution. The chapter argues, however, that the complexities involved in the peace process necessitate the urgency of sustained efforts of regional and international powers towards gradual transformation of conflict in Afghanistan.

Conflict in brief

The scope of the chapter does not necessitate an elaborate study of the history of Afghanistan, as its major thrust is on the current peace process and prospects of its success. There is vast literature on the conflict in Afghanistan (Wilber 1956; George 1990; Schneierson 1986; Klass 1987; Mukherjee 1984; Gall 1988). This section aims at providing a brief description of the Afghanistan conflict in order to depict the complicated nature of the conflict and how, in this background, the peace process has to confront various challenges resurfacing from the past. The location of Afghanistan as a geo-strategic link between the Middle East, Central Asia and South Asia, its empire experience from Alexander the Great, and later from the Mauryas, Genghis Khan and others made this region crucial to the politics of Eurasia. From Afghanistan various local dynasties such as Safavids, Ghaznavids, Timurids and Ghorids had established their empires and spread to other regions. However, the current borders of Afghanistan state emerged towards the end of the nineteenth century during the period of King Abdur Rahman, who made attempts towards state-building (Kakar 1979: 114). The present border of Afghanistan towards the south with Pakistan was demarcated in 1893 in what is famously called the Durand Line, amidst contentions between British India and Afghanistan. The last dynasty that ruled the country in its present shape was the Durrani dynasty, with King Zahir Shah as the last monarch.

The conflict in Afghanistan since its emergence as a buffer state in 1919 in the aftermath of its independence from a brief British rule under the Treaty of Rawalpindi passed through multiple phases of turmoil. The great game in the form of Anglo-Russian rivalry, or the turbulent British–Afghan relations and ensuing wars in 1839–1842, 1878–1880 and 1919, led to the perception that colonialism or subordination is alien to the soil of Afghanistan and its culture. According to Louis Dupree, the noted historian of Afghanistan, four factors contributed to the British disaster in Afghanistan: (1) the occupation of Afghan territory by foreign troops; (2) selecting an unpopular ruler for the throne; (3) the harsh acts of the British-supported Afghans against their local enemies; and (4) the reduction of the subsidies paid to the tribal chiefs by British political agents (Bearden 2001: 18). The Soviet aim to control the territory by invading it in 1979 ended in disaster within the span of a decade. Though Afghanistan was poised to be a buffer state, and to that effect it signed a treaty on Neutrality and Mutual Non-Aggression with the Soviet Union in 1931, further extended in 1955, its strategic location and common border with the Soviet Union pushed Afghanistan to be embroiled in Cold War politics, thus affecting its traditional policy of isolationism (Ramazani 1958: 144).

The diverse character of Afghan society, its warring tribes and various ethnic communities, propped up by either of the great powers during the Cold War ensured that the conflict and unstable nature of the Afghan society continue. Though Afghanistan remained unstable throughout the 1970s,[1] it was the seizure of power in Kabul by Nur Mohammed Taraki that changed the equation in the region, as the involvement of super powers appeared imminent. The kidnapping and later killing of the US Ambassador to Kabul, Adolph Dubs, in February 1979 heightened superpower rivalry in the region. The Soviet invasion in 1979 propelled the country towards chaos that continued even after the end of the Cold War. The invasion propelled the US to launch Operation Cyclone by recruiting, financing and arming mujahideen, with the support of Pakistan. The rise of the mujahideen to fight the Soviet forces, their role after the Soviet withdrawal and very fractious nature of polity continue to shape Afghanistan even to this day.

Pakistan's interest in Afghanistan has been a factor since the partition of the Indian subcontinent and emergence of India and Pakistan as independent states in 1947. After the independence of Pakistan, Afghanistan staked its claim to the region across the Durand Line (largely the current Pakistan province of Khyber Pakhtunkhwa, previously called North West Frontier Province), a region inhabited by majority Pashtuns. Pakistan strongly resisted this attempt and adopted retaliatory measures such as cutting off the supply route from Karachi to Kabul through the Khyber Pass. It also cut off the importation of petroleum products into Afghanistan for about three months in 1950 by closing the transit route. Under these circumstances, and in dire need of petroleum, Afghanistan relaxed its traditional cautious and suspicious attitude towards its northern neighbour, the Soviet Union (Ramazani 1958: 146). Pakistan used the Pashtun card to gain strategic depth in the region, as there are more Pashtuns in Pakistan than in Afghanistan.[2] When, after the Soviet withdrawal, there were violent clashes between the various ethnic groups represented largely by the United National Front and the Taliban, Pakistan supported the Pashtun Taliban,[3] led by Mullah Omar. The Taliban captured Kabul in 1996. While India followed a wait-and-see policy, Pakistan used the Afghanistan situation to its advantage. Particularly after the disturbances in the Indian part of Kashmir in the late 1980s, Pakistan's interests in Afghanistan were renewed with the objective of using it to support militancy in Kashmir, which became 'the prime mover behind Pakistan's Afghan policy and its support to the Taliban' (Rashid 2000: 186). According to Patricia Gossman (2001: 11), since 1990 the intelligence agency of Pakistan – Inter Services Intelligence (ISI) – has fought a covert war on two fronts: one in Afghanistan and the other in Kashmir, and of the two, Kashmir has always taken precedence.

After the departure of the Soviet forces in 1989, the Najibullah government in Kabul was toppled within a few years. The Peshawar Accord on a peace and power-sharing agreement in 1992 could not last long due to internecine rivalries and involvement of the regional rivals Pakistan and Iran, and other players like Saudi Arabia, in supporting various rival groups. Though the accord established the Islamic state of Afghanistan, it received strong opposition from the Pashtun Hezb-e-Islmai led by Gulbuddin Hekmatyar and supported by Pakistan.

According to Amin Saikal (2006: 352), 'Had it not been for the ISI's logistic support and supply of a large number of rockets, Hekmatyar's forces would not have been able to target and destroy half of Kabul.' The Islamabad Accord of 1993, which appointed Hekmatyar as prime minister, failed to broker peace; similarly, the Jalalabad Accord, which urged the militias to give up arms, failed. The year 1993 witnessed violent clashes between the rival forces. While Iran supported the Shia Hazara Hezb-i Wahdat forces of Abdul Ali Mazari as a counter to Sunni forces of Hekmatyar, Saudi Arabia supported the Wahhabite Abdul Rasul Sayyaf and his Ittihad-i Islami faction (Human Rights Watch 2005). The rise of Pashtun-dominated Taliban (plural of Talib, literally meaning student or seeker) in 1994 from Kandahar, initially as a religious force against corruption and criminalisation of politics, changed the equation in the region. Within two years, the Taliban emerged as the most powerful force and captured Kabul in 1996.

However, besides the Taliban's orthodox rule, it was its link with Al Qaeda, and its support of the latter's objective of a global jihad that raised international concern over its rule in Afghanistan, corroborated in a series of attacks on US embassies in Kenya and Tanzania in 1998, and later the 2001 attacks in the United States. While the Taliban was confined to the Islamic Emirate of Afghanistan, recognised by only three countries – Pakistan, Saudi Arabia and the United Arab Emirates – Al Qaeda had a global plan. The leader of the Taliban, Mullah Omar, and the leader of Al Qaeda, Osama bin Laden, had fought the Soviet forces, and shared camaraderie since. The persecution of Osama at his home in Saudi Arabia led him to shift his base to Afghanistan and emerge as a patron-advisor to Mullah Omar. The influence of Osama on Omar was devastating; for instance, following his advice Omar ordered the destruction of the ancient Bamiyan Buddha in March 2001 (Gunaratna 2002: 49). From rugged terrains of Afghanistan, global jihad's spread across globe – towards Kashmir, Xinjiang, Chechnya, Mindanao, Yemen and other parts of the world – was planned.

Like any other conflict, the Afghan conflict had its tangible and intangible costs. As per estimates, the Soviet occupation alone resulted in the deaths of between 600,000 and two million Afghans, mostly civilians (US Department of State 2011). About six million fled as refugees to Pakistan and Iran. The departure of the Soviet forces did not cause tranquillity, as rival factions staked their claim to rule the country and fought bloody wars to achieve the objective. It was civilians who bore the brunt of the violence. According to one estimate, the forces of Hekmatyar's Hezb-i Islami and the Junbish-i Milli of Abdul Rashid Dostum killed about 25,000 people in 1994 alone (Afghanistan Justice Project 2005). The period from 1992 to 1996 was one of intense rivalry as agreements between rivals collapsed within days. Organisations such as the International Committee of the Red Cross (ICRC) or the UN failed to broker peace. A Human Rights Watch report (2005) titled 'Blood Stained Hands: Past Atrocities in Kabul and Afghanistan's Legacy of Impunity' details the incidents of killings, abductions, disappearances and other cases of human rights violations such as forced labour in the early 1990s. The Taliban, in a bid to capture Kabul, engaged in a bitter fight with rival forces and in the process killed thousands of people. In particular, Shia and Hazara people bore the brunt of the Taliban violence. The complicity of radical forces like Al Qaeda along with the Taliban in perpetrating violence in those days has also come to the surface. According to a UN report, 'eyewitnesses in many villages report how Arab fighters were carrying long knives used for slitting throats and skinning people' (Gargan 2001).

The peace process and inclusion of the Taliban

The peace process in Afghanistan that was initiated after the fall of the Taliban government in 2001 is beset with hurdles despite the common agreement that the troublesome region is in urgent need of peace. The Bonn Agreement endorsed by the UN Security Council in Resolution 1383 in December 2001 envisioned an interim administration to be assisted by the ISAF. Led by an ethnic Pashtun leader, Hamid Karzai, initially for six months, the period of the transitional government was increased by the Emergency Loya Jirga (tribal council) till 2004. Karzai was elected president of Afghanistan in 2004 elections, and re-elected in 2009 amidst contestations. While taking into account the nature of the transition process in the war-ravaged country, one of the issues that has complicated the peace process is the prospect of reintegration of the Taliban into the mainstream. Other issues such as streamlining administration by weeding out corruption and handing over the administration to the Afghans by phasing out foreign forces, and most importantly the adoption of a regional strategy to resolve the conflict, have factored in recent years. Suhrke *et al.* (2002: 875) refer to the post-Bonn peace process in Afghanistan as 'conflictual' as the Bonn Agreement excludes 'the defeated party, the Taliban, while seeking to commit the remaining groups to a long-term and loosely defined peace process'. They further argue that 'with Afghan regionally based political–military groups defined largely along ethnic lines, and closely linked to external powers, rebuilding national authority will be a slow and conflictual process'.

Other international conferences on Afghanistan at Berlin (2004), London (2006 and 2010), Rome (2007), Paris (2008), Moscow (2009), The Hague (2009) and Kabul (2010) have emphasised one or other aspects of the peace process in Afghanistan. The second London conference could be considered a landmark in the process as it brought forth innovative ideas. Importantly, perhaps for the first time, the London conference communiqué mentioned the regional organisations such as the Shanghai Cooperation Organization (SCO), South Asian Association for Regional Cooperation (SAARC) and Economic Cooperation Organization (ECO), which can play important roles towards fostering peace and stability in Afghanistan. Organisations such as the Organization of Islamic Conference and countries such as Saudi Arabia have expressed keen interest in mediating between the Taliban and the Afghan government. Another crucial idea was to let the Afghans manage affairs on their own (London Conference Communiqué 2010). This agenda is predicated on the principle of gradual phasing out of ISAF, and gradual shifting of power to the Afghan National Security Forces (ANSF) and other Afghan government agencies. The conference communiqué predicated that initially the Afghan provinces which are less turbulent can be handed over to the ANSF. From other provinces the international force will gradually withdraw by playing a supportive role, while simultaneously training and enlarging the Afghan forces. Though the process of draw down of forces is a complicated one, the killing of Osama bin Laden may foster the process of withdrawal, thus providing the Afghan people with the leverage to handle their affairs. It will be a difficult task due to prevailing differences among the Afghan groups, and it will also depend on how things actually work on the ground, and how the immediate neighbours shape their strategy towards the situation.

The pertinent issue that needs to be focused on in the ongoing peace process is whether a dividing line can be drawn in the ranks of the Taliban between moderate and radical varieties. Perhaps that was a tactical move to weaken the Taliban movement and urge the majority of its members who appear to be drawn to the movement due to various reasons other than fundamentalist ideology. This idea was put forward vigorously in 2010 when Hamid Karzai added a new term, Talibjan, to peace discourse in Afghanistan. The term Talibjan (a combination of Talib, meaning student or seeker, and Jan, meaning darling) is coined to impart a new meaning to the Taliban in Afghanistan in order to bring them into the orbit of the reintegration process. Taliban forces are enthusiastically goaded to the peace efforts by the Afghan leadership with the support of regional and international powers with the 'jan' suffix. The underlying significance of this change in approach towards reconciliation and reintegration efforts is quite crucial as it aimed at accommodating the diverse forces, including the Taliban in the peace process. The Taliban, mainly belonging to the ethnic Pashtun community, to which Karzai also belongs, have increasingly asserted their stakes in the recent years. Karzai has repeatedly emphasised that the peace process will continue with moderate Taliban, and the prospective power-sharing at Kabul will aim at the reintegration of the Taliban with mainstream society towards 'ultimate peace, stability and prosperity'. However, the evolving scenario has to be seen in a wider framework of ethnic pluralism and unique problems that Afghanistan is currently undergoing, particularly when members of other communities in Afghanistan have expressed scepticism about inclusion of the Taliban in the peace process. The ethnic groups such as Tajiks, Hazaras and Uzbeks have protested such moves. One of the prominent Tajik leaders, Abdullah Abdullah, also a former foreign minister of Afghanistan, criticised this move in unequivocal terms: 'It's not just the language he [Hamid Karzai] has used for months about "disaffected brothers"; now he says, "Talib-jan," which is like calling them "darling." To me, it shows the lack of a sense of direction and vision' (King 2010).

The Kabul conference of July 2010 reiterated the same inclusive mantra as a step towards the reconciliation process. The huge gathering in the Afghan capital, attended by 70 countries including 40 foreign ministers, and international bodies and donor agencies, issued a 32-point communiqué which in fact did not spell out anything novel, though its positive achievement is that it further committed the Afghan leadership towards evolving an inclusive approach to solve contentious issues in a transparent manner. The image of the Afghan government in the international arena has been plagued by cases of rampant corruption and inefficiency. However, Karzai appeared confident during the conference when he stated: 'I remain determined that our Afghan National Security Forces will be responsible for all military and law enforcement operations throughout our country by 2014' (Farmer 2010). Though it is expected that within a few years the international forces will depart, handing over control of Afghanistan to Afghan people, it has to be seen how far the transition takes place in a smooth manner, with a wily Taliban and vacillating Pakistan, the two important players in Afghanistan politics, to contend with.

The back channel diplomacy of the past few years has indicated that in order to bring peace to Afghanistan there is no other alternative but to invite the Taliban to be part of the peace process. But this effort led to the complex debate over the distinctive characteristics of moderate Taliban and radical Taliban. As such, there is no clear-cut demarcation between moderate and radical Taliban. These forces which emerged during the Cold War were intoxicated with the radical and orthodox dogmas. The collusion of these forces with extremists such as Al Qaeda made these dogmas further dreaded. The back channel diplomacy notwithstanding and despite the efforts by the UN, such as meeting the Taliban representatives in Dubai in 2010 and peace talks in Qatar in 2011, there is no sign that the Taliban has given up violence. None of the Taliban leaders have declared that the group will shun violence once they are part of the reintegration process; rather, the Taliban leader, Mullah Omar, has openly expressed his resentment of the peace process.

The major dilemma in the peace process continues to be how to convince the Taliban of the utility and importance of dialogue and deliberation towards transformation of the conflict. While describing the Afghan situation in 2004–2005, Sean Maloney (2005: 24) identified three distinct enemies of the Afghan government and its coalition partners – Hizb-I Islami Gulbuddin, Taliban and Al Qaeda – and argues that while the first and the last still pose threats to the peace process, the middle one has been 'completely reduced by OEF [Operation Enduring Freedom] operating methods'. He further argues that with the decimation of Al Qaeda leadership and sidelining or acquiescing of goals of Taliban and Hizb-I Islami, the Taliban has emerged as one of the most significant challenges to the peace process. The Taliban enjoys mass support and consists of the majority Pashtun community and is no longer confined to Afghanistan alone. The recent developments in Afghanistan indicate the rising prowess of the Taliban in turning the tide of developments in their favour. While the organisation is considered strong in the southern parts of Afghanistan, the killing of Wahid Omarkhel, the district governor of Chardara in Kunduz province in northern Afghanistan, in February 2011 reinforced the suspicion that the Taliban is strengthening its hold in the northern parts as well. The killing of Barhanuddin Rabbani, an ethnic Tajik and leader of the High Peace Council to broker peace in the conflict-torn country, in September 2011 in Kabul by the Taliban is certainly an indication of rising prowess of the Taliban. The ISAF forces have so far been unable to completely dismantle the Taliban structure. The Taliban's tactics of avoiding direct confrontation and adopting guerrilla-type methods have remained challenging. The strategy appears to be a wait-and-see till the vacuum emerges after the withdrawal of the ISAF so that they can, with the support from Pakistan, fill it. Adding to this zeal of reviving the Taliban regime in a post-ISAF scenario, the Taliban has in advance issued guidelines for the prospective government. One of the radical websites, Voice of Jihad, in January 2011, published an article written by Ikram Miyundi, outlining the detailed structure of the Afghanistan under the Taliban. While pronouncing Afghanistan to be an Emirate, the article outlined how the future Afghanistan will be governed strictly according to Sharia law, with the supreme religious head called Amir al-Mu'minin (Commander of the Faithful) (Terrorism Monitor 2011). It divided the administrative structure of the proposed Emirate into 34 provinces, which are further divided into directorates and villages. This outline brings back memories of the Taliban rule of 1996–2001, marked with brutalism, intolerance and dogmatism. Reports suggest that the Taliban already has a shadow government which is consolidating the gains acquired by the Taliban forces and their supporters in southern Afghanistan, which has become the renewed focus of the ISAF. In Andar and Deh Yak districts the Taliban runs 28 known schools, adjudicates disputes and circulates public statements by leaflets at night. The 2009 parliamentary elections and its poor turn-out in southern parts have vindicated the Taliban influence in the region. As per a report, in the Andar region, which has a population of about 110,000, only three people voted (Chivers 2011). A report in Pakistan's noted news daily, *The Dawn*, observes that 'the Taliban's shadow governance structure has thrived in the area amid weak local bureaucracy' (*The Dawn* 2011). The role of Pakistan is noteworthy as it not only shares a common border with Afghanistan, but also has a significant population of the same ethnic stock. The Taliban enjoys the patronage of Pakistan, and, as already mentioned, Pakistan was one of three countries that recognised the Taliban government in the 1990s. Hence, the future course of peace and development in Afghanistan will largely depend on the policy matrix of Pakistan and how its civilian government and the dominant army apparatus perceive the situation. Pakistan, which has considered Afghanistan to be within its sphere of influence, can play a major role in the reconciliation and reintegration effort by urging the radical elements under its control to shun violence.

Perception of players and stakes involved

The difficulties in securing peace in Afghanistan are numerous, taking into account the historical nature of conflict in Afghanistan, the emergence of the region as a hub of terrorism and religious fundamentalism, the nature of shifting regional alliances and their peace potentials, and also perceptions of players in the region. The turmoil is so deep and entrenched, it necessitates a format in which international, regional and national players can work together to confront multiple challenges ranging from terrorism to religious fundamentalism, drug trafficking to poverty and underdevelopment to corruption. While the ISAF appears hasty in minimising its losses in Afghanistan by withdrawing its forces in a phased manner, the power vacuum will surely put forth new challenges as well as constraints, not only before Afghanistan but also the regional and global players in the region.

The developments in and around Afghanistan since 2001 indicate a new architecture of relations emerging in Eurasia, in which the major stakeholders vie for control over the geo-strategic space of the region. The debates regarding supply routes to the war-torn Afghanistan have provided enough clues that the ISAF will not be able to follow the old policy of solely relying on Pakistan for supply of reinforcements, especially after repeated obstructions by the radical elements in the route from Karachi port to Afghanistan, particularly through the Khyber Pass. The turning point emerged when the Obama administration in Washington announced that it will seek cooperation from Russia and the countries of Central Asia to supply goods to the war-torn country. The Bush period from 2001–2008 witnessed tense United States–Russia relations, particularly after the efforts of the United States to woo the Central Asian countries, attempts to draw the countries like Ukraine and Georgia into the NATO fold, announcement of an anti-missile shield in Czech and Poland and irritants such as the Luguvoi controversy (Mahapatra 2007). The initial bonhomie generated in the wake of 9/11 withered away gradually with the uncompromising and antagonistic policies in the strategic and energy-rich Eurasia. The Kosovo crisis and later South Ossetian crisis also marked the differing contours of policies in the region. The Afghan issue was no exception to this overall power rivalry in the wider Eurasian region.

The Afghanistan problem, particularly the issue of supply routes, is a point of contention, but it can also provide scope for bilateral and multilateral cooperation. It will depend on how far the United States, European Union, Russia and other powers in the region come together and eschew their old rivalries and develop a common goal towards peace in Afghanistan and dismantle radical forces like the Taliban, which is one of the beneficiaries of a lack of a coordinated agenda on the part of the international players. While Russia argues that its experiences in Afghanistan in the 1980s can be useful in the reconstruction process, NATO forces appear to view the Russian offer with suspicion. This suspicion might have rationale behind it, as it was the US-supported forces which fought a decade-long war against the Soviet forces in Afghanistan. Russia argues that this region is well connected by the Soviet era railroad system. The route from Russia, and then through Kazakhstan, Turkmenistan and Uzbekistan to Afghanistan can help the NATO to achieve its targets with Russian cooperation. There are some positive signs, however feeble, towards possible NATO–Russia cooperation after Moscow gave the green light to NATO by allowing 'non-lethal' supplies to use Russian territory for transit to Afghanistan in November 2008. The US option to avoid the Iran route can be attributed to the nuclear issue, and Iran's apparent non-cooperation towards dismantling or neutralising its nuclear weapons-making programme. Similarly, the ISAF may not be enthusiastic about another route that starts from Shanghai port straight across China to Tajikistan and to Afghanistan. The proposed plan to build a new route from the Black Sea to the port of Poti in Georgia to Azerbaijan, and then onward to Kazakhstan and Turkmenistan to Afghanistan will likely intensify rivalry in the region as such a route will completely bypass Russia and China (Vahabov 2009). Russia's plans to sell Iran the S-300 missile defence system and SA-20 missile systems, and its relations with Central Asian countries will also play a crucial role in determining contours of peace politics in the region. Situations like the Kyrgyz plan in early February 2009 to ask its parliament to approve closure of the US military base on its soil, a major base of operations in Afghanistan, will frustrate NATO efforts to go solo in Afghanistan (Bumiller and Barry 2009). It is comprehensible that the competing interests of nations clash while confronting the Afghan issue, but as past experience shows, any unilateral or sectarian approach is not going to usher peace and stability in Afghanistan. The partnership between the international players will help defuse tensions in the region, besides helping to tackle the radical elements and menaces like drug trafficking. Lack of any such cooperation will only aid the radical forces, and as the developments indicate so far, there are signs that the two Cold War rivals will come together in Afghanistan in a full-fledged agenda of peace and development. Barnett R. Rubin (2006: 175) rightly argues that sustainable peace and stability in Afghanistan require international actors to delegate some sovereign functions to a multilateral entity that can reinforce rather than undermine the institutions responsible for the reconstruction of the nation-state.

Any policy to bypass countries of influence in the region may lead to tense atmosphere with wide-ranging consequences. Bringing regional powers to a common platform towards addressing conflict in Afghanistan will be an enormous task, further made complex due to a lack of synchronisation of policies of immediate neighbours of Afghanistan and the forces, including international assistance forces, present in Afghanistan. While the United States abhors any solution format that includes Iran as a player, Pakistan intermittently uses its regional clout to break away from such a policy when it suits its interests. The Tehran summit in May 2009 is a case in point. The summit involving three Muslim majority nations – Afghanistan, Pakistan and Iran – demonstrated the growing influence of Iran among the neighbouring countries with which the United States has developed a special relationship. At the Tehran summit, Mahmoud Ahmedinejad, Asif Ali Zardari and Hamid Karzai, leaders of Iran, Pakistan and Afghanistan, respectively, while emphasising historical, religious and cultural links between these countries, expressed concern against rising insecurity, terrorism, extremism and drug production and trafficking in the region. The 24-item declaration (*Tehran Times* 2009) in its first point aimed at establishing a mechanism for holding regular and periodical trilateral consultations on special issues by senior officials, foreign ministers and the heads of state/government of the three countries. The declaration also emphasised trilateral institution-building to establish economic and industrial planning commissions and chambers of commerce. Item 2 encouraged the joint commitment to make every effort to tackle the regional issues and address their root causes. The declaration called for a trilateral approach to fight the menace of religious extremism, terrorism and drug trafficking, thus giving rise to the prospects of exclusion of other powers in resolving regional issues. Iran's criticism of the foreign troops (an indirect reference to the presence of ISAF troops in Afghanistan) and its leverage with certain factions in Afghanistan might further complicate the peace process.

There are issues that need to be factored with regard to feasibility of any narrow approach as envisaged by the Tehran declaration. Whether Pakistan and Afghanistan will follow the line of Iran, which perceives the US role in the region to be antithetical to their interests, and whether Iran will have a foothold in the Afghan peace process is difficult to predict, but it is unlikely to happen, at least in the near future. Unless Iran fulfils its global obligations towards a nuclear weapon-free regime, it will have the least acceptability among the other players involved in the peace process. Though international powers have different approaches on how to tackle the Iranian nuclear programme, there is nonetheless unanimity on the issue that Iran must stop using its nuclear facilities for building nuclear weapons. Ahmedinejad may be critical of the presence of foreign troops in the region, arguing, 'Although the presence of foreign forces in our region was under the pretext of establishing security … it has not been much of a help to the establishment of permanent security and political and economic growth' (Jaseb and Dahl 2009); but his acceptability, particularly after the popular protests in Iran, has been significantly eroded. That Iran and Pakistan have not always been on good terms owing to their sectarian differences (Pakistan is Sunni dominated while Iran is Shia dominated), as well as their approaches to international issues, make the success of the trilateral framework a difficult proposition. Turkey's interest has been in salience with NATO, its patron organisation, and as the Istanbul conference of January 2010 indicated, Turkey has not hidden its aspirations to play a major role in the region.

Pakistan, particularly, has evinced major interest as it views the region as its strategic backyard, and its past role in supporting the mujahideen and the Taliban against the erstwhile Soviet Union place it in a special relationship with the United States and NATO. Drawing a parallel between the Soviet invasion and Pakistan's 'creeping' invasion in late 1990s, particularly after the military coup of 1999, Peter Tomsen (2000: 181), who served as the US special envoy to the Afghan resistance, 1989–1992, points out, 'Just as the Soviets tried saving their communist asset in Kabul by invading Afghanistan, Islamabad has been funnelling more troops and military resources to save its own asset, the Taliban.' However, one of the important players for conflict transformation in Afghanistan will be Pakistan. The international forces present there appear to have recognised this dimension, and in turn have provided Pakistan a leveraged position in the process. The US Congress, under the Biden-Lugar Bill of 2009, tripled civilian aid to Pakistan to fight terrorism and fundamentalism. It is a temptation hard to resist for Pakistan. The same is the case with Afghanistan. There are tens of thousands of US and NATO troops stationed in Afghanistan. A report suggests that within a year from 11 September 2001 to 31 December 2002, the United States spent $40 billion on its war efforts in Afghanistan and Pakistan and some other areas (Bailey 2003). Pakistan has used its strategic and bargaining clout in dealing with other players involved in the peace process in the region. Its closure of the Khyber Pass, about 35 km route in the Hindu Kush mountain range, in October 2010 pointed to its increasing assertiveness. The Khyber Pass at present is the most important among other routes for supplies to NATO forces in Afghanistan. The route is considered to be vital for the success or failure of the war against terrorism and dismantling of Taliban fundamentalism in Afghanistan, as about 75 per cent of ammunition, food and fuel for the NATO forces pass through it (Synovitz 2008). This mountainous route has been subject to attacks by the militant Taliban groups. In 2008 about 500 vehicles were attacked by the Taliban. On 7 December 2008 alone, the militants destroyed more than 100 trucks loaded with supplies for American and allied forces in Afghanistan (Perlez 2008). There are also differences emerging in a more protracted way between the United States and Pakistan in recent years. The arrest of Raymond Davis, a member of the US diplomatic staff in Pakistan, by Pak police for his alleged killing of two Pakistani citizens in Lahore in January 2011 has further heightened tension between the two allies. This row threatened bilateral relations, with the United States threatening to cut aid to Pakistan. One commentator observed that 'while Davis' release may improve ties between Washington and Islamabad, it is further inflaming the Pakistani public, with whom the case had generated a fierce wave of anti-American sentiment' (Waraich 2011). The drone attacks have also been a sore point between Pakistan and the United States, though the Pakistan government appears to have given tacit consent for such attacks; notwithstanding, a section of the Pak population view it as an encroachment into the sovereignty of the country.

The stalemate in bilateral relations after the killing of Osama bin Laden in the garrison town of Abbotabad of Pakistan may cause Pakistan to further drift away from the United States, thus impacting the peace process. The visit of the Pakistani president to Russia and prime minister to China in May 2011 are noteworthy in this context. In an interview with the local media, President Zardari invited Russia to use Pakistani territory to access 'southern seas' (*The Hindu* 2011). The visit of the Pakistani prime minister to China in the same month to participate in celebrations to mark 60 years of bilateral relations cannot be ignored in this context. In the aftermath of the Abbotabad episode, China was at the forefront in backing Pakistan's policies on 'implementing counterterrorism strategies' and reiterating its promise to build a nuclear reactor in Chashma of Pakistan, despite objections from other countries. There are also reports that Pakistan has been persuading the Afghanistan leadership to give up the special relationship with the United States and move closer to China (Mohan 2011). China has projected itself as a bridge between Washington and Islamabad and has been interested in playing a major role in developing a regional framework involving Beijing, Kabul and Islamabad. Chinese commentator Li Xiguang argued: 'China, Pakistan and Afghanistan need to form a Pamir group, a strategic trilateral partnership to support sustainable peace and prosperity in the region' (ibid.).

India–Pakistan rivalry on various issues, including Kashmir, impact the peace politics in the region. India-educated Karzai, known as an advocate of the regional format for peace, argues that India can play an effective role in this regional and inclusive format. In his first visit to India after his election as president of Afghanistan in October 2009, Karzai received a warm welcome in New Delhi. India, which is the third largest donor to Afghanistan, with a commitment of about $2 billion, has emphasised the historical link between the two countries. Many Indian stories and myths are related to ancient and medieval Afghanistan and are etched in public memory. The famous Sanskrit Grammarian Panini of India was born in Kabul (Sen 2005: 84). There is overall unanimity in Indian public and policy circles that New Delhi should continue its reconstruction activities in Afghanistan (Mahapatra 2010). According to a poll conducted in December 2009 by the Afghan Centre for Socio Economic and Opinion Research, 71 per cent of 1,534 respondents in 43 Afghan locations have overwhelmingly welcomed India's role in developmental activities in Afghanistan. India has completed the Zaranj-Delaram road project and the Pul-e-Kumri to Kabul transmission line project, and is involved in projects such as the Salma dam hydropower project in Herat and the construction of the Afghan parliament. The Indian national budget for the last few years has allocated funds for reconstruction efforts in Afghanistan. Pakistan suspects India's reconstruction activities in Afghanistan are a cloak to foster India's strategic objectives in the region at the cost of Pakistan. It considers Afghanistan as its strategic backyard, so it must have the determining role in the affairs of the region. According to Pakistani analyst Rasul Bakhsh Rais (*Pak Tribune* n.d.), 'There is a degree of disappointment with him [Karzai], in particular over the way he has provided Afghanistan as a playing field for India.'

India has objected to any peace format that includes the Taliban, which have been vocal in their contempt of India. The Taliban government's deliberate inaction during the hijacking of an Indian Airlines flight to Kandahar in 1999 is undoubtedly a grim memory, and the Taliban's open support to militant groups in Kashmir is a major bone of contention, not only between India and the Taliban, but also between India and Pakistan. Pakistan perceives India as its rival in Afghanistan and used the Taliban as leverage against India. The statement of the late Pakistani Taliban leader, Baitullah Mehsud, that in the case of India–Pakistan war the Taliban will fight in support of Pakistan is a case in point (Mahapatra 2009). Being a target of the Taliban, India has become wary of the prospects of inclusion of the Taliban in the reintegration process by allowing the group into the power-sharing arrangement. India has alleged that the attacks on Indian officials and workers in Afghanistan, for instance the attacks on the Indian embassy in Kabul in October 2009 and July 2010, were orchestrated by Pakistan's official intelligence agency, which Pakistan has denied. The six decades of rivalry and four wars between these two countries contribute to this suspicion factor. Pakistan and India are engaged in bitter rivalry over many issues, including the issue of Kashmir, and that rivalry colours their policies towards Afghanistan.

When the United States pressured Pakistan to attack the militants in north Waziristan in 2010, the Pakistan army cited two main reasons behind its reluctance to divert forces in that direction. While the reason that the military is involved in activities to ameliorate the conditions of the victims of the floods that devastated the Indus basin area in Pakistan appeared well founded, the second reason as articulated by the Pakistani military could be construed a strategy. Pakistan raised the India factor, particularly the threat of India to its east, as another factor for the hesitation of the army to divert to the north to fight the militants. Perhaps this argument of Pakistan in a way emboldened the United States to fight the militants solo in 'hot pursuit' by using gunships and drone attacks. While Pakistan has not appreciated the US 'hot pursuits' in its territory owing to popular dissatisfaction, they are tolerated due to its heavy dependence on US aid; some sections in the US policy establishment have expressed disillusionment over the Pak cooperation in counter-terrorism activities, particularly after the Osama episode. Bob Woodward's *Obama's Wars* (2010) has reflected this sentiment as he argues how, despite the heavy US investments in Pakistan, it has become difficult to realise the US objectives in the region.

Conclusion

The decade old post-9/11 Afghanistan is instructive of a process, though not detached from the underlying conflict dynamics in the region, that peace in Afghanistan will be a difficult endeavour, with challenges looming large from within and without the war-torn country. A major challenge emanates from the emphasis on accommodating diverse parties, including the Taliban, which openly preaches violence. Efforts towards wedging a division between moderate and radical Taliban have not produced significant results; the Taliban violence continues unabated, despite the presence of international troops. Their departure may enable the Taliban to revert to the old orthodox rule and violent practices. Against this background, it will be important to see how reintegration of the Taliban with the mainstream makes any headway as the future of the peace process in Afghanistan will depend on the success or failure of such a reintegration process. The transformation of the Taliban from being a part of the problem to being a part of the solution indeed remains an arduous task in Afghanistan.

The diversity of interests among players involved in the region and their contrasting positions make the peace process in Afghanistan a difficult venture. While in conflict situations it may be natural to have differences among the players, in Afghanistan the exclusivity of the goals perhaps has been starker than other conflicts. The religion factor, the sectarian factor, the existence of old hatreds and acrimony, and the shadow of the Cold War, instead of moderating the peace process, further complicate it in a region that has for the most part of its recent history witnessed war and violence. The international forces present in

Afghanistan to an extent loathe full-fledged involvement of other players in the peace process; perhaps the experience of the Cold War spurs such a perception. Regional players such as China, Iran and countries of Central Asia, due to one or other reason, find their acceptability in the peace process complicated. Pakistan perceives India's presence as antithetical to its interests due to their rival positions on various issues. The strategic location of Afghanistan, its resources and its emergence in the post-Cold War world as a centre of extremism and violence makes the region a valid candidate for sustained peace towards stability and development of the region, as well as for international peace and security. Perhaps no players in the region disagree with the broader objectives of the peace process, but the differences among the players on the means to achieve these objectives make the situation complicated, with the risk of returning to the old days of chaos and instability. The crucial issue of how to achieve tangible peace and with what methods looms large as differences among players persist, which will likely be protracted after the departure of the ISAF.

Notes

1 Under its last king, Zahir Shah, Afghanistan attempted a development-oriented approach by shedding the traditional governance system, but his regime was overthrown in 1973 by his cousin Daud Khan, who was subsequently overthrown in the Saur revolution of 1978, and replaced by a communist government with Soviet support.

2 There are about 55 distinct ethnic groups in Afghanistan, of which the majority – Pashtuns – constitute 38 per cent of the population, while three other significant communities – Tajiks, Hazaras and Uzbeks – constitute 25 per cent, 19 per cent and 6 per cent of the population, respectively (Riphenburg 2005: 37). It was the Pashtuns who ruled most of the time in modern Afghanistan. Their location mainly to the south of the country and also in the border areas of Pakistan positioned the Pashtuns to play a significant role in determining the politics of the region.

3 Though the Taliban as an organisation emerged in 1994, its cadres, including Mullah Omar, had fought the Soviet forces under the guidance of Pakistan's security forces and under the watch of American intelligence.

References

Afghanistan Justice Project (2005) www.afghanistanjusticeproject.org/warcrimesandcrimesagainsthumanity19782001.pdf (accessed 5 June 2011).

Bailey, W. Scott (2003) 'War on Terrorism has Cost US $600 billion: Report Shows Costs are Continuing to Escalate', 6 September. www.intlhorizons.com/article-terrorwarcost.htm (accessed 25 June 2011).

Bearden, Milton (2001) 'Afghanistan, Graveyard of Empires', *Foreign Affairs*, 80 (6): 17–30.

Bumiller, Elisabeth and Barry, Ellen (2009) 'U.S. Searches for Alternative to Central Asian Base', *New York Times*, 4 February.

Chivers, C.J. (2011) 'Afghanistan's Hidden Taliban Government', *New York Times*, 7 February.

The Dawn (2011), 'US Troops Hope for Winter Breakthrough in Afghanistan', 11 January.

Farmer, Ben (2010) 'Hamid Karzai Calls for NATO Troop Withdrawal by 2014', *Telegraph*, 20 July.

Gall, Sandy (1988) *Afghanistan: Agony of a Nation*, London: Bodley Head.

Gargan, Edward A. (2001) 'Taliban Massacres Outlined for UN', *Chicago Tribune*, 12 October. http://articles.chicagotribune.com/2001-10-12/news/0110120312_1_taliban-fighters-massacres-in-recent-years-mullah-mohammed-omar (accessed 25 May 2011).

George, Arney (1990) *Afghanistan: The Definitive Account of a Country at Crossroads*, London: Mandarin.

Gossman, Patricia (2001) 'Afghanistan in the Balance', *Middle East Report*, 221: 8–15.

Gunaratna, Rohan (2002) *Inside Al Qaeda: Global Network of Terror*, New Delhi: Roli Books.

The Hindu (2011) 'Zardari in Russia, on First Foreign Visit Since Osama Killing', 11 May.

Human Rights Watch (2005) 'Blood-Stained Hands: Past Atrocities in Kabul and Afghanistan's Legacy of Impunity'. www.hrw.org/en/reports/2005/07/06/blood-stained-hands (accessed 22 June 2011).

Jaseb, Hossein and Dahl, Fredrik (2009) 'Iran Says Foreign Troops no Help to Region's Security', 24 May. www.reuters.com/article/idUSTRE54N0HM20090524 (accessed 4 June 2011).

Kakar, Hasan (1979) *State and Society in Afghanistan*, Austin, TX: University of Texas Press.

King, Laura (2010) 'Ethnic Divide Threatens in Afghanistan', *Los Angeles Times*, 17 July.

Klass, Rosanne (1987) *Afghanistan: The Great Game Revisited*, New York, NY: Freedom House.

London Conference Communiqué (2010) www.isaf.nato.int/images/stories/File/factsheets/Documents_Communique%20of%20London%20Conference%20on%20Afghanistan.pdf (accessed 4 June 2011).

Mahapatra, Debidatta Aurobinda (2007) 'Luguvoi Controversy: Implications for Russia–EU Relations', *World Focus*, 28 (9): 329–333.

—— (2009) 'What Death of Baitullah Mehsud Means for Terrorism', *Strategic Culture Foundation*, 12 August. http://en.fondsk.ru/article.php?id=2389 (accessed 14 November 2010).

—— (2010) 'New Dimension to the Regional Conflict', *Strategic Culture Foundation*, 22 January. http://en.fondsk.ru/article.php?id=2717 (accessed 4 December 2010).

Maloney, Sean M. (2005) 'Afghanistan Four Years On: An Assessment', *Parameters*, autumn: 21–32.

Mohan, C. Raja (2011) 'The Pamir Group?', *Indian Express*, 8 June.

Mukherjee, Sadhan (1984) *Afghanistan from Tragedy to Triumph*, New Delhi: Sterling.

PakTribune (n.d.) 'Pakistanis Look Beyond Afghan Vote to Greater Role'. http://paktribune.com/news/print.php?id=218490 (accessed 25 May 2011).

Perlez, Jane (2008) 'Militants in Pakistan Destroy NATO Trucks', *New York Times*, 8 December.

Ramazani, R.K. (1958) 'Afghanistan and the USSR', *Middle East Journal*, 12 (2): 144–152.

Rashid, Ahmed (2000) *Taliban: Militant Islam, Oil and Fundamentalism in Central Asia*, New Haven, CT: Yale University Press.

Riphenburg, Carol J. (2005) 'Ethnicity and Civil Society in Contemporary Afghanistan', *Middle East Journal*, 59 (1): 31–51.

Rubin, Barnett R. (2006) 'Peace Building and State-Building in Afghanistan: Constructing Sovereignty for whose Security?', *Third World Quarterly*, 27 (1): 175–185.

Saikal, Amin (2006) *Modern Afghanistan: A History of Struggle and Survival*, London: I.B. Tauris.

Schneierson, Lev Nikolayev (1986) *Afghanistan between the Past and the Future*, Moscow: Progress Publishers.

Sen, Amartya (2005) *The Argumentative Indian: Writings on Indian Culture, History and Identity*, London: Penguin Books.

Suhrke, Astri, Harpviken, Kristian Berg and Strand, Arne (2002) 'After Bonn: Conflictual Peacebuilding', *Third World Quarterly*, 23 (4): 875–891.

Synovitz, Ron (2008) 'U.S., NATO Seek Afghan Supply Routes Other Than Pakistan', Radio Free Europe/Radio Liberty, 11 December. www.rferl.org/content/US_NATO_Seek_Afghan_Supply_Routes_Other_Than_Pakistan/1358749.html (accessed 25 June 2011).

Tehran Times (2009) 'Text of Tehran Declaration of Trilateral Summit', 26 May. www.tehrantimes.com/index_View.asp?code=195443 (accessed 24 June 2011).

Terrorism Monitor (2011) 'Afghan Taliban Issue Guidelines for Establishment of Islamic Emirate', 9 (5), 4 February. www.jamestown.org/single/?no_cache=1&tx_ttnews%5Btt_news%5D=37454&tx_ttnews%5BbackPid%5D=515 (accessed 24 June 2011).

Tomsen, Peter (2000) 'A Chance for Peace in Afghanistan: The Taliban's Days Are Numbered', *Foreign Affairs*, 79 (1): 179–182.

US Department of State (2011) 'Background Note on Afghanistan', 28 November. www.state.gov/r/pa/ei/bgn/5380.htm (accessed 30 November 2011).

Vahabov, Tamerlan (2009) 'NATO Supply Routes Through the South Caucasus', *Eurasia Daily Monitor*, 6 (168), 15 September. www.jamestown.org/single/?no_cache=1&tx_ttnews%5Btt_news%5D=35493 (accessed 15 October 2011).

Waraich, Omar (2011) 'Pakistan: How Shari'a Freed American Ray Davis', 16 March. www.time.com/time/world/article/0,8599,2059330,00.html (accessed 15 October 2011).

Wilber, Donald N. (ed.) (1956) *Afghanistan*, New Haven, CT: Human Relations Area Files.

Woodward, Bob (2010) *Obama's Wars*, New York, NY: Simon and Schuster.

10 Resolving Uyghur conflict through a participatory rights-based approach to development

Henryk Szadziewski

Introduction

Conflict in Xinjiang (also known as East Turkestan) in the far west of present-day China has political, economic, social and cultural derivations. Recurrent sources of unrest centre on Chinese government policies towards the Turkic Uyghur people in the region. Han Chinese migration to the region, political and economic marginalisation of the Uyghur people, as well as curbs on Uyghur cultural rights, such as religious and linguistic freedoms, are all issues of contention between Uyghur civil society and the Chinese government. Uyghur manifestation of discontent with Chinese government policy is neither new nor infrequent. Successive imperial, republican and communist Chinese administrations have all considered the western regions a strategic area for the protection of the Chinese heartland. Chinese governments have laid claim to the territory of Xinjiang on predominately historical grounds; however, Chinese control of Xinjiang has fluctuated. Present Chinese Communist Party rule is the most consolidated Chinese administration yet experienced in Xinjiang, but was preceded by an independent East Turkestan Republic (1944–1949). Although it is not within the scope of this chapter to discuss the legality of Chinese claims to the territory, it is important to note that Chinese domination of the region has been contested by Uyghurs for many years.

Unrest has grown in recent years. The present rate at which unrest is occurring was established in the 1990s, at the end of which the provincial governor, Abdulahat Abdurixit, admitted publicly in March 1999 that the number of incidents in the decade numbered a few thousand (Bequelin 2000: 87). Incidents of unrest are mainly concentrated in three areas of the region: the Kashgar-Khotan area of southwestern Xinjiang; the Ili area of western Xinjiang; and the regional capital of Urumchi, most notably in July 2009. When unrest occurs, Chinese authorities move quickly to quell it, often using force, and then follow such actions with intensified repressive measures. The peaceful demonstration that preceded the eruption of violent unrest in Urumchi on 5 July 2009 sharply illustrated that the dimensions of Uyghur protest had shifted from a focus on increased political autonomy to issues of meaningful political participation, social justice and economic rights.

A rights-based approach to development has increased in prominence in recent development discourse and practice. The approach is characterised by the empowerment of marginalised people through the realisation of human rights – human rights which have been defined and legally represented in the international instruments of the UN system. The approach, usually in states with established civil societies, also offers the potential for marginalised people to systemically realise social and economic rights in order to achieve peaceful resolutions of contentious issues with governments. This chapter argues that while realisation of rights is central to the theory of a rights-based approach, participation is integral to its practice. In addition, this chapter seeks to understand how non-governmental Uyghur actors in Xinjiang can operate in an authoritarian and repressive context to operationalise a participatory rights-based approach to development. It explores the opportunities for leverage that exist for marginalised Uyghur people and assesses whether a rights-based approach can at all exist in such repressive environments.

In this chapter an operational framework is drawn from development literature to build a series of suggested opportunities for encouraging a participatory rights-based approach to development among marginalised people. These opportunities are scrutinised using the current experience of the Uyghur people to understand the potential for the approach to encourage meaningful development and conflict resolution in Xinjiang. The chapter argues that a significant opportunity for peace is possible should such an approach take root in the region.

Rights-based approaches to development: a definition framework

In 1997 Julia Häusermann published *A Human Rights Approach to Development*, which was a milestone in the field of rights-based approaches to development. Concurrently, work began on the United Nations Development Programme's (UNDP) Human Development Report for 2000, *Human Rights and Human Development*. Both publications sought to define and stimulate development through the 'use of human rights principles and legal norms as a coherent framework for poverty elimination' (Häusermann 1998: 59). It is from these two landmark publications that this chapter outlines the framework of a rights-based approach to development. Häusermann (ibid.: 60) contends that the guiding principle of human rights is to affirm that all people are born equal and that the condition of poverty is a violation of human rights. Deprivation of basic human needs such as food, water, housing, employment, education and health run contrary to that fundamental guiding principle. Häusermann places equality at the core of a rights-based approach to development by stating that a rights-based approach to development

> promotes equal opportunities and choices for all so that everyone can develop their own unique potential and have a chance to contribute to

> development and social progress.... Promotes national and international systems based on economic equity, equity in the access to public resources, and social justice.
>
> (Ibid.: 32)

A rights-based approach to development seeks to empower through grass-roots claims to rights from the state. Marginalised people and communities lead the struggle for equality by confronting state rights violations and/or oversight by invoking the articles of international human rights instruments. Häusermann (ibid.: 61) adds that 'By contrasting their current situation with what they are entitled to pursuant to human rights law, they are encouraged to work for change and seek their rights.' This dimension to a rights-based approach to development calls for the participation of marginalised people in development policy formation. Participation and empowerment of marginalised people is also a central theme of UNDP's HDR 2000. However, in contrast, the report suggests that the state plays an important facilitating role in this process by

> Ensuring civil and political rights – freedom of speech, association and participation – to empower poor people to claim their social, economic and cultural rights ... meeting its human rights obligations to implement policies and policy-making processes that do the most to secure economic, social and cultural rights for the most deprived and to ensure their participation in decision-making.
>
> (UNDP 2000: 8)

Consequently, the basic elements underpinning a rights-based approach to development are participation and rights negotiated between state and non-state actors. Indeed, VeneKlasen *et al.* (2004: 1) add that 'It is in this convergence between strands of rights and participation ... where we see the most potential for "rights-based approaches".' The subsequent sections look to outline the understanding of these two elements within a rights-based approach to development.

Participation in a rights-based approach to development

Participation of marginalised people in the formation of government development policy is often viewed by some political analysts as existing more in the realm of theory than practice. If the vast disparities in political power are considered, the potential for meaningful involvement in government decision-making by disenfranchised individuals is an occurrence that can be easily rejected. However, a rights-based approach to development challenges such perceptions in the realm of practice. Participation in development theory and practice can be traced further back than its popularisation at the end of the twentieth century. Community development strategies from the 1950s through to the 1970s explored the involvement of marginalised people in development interventions planned for their community. The extent of this involvement was initially limited to project execution rather than design. Yet in the 1980s, a shift in thinking took place to challenge this limited involvement: 'development policy makers and planners began to argue for societal level political participation and also to devise strategies whereby poor people could become more directly involved in development efforts' (UNDP 2000: 2). The new direction in participatory ideas split the method into two approaches:

> Participation as a means: participation is seen as a process whereby local people cooperate or collaborate with externally introduced development programmes or projects.… Participation as an end: participation is seen as a goal in itself. This goal can be expressed as the empowering of people in terms of their acquiring the skills, knowledge and experience to take greater responsibility for their development.
>
> (Ibid.: 4)

With its focus on transformation through self-empowerment, a rights-based approach to development is allied to the latter of these two approaches (Lumbantobing and Zulminarni 2004: 30). As a result, the right to participation is an integral feature of a rights-based approach to development. It also stands to reason that the right to participation within a rights-based approach to development is pivotal for the achievement of social, economic and cultural equality. Since rights occupy an integral place in a rights-based approach to development, the next section seeks to define their interpretation in the context of this chapter.

Rights in a rights-based approach to development

Human-rights thought is driven by the belief that all human beings are equal (Donnelly 1999: 612). Although this statement is common throughout rights literature, there are differing opinions as to the derivation of rights. This is exemplified in the different positions taken by the UNDP and Julia Häusermann. In the UNDP's view, human rights originate from moral claims, while Häusermann asserts that human rights stem from legal claims. The following quotes evidence their dissimilar viewpoints:

> Human rights are the rights possessed by all persons by virtue of their common humanity, to live a life of freedom and dignity. They give all people moral claims on the behaviour of individuals and on the design of social arrangements.
>
> (UNDP 2000: 16)

> [Human rights are] … a global vision backed by state obligations. The term 'human rights' refers to those rights that have been recognized by the global community and protected by international legal instruments.
>
> (Häusermann 1998: 25)

A rights-based approach to development is consistent with both viewpoints, by taking its ethical outlook from the stance of the UNDP and its operational outlook from Häusermann. Although this work acknowledges each viewpoint, the focus of this chapter on rights operationalisation means greater emphasis is given to Häusermann's perception. Häusermann elaborates on the legal interpretation of human rights by grouping human rights upheld by international human rights instruments into three broad types; cross-referenced by equal rights for men and women and freedom from discrimination, these are rights necessary for

> survival and dignified living [such as] the rights to food and housing; human dignity, creativity and intellectual and spiritual development [for example] the right to participate in the political process; and liberty and physical security [such as] the right to be free from arbitrary arrest or imprisonment.
> (ibid.: 56)

The above grouping illustrates how rights can have positive and negative obligations on states in the multilateral system of international human rights instruments. In order to meet their international obligations, states must either refrain from or be active in promoting certain policies.

Within the context of global post-Second World War ideological differences, the positive–negative rights dichotomy led to the formation of two separate international instruments; one for political and civil rights, the International Covenant on Civil and Political Rights (ICCPR), and the other for economic, social and cultural rights, the International Covenant on Economic Social and Cultural Rights (ICESCR). Broadly reflected in their ratification status, the positive rights contained in the ICESCR were championed by communist states and the negative rights encompassed in the ICCPR were highlighted by capitalist Western states. Nonetheless, Häusermann (ibid.: 64) and the UNDP agree that all types of human rights are 'inter-related and indivisible'.

Brocklesby and Crawford (2005: 25) believe that a rights-based approach to development is a move from needs-based approaches dominant in development discourse in the twentieth century. In a rights-based approach to development, 'participation, rights, and power' are the key elements in leveraging opportunities for equality among marginalised people (VeneKlasen *et al.* 2004: 1). A rights-based approach to development involves marginalised people not only at the implementation level, but also the formation level of development policy. In essence, the rights-based approach to development, as Häusermann (1998: 32) states 'moves the focus from handouts to empowerment, from charity to rights'.

Legal and operational framework

Participation and rights are inherently connected in a rights-based approach to development (Brocklesby and Crawford 2005: 23; DfID 2000: 12; Hamm 2001: 1018; Piron 2003: 4; VeneKlasen *et al.* 2004: 10). The process of claiming and negotiating human rights not only creates intersections between participation and rights but also between government and non-government actors (Júnior *et al.* 2004: 66; Lumbantobing and Zulminarni 2004: 32; VeneKlasen *et al.* 2004: 8, 16). States bear the responsibility of rights obligations, whereas civil society exerts pressure on governments to uphold those obligations. Positive rights obligations of governments often entail the formation of development initiatives to achieve equality for marginalised people. This chapter, through a review of literature, examines how participation and rights work together to create an eight-point operationalisation framework for a rights-based approach to development. The literature focusing on non-governmental actors is generally contextualised in established civil societies, which have experience in advocating for marginalised people. While the context of this chapter is centred on the authoritarian system prevailing in China (White *et al.* 1996: 208), non-governmental research is relevant in understanding how a rights-based approach to development can transpire from its earliest stages.

Bringing participation into rights: an operational framework

The concept of rights 'often conjures up the image of a legalistic approach that is more technical than empowering' (VeneKlasen *et al.* 2004: 7). A rights-based approach to development offsets the too common estrangement between marginalised people and rights work through participation. This chapter has previously discussed the dichotomies of participation; between participation as a means and participation as an end as well as moral and legal obligations for its realisation as a right. While a rights-based approach to development favours participation as an end to empower marginalised people, it also emphasises self-empowerment through policy engagement and understanding (DfID 2000: 17). Participation in rights work according to VeneKlasen *et al.* (2004: 14) means engaging 'people in understanding the many forces of power in their lives or explicitly helping them develop a sense of citizenship or political consciousness that reflects these complexities'. The process of developing political consciousness through participation is a starting position for rights work in a rights-based approach to development, which has been encouraged by '[g]ood development practice [which] emphasizes the importance of starting where people are' (VeneKlasen *et al.* 2004: 7).

In a rights-based approach to development, established civil society organisations (CSOs) are not intended to act as the surrogate for marginalised people engaged in rights work. Research illustrates the importance of the source of rights claims for levels of participation (Júnior *et al.* 2004: 67; Jasis and García 2004: 25). Toyo (2003: 33) report that in Nigeria 'Many CSOs become intermediary groups to facilitate the accessing of rights, and their actions often leave a gap between what the people can do for themselves and what the CSOs are actually doing on behalf of the people.' This facilitating role of CSOs runs contrary to achieving empowerment for marginalised people and leaves questions as to the necessity of the rights claims made on their behalf. On the other hand,

DfID (2000: 7) advocates for the strong involvement of CSOs in supporting marginalised people to initiate rights claims; this is due to the extreme difficulties experienced by marginalised people in 'getting started'. From this standpoint, existing CSOs already possess social, human and financial capital that can be used as a vehicle to initiate rights claims.

The who and how of initiating rights claims through participation is complicated by access to political institutions. Júnior *et al.* (2004: 36) detail the obstructions to political participation in Brazil created by clientelism and entrenched inequities of power, where 'rights are treated as favours, leaving no possibility for the construction of citizenship'. Not only do power inequities create barriers to participation in what Mohan and Holland (2001: 182) describe as 'elections, lobbying, advocacy and the day-to-day interaction with the local state', but also with the development of political consciousness. It is therefore essential in this context to conduct an analysis of the relationships between power and participation.

VeneKlasen *et al.* (2004: 5) characterise the forms of power and participation between governmental and non-governmental actors into three categories: closed, invited and claimed spaces. In the context of this chapter, closed spaces are completely restricted to government actors with no possibility of participation from non-governmental actors; invited spaces occur when non-governmental actors are invited to participate in a predetermined agenda set by governmental actors; and claimed spaces arise when agendas are claimed by non-governmental actors. The ability of marginalised people to effectively initiate rights claims can be determined by the kind of participation in which they find themselves engaged.

According to Brocklesby and Crawford (2005: 23), political participation must include marginalised people in a rights-based approach to development, but if participation is token it can become counter-productive. Research by Jasis and García (2004: 10) into participation and rights in Mexico found that

> on the one hand the government [of Mexico] maintains a facade of 'support for the promotion and advances in the activities of the civil society concerning human rights', and on the other, it discourages participation from civil society organizations by hindering access.

This kind of role, if seen in a broader context 'can lead to alienation, cynicism and an actual decrease in the willingness of the poor and marginalised to participate' (VeneKlasen *et al.* 2004: 36). Furthermore, in order to avoid such issues as token participation and the prevalence of closed power spaces, the participation of governmental or non-governmental community leaders must be meaningful. Governmental or CSO leaders, operating as figureheads for the government, are unlikely to claim the power spaces required to initiate rights claims from the state (Júnior *et al.* 2004: 67–68; Jasis and García 2004: 25).

Before turning to an analysis of the role of rights in participatory work, the role of participation in rights work can be summarised as follows:

- Participation empowers and is an end.
- Individuals and communities must discover their level of political consciousness.
- Power spaces in participatory processes require understanding.
- Participation and leadership should be meaningful.

Bringing rights into participation: an operational framework

In a participatory rights-based approach to development, rights work is often seen as related to theory and policy, while participation is concerned with application and practice (VeneKlasen *et al.* 2004: 3–4). This impression of the former is a legacy of the legalistic manner in which rights groups have traditionally voiced concerns about rights violations. However, rights work is not merely restricted to explaining the law. In the following section broader suggestions from the development literature are proposed to operationalise rights within the practise of participation. It attempts to answer two questions: first, what are the main rights considerations in participatory work? Second, to whom should marginalised people direct rights claims?

Earlier, the assertion was made that power inequities directly influence the effectiveness of participation; as a consequence they also affect the realisation of rights. Realising positive rights requires a considerable input of resources by the state. In an environment of fiscal constraint common in almost all states, access to the decisions regarding distribution of resources is highly contentious. As a starting point for participatory rights work, a rights-based approach to development must ultimately guarantee the right of equal access to resource management decision-making (Brocklesby and Crawford 2005: 23; DfID 2000: 8). Access to the decision-making process can either assume hidden or visible forms. Visible forms of decision-making refer to branches of government such as the legislative and judicial, while hidden forms manifest in 'behind the scenes' deals apparent in clientelism. Either form has the power to discriminate in an environment of contending interests (VeneKlasen *et al.* 2004: 8). VeneKlasen *et al.* (ibid. 12) further suggest increased honesty in visible forms of decision-making and an elimination of the closed spaces evident in hidden forms. For example, this dual process has been ongoing in India, where the National Centre for Advocacy Studies (2004: 10) reports 'a sustained movement in transparent government'.

Mapping access rights in the decision-making processes of resource management contains an additional dimension, which is legitimacy of competing rights claims made by stakeholders from numerous sectors of society (VeneKlasen *et al.* 2004: 4). For example, the case study of this chapter relates how the Chinese government is developing a natural resource in Xinjiang, oil, to meet domestic energy needs and to generate revenue across the country. Yet, many Uyghurs in the region would like to see the greater proportion of benefits accrued from oil staying within Xinjiang. The example shows Toyo's (2003: 32) observation that rights claims are not always made for the benefit of all citizens and may even exclude sectors of society. The literature reveals that in both claimed spaces and visible forms of power, states have been more responsive to participatory non-governmental actors who have specific rights claims (DfID 2000: 17). An illustration of rights claims leading to directed participatory action and ultimately to government action is found in Nyamu-Musembi and Musyoki's (2004: 24) Kenyan study, where 'community-based movements are strategizing to better organize to demand accountability from government'. The Kenyan study of participation and rights, among numerous examples, includes the 'Mombassa council tenants who, since the mid-1990s, have succeeded in thwarting plans for irregular sale of the estates to private developers' (ibid.: 25). Successful participatory rights work also entails directing rights claims to the institutions that have an obligation to meet them. Piron (2003: 12) summarises the importance of this point by stating that rights work not only focuses 'on the demand side of rights-claiming, but also on the legitimate nature of these claims, and the obligation of the state to respond to them'.

VeneKlasen *et al.* (2004: 4) add that effective rights claims can only be made from institutions that marginalised people can access. They propose local and national forms of government as appropriate institutions from which to claim rights. However, the origins of international human rights instruments are in the multilateral system of nation states. Galtung (1998: 216) argues that there is a case for claiming rights from global institutions. In this paradigm, states are duty-bearers of the articles in international human rights instruments and are responsible to multilateral organisations for compliance. Yet citizens in authoritarian societies, such as China, are generally unable to put pressure on their states at this level as the central government remains in firm control over information to the wider world:

> [T]he pervasive control and regulation of information by the PRC government through State Secrets, State Security, and other laws, social and police controls, and censorship technology, not only undermines effective monitoring and review of the PRC government's compliance with … [ICESCR], but also impedes its ability to formulate properly designed policies and programs that facilitate public scrutiny and participation.
>
> (HRIC 2005: i)

As an additional layer of state accountability to counter-balance the lack of information on international human rights instruments in controlled societies, this work, in accordance with VeneKlasen *et al.* (2004: 19), proposes that nationally generated documentation, such as constitutions, be taken into consideration for rights claims by advocates of a rights-based approach to development.

As a summary, the subsequent points on the effective operationalisation of rights work in participation are offered to complete the eight-point framework for the operationalisation of a rights-based approach to development in Xinjiang:

- Access to the decision-making process of resource distribution is central.
- Claimants operate in an arena of competing and conflicting rights claims.

- Specific claims are more successful than broad claims to equality.
- Claims should be addressed to accessible institutions.

There is considerable overlap between participation and rights within a rights-based approach to development. Both concepts work in synergy to form a comprehensive and integrated method to promote empowerment and development. Operationalising participation and rights within a rights-based approach to development is 'not simply a matter of "giving permission" for marginalized people to join in, but of dealing with the barriers which prevent them joining in and encouraging their acceptance by the rest of society' (Brocklesby and Crawford 2005: 23).

Eight-point framework

Participation empowers and is an end

The development of an electoral system for village and neighbourhood committees in China seemingly offers an opportunity to explore new interpretations of participation among Uyghurs. Uyghur participation in state-led development initiatives, at the very least, has taken the form of forced inputs of labour (known as *hashar*). This kind of participation is exemplified in Xinjiang by village irrigation projects, which are characterised by the forced and free input of physical labour over any kind of contribution of opinion on project implementation from the community.[1] Such projects in Plummer and Taylor's (2004: 48) opinion 'can fundamentally misdirect the very nature of the participatory project away from decision-making and towards exploitative use of poor households'. Whereas village and neighbourhood committees are mobilised to implement projects, they also have the potential to embody the rights claims of marginalised communities. In essence, the committees provide a previously unavailable representative platform. Nevertheless, the continuing dominance of the centre in China will dictate levels of participation available to Uyghurs. Plummer and Taylor (2004: xviii) observe that 'Expanding the power of local institutions, with participation as part of their mode of operation, would be zero-sum only when and to the extent that decision-makers at the centre did not want for communities at the periphery what those communities want for themselves'.

Individuals and communities must discover their level of political consciousness

Uyghur protests over social and political issues suggest that public consciousness over issues of inequality is high. While the nature of Uyghur protest is frequently viewed through the lens of ethno-nationalist grievances over genuine self-determination, demonstrations have also been motivated by instances of discrimination. For example, the July 2009 demonstration that preceded an outbreak of unrest in the regional capital of Urumchi was characterised by calls for greater protection by the Chinese state against economic and social discrimination. Therefore, the development of a political consciousness that the protests reflect ostensibly stems from the continuing repressive experiences of Uyghurs under Chinese rule. However, political consciousness originating from an increased knowledge of the processes of political institutions is an alternative form that has the potential to advocate for rights through more formalised paths. First, there is the contention that political bodies at the local level are becoming more representative and open: 'Since the income and expenses of the village and its decision-making activities are transparent, villagers can exercise effective supervision over cadres' (Yu 2004: 14). Second, representative bodies provide opportunities to educate and address rights violations:

> [V]illage elections are a process of practicing democracy as well as a process of educating and training peasants and village cadres, enhancing their consciousness of democracy and law while strengthening their ability to implement democracy. Recently, there have been an increasing number of administrative appeals by peasants who are distraught with village elections. This fact shows, on the one hand, that there still exists much resistance to village democracy. On the other hand, it clearly evidences a gradual awakening of peasants' consciousness of democracy and rule of law.
>
> (Xiang 2000)

Power spaces in participatory processes require understanding

Chinese government development strategies in Xinjiang are formulated at the centre, as the Work Forum in 2010 clearly illustrated, and implementation of those strategies is ultimately the responsibility of local authorities. The 'top-down' character of development policy formulation displays the form of power relationships. Participatory rights for marginalised people in state-led development initiatives appear to run contrary to the existing power structure. Equality and development as viewed by the Chinese formulators of state-led development initiatives are measured in economic and not political terms, which de-emphasise the importance of political participation at the local level. Consequently, state-led development initiatives seek to use macroeconomic solutions to transform regions, with less importance placed on the input of and outcomes for marginalised people. The lack of input from marginalised people in policy formation is significant. If decision-making over state-led development initiatives continues only at the highest levels, the inequalities experienced by marginalised people will persist. Central authorities must see the necessity of consulting with village and neighbourhood committees or permit the formation of independent NGOs in the region. This suggestion entails a transition from closed to invited spaces. While a rights-based approach to development ideally operates in claimed spaces, the approach is not 'one size fits all'. The gradual emergence of a non-governmental sector in Xinjiang's development necessitates working through the government to achieve claimed spaces in the future.

Participation and leadership should be meaningful

Meaningful participation for Uyghurs requires the establishment of organisations or social networks directly outside the jurisdiction of the Chinese government. Uyghurs currently have their interests articulated by a distant central government in a non-consultative manner rather than the ability to initiate rights claims through a non-governmental process. Uyghurs have made attempts to do this, most notably through traditional gatherings called *mäxräp*, but the repressive climate in the region has made sustaining this next to impossible. Indeed, the demonstrations in Ghulja in 1997 centred on the closing of independent groups working on social issues. The expansion of NGOs nationwide, even in the face of fluctuating support, is a pattern that should be operating in Xinjiang, but does not. The central government's policy of repressing Uyghur rights to provide the perceived stability for long-term development goals requires reassessment. The Chinese government cannot act alone in achieving progress towards the realisation of rights. Zhang (2003: 20)states:

> As China becomes more diversified and pluralized, the government alone cannot deal with all of the issues and concerns facing society. New institutions such as NGOs can mobilize large amounts of social capital that are instrumental to China's social and economic development. To facilitate NGO development in China, the government needs to put in place a more constructive legal framework in which NGOs can function in partnership with the government.

In addition, minority leadership in local government is also fundamental in the meaningful participation of Uyghurs. According to official statistics, the number of minority cadres has increased throughout CCP administration of Xinjiang. The Chinese government (2003: 648) reports that 'In 1955, when the Xinjiang Uygur Autonomous Region was established, there were 46,000 ethnic-minority cadres. Today, there are as many as 348,000, accounting for 51.8 per cent of the total number of cadres in the autonomous region.' However, the inclusion of Uyghur cadres in the political institutions of Xinjiang does not necessarily mean that Uyghur concerns are represented. Real power does not lie with ethnic minority officials but with a select group of centre-appointed, and Han Chinese, cadres who ensure consistency with central government policy. This belief has been challenged, making the point that present forms of Uyghur representation in government are beneficial because they provide a two-way channel between government and ethnic minorities:

> Contrary to a common assumption, the absence of real power does not mean that the ethnic-minority leaders do not play a significant role.... Even if they have only formal power in the structure they are the only mediation between the state and the society.
>
> (Bequelin 2000: 86)

An appreciation of the decision-making process is central

Chinese citizens nationwide, through village and neighbourhood committees, are theoretically presented with an opportunity to access visible forms of the decision-making process at the local level. Uyghur representation and leadership of village and neighbourhood committees signifies a *possible* new source of political power and participation if the system were implemented transparently. In the opinion of Taylor (2004: 32):

> The establishment of VCs [village committees] has created a new basis for political power – through popular election. It also appears to be producing a changing distribution of power within China's villages ... not only has the basis for involvement in decision-making become broader, but the focus of power within villages has also changed.

Increased access to local government is a trend complemented by rising pressures on corruption. In Altay, in the far north of Xinjiang, officials are now required to declare assets and incomes publicly in an attempt at transparency (*China Daily* 2009). However, both governmental and non-governmental actors in Xinjiang must constantly reappraise their decision-making relationships if change is to happen. Reform in this area moves away from the government-led decision-implementation model to a more dynamic decision-making process. 'Participation, in this sense, involves conflict, and demands a capacity to analyze, negotiate and alter unequal relations at all levels' (VeneKlasen *et al.* 2004: 5).

Claimants operate in an arena of competing and conflicting rights claims

Since the beginning of the reform period, China has moved from the security of the 'iron rice bowl'[2] to competition for economic and social resources. In the context of increased Han in-migration and the shortages of land consummate with Xinjiang's physical terrain, Uyghurs are involved in an intensified struggle for finite resources in the region. In this context, increased Han Chinese in-migration has created an unlikely alliance between some Uyghurs and the older generation of Han in-migrants to Xinjiang from before the reform period: 'In some villages, elderly Chinese farmers are complaining that the arrival of new migrants has destroyed the modus vivendi they have developed with Uyghurs, and has heightened competition for the already limited supply of water, fertilizer and seeds' (Bequelin 2000: 85). Bequelin's observations show that relationships in rights claims are dynamic and that interests can often overlap ethnic delineations that have dominated views of discontent in Xinjiang.

Specific claims are more successful than broad claims to equality

Ongoing Uyghur unrest is a clear indicator that local and central Chinese authorities are not addressing Uyghur grievances or listening to Uyghur voices. In a rights-based approach to development, non-governmental actors direct specific rights claims to state authorities. The Chinese state's large investment in natural resource extraction in the region requires corresponding investment in social programmes that target specific Uyghur objections to shortages of economic opportunity, linguistic rights, religious rights and participatory rights. In the current absence of independent NGO activity and limited autonomy among village and neighbourhood committees, there are few accessible channels to pursue these rights claims. In fact, village and neighbourhood committees have proved effective in achieving rights claims from higher levels of government than from the regional authorities. Across China, they have been, as Taylor (2004: 31) records, 'successfully reducing charges and levies, securing funds for village services, arranging infrastructure improvements … reducing illegal land seizures, defraying hospital charges and mobilizing uncompensated workers for local employment'. This phenomenon may be explained by the willingness of local authorities to display a harder line in order to avoid censure by central authorities.

Claims should be addressed to accessible institutions

Although the existence of village and neighbourhood committees points to theoretical support for the rights claims of marginalised people nationwide, the accountability, much as the capacity of these committees, exists at the local level. However, compliance with the articles contained in the ICCPR and ICESCR also requires greater accountability on the part of the Chinese central government in the multilateral arena. International human rights instruments provide a legal basis for rights claims, but if Uyghurs are to initiate rights claims through these instruments, the accessibility of the multilateral system must be increased.

The multilateral system is a monitoring tool to which stronger enforcement of international human rights instruments would be beneficial. Alternatively, and in addition to international instruments, domestic instruments can also be utilised on which to base rights claims. The Chinese government 'is under an obligation to give effect to the Covenant [ICESCR] in its domestic legal order' (HRIC 2005: ii), and in its provisions the Chinese Constitution could provide Uyghur advocates with an accessible means of address. The constitution states that

> All ethnic groups in the People's Republic of China are equal. The state protects the lawful rights and interests of the ethnic minorities and upholds and develops a relationship of equality, unity and mutual assistance among all of China's ethnic groups. Discrimination against and oppression of any ethnic group are prohibited.
>
> (Chinese government 2003: 646)

Compliance in this instance rests with the CCP administration. While pressure can be brought to bear by non-governmental actors in this regard, the character of a participatory rights-based approach to development in Xinjiang inevitably involves the non-infringement of the state:

> [W]hereas elsewhere participatory processes emerge from partnerships formed in civil society – partnerships that build on diversity of relationships and benefit from non-governmental demonstration projects – in China, the partner is invariably the government and the interface role is restricted to government officials.
>
> (Plummer 2004: 8)

The eight-point framework provides an outline of the possibilities that exist for a Uyghur-initiated rights-based approach to development. The framework does not indicate the inevitability of these opportunities coming to pass. In some cases the framework discusses nationwide trends that may arrive in Xinjiang in the future. The framework does emphasise that the operationalisation of a rights-based approach to development will involve a partnership of governmental and non-governmental actors. While China's state apparatus is decentralising, the pace of that change in Xinjiang is vastly slower due to the state's security concerns. State-led economic policies are currently being used as a stabilising panacea to mollify those security concerns; however, 'the forces of history are certainly moving China, like other countries, in the direction of more participatory governance and management (Uphoff 2004: xvii).

Conclusion

State-led development initiatives alone do not bring participation, rights and developmental equality to marginalised people. The formulation of Chinese government development policy in Xinjiang invariably happens in the closed spaces of central government and does not include the opinions of the people they are designed to assist. Development initiatives are in essence centre-led policies that local government is mobilised to carry out. These directives are highly politicised, with the aim of bringing Xinjiang firmly into the Chinese fold. The Chinese government rhetoric of equality is rarely implemented in the region and often exacerbates economic and social inequalities. Han Chinese are often more prepared for the kinds of economic and developmental incentives offered by the Chinese government-led development than Uyghurs. They are prepared in terms of marketable skills, language and education. The Chinese government has not prioritised development on Uyghur terms. Indicators show that in terms of education, health and employment rights, Uyghurs lag far behind their Han counterparts. Consultation between the centre and the periphery on this issue is not encouraged.

Operationalising a rights-based approach to development in Xinjiang for Uyghurs will involve a transition by the Chinese government to operate in less closed spaces and view participation more as an end than a means. In this light, the Chinese government will have to open the field to independent NGO work in

Xinjiang. The village and neighbourhood committees theoretically open the *possibility* at some time in the future of raising political consciousness, increasing the accountability of officials and eliminating hidden decision-making processes. The value of participation is not lost on Uyghurs despite the environment of closed spaces, and the process of establishing trust between Uyghurs and the state is an ongoing task.

While the eight-point framework for operationalising a rights-based approach to development is gleaned from studies of countries with strong civil societies, the flexibility of a rights-based approach to development means that it also points to opportunities for emerging civil societies. China's emerging civil society also illustrates that not only do state-led development initiatives require the input of non-governmental actors, but also that non-governmental actors must work in partnership with the state. In politically controlled environments such as Xinjiang, rights claims can only be made through existing political channels. This means one of the most important tasks is to build trust in political institutions through increased transparency. Nevertheless, a participatory rights-based approach to development in partnership with the state presents a perspective in realising rights for marginalised people in whatever political environment they may find themselves.

International human rights instruments and the multilateral UN system designed to enforce their obligations play a major role in the legal basis of rights claims. The case of Xinjiang shows how the international community has responsibilities to marginalised people, such as ethnic minorities, to strengthen its monitoring of rights abuses. Without proper enforcement, marginalised people will need to seek alternative means of address. As an addition to the eight-point framework presented from the literature, this work suggests the addition of: What is the most appropriate and effective way to make rights claims in the present political environment?

This work suggests that research undertaken on a rights-based approach to development points to the partnership of state and non-state actors in realising rights claims, though the argument requires further investigation. The assumption that trends in China will translate into Xinjiang cannot be substantiated at this point. The sheer size and diversity of China means that what is happening in one part of the country does not necessarily happen in another. Provinces in the east are less complex in their ethnic composition and politically more stable than Xinjiang. The widespread development of NGOs in Xinjiang may never happen and the government may persist in its pursuit of state-led development initiatives. Its lack of stability means that Xinjiang is less likely to see innovation.

A participatory rights-based approach to development is a significant opportunity for marginalised people to rewrite the nature of political power relationships. It embodies the self-empowerment of marginalised people in their development, derived from solid international and domestic legal foundations. The approach also integrates both the moral and legal arguments for rights claims. A participatory rights-based approach to development has the potential to operate in authoritarian and repressive contexts, and may be able to steer state-led development initiatives towards more grass-roots concerns. In the wider context, the partnership of a participatory rights-based approach to development and a consultative state-led development initiative attached to the benchmarks of the Millennium Development Goals presents a meaningful path to poverty alleviation, addressing rights issues and conflict resolution.

Notes

1 Author's observation of an irrigation project in Artush village in 1996. For more on the forms of participation in China, see Uphoff (2004: xvi).

2 '[A] reasonably comprehensive welfare system – the so-called "iron rice bowl" – of housing, education, employment, maternity leave and pension benefits provided for each worker in a state-owned enterprise' (Taylor 2004: 24).

References

Bequelin, Nicolas (2000) 'Xinjiang in the Nineties', *The China Journal*, 44: 65–90.

Brocklesby, M.A. and Crawford, S. (2005) *Rights Based Development: A Guide to Implementation*, Swansea: Centre for Development Studies.

China Daily (2009) 'Officials' Pay to be Publicized'. www.chinadaily.com.cn/language_tips/cdaudio/2009-01/12/content_7388181.htm (accessed 16 July 2010).

Chinese government (2003) 'History and Development of Xinjiang', White Paper, Beijing, Information Office of the State Council of the People's Republic of China.

DfID (2000) 'Realising Human Rights for Poor People', Department for International Development.

Donnelly, Jack (1999) 'Human Rights, Democracy, and Development', *Human Rights Quarterly*, 21 (3): 608–632.

Galtung, Johan (1998) 'The Third World and Human Rights in the Post-1989 World Order', in Tony Evans (ed.) *Human Rights Fifty Years On: A Reappraisal*, Manchester: Manchester University Press, pp. 211–232.

Hamm, Brigitte (2001) 'A Human Rights Approach to Development', *Human Rights Quarterly*, 23 (44): 1005–1031.

Häusermann, Julia (1998) *A Human Rights Approach to Development*, London: Rights and Humanity.

HRIC (2005) *Implementation of the International Covenant on Economic, Social and Cultural Rights in the People's Republic of China*, New York, NY: Human Rights in China.

Jasis, M. and García, M. (2004) *Linking Rights and Participation: Mexico Country Study*, Brighton: Institute of Development Studies.

Júnior, A.P., Antunes, M. and Romano, J.O. (2004) *Linking Rights and Participation: Brazil Country Study*, Brighton: Institute of Development Studies.

Lumbantobing, D. and Zulminarni, N. (2004) *Linking Rights and Participation: Indonesia Country Study*, Brighton: Institute of Development Studies.

Mohan, G. and Holland, J. (2001) 'Human Rights and Development in Africa: Moral Intrusion or Empowering', *Review of African Political Economy*, 88 (28): 177–196.

National Centre for Advocacy Studies (2004) *Linking Rights and Participation: India Country Study*, Brighton: Institute of Development Studies.

Nyamu-Musembi, C. and Musyoki, S. (2004) *Kenyan Civil Society Perspectives on Rights, Rights-Based Approaches to Development and Participation*, Brighton: Institute of Development Studies.

Piron, Laure-Hélène (2003) *The Right to Development: A Review of the Current State of the Debate for the Department for International Development*, London: Overseas Development Institute.

Plummer, J. (2004) 'Introduction', in Janelle Plummer and John G. Taylor (eds) *Community Participation in China: Issues and Processes for Capacity Building*, London: Earthscan, pp. 1–20.

Plummer, J. and Taylor, J.G. (2004) 'The Characteristics of Community Participation in China', in Janelle Plummer and John G. Taylor (eds) *Community Participation in China: Issues and Processes for Capacity Building*, London: Earthscan, pp. 36–54.

Taylor, John G. (2004) 'The context for community participation in China', in Janelle Plummer and John G. Taylor (eds) *Community Participation in China: Issues and Processes for Capacity Building*, London: Earthscan, pp. 23–35.

Toyo, Nkoyo (2003) *Linking Rights and Participation: Nigeria Country Study*, Brighton: Institute of Development Studies.

UNDP (2000) *Human Development Report 2000*, New York, NY: UNDP.

Uphoff, Norman (2004) 'Foreword', in Janelle Plummer and John G. Taylor (eds) *Community Participation in China: Issues and Processes for Capacity Building*, London: Earthscan, pp. xvi–xviii.

VeneKlasen, Lisa, Miller, Valerie, Clark, Cindy and Reilly, Molly (2004) *Rights-Based Approaches and Beyond: Challenges of Linking Rights and Participation*, Brighton: Institute of Development Studies.

White, G., Howell, J.A. and Shang, X. (1996) *In Search of Civil Society: Market Reform and Social Change in Contemporary China*, Oxford: Clarendon Press.

Xiang, Jiaquan (2000) 'Self-Government in Chinese Villages: An Evaluation', *Perspectives*, 1 (4), 29 February. www.oycf.org/Perspectives2/4_022900/self_government.htm (accessed 16 July 2010).

Yu, Keping (2004) 'The Emergence of Chinese Civil Society and its Significance to Governance'. www.ids.ac.uk/ids/civsoc/final/china/chn8.doc (accessed 16 July 2010).

Zhang, Ye (2003) *China's Emerging Civil Society*, Beijing: The Asia Foundation.

11 Linking peace and development

An imperative for conflict transformation in Kashmir

Seema Shekhawat

Introduction

This chapter explores the issue of whether Kashmir can be a model of conflict transformation in which peace process and development activities can be conducted simultaneously even as the conflict continues and parties negotiate their positions. Peace as a means of conflict resolution dawned in Kashmir in its full import only in the late 1990s, when parties to the conflict, particularly India and Pakistan, realised the futility of armed conflict in Kashmir. Though it is difficult to identify a steady conflict pattern in Kashmir, since its inception in the late 1940s, its emergence in the regional as well as wider Eurasian matrix as one of the most protracted conflicts in a volatile region with subsequent heavy costs propelled the parties to seek non-violent resolution as violence had failed to resolve the conflict. While factors like religious fundamentalism and terrorism emerged in later years as crucial factors in determining the contours of the Kashmir conflict, its location between three nuclear powers with complex equations between them, and its geopolitical relevance in the power rivalry in the wider regions makes Kashmir different from many other conflicts. Tangible and intangible costs aside, the region has not witnessed resolution of the conflict, partly owing to the rigid positions of the parties and partly due to persistence of violence, though intermittent. The post-2008 stalemate in India–Pakistan relations also brings into focus the way in which the Kashmir conflict is subject to shifting bilateral relations between India and Pakistan. Despite its own dynamics, the bilateral relations play a crucial role in determining the nature of conflict and peace in the region.

The parties to the conflict recognise the futility and the heavy cost of resorting to violence as a means for conflict resolution. Though this realisation perhaps has not dawned in full among the parties, the peace overtures and negotiations, particularly in the 2000s, stalled after the 26 November 2008 Mumbai attacks, to be resumed again in 2010, indicate that despite the troublesome pace of peace in the region, the past decades of violence are unlikely to return. As the Indian leadership envisages a *Naya*[1] (new) Kashmir free from violence, and the Pakistan leadership envisages its solution through peace and dialogue,[2] it appears peace has gained supremacy over violence in the region. Violent conflict has devastated development prospects within the region, escalating poverty and degradation, thus providing another spur to violence in an almost cyclic fashion. This symbiotic relationship between poverty and violence has been emphasised in recent years in policy circles; hence the emphasis that development processes cannot wait till the conflict has run its full course. Though economic development cannot be the sole guarantor of peace and ultimate conflict resolution, it undoubtedly can act as a catalyst to moderate the violent activities resulting from poverty and unemployment, and motivate the parties towards peaceful resolution of the conflict. While conceding a holistic view of development will encompass more than economic development, the chapter confines its analysis mainly to economic development and its impact on the peace process.

Kashmir's location at the strategic crossroads between China in the east, Pakistan in the west, India in the south and Afghanistan and Central Asia to the north, its past legacies – particularly the silk route trade – and its cultural connections with the northern regions make Kashmir a crucial part of the Eurasian region (Schoeberlein 2002; Mahapatra 2008, 2009).[3] While admitting the fluid and ambiguous nature of the term 'conflict', for the purpose of this chapter, conflict in Kashmir refers specifically to the militancy-related violence in the Indian part of Kashmir, called Jammu and Kashmir (J&K). The present analysis has been confined to J&K because the Pakistani side of Kashmir has not witnessed militant violence, and comparisons between the two sides are generally difficult to make due to different social, political and economic systems in both parts of Kashmir (Mahapatra and Shekhawat 2008a).

The main arguments of this chapter follow this course. The first section will focus on conflict, particularly its tangible and intangible costs, identifying the devastating consequences of violence, both material and psychological, and hence the urgency for economic reconstruction and development of the region. The second section argues how the study of the symbiotic relationship between peace and development is crucial for conflict resolution in Kashmir. The third section focuses on the peace process as it is not only crucial for development, but also a necessary condition for conflict resolution in the region. The fourth section identifies some of the areas indigenous to the region of Kashmir which need special attention in the development drive. The final section summarises the main conclusions.

Conflict and its costs

The conflict in Kashmir is one of the most protracted conflicts involving, among others, two sovereign states – India and Pakistan – both of which possess nuclear weapons. The conflict over the region has persisted since 1947, when, following independence both countries staked a claim to the region of Kashmir, a princely state under British rule.[4] The conflict has led to four wars between India and Pakistan in 1947, 1965, 1971 and 1999, and to the division of the Kashmir region,[5] with one part remaining within India and the remainder divided between Pakistan and China. The total area of the Kashmir region is

222,236 km^2, including 78,114 km^2 under the control of Pakistan and 42,685 km^2 under China, of which Pakistan handed over 5,130 km^2 (Jammu & Kashmir: A Profile n.d). The conflict has two broad and interlinked dimensions: the external, in which India and Pakistan are antagonists, with four wars fought between them since 1947; and the internal, arising from a separatist movement in the Indian part of Kashmir. The internal dimension of the conflict is characterised by violent militancy, particularly in the Kashmir valley, which is predominantly inhabited by Sunni Muslims. The valley witnessed a surge of popular support for independence in 1989–1990 that later spread to other highland areas of Jammu and Kashmir, including Poonch and Rajouri. Analysts have proffered a number of overlapping theories to account for this rise in militancy; their arguments include such factors as unfulfilled promises of self-determination made by India, the dilution of regional autonomy by the Indian government, lack of democracy, religious extremism and Pakistani intervention. This chapter does not go into details of the conflict and its multiple dimensions as its main argument does not necessitate such a study; one may refer elsewhere for a detailed study of the Kashmir conflict and its history (Ganguly 1997; Lamb 1992; Schofield 2004; Puri 1993).

The tangible and intangible costs of violence in Kashmir include far-reaching economic, cultural and social devastation in the region (Mahapatra and Shekhawat 2008b; Shekhawat 2009: 976–981). Even by conservative estimates, thousands have lost their lives. The number of missing people also runs into the hundreds. Civilians have suffered from pervasive violence, fear and coercion and have become indirect victims through arrest, torture, disappearance and loss of their loved ones. The conflict has created an atmosphere in which violence is an integral part of day-to-day life, inducing a sense of resignation and frustration among people and negatively affecting their physical and mental health. The conflict has also led to large-scale population displacement among several demographics (Shekhawat 2006: 64–66). Sources of livelihood including agriculture, horticulture and handicraft industries are sufficient only for subsistence rather than for business growth or profit. Essential infrastructure in the form of electricity, roads, communications and drinking water remains underdeveloped due to the impact of militancy on the state resources.

Tourism, one of the main industries in the Kashmir valley, has suffered tremendously due to violent activities. It has declined substantially since the late 1980s, when militancy gained momentum. The number of tourists visiting the state per year went down from around 7,000,000 in the pre-militancy days to a few thousands in the following years. It is estimated that the state lost 27 million potential tourists in 1989–2002, leading to tourism revenue loss of $3.6 billion (Strategic Foresight Group 2005: 69). According to the records, although as many as 557,974 tourists visited the state in 1989, in 1993 the number reduced to 8,026. In 2002, 27,358 tourists visited the state. The number of tourists is dependent on the level of violence at a particular time. Violence has also directly affected other important sources of livelihood such as agriculture, horticulture and the handicraft industry as it discourages investment from within and outside the region and also negatively impacts the morale of the local population. These sectors have become the survival mechanisms for the local people, but are not flourishing.

The sacrifice of the Kashmir conflict as described above is a glimpse of the overall dismal scenario in the state. The human and material costs of the conflict are much greater than described above, and need elaborate study and research. However, the above analysis provides enough indication of the bleak economic scenario in the state. There is no doubt that there are political, socio-cultural and economic challenges that need understanding as well as pragmatic action. It has been argued, among many reasons for the continuation of militancy that it is 'frustration at a lack of economic opportunities' (Pasricha 2011). Hence, it is necessary to see conflict in Kashmir not only in terms of religious antagonism or clashes of national interests, but also in terms of poverty and underdevelopment, which any peace process in the region must take into account.

Development for peace

Recent decades have seen the emergence and escalation of a variety of violent conflicts around the world. Regardless of the motives, violent conflicts are usually disastrous socially as well as culturally, and economically as well as politically. Apart from a few beneficiaries in the arms industry, economic disruption is an integral part of conflict, negatively affecting people's livelihoods and development processes. With violence becoming a part of everyday life, the affected region becomes 'conflict habituated'. The aim of parties involved in the conflict becomes maximising advantage over rival groups. In this scenario development is not prioritised. Such a scenario gives rise to the question of whether sustainable development can be advanced during times of protracted armed conflict. Earlier development theory and practice were largely conflict-neutral, and even when they attended to conflict, the scope was quite limited. Traditional approaches to development presupposed that development takes place under conditions of peace. Yet that is rarely the case. The absence of peace is a pervasive global reality. Most countries have to strive for development against a background of past, present or threatened conflict (Secretary General of the United Nations 1994). The modern development theories, thus, largely focus on conflict and development in a holistic framework. This argument is equally applicable to the situation in Kashmir.

The cause of conflict in many cases is a lack of development – economic, political or social – or a varied combination of all three. The relationship between conflict and development is strong, and is a two-way process: conflict retards development, and equally, failures in development substantially increase the tendency for conflict. There arises a 'conflict trap' – a cycle of conflict-related violence and economic retardation (Collier and Hoffler 1998). Modern analysts thus subscribe to the inclusive view that development cannot be reserved solely for peace and conflict-free environments. Collier and Hoffler argue that development activities in conflict zones can play a crucial role in defusing violent situations by addressing problems of poverty and underdevelopment. They reason that, among many other factors, poverty and underdevelopment fuel violence in conflict situations. Several studies have shown that the influence of conflict on development, and vice versa, is significant in both exacerbating tensions and minimising them (Buckles 1999; Anderson 1999). The OECD (1997), in its 'Policy Statement and Guidelines on Conflict, Peace and Development', also argues that sustainable development cannot be achieved without peace and stability, and peace and security are not possible without meeting the basic needs of the people.

Studies from conflict-affected areas show that economic reconstruction contributes positively to long-term political harmony (Junne and Verhoken 2004). In one of its reports, the Secretary General of the UN points out that, among other things, the promotion of sustainable economic development is an essential aspect of conflict prevention or resolution (Secretary General of the United Nations 1992). The research described here is consonant with the UN Secretary General's assumption and puts forth the argument that sustainable development in Kashmir, with a people-centric approach, can deter much of the violence and foster a process of conflict resolution. In the majority of cases, the development process can continue even during conflict, and the pace of development can be effectively increased, parallel to peace processes. Benefits of continued development during conflict include: minimising the cost of the conflict; providing a means of survival for the people; and more importantly, avoid the probability of a development vacuum in the post-conflict situation, which increases the chances of conflict revival.

Negotiations and peace processes

In the 1990s, geopolitical changes brought about by the end of the Cold War altered the dynamics of international relations with implications for conflicts around the world. Conventional armed disputes have been transformed by the intensification of globalisation and increasing acceptance of peaceful means for conflict resolution (Mahapatra 2007: 31). The multiple players involved in the complex Kashmir conflict, namely India, Pakistan, Kashmiri people and the international community have been influenced by these developments in the global scenario. The result has been the historic peace process in the region. A multi-pronged strategy for conflict resolution has evolved, which included, among others, the initiation of dialogue between India and Pakistan as well as between New Delhi and J&K. These talks gathered momentum with the accession of the National Democratic Alliance (NDA) to power in New Delhi in 1998. The NDA government furthered peace efforts, starting notably with a historic bus journey from New Delhi to Lahore on 20 February 1999 with the then Indian Prime Minister Atal Behari Vajpayee on board.

In October 2003 India proposed a series of confidence-building measures aimed at improving communications by road, rail and sea between India and Pakistan. On 26 November 2003, India announced a ceasefire on the dividing line in Kashmir. Despite reports of occasional violations, the ongoing ceasefire is significant as the first formal ceasefire agreement between India and Pakistan since the outbreak of militancy in J&K. Its continuation to the present has brought perceptible normalcy to border areas. On the sidelines of the 2004 SAARC summit, India and Pakistan collectively expressed their willingness to engage in a composite dialogue aimed at the peaceful settlement of all bilateral issues, including Kashmir. Since then, Indian and Pakistani officials have met a number of times to discuss issues of common concern, and have agreed to cooperate in many areas such as opening intra-Kashmir routes, facilitating people-to-people contact and bilateral trade. The process was adversely affected in the aftermath of the 2008 Mumbai terror attacks when India accused Pakistan of not taking action against the terrorist organisation Lashkar-e-Toiba for orchestrating the attack. This development was a setback to the peace process, but there is an overall perception that the peace process between the two countries is beneficial and should continue.

Alongside Indo-Pak negotiations, India launched a major peace mission in J&K to involve the civilians as well as separatist groups in the peace process. On 19 November 2000, India announced a unilateral ceasefire aimed at persuading militants to renounce violence and join the peace process. This ceasefire initiative was extended twice, lasting until 26 February 2001. Since then, New Delhi has refused any further ceasefire extensions. This has been partly due to alleged violations of the original ceasefire by militants. In 2001 J&K held its first panchayat (grass-roots body at the village level) elections in more than two decades, followed by another election in 2011. These elections were a turning point in light of J&K's electoral history. In 1996, after nearly six years of the president's rule, state assembly elections returned the National Conference to power. This party had governed single-handedly, or in a coalition with the Indian National Congress, since the start of electoral politics in the state in 1951. In 2002 elections brought unprecedented change to the state assembly's composition by bringing a coalition of the People's Democratic Party and the Indian National Congress into power. J&K held another state assembly election in 2008. Despite calls from separatist groups, such as the Hurriyat Conference, and advocates of a Pakistan union or an independent Kashmir to boycott the polls, an overwhelming number of residents participated in these elections. The 2008 elections witnessed 61.49 per cent of the electorate voting, as compared to the 43.69 per cent who voted in the 2002 elections (Kumar 2008). These democratic exercises are significant because lack of electoral democracy was a significant reason for the onset of militancy in J&K in the late 1980s (Shekhawat 2006: 51–56).

New Delhi convened a meeting of the people of J&K on 24 April 2007 to have dialogue in what is referred to as a round table conference (RTC). It was the third such conference, the first one being held in 2005. The main agenda of the conference was to discuss the reports presented by the four working groups (out of five working groups) established in the second RTC in Srinagar in May 2006. The first working group focused on confidence-building measures; the second focused on strengthening relations across the line of control between

India and Pakistan; the third dealt with economic development of the state; and the fourth working group aimed at providing good governance to people. The fifth working group that worked on centre-state relations submitted its report in 2009.

The debates over prospects for dialogue between India and Pakistan took priority in Indian policy discourse since the bilateral peace process became stalled when Pak-based terrorists attacked India's commercial capital, Mumbai, in November 2008. The 26 November attack pulled the bilateral relations down to a new low. However, the joint statement on 16 July 2009 at Sharm el Sheikh not only revived the prospects of bilateral dialogue, but also brought to the surface the common ground of both countries on issues of terrorism, with Pakistan's promise to do 'everything in its power' to bring the perpetrators of the Mumbai attacks to justice. The joint statement also noted 'India's interest in a stable, democratic Islamic Republic of Pakistan' (*The Hindu* 2009). How far both countries will work together for a better future of the subcontinent is yet to be seen, as the mutual suspicion is quite deep; both sides find it difficult to erase the old sheltered menace of distrust, particularly on the issue of Kashmir. However, an infinite distrust or hatred is neither sustainable nor practicable between the two neighbours. It is in this context that the meeting of foreign secretaries of India and Pakistan on 25 February 2010 in Hyderabad House in New Delhi far exceeded its immediate outcome, primarily owing to two reasons. First, though the meeting did not produce any tangible result, both parties agreed on the importance of dialogue. Second, following the Mumbai terror attack, it was the first official bilateral interaction to take place. Equally importantly, the meeting showed the reality that the process of peace in South Asia cannot effect far-reaching changes in a short span of time as the complex situation demands small and significant steps over a long period of time.

Since February 2010, when direct official talks started between India and Pakistan, after a gap of about 1.5 years, hopes have gathered momentum among civil society members that something positive will gradually come about. The meeting of prime ministers of both countries in the Bhutanese capital of Thimpu on 30 April 2010 on the sidelines of the SAARC summit further increased the peace accord and raised hopes. Both prime ministers emphasised the initiatives to bridge the trust deficit between the two countries.[6] Prime Minister Singh of India, known for his peace overtures to Pakistan despite criticism from groups at home, promised to 'walk the extra mile'[7] to promote friendly relations with Pakistan. The Indian leadership is optimistic that peace and dialogue is the only way forward to resolve the contentious issues. This sentiment was echoed by Pak Prime Minister Yusuf Raja Gilani during his visit to the Indian city of Mohali to watch the world cup semi-final cricket match between India and Pakistan on 30 March 2011. The prime minister told reporters at Chaklala military airbase in Rawalpindi before taking off for Mohali, 'As far as our relations are concerned, I am happy that our talks have resumed', and while appreciating the role of his Indian counterpart, Gilani stated, 'He [Singh] wants to work for peace and prosperity in this region. We are both committed to this and we want the environment to improve so that we can serve the people' (*Times of India* 2011a). It can be argued against this background that though the Mumbai attack dampened the peace process temporarily, it failed to completely neutralise the peace process and its achievements.

Opportunities and challenges

The revival of the economy in Kashmir in the atmosphere of peace gained ground with the realisation that peace attempts and development must go in tandem in Kashmir. There was a noticeable shift in India's policy as the earlier provision of providing central largesse to the state has been transformed into policies for development of the state by launching projects, as well as providing incentives to the private sector to contribute to economic growth. This change in approach is fruitful in two ways. First, it helped address some of the grievances of the people by engaging them in the development process, thereby further contributing to the peace process. Second, it contributed to the prospects of minimising the revival of violence as poverty and unemployment are, among other factors, catalysts of violence. Hence, it may prove not only costly but also imprudent to wait for the conflict to be settled fully before initiating processes of economic development.

The economic revival is an uphill task and is fraught with multiple challenges, ranging from renewing the degenerating industries to tapping new resources and attracting private investment to developing infrastructure. However, the opportunities, especially in the context of economic development, are enormous as the country is not only endowed with rich flora and fauna and scenic beauty, but also has a past record of having a rich economy in the pre-independence era, partly due to its trade with neighbouring regions like China, Central Asia and West Asia via the famous silk route (Mahapatra 2008: 149–155). Tourist destinations like Sonmarg and Gulmarg are known internationally for winter games such as skiing. Gulmarg is also known as the highest green golf course in the world, and boasts the world's largest cable car lift. The famous Dal Lake in the Kashmir valley needs special mention in this context. Adventure sports available include trekking, mountaineering, winter sports, water sports, golf and fishing. However, most of these tourist attractions remain underdeveloped. Many other tourist attractions in the state remain untapped, partly due to the heightened atmosphere of conflict. As in the Kashmir valley, the regions of Jammu and Ladakh also have much tourism potential. Some of the tourist spots in Jammu that need development are Patni Top, the forts of Ramnagar, the temples of Babor and Krimchi, Sudh Mahadev and Mantalai, Shiv Khori, the saint-soldier Banda Bairagi's memorial, as well as the Kishtwar and Bhaderwah hills, all of which can be developed with modern facilities in order to attract a wide cross-section of people from different parts of the world.

Many Kashmiris are engaged in making shawls, silk carpets, rugs and embroidered clothes. The region is also known for silver-work, papier-mâché work, wood-carving and silk-weaving. The ancient art of stone carving is another area of prominence. Tombstones are a specialty of the state's stone carvers. Many stone artisans of the area also build houses and mosques with different stones for each season. This is another area in which Kashmir has its own niche and could be used to boost its economy. Kashmir's economy is highly dependent on agriculture, supporting about 80 per cent of its population. Traditionally, the staple crop of the valley is rice, followed by Indian corn. Wheat, barley and oats are also grown in the region. Blessed with a temperate climate, unlike much of the Indian subcontinent, J&K is well-suited to the production of crops like asparagus, artichoke, seakale, broad beans, beetroot, cauliflower and cabbage. The Pampore region, about 9 km from Srinagar, is home to the finest saffron in the world. The R.S. Pura region in Jammu district is home to one of the best qualities of rice. Nearly 75 per cent of temperate fruits in India are grown in the state. The cultivated orchards yield fine-quality pears, apples, peaches, cherries, walnut, almond, saffron, apricot, strawberry and plums. The industry earns revenue of over INR 500 million annually and provides jobs for the thousands of people directly and indirectly involved in the agricultural sector. Considering the growth prospects of this sector, the state government needs to plan for more and better-quality production. The state should shift its agriculture development strategy from food-security mode to that of value addition by growing certain products like high-value fruits, vegetables and cash crops like saffron that can give high returns.

Sericulture is the traditional occupation for a large section of the population, but due to inadequate infrastructural and agricultural inputs the silk industry, which has seen a glorious past, is in decline. As an important activity related to agriculture, fisheries can also strengthen the productive base of the agricultural economy and generate self-employment, as well as attract tourists if fishing festivals or tournaments are organised. Keeping in view the potential of this sector, the 27,781 km of rivers and streams in the state could provide the facility for the farming of over 40 million tons of fish. There has been a big gap between the demand and supply of fish, and the right strategy cannot only cater to local demands, but also enable the state to export. Some other areas that could be explored include floriculture, medicinal and aromatic plants, mushroom production and apiculture. The recent initiative by the state government under the Technology Mission Programme to establish a local floriculture industry is showing some promise in this context.

Animal husbandry with a diverse livestock in the form of cattle, sheep, goats and poultry also plays a role in the state economy. The production of pashmina (a kind of fine Kashmiri wool) shawls, carpets and blankets depend on the livestock and can render handsome economic returns. The huge gap between the demand and supply in terms of meat consumption compels the state to purchase meat from other parts of India. The state provides a suitable climate for cattle breeding and it could be sufficient. As the demand for milk and milk products is increasing at a fast rate, there is vast scope for dairy development. The modernisation of all of these sectors can play a vital role in economic reconstruction of the state. Besides being provided with professional guidance, there is a need to ensure availability of basic inputs such as seeds, fertilisers, pesticides and storage facilities to develop agriculture and allied sectors. There is also a need to develop proactive sector-specific marketing strategies and explore new markets.

Industrial growth

Kashmir is an industrially backward state, partly because most of the industries are state-owned, and in turn have proved to be burdens on the state exchequer. There is a need to make a functional policy in terms of efficient management of public sector units and their disinvestment. There are many small-scale industries that export products such as textile items, cricket bats and other sports items, walnut and walnut kernels, bitter apricot nuts, foundry fluxes and chemicals and handicraft to various countries, especially European and Gulf countries. While there is a vast scope to increase the export levels of these products, there are many other potential areas for industrial development as well. Potential investment areas include biotechnology, processed food, fruit processing, leather goods, processing of gems and precious stones, honey and other hive products and watershed development. Mineral industry is another potential area of growth since the state is rich in bauxite, limestone, sapphire, gypsum, coal and marble. The forests of the state have vast natural resources that need to be tapped judiciously. Kashmir has a long tradition of wooden furniture-making, and the forests can also contribute to the growth of the herbal industry. Another major area that has yet to attract attention is communication technology in the state in terms of setting up technology parks, providing telephone and internet connections to people living in difficult terrains and facilitating use of communication technology for overall development. The region being an important tourism destination, the hotel industry is another area with tremendous possibilities for growth.

The private sector has yet to join the mission of economic reconstruction of the devastated state. An important strategy for economic development of the state will be to engage the private sector, at national and international levels. In order to flag such policies, the first requirement will be to identify the potential investors, financial institutions and donors. The next step can be to identify the potential areas of investment, followed by an integrated course of action to achieve sustainable development. The region needs attention from national and international financial institutions as well as aid agencies. The international financial institutions like the World Bank and Asian Development Bank (ADB) can significantly contribute towards the development of the region. In November 2004 the World Bank pledged economic assistance for Kashmir to promote peace in the region.[8] The ADB is currently funding road-connectivity projects that were devastated during the years of turmoil. In March 2007 the World Bank approved INR 4,000 million for the improvement of roads in the eight districts of the state under the scheme Pradhan Mantri Gram Sadak Yojana. Some other sectors such as the power sector could be developed with help from these institutions.

Infrastructure growth

Infrastructure renewal and growth is necessary for the economic revival of the state as the violent conflict has exacted extensive damage to existing infrastructure. Some of the important sectors of infrastructure that need immediate attention include power and connectivity. Kashmir is endowed with huge water resources, but tapping these resources for the benefit of the economy has not been done adequately. The state, with huge power potential, has the largest power deficit among the states of India. The region, capable of generating close to 20,000 MW of hydroelectric power, is capable not only of meeting its power demand, but could become an exporter of power.

The difficult terrains of the state coupled with law-and-order problems have contributed to the poor connectivity in the region. The railroad mix of transport in the state is insignificant. As Jammu city is the railhead for the state, Kashmir valley as well as Ladakh are dependent on road transport or expensive air transport. The rural road connectivity scheme of the Bharat Nirman Programme, an Indian government scheme, aims to bring about required changes in infrastructure. There is further need to build alternative roads in places to ensure better connectivity. The government is planning to build an alternative road to the existing national highway connecting the Kashmir and Ladakh regions of the state with the rest of India, as it remains closed for long periods of the year due to bad weather and landslides. There is also a need to upgrade many of the existing roads from two lanes to four lanes. As far as spreading rail connectivity to the whole of J&K is concerned, rail projects such as Hampur–Katra and Qazigund–Baramulla and sections of Udhampur–Baramulla need to be given high priority. In a step forward in this direction, the Indian Prime Minister Manmohan Singh inaugurated the first train service in Kashmir valley on 11 October 2008. The state, sparsely populated and scattered as it is, also needs more airports and better air connections. Remote places like Kupwara, Poonch, Rajouri and Kishtwar need to be connected by air.

The revival of indigenous industries, tapping of new areas with the help of the private sector, opening of the intra-Kashmir routes, the infrastructural development – all of these would not only revive and boost the state economy but would also lead to employment. Citing unemployment and lack of infrastructure as main reasons for militancy, former chief minister of the state, Ghulam Nabi Azad, emphasised the need to pay attention to these areas. He was confident that 80 per cent of militancy will go away 'if we are able to give employment to the youth' (Bukhari 2006). In this context, a survey conducted by the British group Market and Opinion Research International in the state in March 2002 is noteworthy. According to the survey, 93 per cent of respondents[9] believed that the correct way to bring peace to the region will be through economic development, which can provide more job opportunities and reduce poverty (International Crisis Group 2002: 19–20). One of the crucial steps in this direction is the commencement of construction of a 592 metre cable-stayed bridge at Basoli in the Kathua district of Jammu region, the foundation stone of which was laid by

United Progressive Alliance-II (the coalition of political parties in power in New Delhi) chairperson, Sonia Gandhi, on 23 May 2011. Scheduled to be constructed by September 2014, the bridge will open up avenues for commercial mining of gypsum and limestone, besides connecting the states of Punjab, Himachal Pradesh and J&K, thus promoting tourism and development (www.constructionweekonline.in 2011). According to Gandhi, the Indian government will provide training facilities for 100,000 young people in the region over the next 3–5 years (Pasricha 2011). Indian Defence Minister A.K. Antony, who was present on the occasion of the foundation ceremony, emphasised that Kashmir will be the government's 'undivided priority', and 'the development of infrastructure will ensure accelerated economic progress for the region as well for India'. The J&K chief minister, Omar Abdullah, has emphasised the urgency of construction of 'two tunnels at Chattergala between Basoli-Bhaderwah and Singhpora-Vailoo between Kishtwar-Anantnag to link Kishtwar belt with Kashmir Valley', as it will provide an alternate route from Kashmir valley to Jammu, Himachal Pradesh and Punjab, thus facilitating trade, tourism and development.

Opening roads between two Kashmirs

The opening of roads across the line of control (LOC) has encouraged the prospects of both development and peace in the state. The opening of Srinagar-Muzaffarabad road in April 2005 followed by Poonch-Rawalakote in June 2006 and the likely opening of other roads such as Jammu-Sialkot and Jhanger-Mirpur will aid the process of economic revival in the undivided Kashmir region. The roads will not only help divided families to meet each other, but will also boost trade and tourism. The prospective opening of the Kargil-Skardu road will merge Gilgit and Baltistan with the cultural heritage of Ladakh and the Tibetan Buddhist region that already attracts thousands of tourists every year. The re-opened road is set to turn the world's highest mountain region into an even larger theatre of mountain tourism. From the foothills of Mount Everest in Nepal to the Karakoram in Pakistan, the road connection may encourage adventure tourism in the region. The trans-LOC trade through these routes can further bring development to the region as a whole, as these routes are more accessible than other currently used routes within the state. Besides the economic advantage to Kashmir, it will help build trust across people, thus further lessening chances of future violence. The Indian *Economic Survey* 2007–2008 has also emphasised the need for opening the roads between the two Kashmirs. It observed that:

> creating intra-Kashmir economic linkages might begin to give Kashmiris a greater sense that peace is possible. Creation of economic institutions across the LOC will be a step towards the kind of practical and honourable arrangements that most people believe are essential for a lasting Kashmir settlement.
>
> (Quoted in Pargal 2008)

One positive step in this direction despite differences is commencement of trade between the two sides of Kashmir from October 2008 (Mahapatra 2012; Shekhawat and Mahapatra 2009).

Conclusion

Kashmir has not witnessed peace as it has now, where development-oriented peace has evolved as a means of resolving the conflict. Besides reducing the costs, the peace and development agenda with a participatory approach will mitigate any future prospects of violence, and may motivate people towards thinking of innovative ways of conflict resolution. Poverty and unemployment play a major role in violence, hence development-oriented peace processes can play a vital role towards resolving the conflict as it will enable people to feel ownership in the affairs of Kashmir; with better opportunities it will usher in an era in which development and freedom can go together. As well as economic development, the decentralisation of power at the grass-roots level and the recent local elections indicate that peace is not an impossible proposition in Kashmir, but it must be tempered with an agenda with careful planning and persistence towards empowering people. The peace constituency appears to assume strength in recent years despite hard-line pronouncements by some leaders or silencing of some of the moderate separatist leaders.[10] The resilience of the Kashmiri society and its traditional harmonious culture has been strong enough to adopt a peaceful world view.

Whether Kashmir is more dangerous or not in comparison with other conflicts in the world, its strategic location and its significance in the wider politics of South Asia and Eurasia cannot be ignored. However, as recent developments indicate, Kashmir has not shown signs, despite intermittent violence, of sliding back to earlier periods of chaos as witnessed during the heights of militancy in the 1990s. It must be emphasised that two of the major parties to the conflict – India and Pakistan – and their policies in the region impact on Kashmir more than any other dynamics. The Pakistani prime minister rightly echoes the mood in the subcontinent that it is difficult to afford another war between the nuclear weapon-powered neighbours, complemented by his Indian counterpart that peace and dialogue are the only means for conflict resolution in Kashmir. There may be dissenting voices in respective establishments, but as the developments of past decades show, and despite turmoil and setbacks as the post-Mumbai terror attack displayed, the countries have not resorted to or instigated violence. It appears that peace is to stay in Kashmir, and this realisation has been more prominent in recent years. The post-Cold War developments – particularly the increasing realisation of utility of democratic means of conflict resolution, globalisation and developments in information technology and communications – and also the people's denunciation of violent methods and embracing of democratic norms, as the recent elections in J&K indicate, have had positive impacts in Kashmir.

The peaceful atmosphere raises the urgency for economic development. The Kashmir region is not only full of natural bounties in terms of natural resources, but also in terms of human resources. The current opportunity to bring peace by means of development in the region needs to be utilised instead of waiting for the conflict to be resolved fully. In an era of globalisation, when political issues are guided mostly by economic imperatives, it is necessary to bring the same realisation to Kashmir. The conflict has brought innumerable losses for both India and Pakistan, but it is the people of the region who suffer the most. The current opportunity must be used to better the living standards of the people of this troubled region, as economic development will steer the peace process further and help realise a peaceful solution to the Kashmir issue. It is a three-way process: addressing underdevelopment; involving people in the development process, thus bringing empowerment and help to address the issues related to alienation; and using the development process and its results as a deterrent to violence.

Notes

1 Prime Minister Manmohan Singh during his closing remarks at the third round table conference on J&K on 24 April 2007 envisaged a 'Naya [new] Jammu, Kashmir and Ladakh which is symbolized by peace, prosperity and people's power', adding 'I am sure that this dialogue process is the best way forward among others.' The complete remarks are available at http://pmindia.nic.in/speech/content.asp?id=528 (accessed 22 June 2007).

2 In a speech at a Kashmir conference in Muzaffarabad in Pakistan-controlled Kashmir on 23 May 2011, Pakistan Prime Minister Yusuf Raja Gilani reiterated the commitment of Pakistan to 'dialogue process' to resolve conflict in Kashmir and emphasised 'We cannot afford another war' (Bukhari 2011).

3 John Schoeberlein attempts to give a broad definition of central Eurasia under which he includes 'lands from the Iranian Plateau, the Black Sea, and the Volga Basin through Afghanistan, Southern Siberia, and the Himalayas to Muslim and Manchu regions of China and the Mongol lands' (Schoeberlein 2002: 5). The undivided Kashmir region includes segments of Karakoram and Himalaya mountain ranges.

4 There were 550-odd princely states under the British rule, who owed direct allegiance to the British government. Under the Mountbatten Plan of 1947 the rulers of these states had to decide, while taking into account the popular wishes, whether to join India or Pakistan.

5 The entire partition line between India and Pakistan in and surrounding Kashmir is divided into three segments: 198 km of international border; a 778 km line of control, extending from Akhnoor to NJ 9842 till Siachen Glacier; and then the undefined actual ground positioning line, not clearly defined.

6 The Indian foreign minister, S.M. Krishna, stated

> The genesis of all this (revival of dialogue process) was the Prime Ministers, when they met in Thimphu, they mandated the Foreign Ministers and Foreign Secretaries to bridge the trust deficit between the two countries. So, all these meetings at the level of Foreign Secretaries and Foreign Ministers are going to achieve that purpose.
>
> (*Times of India* 2011b)

7 During his visit to Saudi Arabia, Singh stated: 'If Pakistan cooperates with India, there is no problem that we cannot solve and we can walk the extra mile to open a new chapter in relations between our two countries' (*Indian Express* 2010).

8 Then World Bank president, James D. Wolfensohn, stated on 18 November 2004, in the context of Kashmir, 'Economic development along with peace is essential. When young people don't have economic hope, they tend to do all sorts of things.'

9 The group conducted a poll of 850 people in J&K in 2002 in anticipation of the 2002 elections.

10 One of the hard-line Hurriyat leaders, Syed Ali Shan Geelani observed the day after the killing of Osama bin Laden: 'Osama has died a martyr.... But his martyrdom won't end the resistance against the US in Afghanistan and elsewhere in the Muslim world' (Wani 2011). A prominent separatist leader of Kashmir, Maulana Showkat Ahmed Shah, was killed on 8 April 2011, one of the reasons being that he opposed the violent protests in the valley in 2010.

References

Anderson, M.B. (1999) *Do No Harm: How Aid Supports Peace – Or War*, London: Lynne Rienner.

Buckles, Daniel (ed.) (1999) *Cultivating Peace: Conflict and Collaboration in Natural Resource Management*, Washington, DC: World Bank Institute.

Bukhari, Shujaat (2006) 'Unemployment, the Root Cause of Militancy: Azad', *The Hindu*, 6 February.

Bukhari, Shujaat (2011) ' "Resolve Kashmir Issue for Peace and Progress in South Asia",' *The Hindu*, 24 May.

Collier, Paul and Hoffler, A. (1998) 'On Economic Causes of Civil War', *Oxford Economic Papers*, 50 (4): 563–573.

Ganguly, Sumit (1997) *The Crisis in Kashmir: Portents of War, Hopes of Peace*, New Delhi: Foundation Books.

The Hindu (2009) 'Joint Statement of Prime Minister Manmohan Singh and the Prime Minister of Pakistan Syed Yusuf Raza Gilani,' 17 July.

Indian Express (2010) 'India Ready to Walk Extra Mile if Pak Acts Against Terror: PM,' 2 March.

International Crisis Group (2002) 'Kashmir: The View from Srinagar', ICG Asia Report no. 41.

'Jammu & Kashmir: A Profile' (n.d.) http://jammukashmir.nic.in/profile/welcome.html (accessed 15 June 2011).

Junne, Gerd and Willemijn, Verkoren (2004) *Postconflict Development: Meeting New Challenges*, London: Lynne Rienner.

Kumar, Vijay (2008) '2008: Election of Many Firsts in Jammu & Kashmir', 26 December. www.groundreport.com/World/2008-Election-of-many-firsts-in-Jammu-Kashmir-2008_2/2877780 (accessed 14 January 2009).

Lamb, Alastair (1992) *Kashmir: A Disputed Legacy, 1846–1990*, Hertingfordbury: Rexford Books.

Mahapatra, Debidatta Aurobinda (2007) 'A Perspective on Peace in Kashmir', *ICFAI Journal of Governance and Public Policy*, 2 (4): 43–55.

—— (2008) *Central Eurasia: Geopolitics, Compulsions and Connections*, New Delhi: Lancers Publishers.

—— (2009) 'Silk Route in Kashmir', *Central Eurasian Studies Review* 8 (1): 13–15.

—— (2012) *Making Kashmir Borderless*, Colombo: RCSS (forthcoming).

Mahapatra, Debidatta Aurobinda and Shekhawat, Seema (2008a) *Kashmir Across LOC*, New Delhi: Gyan Publishing House.

—— (2008b) 'The Peace Process and Prospects for Economic Reconstruction in Kashmir', *Peace & Conflict Review* 3 (1): 1–17.

OECD (1997) 'Conflict, Peace and Development: Cooperation on the Threshold of the 21st Century'. www.oecd.org/dataoecd/31/39/2755375 (accessed 25 August 2007).

Pargal, Sanjeev (2008), 'Pre-budget Survey for End to Subsidies, Freebies', *Daily Excelsior*, 17 January.

Pasricha, Anjana (2011) 'India Promises to Build Infrastructure in Jammu and Kashmir', 23 May. www.voanews.com/english/news/India-Promises-To-Build-Infrastructure-in-Jammu-and-Kashmir-122438954.html (accessed 25 May 2011).

Puri, Balraj (1993) *Kashmir Towards Insurgency*, New Delhi: Orient Longman.

Schoeberlein, John (2002) 'Setting the Stakes of a New Society', *Central Eurasian Studies Review*, 1 (1): 4–9.

Schofield, Victoria (2004) *Kashmir in the Crossfire: India, Pakistan and the Unending War*, New Delhi: Viva Books Pvt. Ltd.

Secretary General of the United Nations (1992) 'An Agenda for Peace, Preventive Diplomacy, Peacemaking and Peace-keeping'. www.un.org/Docs/SG/agpeace.html (accessed 17 September 2007).

—— (1994) *An Agenda for Development*, New York, NY: United Nations.

Shekhawat, Seema (2006) *Conflict and Displacement in Jammu and Kashmir: The Gender Dimension*, Jammu: Saksham Books International.

—— (2009) 'Fragile Kashmir, Costs and Hopes for Peace', *Journal of Alternative Perspectives in the Social Sciences*, 1 (3): 976–981.

Shekhawat, Seema and Mahapatra, Debidatta Aurobinda (2009) *Contested Border and Division of Families in Kashmir: Contextualizing the Ordeal of the Kargil Women*, New Delhi: WISCOMP.

Strategic Foresight Group (2005) *The Final Settlement: Restructuring India–Pakistan Relations*, Mumbai: Strategic Foresight Group.

Times of India (2011a) 'Pakistan PM Yousuf Gilani, PM Manmohan arrive in Chandigarh for High-voltage India-Pak Semifinal,' 31 March.

Times of India (2011b) '"Indo-Pak Meeting Lays a 'Solid Foundation," says Krishna,' 8 February.

Wani, Riyaz (2011) 'Osama a Martyr, Says Geelani,' *Indian Express*, 3 May.

www.constructionweekonline.in (2011) 'J&K to have its first cable-stayed bridge' 24 May. www.constructionweekonline.in/article-7266-jammu_kashmir_to_have_first_cable_stayed_bridge (accessed 24 June 2011).

Index

Abbotabad 170
Abkhazia, Abkhazian 3, 6, 12, 14, 16, 18, 27, 37, 40, 41, 43–6, 48, 50, 51, 86–8, 91–101, 136
Afghanistan, Afghan 6, 8, 9, 12, 13, 17, 18, 27, 32, 100n2, 112, 114, 121, 126, 167, 168, 170, 171, 173, 173n1, 173n2, 195, 207n3, 208n10; Afghan National Security Forces (ANSF) 163, 165; conflict 159, 160, 162, 166; peace process 164, 165, 166, 169, 172; society 160, 161; Taliban 8, 9, 10
Africa 6, 28, 34
African Union 25
Ahmadinejad, Mahmoud 148
Akayev, Askar 119, 120, 124, 130n1
Al Qaeda in Iraq 141
Aliyev, Ilham 73, 78
alternative dispute resolution (ADR) 74
al-Zawahiri, Ayman 114, 124
Andijan 38
Armenia 8, 10, 14, 15, 27, 33, 42, 46, 47, 50, 60, 61, 73–85, 86n6, 86n7, 86n8, 86n9, 93, 95, 153n1
arms race 24
Asian Development Bank 203
Association of South East Asian Nations (ASEAN) 23, 25–7, 33
asymmetrical relations 10
Australia 25, 137
Azerbaijan 8, 11–15, 27, 42, 46, 47, 50, 60, 73–85, 93, 134, 136, 145–7, 149–52, 153n1, 168

Bakiyev, Kurmanbek 9, 10, 16, 119–24, 130n1, 130n2
Baku-Tblisi-Ceyhan (BTC) pipeline 43, 80, 81
balkanisation 49
Balkans 49, 50
Baltistan 205
Bamiyan Buddha 162
Basaev, Shamil 111
Bashmakh 147–9, 154n5
Belarus 10, 47, 61, 126, 130
Beslan 39, 57
Bharat Nirman Programme 204
Biden-Lugar Bill 169
bipolar politics 1
Black Sea 9, 40, 60, 91, 96, 168, 207n3
Bolshevik revolution 75, 110
Bosnia-Herzegovina 33, 38, 43, 46, 50
Brazil 182
Brzezinski, Zbigniew 11
Budennovsk 57, 59–60
buffer state 160

Canada 35n3
Caucasian Caliphate/Emirate 9, 16
Caucasian community 33
Caucasus 3, 8, 12, 14, 15, 36, 37, 40, 41, 44–8, 50, 59, 74, 76, 82–4, 85n4, 100, 107, 109, 145; and Central Asia 1, 45; North 15, 39, 54, 55, 57–62, 66–9, 70n4, 86n10, 105–7, 110, 113, 115–17; South 42, 46, 47, 57, 74, 75, 76, 81, 94
Central Asia, Central Asian 6, 8–11, 13, 16, 24, 42, 46, 47, 93, 123–5, 127–9, 167, 168, 173; and China 12; Electricity Grid 125; community of Afghanistan 27; post-Soviet 119; and South Asia 7, 160
Central Eurasia 207n3
Central Eurasian Studies Society 20
Central Intelligence Agency (CIA) 127, 139
CGT syndrome 30
Chechnya, Chechen 9, 54, 61, 62, 68, 107, 110, 112, 115; aspirations 16; conflict 103; economy 58; fighters 108; first war 59; history 109; intellectuals 109; jihadists 108; movement 106;

nationalism 109; nationalists 108, 109; rebels 16; republic 68; resistance 105, 106, 111, 117; second war 57, 59; state 109, 116; tradition 105; wars 54, 58
China 8, 12, 23, 25–8, 34n2, 56, 96, 104, 126, 130, 168, 170, 171, 173, 176, 181, 184, 185, 187–91, 192n1, 195, 196, 201, 207n3
civic groups 120
civic identity 129
civil rights 180
civil society 8, 10, 14, 28, 29, 84, 85, 123, 128, 176, 181, 182, 190, 191, 200
clientelism 182, 183
climate change 34
coalition forces 141
coalition invasion 136, 143
Collective Security Treaty Organisation 10
colonial languages 27
colonial powers 25, 27
colonialism 27, 30, 160
colour revolutions 120
commercial diplomacy 144, 145, 147
Commonwealth of Independent States (CIS) 41, 88, 93, 97, 100n1, 119
Conference for Security and Cooperation in Europe 32
conflict 1–3, 6–13, 18, 23, 28, 36, 38, 39, 41, 42, 76, 77, 79, 81, 85n2, 89, 90, 92, 93, 95, 99, 100n1, 100n5, 103, 106, 115, 119, 121, 127, 128, 134, 138, 139, 141, 160–2, 165, 168, 176, 188, 196, 201, 204, 207; analysis 15, 48; area 80; armed 7, 91, 94; civil 140; complex 32; critical 24; direct 153; discourse 103; dualistic 5; dynamics 172; ethnic 3, 6, 8, 54, 55, 62–5, 68, 74, 122, 153; ethno-nationalist 54; free environments 197; frozen 2, 36, 41, 42, 80; geopolitical dimension 47; habituated 197; internal 30, 34, 50; international 34, 89; intractable 30; intra-state 7, 91, 94; levels 14; management 14, 15, 55, 56, 63, 67–9, 136; management and cartography 15, 54, 55, 65; mapping 14, 30, 31; military 54, 68, 153; models 37, 47, 49; modern 7; new 45; open 89; over resources 1; paradigms 159; pattern 194; prevention 29, 49, 50, 198; potentials 10, 18; protracted 79, 194, 195; readiness 62; recurrent 136; regional 50; related violence 197; religion based resolution 9; resolution 3, 13–17, 27–9, 31–3, 36, 47–9, 74, 78, 79, 84, 136, 159, 177, 192, 194, 195, 198; resolution formula 27; resolution process 15, 73; situation 14, 36, 128, 172, 198, 206; structural 33; theory 23; transformation 17, 84, 159, 160, 169, 194; trap 197; unresolved 29; violent 10, 15, 46, 68, 194, 197; volatile 18; warning and prevention measures 65; and women 29; zone 15, 17, 85
constitutional crisis 86n1
constitutional order 88
cooperation 11, 17, 81–3, 100, 105, 137, 139, 146–8, 153, 167, 168, 172; cross-border 134; economic 24, 143–5; global 34; international 140; mass 23; multilateral 167; protocol 144; regional 63, 124; security 149; subregional 138, 143
Council of Europe 23, 24, 89
Crimean ASSR 92
critical geopolitics 56
critical peace research 56
cross-border integration 153
cultural repression 140
customs union 126, 130
Cyprus 31, 79
Czarist rule/empire 8, 95

Dagestan 12, 57–62, 114
defensive defence 24, 27
democracy 9, 10, 41, 69, 89, 119, 186, 196; deficit 24; electoral 199; and human rights 11, 31; parliamentary 128, 129
détente 81
development vacuum 198
diplomacy 17, 23, 82, 135, 137, 138, 144, 145, 147, 149, 165
direct allegiance 207n4
direct confrontation 166
direct violence 26, 30
displacement 135, 142, 196
domino effect 45
Dostum, Abdul Rashid 162
drug trafficking 122, 167–9
dualism 30
Dudaev, Dzhokhar 105
Dugin, Aleksandr 4, 5, 111
Durand Line 160, 161
Durrani dynasty 160

East Asia 23, 25, 26, 33
East Asian Community 26
East Turkestan 176
Eastern Anatolia 134
Eastern Europe 1, 47, 80
Eastern Mediterranean Community 31
economic dislocation 58
economic reconstruction 195, 198, 202, 203

economic retardation 13, 197
energy 12, 13, 74, 81, 140, 167, 183; crisis 125; politics 12, 73, 83, 85; resources/ source 2, 6, 11; routes 47; security 34; shortfall 124; supply 43, 83, 96
enlightenment 95, 114
epistemic community 56
Erbil 134, 136–8, 140–50, 153n3
ethnic, ethnicity 2, 3, 5–7, 9, 15, 16, 41, 49, 54, 63, 69, 99, 108, 109, 117, 123, 160; atlas of Stavropol 55, 56, 64, 65, 68; Armenians 77; Azeris 77; balance 66, 68; Caucasians 54, 59, 61, 62; Chechen 54, 62; cleansing 43, 49, 90, 96, 97; differentiation 129; division 8, 75; educational schemes 63; geography 55, 57, 62, 65; Georgians 93, 95, 98; groups 6, 60–2, 66, 68, 89, 106, 110, 111, 161, 164, 173n2, 189; heterogeneity 8; homogeneity 10; Hungarians 38; Kyrgyz 121; linkages 8; migration 64, 66; minorities 62–4, 69, 187, 189, 191; Pashtun 163, 164; pluralism 164; republics 58, 59, 61, 62, 105; riots 54, 70n9, 111; Russians 54, 58–62, 67, 68, 107, 110–13, 116; split 123; state 123; stock 166; structure 62, 66–8; Tajiks 165; territorial policy 77; Uzbeks 38
ethno-cultural consciousness 67
ethno-nationalism 62
Eurasia, Eurasian 1–9, 11–14, 16, 18, 34, 43, 84, 86n7, 111, 134, 160, 167, 194, 195, 206, 207n3
Eurasian Development Bank 125
Eurasianism 4, 5, 112, 113
Europe 1, 4–6, 11, 23, 24, 26, 32, 37, 43, 44, 48, 85, 89, 90, 94–6, 99, 105, 110, 116, 136, 137
European Commission 47
European Court of Human Rights 95
European Economic Community (EEC) 23, 24, 28
European Union (EU) 11, 14, 24–7, 29, 31–3, 34n1, 37, 41, 42, 46, 48–50, 73, 74, 80, 82–5, 91, 96, 97, 99, 100n3, 126, 137
extended neighbourhood 1, 10

Fergana 127
Finland 24
forced labour 162
France 32, 33, 44, 74, 79, 80, 115, 137
free economic zone 94
French Revolution 104, 114, 115

Gali 98, 100n4
Galtung, Johan 14, 23, 24, 28, 69, 74, 184
Gamsakhurdia, Zviad 92–4, 97, 100n1
Gandhi, Sonia 205
Genghis Khan 160
genocide 32, 43, 74, 79, 82, 83, 85, 86n10, 90, 91, 96, 98, 122, 130n6
geography 5, 11, 55, 57, 60, 62, 65, 123, 139; of war and peace 56
geopolitics, geopolitical 2, 5, 6, 11, 54, 56, 57, 59, 60, 66, 74, 83, 94, 134, 194, 198
Georgia 2, 3, 8, 11, 14, 15, 27, 36, 37, 39, 40–7, 50, 60, 61, 74, 75, 80, 86n7, 88–99, 100n1, 100n2, 120, 136, 153n1, 167, 168
Germany 31, 32, 44, 46, 74, 80, 105, 137
Ghaznavids 160
Gilani, Yusuf Raja 200, 207n2
global peace index 46
globalisation 18, 24, 25, 198, 206, 207
globalised world 25
good governance 123, 200
Gorbachev, Mikhail 24
gordian knots 28
great game 6, 160
Greece 24, 46, 114, 115
Greenland 34
Grozny 105

Haji Omaran 145–7
Hakkâri 142
Halabja 141
Han Chinese migration 8, 176
Hekmatyar, Gulbuddin 161, 162
Himalayas 207n3
Hindu Kush 170
Hizb ut-Tahrir 9, 122
Horn of Africa 34
hot pursuit 172
human rights 7, 11, 24, 30, 31, 62, 77, 89, 95, 100n5, 130 n 3, 162, 177–82, 184, 189, 191
Human Systems Dynamics (HSD) 47
Hurriyat Conference 199

Iceland 34
ideational roots 45
ideology, ideological 6, 16, 38, 43, 45, 49, 106, 107, 109–11, 116, 121, 140, 143, 159, 180; bourgeois 104; communist 9; dominant 105; factors 3; functional 104; fundamentalist 164; geographist 4; internationalist revolutionary 103; weapon 11
imperial domination 1
imperial rivalry 6
imperial rule 8
India, Indian 6, 17, 23, 28, 34, 46, 96, 116,

160, 183, 195, 201, 204, 205; and Pakistan 171, 172, 194, 196, 199, 200, 206, 207; subcontinent 12, 161, 202
Indonesia 56
infidels 106, 107, 115
information war 128
Ingushetia 57–9, 70n4, 106
insurgency 142
internally displaced persons (IDPs) 59, 73, 78–82, 85, 95, 98
International Committee of Red Cross 162
International Court of Justice (ICJ) 37, 44, 45, 95
International Covenant on Civil and Political Rights (ICCPR) 180, 189
International Covenant on Economic Social and Cultural Rights (ICESCR) 180, 184, 189
International Criminal Tribunal 44
International Monetary Fund 123
international relations 12, 55, 56, 89, 136–8, 198
International Security Assistance Force (ISAF) 159, 163, 164, 166–9, 173
international security 17, 78, 159
internationalism 106–8
interstate warfare 7
intolerance 9, 166
Iran, Iranian 5, 8, 9, 11–13, 15–17, 27, 74, 79, 80, 86n7, 103, 104, 134, 135, 137–40, 142, 145–53, 161, 162, 167–9, 173, 207n3
Iraq, Iraqi 8, 13, 16, 17, 27, 32, 100n2, 107, 134–49, 153
Islamabad Accord 162
Islamic Movement of Uzbekistan 10, 122
Islamic Party of Rebirth of Tajikistan 122
Islamic puritanical movements 106
Islamic traditions 9
Islamic umma 108, 109
isolationism 160
Israel 11, 25, 27, 30–2, 73
Italy 32, 44, 46, 137
Ittihad-i Islami 162

Jalalabad 121, 122, 162
Jamat Shariat 113
Jammu and Kashmir (J&K) 195, 198, 199, 202, 204–6, 207n1, 208n8
jihad 16, 106–9, 112–15, 162, 166

Kabardino-Balkaria 57–9, 62
Kadyrov, Ramzan 115, 117
Kalinin 65, 70n9
Kalmikiya 60
Kandahar 114, 162, 171
Karachaevo-Cherkessia 57, 58, 60
Karachi 161, 167
Karakalpak ASSR 92
Karakoram 205, 207n3
Kargil-Skardu road 205
Kashmir 9, 10, 12, 17, 161, 162, 171, 172, 194–207, 208n8; *see also* Jammu and Kashmir (J&K)
Kazakhstan 8, 10–12, 120, 124–7, 130, 167, 168
Khasavyurt Agreement 105, 106, 177
Khojaly Massacre 77
Khyber Pass 161, 167, 170
Kodori 41, 88, 98
Kosovo 3, 6, 14, 15, 29, 33, 36–50, 79, 91, 96, 114, 136, 167
Kremlin 5, 73, 81, 99, 105, 106, 113, 117, 120
Kurdistan, Kurdish 13, 16, 17, 32, 134–49, 153
Kuwaiti oil fields 12
Kyrgyzstan, Kyrgyz 9, 13, 14, 16, 36, 124, 125, 128, 168; bazaars 126; conflict 8, 119; economy 126; elite 129; insurgents 122; militia 130n7; oil imports 120; parliament 129; society 123; southern 10, 38, 121; –Tajik border 127; workforce 128

Lachin 77, 84
Ladakh 201, 204, 205, 207n1
Laden, Osama bin 114, 162, 164, 170, 208n10
Latin America 25, 26, 28
Lebanon 31, 32
liberalisation 6, 54, 123
Loya Jirga 163
Luguvoi Controversy 167

Macedonia 46, 47, 96
Mackinder Halford J. 6
Madrid 32, 78, 83, 84
Makhachkala 114
market reforms 6
Marxism 108, 111; -Leninism 104
Medvedev, Dmitri 58, 73
Mehsud, Baitullah 171
Meskhetian Turks 10, 121
Middle East 9, 29, 31, 37, 144, 160
Middle East Community (MEC) 25, 27, 31
migration 8, 12, 54, 59, 61–4, 66, 68, 124, 127–9, 139, 176, 188
militancy 161, 195–7, 199, 204, 206
military bases 11, 79, 81, 93
military coup 169
military forces 7, 135
military pacts 12
military spending 10, 46

millenarianism 103
Millennium Development Goals 192
Mindanao 25, 162
Mitrovica 40
Moldova 37, 41, 47, 93, 136
Montevideo Convention 88
Morocco 25, 32
Mount Elbrus 57
Mount Everest 205
mountain tourism 205
Mountain of World Peace 33
Mountbatten Plan 207n4
mujahideen 107, 108, 161, 169
Mullah Omar 161, 162, 165, 173n3
multi-dimensional endeavour 18
multiethnic states 3, 7, 49
multilateralism 23
Mumbai 194, 199–201, 206
mutual non-aggression 35n2, 160
mutual non-interference 35n2
Myanmar 33

Nabucco pipeline 12
Nagorno-Karabakh 3, 8, 9, 12, 15, 18, 27, 37, 38, 41, 42, 48, 50, 73–9, 81–5, 86n6, 92, 96, 100, 136
Nakhichevan 76, 77, 85n5
narratives 16, 36; contradictory 9; grand 6; historical 4; of victimhood 129
nation building 6, 16, 18
National Bolshevism 104, 105, 111, 116, 117
National Organisation of Russian Muslims (NORM) 112, 113
nationalism 54, 62, 63, 78, 103–10, 115–17, 140
Nauru 45, 88
neo-Eurasianism 4, 5
Nepal 205
Netherlands 25
Nevsky Express 112
new cold war 90
new great game 6
Nicaragua 45, 88, 90
nomadic horsemen 5
non-democratic ways 10
Non-Governmental Organisations (NGOs) 28, 29, 32, 48, 62, 74, 85n2, 98, 100n5, 120, 123, 137, 186, 187, 191
nonviolence 31
North Atlantic Treaty Organisation (NATO) 11, 13, 14, 24, 38, 41–5, 48, 80, 83, 96, 112, 167–70
North Ossetia, North Ossetian 57–9, 90, 92, 97, 98, 100
Norway 24, 32
nuclear arms/weapons 24, 168, 169, 195
nuclear reactor 170
nuclear warhead 39

oasis-routes 6
Obama, Barack 82, 83, 167, 172
oil 13, 27, 32, 74, 75, 80, 83, 96, 120, 124, 125, 140, 148, 183; Oil-for-Food Programme 143; power 43; supplies 12
Operation Atalanta 29
Operation Enduring Freedom 9, 165
Operation Storm 43
Ordzhonikidze 75, 76, 85n4
Organisation of Economic Cooperation and Development 198
Organisation of Islamic Community (OIC) 25–7, 32, 33
Organisation for Security and Cooperation in Europe (OSCE) 38, 42, 46, 78, 79, 84, 85n2, 94, 97
Orthodox Christianity 5, 57
Osh 10, 16, 119, 121, 122, 127–9
Ottoman Empire 8, 30, 32, 33

pacification 14, 33
Pakistan, Pakistani 8–10, 27, 107, 116, 160, 162, 165–7, 173n2, 195, 196, 198–200, 205, 207n2, 207n5; Afghan policy 161, 168–71; army 172; government 170; Inter-Services Intelligence (ISI) 161, 171; leadership 194; North West Frontier Province 161; Taliban 171; *see also* India and Pakistan
Palestine 27, 31, 32
Pamir Group 171
Panchsheel 23, 34n2
Panini 171
parallelisms 9
partnership for peace 11
passportisation 96, 99
Patni Top 201
patrimonial drift 119
peace 1–3, 7, 8, 10, 15, 17, 25, 26, 30, 31, 33, 42, 43, 50, 63, 81, 82, 89, 100n6, 112, 119, 122, 161, 162, 166, 167, 177, 203–5, 208n8; accord 200; building 28, 29, 47, 48, 74, 75; constituency 18, 206; discourse 164; efforts 84, 164, 198; format 171; forced 6; inclusive 14, 19, 159; inner 31; interethnic 55, 67, 69; international 81, 159, 173; manoeuvre 18; mission 199; negative 14, 23, 24, 27, 69; negotiations 73; overtures 17, 174, 200; people centric 15; permanent 37; perspective 23, 159; politics 168, 171; positive 14, 19, 23, 24, 27, 34, 74, 79; process 15, 73, 74, 78, 79, 85, 159, 160, 163–5, 169, 170, 172, 173, 194, 195,

197–201, 206, 207; proposal 98; relative 16; research 55, 56; studies 13, 14; sustainable 168, 171
peaceful coexistence 8, 34n2, 90
peaceful settlement 82, 199
peacekeeping 33, 36, 45, 46, 74, 78, 93, 97, 100n1
peacemaking 29
people-to-people contact 83
perceptions of space 9, 15
Persian Gulf War 135
Peshawar Accord 161
pipeline politics 12
Poonch-Rawalakote 205
Portugal 137
post-Balkan perspective 36
post-Soviet era/period 5, 62
Poti 88, 91, 168
power vacuum 167
Pristina 37, 96
Pul-e-Kumri 171
punitive action 96
Punjab 205
Puntland 136
Putin, Vladimir 42, 57, 58, 60, 69, 106, 110, 112, 113, 115

Rabbani, Barhanuddin 165
Rajouri 196, 204
Red Army 110
refugees 64, 78, 85n1, 120, 122, 149, 162
regional integration 16
religion 2, 5, 9, 12, 18, 30, 33, 57, 117n1, 172
religious antagonism 197
religious extremism 6, 9, 65, 169, 196
religious fundamentalism 9, 166, 167, 194
revolution 16, 56, 75, 80, 90, 94, 95, 97, 103, 104, 108–10, 114, 115, 119–21, 173n1
rights-based approach 176, 177, 185, 190, 191
Roki tunnel 88, 99
Rose Revolution 80, 90, 94
Russia, Russian 1, 3, 4, 8–10, 12–16, 25, 26, 28, 32, 36, 39, 40, 42–4, 46, 57–61, 63, 66–8, 70n5, 73–5, 77–9, 82, 83, 93, 94, 96–8, 100, 103, 107–9, 112, 125, 127–30, 167, 168, 170; diaspora 95; empire 6, 59, 92, 110, 111, 113–15, 117, 120–2, 159; -Eurasia 5; foreign policy 11; gas 85, 95; –Georgia 2, 37, 80, 89, 90, 99; Germans 106; heartland 105; history 104; idea 111; jihadist-Bolshevism 113; –Kazakhstan–Belarus Customs Union 126; media 130n6; military 81, 91, 99, 110; Mongol conquest of 4; nationalism 54, 104, 116; and NATO 41, 45; peacekeepers 88; society 62, 69

Saakashvili, Mikheil 41, 43, 90, 94, 96, 99
Saddam Hussein 16, 134, 142
Salma hydropower project 171
Samara attack 112
Saudi Arabia 161–3, 207n7
Saur revolution 173n1
Sayiid Qutb 107
Scotland 79
security 5, 7, 10, 11, 24, 25, 27–9, 31, 34, 46, 63, 64, 69n2, 78, 79, 81, 83, 99, 100n1, 120, 121, 130, 134–6, 139, 141–9, 153n4, 159, 173, 180, 184, 190, 198; financial 97; food 58, 202; human 15; international 17, 78; maritime 34; national 129; permanent 169
self-determination 3, 33, 185
separatism/separatist movement 17, 41, 45, 90, 196
Serbia 33, 36–46, 91, 96, 120
Shamanism 5
Shanghai Cooperation Organisation (SCO) 12, 25–7, 33, 163
Sharia 166
Sharm el-Sheikh 200
silk route 12, 195, 201
Singh, Manmohan 204, 207n1
soccer diplomacy 82
Sochi 73, 78, 95–7, 99
Somaliland 136
South Asia 7, 8, 25, 160, 163, 200, 206
South Asian Association for Regional Cooperation (SAARC) 25–7, 33, 163, 199, 200
South Ossetia 3, 6, 9, 12, 14, 16, 18, 27, 36, 37, 39–46, 48, 50, 73, 80, 85, 88, 90–100, 136
South Stream pipeline 12, 43
Soviet Union, Soviet 3–5, 24, 42, 64, 75, 76, 85n5, 86n6, 95, 97, 108, 111, 113, 116, 127, 160–2, 167, 169, 173n1, 173n3; command system 6; constitution 77, 93; control of religion 9; domination 6; former republics 9–11, 41, 93, 100n1, 153n1; post-, 1, 2, 6, 9, 12, 14, 16, 54, 55, 57–9, 62, 65, 77, 78, 85, 103, 110, 117n1, 119, 123, 130n6; regime 8, 124; *see also* USSR
Sovietology 4
Spain 29, 32, 137
Sri Lanka 38
Srinagar-Muzaffarabad road 205
Stalin, Joseph 75, 76, 84, 106
Stavropol 15, 54–69, 111

structural violence 26, 27, 30
subregional integration 17, 135, 149–52
sub-state diplomacy 17, 135, 137
Sumgait 77
super powers 25
Svedlovsk Oblast 105
Sweden 24
Syria 17, 31, 32, 134, 135, 138–43, 149, 153

Tajikistan 8–10, 122–5, 168
Taliban 9, 10, 17, 107, 114, 159, 161–7, 169–72, 173n3; *see also* Pakistan Taliban; Afghan Taliban
Tanzania 162
Taraki, Nur Mohammed 161
Tatarstan 105
Tehran 135, 142, 145, 168, 169
Tehrik-e-Taliban 9
Ter-Petrosyan, Levon 81
terror/terrorism 2, 9, 11, 16, 18, 32, 69n1, 104, 111, 115, 138, 166–70, 172, 194, 199, 200, 206
third world 18, 27, 33, 34, 42
Tibet, Tibetan 5, 8, 96, 205
Transnistria 136
Treaty of Rawalpindi 160
Treaty of Rome 24, 32
Trubetskoi, Nikolai 4, 5
Tskhinvali 43, 88, 90, 91, 97, 99
Tulip Revolution 119
Turkey 8, 9, 12, 13, 15, 16, 27, 30, 31, 33, 46, 47, 74, 76, 79, 80, 82–5, 86n7, 129, 134, 138–40, 142, 143, 145, 148, 149, 153, 169
Turkmenistan 8, 12, 46, 124, 167, 168

Ukraine 47, 60, 66, 92, 93, 96, 120, 167
Umarov, Doku 9
unitary state 33
United Nations (UN) 23, 25, 33, 35n4, 44, 48, 74, 79, 86n10, 93, 137, 141, 143, 162, 165, 191, 198; Charter 82; Development Programme (UNDP) 37, 177–80; Economic Commission for Europe in Geneva 24; General Assembly 45; Mission in Kosovo 37; peacekeeping forces 100n1; Security Commission for Europe 24; Security Council (UNSC) 82, 96, 135, 163; veto power 28
Uppsala Conflict Data Project 7
Ural Republic 105
US 11, 24–6, 32, 38, 45, 83, 85n2, 112, 136, 141–3, 154n5, 161, 162, 167–70, 172
USSR 92, 94, 95, 106, 110, 111, 114, 115, 117; *see also* Soviet Union
Uyghur 8, 13, 17, 176, 177, 183, 185–91
Uzbekistan 8–10, 38, 46, 122–6, 167

Vajpayee, Atal Behari 198
Venezuela 45, 88

Walesa, Lech 44
war 4, 9, 14, 15, 17, 18, 31, 32, 37, 41–3, 48, 54, 55, 57–9, 69, 80, 83, 85, 86n10, 88, 90, 91, 96, 97, 99, 106, 108, 109, 115, 116, 135, 140, 141, 143, 144, 163, 170, 171, 180, 195, 196, 207n2; bloody 77, 162; brutal; civil 49, 75, 95, 98, 104, 110, 136; cold 1, 7, 11, 24, 74, 159–61, 165, 168, 172, 198; costly 12; crimes 89, 92; geography of 56; hot 24; information 128; long 167; post-cold 2, 3, 6, 13, 173, 206; short 94; War Participation Index 30
Waziristan 107, 108, 172
World Bank 10, 123, 126, 127, 203, 208n8
World Food Programme 127
World Trade Organisation 123
world war 18, 42, 55, 99, 106, 116, 180

Xinjiang 8, 17, 162, 176, 177, 183–8, 190, 191

Yeltsin, Boris 57, 93, 97, 105
Yemen 162
Yerevan 81, 86n6
Yugoslavia 24, 37, 38, 41, 44

Zebari, Hoshyar 137